BESTSELLING BOOK SERIES

UNIX® For Dummies®, 4th E

Quick list of commands

To Do This	Type or Press This
Cancel a command	Ctrl+U, Ctrl+X, or @
Change the working directory to /usr	`cd/ usr`
Change the working directory back to your home directory	`cd`
Copy a file	`cp` *oldfile newfile*
Copy a file to another directory	`cp` *oldfile dirname*
Copy a bunch of files to another directory	`cp` *budget* dirname*
Copy all the files in this directory and in all its subdirectories	`cp -r *` *newdir*
Erase a file	`rm` *junkfile*
Rename a file	`mv` *oldname newname*
Move a file to another directory	`mv` *oldfile dirname*
List filenames	`ls`
List filenames with sizes and dates	`ls -l`
List hidden files too	`ls -al`
List files and pause when screen is full	`ls | more`
Look at a text file	`cat` *letter*
Look at a long text file	`more` *letter*
Make a new link (name) for a file	`ln` *oldname newname*
Make new links (names) for files in a directory	`ln` *dirname/* newdir*
Combine two files	`cat` *file1 file2* > *newfile*
Compare two files	`diff` *file1 file2*
Look at the manual page for the `ls` command	`man ls | more`
Change your password	`passwd`

Filenames and pathnames

Capital and small letters are different in filenames.

Filenames can contain letters, numbers, periods, and underscores (_). Stay away from other punctuation. Slashes are special (see the last paragraph in this box).

Filenames shouldn't contain spaces.

The ? wildcard stands for a single character in a filename. The * wildcard stands for a bunch of characters in a filename. An * by itself stands for all files in the working directory.

A *pathname* is the path in which you (or UNIX) can find a file or directory. The root (main) directory of the disk is called /.

A pathname consists of directory names separated by slashes (/). If a pathname starts with a slash (/), it begins at the root directory. If a pathname doesn't start with a slash, it begins at the working directory.

...For Dummies®: Bestselling Book Series for Beginners

BESTSELLING BOOK SERIES

UNIX® For Dummies®, 4th Edition

Cheat Sheet

Printing

On System V UNIX:

To Do This	Type This
Print file	`lp` *`textfile`*
Print file on a named *printer*	`lp -d`*`printer textfile`*
Cancel a print job	`cancel` *`requestid`*
Check the printer queue	`lpstat -a all`

On Linux or BSD UNIX:

To Do This	Type This
Print file	`lpr` *`textfile`*
Print file on a named *printer*	`lpr -P`*`printer textfile`*
Cancel a print job	`lprm` *`jobnumber`*
Check the printer queue	`lpq -a`

Your version of UNIX (see Chapter 2):

❑ BSD ❑ System V ❑ Linux

(NetBSD, FreeBSD, OpenBSD, and BSD/OS are all BSD. Solaris 1, OSF/1, and AIX are similar to BSD. Solaris 2 is similar to System V.)

Your UNIX shell (see Chapter 2):

❑ Bourne shell ❑ C shell
❑ Korn shell ❑ BASH shell

Lost and found

To find out where you are, type **pwd**.

To find out who you logged in as, type **who am I**.

To find a file if you remember its name, type

```
find . -name filename -print
```

To find a file if you know that it contains the word *dummies*, type

```
grep "dummies" *
```

General stuff

Log in before you use UNIX. Remember your username and password.

When you see a prompt (usually $ or %), you can type a UNIX command.

To back up and correct typos, try pressing Backspace, Delete, # (Shift+3), or Ctrl+H.

To cancel what you have typed and try again, try pressing Ctrl+U or @ (Shift+2).

Type a space between the command name and any other information on the same line.

When you're typing commands, use the correct capitalization; UNIX distinguishes between CAPITAL and small letters.

When you have typed the command, press Enter (or Return).

When you log in, the working directory is your home directory.

To log out, type **exit** or press Ctrl+D.

Don't turn off your terminal until you have logged out. Don't turn off workstations or PCs.

Cheat Sheet $2.95 value. Item 0419-3.
For more information about IDG Books, call 1-800-762-2974.

...For Dummies®: Bestselling Book Series for Beginners

References for the Rest of Us!®

BESTSELLING BOOK SERIES

Are you intimidated and confused by computers? Do you find that traditional manuals are overloaded with technical details you'll never use? Do your friends and family always call you to fix simple problems on their PCs? Then the *...For Dummies®* computer book series from IDG Books Worldwide is for you.

...For Dummies books are written for those frustrated computer users who know they aren't really dumb but find that PC hardware, software, and indeed the unique vocabulary of computing make them feel helpless. *...For Dummies* books use a lighthearted approach, a down-to-earth style, and even cartoons and humorous icons to dispel computer novices' fears and build their confidence. Lighthearted but not lightweight, these books are a perfect survival guide for anyone forced to use a computer.

"I like my copy so much I told friends; now they bought copies."

— Irene C., Orwell, Ohio

"Quick, concise, nontechnical, and humorous."

— Jay A., Elburn, Illinois

"Thanks, I needed this book. Now I can sleep at night."

— Robin F., British Columbia, Canada

Already, millions of satisfied readers agree. They have made *...For Dummies* books the #1 introductory level computer book series and have written asking for more. So, if you're looking for the most fun and easy way to learn about computers, look to *...For Dummies* books to give you a helping hand.

1/99

V. - aliases

Shift g bottom line.

UNIX®

FOR

DUMMIES®

4TH EDITION

O = insert mode

alias capture (tab) /users/sdds/bin/capt

then escape (out of insert mode)

:WQ (write file & quit)

to make active. first time

source ~/aliases

by John R. Levine
and Margaret Levine Young

IDG Books Worldwide, Inc.
An International Data Group Company

Foster City, CA ♦ Chicago, IL ♦ Indianapolis, IN ♦ New York, NY

UNIX® For Dummies®, 4th Edition

Published by
IDG Books Worldwide, Inc.
An International Data Group Company
919 E. Hillsdale Blvd.
Suite 400
Foster City, CA 94404
`www.idgbooks.com` (IDG Books Worldwide Web site)
`www.dummies.com` (Dummies Press Web site)

Library of Congress Catalog Card No.: 98-87434

ISBN: 0-7645-0419-3

Printed in the United States of America

10 9 8 7 6

4O/RS/QV/ZZ/IN

Distributed in the United States by IDG Books Worldwide, Inc.

Distributed by CDG Books Canada Inc. for Canada; by Transworld Publishers Limited in the United Kingdom; by IDG Norge Books for Norway; by IDG Sweden Books for Sweden; by Woodslane Pty. Ltd. for Australia; by Woodslane (NZ) Ltd. for New Zealand; by TransQuest Publishers Pte Ltd. for Singapore, Malaysia, Thailand, Indonesia, and Hong Kong; by ICG Muse, Inc. for Japan; by Norma Comunicaciones S.A. for Colombia; by Intersoft for South Africa; by Le Monde en Tique for France; by International Thomson Publishing for Germany, Austria and Switzerland; by Distribuidora Cuspide for Argentina; by Livraria Cultura for Brazil; by Ediciones ZETA S.C.R. Ltda. for Peru; by WS Computer Publishing Corporation, Inc., for the Philippines; by Contemporanea de Ediciones for Venezuela; by Express Computer Distributors for the Caribbean and West Indies; by Micronesia Media Distributor, Inc. for Micronesia; by Grupo Editorial Norma S.A. for Guatemala; by Chips Computadoras S.A. de C.V. for Mexico; by Editorial Norma de Panama S.A. for Panama; by American Bookshops for Finland. Authorized Sales Agent: Anthony Rudkin Associates for the Middle East and North Africa.

For general information on IDG Books Worldwide's books in the U.S., please call our Consumer Customer Service department at 800-762-2974. For reseller information, including discounts and premium sales, please call our Reseller Customer Service department at 800-434-3422.

For information on where to purchase IDG Books Worldwide's books outside the U.S., please contact our International Sales department at 317-596-5530 or fax 317-596-5692.

For consumer information on foreign language translations, please contact our Customer Service department at 1-800-434-3422, fax 317-596-5692, or e-mail rights@idgbooks.com.

For information on licensing foreign or domestic rights, please phone +1-650-655-3109.

For sales inquiries and special prices for bulk quantities, please contact our Sales department at 650-655-3200 or write to the address above.

For information on using IDG Books Worldwide's books in the classroom or for ordering examination copies, please contact our Educational Sales department at 800-434-2086 or fax 317-596-5499.

For press review copies, author interviews, or other publicity information, please contact our Public Relations department at 650-655-3000 or fax 650-655-3299.

For authorization to photocopy items for corporate, personal, or educational use, please contact Copyright Clearance Center, 222 Rosewood Drive, Danvers, MA 01923, or fax 978-750-4470.

About the Authors

Margaret Levine Young and **John R. Levine** were members of a computer club in high school — before high school students, or even high schools, *had* computers. They came in contact with Theodor H. Nelson, the author of *Computer Lib* and the inventor of hypertext, who fostered the idea that computers should not be taken seriously and that everyone can and should understand and use computers.

Margy has been using small computers since the 1970s. She graduated from UNIX on a PDP/11 to Apple DOS on an Apple II to MS-DOS and UNIX on a variety of machines. She has done all kinds of jobs that involve explaining to people that computers aren't as mysterious as they may think, including managing the use of PCs at Columbia Pictures, teaching scientists and engineers what computers are good for, and writing computer manuals and books, including *Dummies 101: The Internet For Windows 95* and *Dummies 101: Netscape Navigator* (with Hy Bender), *Dummies 101: WordPerfect 7 For Windows 95* and *Dummies 101: WordPerfect 6.1 For Windows* (with Alison Barrows), *Dummies 101: Access 97 For Windows* and *Dummies 101: Access For Windows 95* (with Rodney Lowe), *The Internet For Windows For Dummies Starter Kit, MORE Internet For Dummies, WordPerfect For Windows For Dummies* (with David C. Kay), *The Internet For Dummies Quick Reference, Understanding Javelin PLUS,* and *The Complete Guide to PC-File.* She has a degree in computer science from Yale University.

John wrote his first program on an IBM 1130 (a computer roughly as powerful as your typical modern digital wristwatch, only harder to use) in 1967. His first exposure to UNIX was while hanging out with friends in Princeton in 1974. He became an official system administrator of a networked computer at Yale in 1975. He started working part-time for Interactive Systems, the first commercial UNIX company, in 1977 and has been in and out of the computer and network biz ever since. He put his company on Usenet so long ago that it appears in a 1982 *Byte* magazine article, which included a map of Usenet sites. He used to spend most of his time writing software, but now he mostly writes books (including *Internet SECRETS* (with Carol Baroudi), *The Internet For Dummies* (also with Carol Baroudi), *The Internet For Dummies Quick Reference,* and *MORE Internet For Dummies,* (all published by IDG Books Worldwide, Inc.) because it's more fun. He also teaches some computer courses, publishes and edits an incredibly technoid magazine called *The Journal of C Language Translation,* and moderates a Usenet newsgroup. He holds a B.A. and a Ph.D. in computer science from Yale University, but please don't hold that against him.

ABOUT IDG BOOKS WORLDWIDE

Welcome to the world of IDG Books Worldwide.

IDG Books Worldwide, Inc., is a subsidiary of International Data Group, the world's largest publisher of computer-related information and the leading global provider of information services on information technology. IDG was founded more than 30 years ago by Patrick J. McGovern and now employs more than 9,000 people worldwide. IDG publishes more than 290 computer publications in over 75 countries. More than 90 million people read one or more IDG publications each month.

Launched in 1990, IDG Books Worldwide is today the #1 publisher of best-selling computer books in the United States. We are proud to have received eight awards from the Computer Press Association in recognition of editorial excellence and three from Computer Currents' First Annual Readers' Choice Awards. Our best-selling *...For Dummies®* series has more than 50 million copies in print with translations in 31 languages. IDG Books Worldwide, through a joint venture with IDG's Hi-Tech Beijing, became the first U.S. publisher to publish a computer book in the People's Republic of China. In record time, IDG Books Worldwide has become the first choice for millions of readers around the world who want to learn how to better manage their businesses.

Our mission is simple: Every one of our books is designed to bring extra value and skill-building instructions to the reader. Our books are written by experts who understand and care about our readers. The knowledge base of our editorial staff comes from years of experience in publishing, education, and journalism — experience we use to produce books to carry us into the new millennium. In short, we care about books, so we attract the best people. We devote special attention to details such as audience, interior design, use of icons, and illustrations. And because we use an efficient process of authoring, editing, and desktop publishing our books electronically, we can spend more time ensuring superior content and less time on the technicalities of making books.

You can count on our commitment to deliver high-quality books at competitive prices on topics you want to read about. At IDG Books Worldwide, we continue in the IDG tradition of delivering quality for more than 30 years. You'll find no better book on a subject than one from IDG Books Worldwide.

John Kilcullen
Chairman and CEO
IDG Books Worldwide, Inc.

Steven Berkowitz
President and Publisher
IDG Books Worldwide, Inc.

Eighth Annual Computer Press Awards 1992

Ninth Annual Computer Press Awards 1993

Tenth Annual Computer Press Awards 1994

Eleventh Annual Computer Press Awards 1995

IDG is the world's leading IT media, research and exposition company. Founded in 1964, IDG had 1997 revenues of $2.05 billion and has more than 9,000 employees worldwide. IDG offers the widest range of media options that reach IT buyers in 75 countries representing 95% of worldwide IT spending. IDG's diverse product and services portfolio spans six key areas including print publishing, online publishing, expositions and conferences, market research, education and training, and global marketing services. More than 90 million people read one or more of IDG's 290 magazines and newspapers, including IDG's leading global brands — Computerworld, PC World, Network World, Macworld and the Channel World family of publications. IDG Books Worldwide is one of the fastest-growing computer book publishers in the world, with more than 700 titles in 36 languages. The "...For Dummies®" series alone has more than 50 million copies in print. IDG offers online users the largest network of technology-specific Web sites around the world through IDG.net (http://www.idg.net), which comprises more than 225 targeted Web sites in 55 countries worldwide. International Data Corporation (IDC) is the world's largest provider of information technology data, analysis and consulting, with research centers in over 41 countries and more than 400 research analysts worldwide. IDG World Expo is a leading producer of more than 168 globally branded conferences and expositions in 35 countries including E3 (Electronic Entertainment Expo), Macworld Expo, ComNet, Windows World Expo, ICE (Internet Commerce Expo), Agenda, DEMO, and Spotlight. IDG's training subsidiary, ExecuTrain, is the world's largest computer training company, with more than 230 locations worldwide and 785 training courses. IDG Marketing Services helps industry-leading IT companies build international brand recognition by developing global integrated marketing programs via IDG's print, online and exposition products worldwide. Further information about the company can be found at www.idg.com.

1/24/99

Dedication

John and Margy both dedicate this book to their dad, wherever he is. When last sighted, he was traveling somewhere in Turkey, tasting wine, unless he was at the beach in the United States — he's a man who knows how to live!

Authors' Acknowledgments

First and foremost, the authors would like to thank Jonathan Weinert for doing most of the work of updating this book to a fourth edition. Jonathan provided his invaluable knowledge of UNIX and the Internet, along with his *Dummies*-compatible twisted sense of humor, and not a moment too late because we had just about run out of jokes.

The authors thank Antonia Saxon, Jordan Young, Sara Willow Levine Saxon, Meg Young, and Zac Young for putting up with us while we updated this book. Thanks also go to our Internet providers: Finger Lakes Technologies Group and the Trumansburg Home Telephone Company (Trumansburg, New York), the Shoreham Telephone Company (Shoreham, Vermont), and SoVerNet (Bellows Falls, Vermont).

Rebecca Whitney did her usual terrific job of shepherding the text from our hazy scribblings (electronically speaking) to a printed book with her usual blend of patience and midnight wit, despite the best efforts of her telephone company to consign her to a permanent offline existence. She got lots of help, of course, from all the folks listed on the other side of this page.

Publisher's Acknowledgments

We're proud of this book; please register your comments through our IDG Books Worldwide Online Registration Form located at `http://my2cents.dummies.com`.

Some of the people who helped bring this book to market include the following:

Acquisitions, Editorial, and Media Development

Project Editor: Rebecca Whitney

Acquisitions Manager: Michael Kelly

Technical Editor: Tara L. Jennings

Editorial Manager: Mary C. Corder

Editorial Assistant: Paul E. Kuzmic

Production

Project Coordinator: E. Shawn Aylsworth

Layout and Graphics: Lou Boudreau, Angela F. Hunckler, Drew R. Moore, Brent Savage, Rashell Smith, Kate Snell

Proofreaders: Kelli Botta, Rachel Garvey, Nancy Price, Ethel M. Winslow, Janet M. Withers

Indexer: Sherry Massey

General and Administrative

IDG Books Worldwide, Inc.: John Kilcullen, CEO; Steven Berkowitz, President and Publisher

IDG Books Technology Publishing: Brenda McLaughlin, Senior Vice President and Group Publisher

Dummies Technology Press and Dummies Editorial: Diane Graves Steele, Vice President and Associate Publisher; Mary Bednarek, Director of Acquisitions and Product Development; Kristin A. Cocks, Editorial Director

Dummies Trade Press: Kathleen A. Welton, Vice President and Publisher; Kevin Thornton, Acquisitions Manager

IDG Books Production for Dummies Press: Michael R. Britton, Vice President of Production and Creative Services; Cindy L. Phipps, Manager of Project Coordination, Production Proofreading, and Indexing; Kathie S. Schutte, Supervisor of Page Layout; Shelley Lea, Supervisor of Graphics and Design; Debbie J. Gates, Production Systems Specialist; Robert Springer, Supervisor of Proofreading; Debbie Stailey, Special Projects Coordinator; Tony Augsburger, Supervisor of Reprints and Bluelines

Dummies Packaging and Book Design: Patty Page, Manager, Promotions Marketing

♦

The publisher would like to give special thanks to Patrick J. McGovern, without whom this book would not have been possible.

♦

Contents at a Glance

Cartoons at a Glance

By Rich Tennant

The 5th Wave By Rich Tennant
THAT'S RIGHT, THE UPPER CASE BUTTON WORKS ON-SCREEN, BUT THEY'RE NOT COMING OUT ON THE DANG PRINTER! HOLD? SURE, I'LL HOLD.
Poet e.e. cummings makes his last service call.

page 305

The 5th Wave By Rich Tennant
WELL HOT DANG!! FINALLY-A FAULT TOLERANT PRETZEL MAKER THAT RUNS UNDER UNIX!
LARRY'S HOMEMADE PRETZELS
LARRY'S HOMEMADE PRETZELS

page 125

The 5th Wave By Rich Tennant
"WELL THIS HAS SURE TURNED OUT TO BE A MICKEY MOUSE SYSTEM."

page 35

The 5th Wave By Rich Tennant
SURE, HE'S A LITTLE DIFFERENT, BUT HE WORKS HARD, AND KEEPS THE SYSTEM FREE OF BUGS.

page 341

The 5th Wave By Rich Tennant
Now take your time and see if you can identify the person who attacked you on e-mail.

page 189

The 5th Wave By Rich Tennant
WHAT DO YOU MEAN THERE'S A UNIX OPERATING SYSTEM IN THE LOBBY?

page 7

Fax:* 978-546-7747 • *E-mail: the5wave@tiac.net

Table of Contents

Part III: Getting Things Done 125

Introduction

Welcome to *UNIX For Dummies,* 4th Edition! Although lots of good books about UNIX are out there, most of them assume that you have a degree in computer science, would love to learn every strange and useless command UNIX has to offer (and there are plenty), and enjoy memorizing unpronounceable commands and options. This book is different.

Instead, this book describes what you really do with UNIX — how to get started, what commands you really need, and when to give up and go for help. And we describe it all in plain, ordinary English.

About This Book

This book is designed to be used when you can't figure out what to do next. We don't flatter ourselves that you are interested enough in UNIX to sit down and read the whole thing. When you run into a problem using UNIX ("I thought I typed a command that would copy a file, but it didn't respond with any message . . ."), just dip into the book long enough to solve your problem.

We have included sections about these kinds of things:

- Typing commands
- Copying, renaming, or deleting files
- Printing files
- Finding where your file went
- Using the Internet from UNIX
- Connecting and communicating with people on other computers

In this fourth edition, we've beefed up the information about Linux, a new, widely used version of UNIX, and about the Internet, to which many UNIX computers are connected, including a new chapter on how to host an Internet site from your very own computer.

Conventions Used in This Book

Use this book as a reference. (Or use it as a decorative paperweight — whatever works for you.) Look up your topic or command in the table of contents or the index; they refer to the part of the book in which we describe what to do and perhaps define a few terms, if absolutely necessary.

When you have to type something, it appears in the book like this:

```
cryptic UNIX command to type
```

Type it just as it appears. Use the same capitalization we do — UNIX cares deeply about CAPITAL and small letters. Then press the Enter or Return key (we call it Enter throughout this book). The book tells you what should happen when you give each command and what your options are. Sometimes part of the command is in *italics*; the italicized stuff is a sample name, and you have to substitute the actual name of the file, computer, or person affected.

Chapter 25 lists error messages you may run into, and Chapter 26 lists common user mistakes. You may want to peruse the latter to avoid these mistakes before they happen.

Foolish Assumptions

In writing this book, we have assumed these things about you:

- You have a UNIX computer or terminal.
- You want to get some work done on it.
- Someone has set it up so that, if you turn it on (in many cases, it's left on all the time), you are talking to UNIX.
- You are not interested in becoming the world's next great UNIX expert.

How This Book Is Organized

This book has six parts. The parts stand on their own — you can begin reading wherever you want. This section lists the parts of the book and what they contain.

Part I: In the Beginning

This part tells you how to get started with UNIX, including figuring out which kind of UNIX you're using. (You need to know this information later because commands can differ from one type of UNIX to another.) You learn how to log in, type UNIX commands, and ask for help. For Linux users, we include a short chapter on what's it's all about, why Linux is cool, and how to get more information about Linux.

Part II: Some Basic Stuff

Like most computer systems, UNIX stores information in files. This part explains how to deal with files — creating, copying, and getting rid of them. It also talks about directories so that you can keep your files organized, finding files that have somehow gone astray, and printing files on paper.

Part III: Getting Things Done

This part talks about getting some work done in UNIX. It gives step-by-step instructions for using the most common text editors to create and change text files, running several programs at the same time (to get confused several times as fast), and making your Linux system behave, and it gives you directions for a bunch of other useful UNIX commands.

Part IV: UNIX and the Net

Most UNIX systems are connected to networks, and many are connected to the biggest network of them all: the Internet. This part prepares you for the world of communications, including instructions for sending and receiving electronic mail, transferring files over the network, logging in to other computers over the Internet, and surfing on the World Wide Web. For those of you with some intestinal fortitude, we include a new chapter on how to have your Internet site running on your very own UNIX computer.

Part V: Help!

If disaster strikes, check this part of the book. It includes information about what to do if something bad happens, what to do about backups, and what to do when you see common UNIX error messages.

Part VI: The Part of Tens

This part is a random assortment of other tidbits about UNIX, including common mistakes and how to get online help — all organized into two convenient ten-item lists, sort of.

Icons Used in This Book

Some particularly nerdy, technoid information is coming up, which you can skip (although, of course, we think that it's all interesting).

A nifty little shortcut or time-saver is explained, or you get a piece of information you can't afford to be without.

Yarrghhh! Don't let this happen to you!

Information that applies only if your computer is on a network. If it isn't, you can skip to the next section.

Something presented in an earlier section of the book or something you need to remember to do.

The friendly penguin alerts you to information specifically about Linux (see Chapter 3 to find out what Linux is).

Where to Go from Here

That's all you need to know to get started. Whenever you hit a snag in UNIX, just look up the problem in the table of contents or index of this book. You will have the problem solved in a flash — or you will know to find some expert help.

Because UNIX was not designed to be particularly easy to use, don't feel bad if you have to look up a number of topics before you feel comfortable using the computer. Most computer users, after all, never have to face anything as daunting as UNIX (point this statement out to your Windows and Macintosh user friends)!

If you have comments about this book and your computer can send electronic mail via the Internet, you can send them to our friendly mail robot (who will write back) at `unix4@gurus.com`. (We authors also read your message and write back if time permits.) Also visit our Web site with book info and updates, at `http://net.gurus.com`. For information about the *...For Dummies* books in general, write to `info@idgbooks.com` or surf on by `http://www.dummies.com`.

Part I
In the Beginning

In this part . . .

Yikes! You have to learn how to use UNIX! Does this mean that you're about to get inducted, kicking and screaming, into a fraternity of hard-bitten, humorless nerds with a religious dedication to a 25-year-old operating system from the phone company? Well, yes and no. We hope that we're not humorless.

If you're like most UNIX users, a zealot stopped at your desk, connected your terminal or workstation, gave you five minutes of incomprehensible advice, demonstrated a few bizarre games (like roaches that hide behind the work on your screen), and disappeared. Now you're on your own.

Don't worry. This part of the book explains the absolute minimum you need to know to get your UNIX system's attention, persuade it that you are allowed to use it, and maybe even accomplish something useful.

Chapter 1

Log Me In, UNIX!

In This Chapter

- Turning your computer on and getting its attention
- Persuading your computer to let you use it
- Using usernames, passwords, and all that
- Logging out when you finish

If you read the exciting introduction to this book, you know that we make some Foolish Assumptions about you, the reader. Among other things, we foolishly assume that someone else has installed and set up UNIX for you so that all you have to do is turn your computer on and tell UNIX that you're there.

If you don't have UNIX already set up on a computer, the best thing you can do for yourself is find a local UNIX guru or system administrator who is willing to get you up and running. Unless you really know what you're doing, installing and setting up UNIX can be painful, frustrating, and time-consuming. We recommend that you find something more enjoyable to do, such as cleaning out the grease trap under your kitchen sink or performing urgent home surgery on yourself. (You can learn how to administer a UNIX system with some patience and perseverance, but explaining how is way beyond the scope of this book because each version of UNIX has its own procedures.)

Turning Your Computer On and Off

If you think that turning your computer on and off is easy, you may be wrong. Because UNIX runs on so many almost-but-not-quite-compatible computers — all of which work somewhat differently — you first must figure out which kind of UNIX computer you have before you can turn it on.

A dumb terminal

The simplest way to hook up to a UNIX system is with what's known (sneeringly) as a *dumb terminal.* You can identify a dumb terminal by a complete absence of mice and floppy disks and all that other stuff that causes confusion in a more advanced computer. Much can be said for dumb terminals: They're simple and reliable. With UNIX, you can do hundreds, if not thousands, of things wrong to totally scramble a more advanced machine; these same boo-boos make no difference to a dumb terminal.

Turning on a dumb terminal is easy. You find the power switch (probably on the back) and flip it on. Because the terminal has no pesky disks and stuff, you can turn it on or off whenever you want and not break anything. People make long, sort of theological arguments about whether to leave the picture tube on all the time. Personally, we turn off our terminals overnight and don't worry about them at other times.

After you turn on the terminal, you use it to communicate with the computer that is running UNIX. If the terminal is wired directly to the computer, UNIX asks you to log in before you can do anything else (see the section "Hey, UNIX! I Want to Log In," later in this chapter). If not, you may have to perform some additional steps to call the computer or otherwise connect to it.

The PC masquerade ball

Because PCs are so cheap these days, they're commonly pressed into duty as terminals. You run a *terminal emulator* program on a PC, and suddenly the mild-mannered PC turns into a super UNIX terminal. (Truthfully, it's more the other way around: You make a perfectly good PC that can run Leisure Suit Larry and other business productivity-type applications that act like a dumb terminal that can't do much of anything on its own.)

When you finish with UNIX, you leave the terminal emulator, usually by pressing Ctrl+X or some equally arcane combination of keys. (Consult your local guru: No standardization exists.) Like Cinderella at the stroke of midnight, the terminal-emulating PC turns back into a real PC. To turn it off, you wait for the PC's disks to stop running (carefully scrutinize the front panel until all the little red or green lights go out) and then reach around and turn off the big red switch. If you don't wait for the lights to go out, you're liable to lose some files.

If you have a network installed, which these days has become so cheap that nearly everyone does, your PC running Windows may have a network connection to your UNIX system. Windows 98, Windows 95, Windows NT, and the MacOS (the Macintosh operating system) have the network stuff built in; on Windows 3.1, however, you have to add extra network software with names such as Trumpet or Chameleon.

What you were hoping we wouldn't tell you: The difference between a PC and a workstation

First, you have to understand that this isn't a technical question — it's a theological question. Back in the olden days (about 1980), telling the difference was easy. A workstation had a large graphical screen — at least, large by the standards of those days — 1,000K of memory, a fast processor chip, and a network connection, and it cost about $10,000. A PC had a lousy little screen, 64K of memory, a slow processor chip, and a floppy or two, and it cost more like $4,000.

These days, your typical $1,200 PC has a nice screen (much nicer than what the workstation used to have) 16,000K of memory, a fast Pentium processor, a big disk, speakers, and a network connection. That's much better than what people used to call a workstation. Does that make a PC a workstation? Oh, no. Modern workstations have even better screens, buckets of memory, a turbocharged processor chip — you get the idea. What's the difference?

Maybe it's the software that people use: Most workstations are designed to run UNIX (or, in a few cases, proprietary systems similar in power to UNIX), whereas PCs run DOS or Windows or Macintosh software. Wait — some perfectly good versions of UNIX run on PC hardware, and Windows NT runs on many boxes that everyone agrees are workstations. Now what? You can get into esoteric arguments about the speed of the connection between the guts of the computer on one hand and the disks, screens, and networks on the other hand and argue that workstations have faster connections than PCs, but some examples don't fit there, either.

As far as we can tell, if a computer is *designed* to run DOS or Windows or the MacOS, it's a PC. If it's *designed* to run UNIX, it's a workstation. If this distinction sounds feeble and arbitrary to you, you understand perfectly. Here at UNIX For Dummies Central, we have a couple of large PCs running UNIX (which makes them look, to our eyes, just like workstations) and a couple of other, smaller ones running Windows. Works fine for us.

If you do have a network connection, you can use a program called `telnet` (described in Chapter 16) to connect to your UNIX system. After telnet is running and connected to your UNIX system, within your telnet program's window you get a faithful re-creation of a 1970s dumb terminal and you can proceed to log in, as described in the next section.

If a train stops at a train station, what happens at a workstation?

A *workstation* is a computer with a big screen, a mouse, and a keyboard. You may say, "I have a PC with a big screen, a mouse, and a keyboard. Is it really a workstation?" Although UNIX zealots get into long arguments over this question, for our purposes, we say that it is.

Turning on a workstation is easy enough: You reach around the back and turn on the switch. Cryptic things that appear on-screen tell you that UNIX is going through the long and not-at-all-interesting process of starting up. Starting up can take anywhere from ten seconds to ten minutes, depending on the version of UNIX, number of disks, phase of the moon, and so on. Sooner or later, UNIX demands that you log in. To find out how, skip to the section "Logging In: U(NIX) Can Call Me Al," later in this chapter.

Turning *off* a workstation is a more difficult problem. Workstations are jealous of their prerogatives and *do* punish you if you don't turn them off in exactly the right way. Their favorite punishment is to throw away all the files related to whatever you were just working on. The exact procedure varies from one model of workstation to another, so you have to ask a local guru for advice. Typically, you enter a command along these lines:

```
shutdown +3
```

This command tells the workstation to shut down (in three minutes, in this example). With some versions of UNIX, that command would be too easy. The version we use most often uses this command:

```
halt
```

If you use Linux, type this command to shut down the system right away:

```
shutdown now
```

The workstation then takes awhile to put a program to bed or whatever else it does to make it feel important because it knows that you're waiting there, tapping your feet. Eventually, the workstation tells you that it's finished. At that point, turn it off right away, before it gets any more smart ideas.

An approved method for avoiding the hassle of remembering how to turn off your workstation is never to shut off your computer (although you can turn off the monitor). That's what we do.

X marks the terminal

An *X terminal* is similar to an extremely stripped-down workstation that can run only one program — the one that makes X Windows work. (See Chapter 4 to find out what X Windows are — or don't. It's all the same to us.) Turning an X terminal on and off is pretty much like turning a regular dumb terminal on and off. Because the X terminal doesn't run programs, turning it off doesn't cause the horrible problems that turning off a workstation can cause.

Hey, UNIX! I Want to Log In

Whether you use a terminal or a workstation, you have to get the attention of UNIX. You can tell when you have its attention because it demands that you identify yourself by logging in. If you use a workstation, whenever UNIX has finished loading itself, it is immediately ready for you to log in (skip ahead to the section "Logging In: U(NIX) Can Call Me Al"). You terminal users (X or otherwise), however, may not be as lucky.

Direct access

If you're lucky, your terminal is attached directly to the main computer, so it immediately displays a friendly invitation to start working, something like this:

```
ttyS034 login:
```

Well, maybe the invitation isn't that friendly. By the way, the `ttyS034` is the name UNIX gives to your terminal. Why doesn't it use something easier to remember, like Fred or Muffy? Beats us!

This catchy phrase tells you that you have UNIX's attention and that it is all ears (metaphorically speaking) and waiting for you to log in. You can skip the next section and go directly to "Logging In: U(NIX) Can Call Me Al."

If your UNIX system displays a terminal name, make a note of it. You don't care what your terminal's name is, but, if something gets screwed up and you have to ask an expert for help, we can promise you that the first thing the guru will ask is, "What's your terminal name?" If you don't know, the guru may make a variety of nerd-type disparaging comments. But, if you can say, "A-OK, Roger. That's terminal `tty125`," your guru will assume that you are a with-it kind of user and may even try to help you. (Even if her name isn't Roger.)

Yo, UNIX! — not-so-direct access

If you're using a PC with a modem, you probably have to tell the modem to call the UNIX system. Although all terminal emulators have a way to make the call with two or three keystrokes, all these ways are different, of course. (Are you surprised?) You have to ask your local guru for info.

After your terminal is attached to the computer, turned on, and otherwise completely ready to do some work, UNIX, as often as not, doesn't admit that you're there. It says nothing and seems to ignore you. In this way, UNIX resembles a recalcitrant child — firm but kind discipline is needed here.

The most common ways to get UNIX's attention are

- Press the Return or Enter key. (We call it the Enter key in this book, if you don't mind.) Try it two or three times if it doesn't work the first time. If you're feeling grouchy, try it 20 or 30 times and use a catchy cha-cha or conga rhythm. It doesn't hurt anything and is an excellent way to relieve stress.
- Try other attention-getting keystrokes. Ctrl+C (hold down the Ctrl key, sometimes labeled Control, and press C) is a good one. So is Ctrl+Z. Repeat to taste.
- If you're attached to UNIX through a modem, you may have to do some speed matching (described in a minute): Press the Break key a few times. If you're using a terminal emulator, the Break key may be disguised as Alt+B or some other hard-to-find combination. Ask your guru.

Two modems can talk to each other in about 17,000 different ways, and they have easy-to-remember names, such as B212, V.32, and V.32bis. (*Bis* is French for "and a half." Really.) After you call the UNIX system's modem with your modem, the two modems know perfectly well which way they're communicating, although UNIX sometimes doesn't know. Every modem made since about 1983 announces the method it's using when it makes the connection. Because the corresponding piece of UNIX code dates from about 1975, though, UNIX ignores the modem's announcement and guesses, probably incorrectly, at what's being used.

If you see something like `~xxx~~r.!"` on-screen, you need to try *speed matching.* Every time you press Break (or the terminal emulator's version of Break), UNIX makes a different guess at the way its modem is working. If UNIX guesses correctly, you see the login prompt; if UNIX guesses incorrectly, you see another bunch of `~xxx~~~@(r)!"` or you see nothing. If UNIX guesses incorrectly, press Break again. If you overshoot and keep Breaking past your matched speed, keep going and it'll come around again.

After a while, you learn exactly how many Returns, Enters, Breaks, and whatnots your terminal needs in order to get UNIX's attention. It becomes second nature to type them, and you don't even notice what a nerd you look like while you do it. You have no way around that last part, unfortunately.

Logging In: U (NIX) Can Call Me Al

Every UNIX user has a username and password. Your system administrator assigns you a username and a password. Although you can and should change your password from time to time, you're stuck with your username.

Before you can start work, you must prove your bona fides by logging in; that is, by typing your username and password. How hard can it be to type two words? Really, now. The problem is this: Because of a peculiarity of human brain wiring, you will find that you can't enter your username and password without making a typing mistake. It doesn't matter whether your username is `al` — you will type `Al`, `la`, `a;L`, and every other possible combination.

UNIX always considers upper- and lowercase letters to be different: If your username (sometimes also called your *login name*) is egbert, you must type it exactly that way. Don't type Egbert, EGBERT, or anything else. Yes, we know that your name is Egbert and not egbert, but your computer doesn't know that. UNIX usernames almost always are written entirely in lowercase. Pretend that you're a disciple of e. e. cummings.

When you type your username and password and make a mistake, you may be tempted to press Backspace to clear your mistake. If only life were that easy. Guess how you clear typing errors when you type your username and password? You press the # key, of course! (We're sure that it made sense in 1975.) Some — but not all — versions of UNIX have changed so that you can use Backspace or Delete; you may have to experiment. If you want UNIX to ignore everything you have typed, press @, unless your version of UNIX has changed the command key to Ctrl+U (for *untype,* presumably — doubleplus-ungood). So, Egbert (as you typed your username), you may have typed something like this:

```
ttyS034 login: Eg##egberq#t
```

Finish entering your username by pressing Enter or Return.

After you type your username, UNIX asks you to enter your password, which you type the same way and end by pressing Enter (or Return, but we call it Enter). Because your password is secret, it doesn't appear on-screen as you type it. How can you tell whether you've typed it correctly? You can't! If UNIX agrees that you've typed your username and password acceptably, it displays a variety of uninteresting legal notices and a message from your system administrator (usually `delete some files, the disk is full`) and passes you on to the shell, which you learn about in Chapter 2.

If UNIX did not like either your username or your password, UNIX says `Login incorrect` and tells you to start over with your username.

Password Smarts

Like every UNIX user, you should have a password. You can get along without a password only under these circumstances:

- You keep the computer in a locked, windowless room to which you have the only key, and it's not connected to any network.
- You don't mind whether unruly 14-year-olds borrow your account and randomly insert dirty knock-knock jokes in the report you're supposed to give to your boss tomorrow.

The choice of your password deserves some thought. You want something easy for you to remember but difficult for other people to guess. Here are some bad choices for passwords: single letters or digits, your name, the name of your spouse or significant other, your kid's name, your cat's name, or anything fewer than eight characters. (Bad guys can try every possible seven-letter password in less than a day.)

Good choices include such things as your college roommate's name misspelled and backward. Throw in a digit or two or some punctuation, and capitalize a few letters to add confusion, so that you end up with something like `yeLLas12`. Another good idea is to use a pair of words, like `fat;Head`.

You can change your password whenever you're logged in, by using the `passwd` program. It asks you to enter your old password to prove that you're still who you were when you logged in (computers are notoriously skeptical). Then the `passwd` program asks you to enter your new password twice, to make sure that you type it, if not correctly, at least consistently. None of the three passwords you type appears on-screen, of course. We tell you how to run the `passwd` program in Chapter 2.

Some system administrators do something called *password aging;* this strategy makes you change your password every once in awhile. Some administrators put rules in the `passwd` program that try to enforce which passwords are permissible, and some even assign passwords chosen randomly. The latter idea is terrible because the only way you can remember a password you didn't choose is to write it on a Post-It note and stick it on your terminal, which defeats the purpose of having passwords.

In any event, be sure that no one other than you knows your password. Change your password whenever you think that someone else may know it. Because UNIX stores passwords in a scrambled form, even the system administrator can't find out what yours is. If you forget your password, the administrator can give you a new one, but she can't tell you what your old one was.

Ciao, UNIX!

Logging out is easy — at least compared to logging in. You usually can type **logout**. Depending on which shell you're using (a wart we worry about in Chapter 2), you may have to type **exit** instead. In many cases, you can press Ctrl+D to log out.

Chapter 2

What Is UNIX, Anyway?

In This Chapter

- Why you care: A little boring UNIX history
- How to tell which version of UNIX you have
- How to use the UNIX shell
- Shell traps and pitfalls

This entire chapter tells you how to figure out which kind of UNIX system you have gotten involved with. If you *really* don't think that you care, skip this chapter. As you read the rest of this book and run into places where you need to know which kind of UNIX or shell you are using, you can always come back here.

Why Do We Ask Such Dumb Questions?

"What is UNIX?" UNIX is UNIX, right? Not entirely. UNIX has been evolving feverishly for close to 30 years, sort of like bacteria in a cesspool — only not as attractive. As a result, many different varieties of UNIX have existed along the way. Although they all share numerous characteristics, they differ (we bet that this doesn't surprise you) just enough that even experienced users are tripped up by the differences between versions.

May a thousand UNIXes flower

Indulge us while we tell a historical parable. Imagine that UNIX is a kind of automobile rather than a computer system. In the early days, every UNIX system was distributed with a complete set of source code and development tools. If UNIX had been a car, this distribution method would have been the same as every car's being supplied with a complete set of blueprints, wrenches, arc-welders, and other car-building tools. Now imagine that nearly all these cars were sold to engineering schools. You may expect that the students would get to work on their cars and that soon no two cars would be the same. That's pretty much what happened to UNIX.

Bell Labs released the earliest editions of UNIX only to colleges and universities. (Because Bell Labs was The Phone Company at that time, it wasn't supposed to be in the software business.) From that seed, a variety of more-or-less scruffy mutants sprang up, and different people modified and extended different versions of UNIX.

Although about 75 percent of the important stuff is the same on all UNIX systems, it helps to know which kind of UNIX you're using, for two reasons. First, you can tell which of several alternatives applies to you. Second, you can impress your friends by saying things like "HP-UX is a pretty good implementation of BSD, although it's not as featureful as SunOS." It doesn't matter whether you know what it means — your friends will be amazed and speechless.

Throughout this book, we note when a command or feature being discussed differs among the major versions of UNIX. When we talk about the popular new Linux system, you see our cute Linux icon in the margin. We don't waste your time with a family tree of UNIX systems. The following sections describe the most common kinds.

The two main versions of UNIX are BSD UNIX and System V. Although they differ in lots of little ways, the easiest way to tell which one you're using is to see how you print something. If the printing command is `lp`, you have System V; if it's `lpr`, you have BSD. (If the command is `print`, you cannot be using UNIX; nothing in UNIX is that easy.)

Here are the major types of UNIX you're likely to run into:

- **Berkeley UNIX:** One of the schools that received an early copy of UNIX was the University of California at Berkeley. Because no student's career was complete without adding a small feature to Berkeley UNIX, you can still see on every part of BSD UNIX the greasy fingerprints of a generation of students, particularly a guy named Bill, about whom you hear more later.

  The Berkeley people made official Berkeley Software Distributions of their code (named BSD UNIX) and gave numbers to its versions. The most widely used versions of BSD UNIX are Versions 4.3 and 4.4. Berkeley graduates fanned out across the country, working for and even starting new companies that sell descendants of BSD UNIX, including Sun Microsystems (which markets SunOS and Solaris), Hewlett-Packard (HP-UX), Digital Equipment (Ultrix), and IBM (AIX). Most workstations run some version of BSD UNIX.

- **Post-Berkeley BSDs:** Shortly before 4.4BSD came out, the folks at Berkeley realized that they had made so many changes to BSD over the years that practically none of the original Bell Labs code was left. Several groups quickly rewrote the missing 1 percent, adapted the BSD code for 386 and newer PC-compatible machines, and made all the code available over the Internet. Three projects (called FreeBSD, OpenBSD, and NetBSD) continued to improve and update the freely available BSD, and a company called Berkeley Software Design offers a commercially supported version of BSD/OS.

- **System V:** Meanwhile, back at The Phone Company, legions of programmers were making different changes to UNIX. They gave their versions of UNIX Roman numerals — which are classier than plain ol' digits. Their current version of UNIX is known as System V. The many subversions of System V are known as System V Release 1 (SVR1) and SVR2, SVR3, and SVR4. Most nonworkstation versions of UNIX are based on System V or, occasionally, its predecessor, System III. (What happened to System IV? Not ready for prime time, we guess.)

  Sun Microsystems, from the BSD camp, and AT&T, of the System V camp, decided to bury the hatchet and combine all the features of BSD and System V into the final incarnation of System V, SVR4. SVR4 has so many goodies that it's only slightly smaller than a blimp. If your system runs SVR4 or its descendants, you have to pay attention to our hints about both BSD *and* System V. The last version of SVR4 was SVR4.4. (Where *do* they get these numbers?) System V was eventually sold to Novell (the NetWare people), which retitled it UNIXWare. Novell eventually sold it to a Microsoft affiliate called the Santa Cruz Operation (better known as SCO), which retitled it UnixWare (don't ask).

  Helpful advice to Sun users: Although Sun changed the name of its software from SunOS to Solaris, it didn't change the way the software worked (at least in Solaris 1.0, which is still a BSD-flavored UNIX). If you use Solaris 1.0, follow the instructions for BSD UNIX. Because Solaris 2.0 is based on SVR4, however, you have to worry about both BSD and System V. Is this stuff clear? We're still confused about it.

- **OSF/1:** When System V and BSD UNIX merged to form SVR4, many UNIX vendors were concerned that, with only one version of UNIX, the market confusion would be insufficient. They started the Open Software Foundation, which makes yet another kind of UNIX: OSF/1. Although OSF/1 is mostly BSD, it is also a goulash of some System V and many other miscellaneous eyes of newts and toes of frogs.

  OSF/1 has largely disappeared; if you use OSF/1, however, pay attention to the BSD advice in this book, and you should be okay.

- **Linux:** Without a doubt, the most surprising UNIX development in recent years has been the appearance — seemingly from nowhere (but actually from Finland) — of Linux, a rather nice, freely available version of UNIX. Linux is such a big deal that we devote an entire chapter to it (the next one, in fact). Chapter 14 also has stuff about Linux for those brave souls who run their own Linux systems.

  Linux resembles SVR4 as much as it resembles any other version of UNIX.

Why you should fight rather than switch

The question "Which is better: UNIX or Windows NT?" has sparked a religious war between UNIX crusaders and the high priests of marketing at Microsoft Corporation. Microsoft would have you believe that NT, its industrial-strength version of Windows, is a snazzy new alternative to UNIX, a tired old system that wore out its welcome in the last days of disco. According to Microsoft, UNIX is expensive and impossible to use without a degree in computer science. NT is cheaper and easier to use, and, because it's a Microsoft product, it's just plain better. So you should junk your UNIX computers and replace them with NT servers and workstations *right now, before it's too late!* (If we were cynical, we would point out that Microsoft has no UNIX version of its own to sell. But we're not cynical. Are we?)

In spite of rather extravagant Microsoft claims of NT superiority, the evidence is decidedly mixed. Although many businesses seem to have made the switch from UNIX to NT successfully, they're usually on the small- to medium-size end of the spectrum. If you have to support a large company that depends on an extensive network to handle high volumes of traffic and to serve critical applications and information, you're much better off sticking with UNIX.

In case your system administrator is considering making an ill-advised switch from UNIX servers to NT servers, here are a few points you should try to work in during your next conversation at the company water cooler.

NT servers tend to *go down* — stop working properly for one reason or another — fairly regularly. UNIX servers, on the other hand, tend to work perfectly for months on end. Running your company's phone sales department on an NT server means running the risk of cutting off all your callers until you can get your server to *reboot,* or recover from one of its little episodes.

According to various independent reports, more NT security *bugs* (problems with the way the system behaves) than UNIX bugs get reported every week. NT simply doesn't have the built-in security and permissions features that UNIX has always had.

As far as processing power goes, NT can't hold a candle to UNIX. NT servers now have a four-processor limit, although UNIX machines can handle many, many more. UNIX can handle larger files, and its architecture provides as much as 4 *billion* times more data space than NT (yup, we said *billion*). In practice, this statement means that you have to replace each of your UNIX machines with multiple NT machines to maintain the same amount of computing power.

Which brings us to the question of cost. Although individual NT servers may be cheaper than individual UNIX servers, the apparent price advantages quickly evaporate when you consider the number of servers you need and the cost of administering and maintaining them, not to mention hidden costs from server downtime and data loss.

We could go on (and if you want to meet us over a couple of beers, we certainly will). Suffice it to say that the Microsoft rumors about the imminent death of UNIX have been greatly exaggerated.

Oh, and by the way, UNIX stills leads the way when it comes to serving Web sites. The Apache server, which we discuss in Chapter 21, is still the most widely used Web server in the world today. And it doesn't cost much. In fact, it's free.

- **XENIX:** A few older versions of UNIX just won't die. The most notable version is XENIX, originally from Microsoft Corporation and later sold by the aforementioned SCO. XENIX is considered hopelessly obsolete. It occupies much less disk space than do more modern versions of UNIX, and it runs much faster. (To be fair, it's missing some of the more modern versions' zoomy features, although you're not likely to notice.) Because XENIX is based on one of the ancestors of System V, most System V advice applies to XENIX. SCO has now moved most of its XENIX customers to UnixWare, which is based on System V.

What's GNU?

No tour of UNIX versions is complete without a visit to the Free Software Foundation, in Cambridge, Massachusetts (not to be confused with the OSF, Open Software Foundation, which is about six blocks down the street). The FSF was founded by a brilliant but quirky programmer named Richard Stallman, who came from MIT, where people wrote lots and lots of software and gave it all away. He firmly (some would say fanatically) believes that all software should be free, and he set up the FSF to produce lots of high-quality free software, culminating in a complete, free version of UNIX. Despite quite a bit of initial skepticism, the FSF has raised enough money and been given and lent enough equipment to do just that. The FSF's project GNU (for *G*NU's *N*ot *U*NIX) has so far produced versions of most of the UNIX user-level software. The best known and most widely used pieces are the text editor GNU Emacs (which we discuss in Chapter 10), most of the other basic UNIX utilities, and the GNU C compiler (GCC), which is now used on all the free versions of UNIX, including Linux, as well as on a few commercial ones.

The GNU crowd continues to work on new stuff, including its *pièce de résistance,* the GNU Hurd, a complete working version of the guts of the UNIX system. Early on, fans of free software awaited the GNU Hurd with great eagerness; now that Linux and the freely available BSD versions have arrived, however, their eagerness has abated somewhat. Hurd or no Hurd, GNU Emacs, GCC, and the GNU utilities are here to stay.

What the FSF means by "free" software is a little different from what you may expect: It means freely available, not necessarily available for free. It means that if you can find someone willing to pay you a million bucks for some GNU software, that's perfectly okay. That person, and anyone else to whom you give or sell GNU software, however, must be free to give or sell it, in turn, to other people without restriction. The intention is that people can make money by supporting and customizing software, not by hoarding it. Although opinions vary about the long-term practicality of this plan, for now the FSF surely has written some popular software, and at least one company, Cygnus Support, makes a good business supporting it.

How Can You Tell?

When you log in to your UNIX system, a variety of copyright notices usually flash by, with an identification of the type of UNIX you are accessing. Carefully scrutinize the information on-screen, and you may be able to tell which version you have.

Another approach is to type the command **uname** and press Enter. Sometimes this command displays the name of your computer (such as `aardvark` or `acctg3`). Sometimes, however, the command displays the version of UNIX you are running. On Linux systems, it says `Linux`.

If you can't tell which UNIX version you have, break down, grovel, and ask your local UNIX expert. When you figure out which type of UNIX you are running, write it down on the Cheat Sheet in the front of this book. You never know when you may need to know this stuff.

If you're using a dumb terminal or an X terminal (or a PC acting like a dumb terminal or connected to your UNIX system by means of a network), the type of UNIX you're using depends on the maker of the main computer you're attached to — not on the maker of the terminal. You generally see the identification of the main computer in a message it sends to the terminal just before or just after you log in.

Cracking the Shell

Now that you have figured out which general variety of UNIX you have, you must figure out one other vital consideration: which shell you're using. Although you may say, "I don't want to use *any* shell; I just want to get some work done," the shell is the only way to get to where you want to be.

The guts of UNIX are buried deep in the bowels of the computer. The guts don't deign to deal with such insignificant details as determining what users may want to do. That nasty business is delegated to a category of programs known as shells. A *shell* is a program that waits for you to type a command and then executes it. From the UNIX point of view, a shell is nothing special, other than the first program UNIX runs after you log in. Because you can designate any old program to run when you log in, any fool can write a shell — indeed, many have done so. About a dozen UNIX shells are floating around, all slightly incompatible with each other (you probably guessed that).

Fortunately, all the popular shells fall into two groups: the Bourne (or Korn or BASH) shell and the C shell. If you can figure out which of the two categories your shell is in, you can get some work done. (You're getting close!)

You can disregard this discussion about the true nature of shells

What UNIX calls a shell, many other people — especially DOS users — call a *command processor.* What DOS users call a shell is a fancy graphical program that is supposed to make the computer easier to use by displaying cute little icons for programs and files and other such user-friendly goodies.

Because the people who wrote UNIX didn't go for all this wimpy, fru-fru, hand-holding stuff, their idea of a shell was a program in which you could type **zq** to run a program called `zq`. (These guys were notoriously lazy typists.) Although user-friendly shells are available for UNIX, they're not widely used, and we don't mention them again in this book.

If a Windows or Macintosh fanatic says rude things about the UNIX shell, you can respond that, although UNIX may be somewhat challenging to use, as a UNIX user, at least you're not a wimp.

You can easily tell which kind of shell you're using. If UNIX displays a `$` after you log in, you have a Bourne-style shell; if UNIX displays a `%`, you're using the C shell. Traditionally, System V systems use the Bourne shell, and BSD systems use the C shell. These days, however, because all versions of UNIX come with both shells, you get whichever one your system administrator likes better. Preferences in command languages are similar to preferences in underwear: People like what they like, so you get what you get, although these days most of the people we know like BASH, a souped-up Bourne-style shell.

Linux systems usually come with the BASH shell, a Bourne-style shell.

After you have determined whether you have a Bourne-style shell (`$`) or a C shell (`%`), note this fact on your Cheat Sheet in the front of this book.

If you use a GUI (see Chapter 4), you see windows and icons, not a boring little UNIX prompt, after you log in. You still need to use a UNIX shell from time to time, however, usually to perform housekeeping tasks.

The Bourne and Bourne Again shells

The most widely used UNIX shell is the Bourne shell, named after Steve Bourne, who originally wrote it. The Bourne shell is on all UNIX systems. It prompts you with `$`, after which you type a command and press Enter. Like all UNIX programs, the Bourne shell itself is a program, and its program name is `sh`. Clever, eh?

A few alternative versions of the original Bourne shell exist, most notably the Bourne Again shell (or BASH, whose program name is `bash`) from the GNU crowd. This version of the Bourne shell is used in many places because of its price — it's free. Some people claim that it's still overpriced, but we don't get into that. BASH is enough like the original Bourne shell that anything we say about the Bourne shell applies also to BASH. The most notable advantage of BASH is that it has "command editing," a fancy way of saying that you can press the arrow keys on your keyboard to correct your commands as you're typing them, just as you can with DOS (oops, better not say that when any UNIX fans are listening).

The Korn-on-the-cob shell

After the Bourne shell was in common use for a couple of years, it became apparent to many people that the shell was so simple and coherent that one person could understand all its features and use them all effectively. Fortunately, this shameful situation was remedied by a guy named Dave Korn, who added about a thousand new features to the Bourne shell and ended up with the Korn shell (called `ksh`). Because most of the new features are of interest only to people who write *shell scripts* (sequences of shell commands saved in a file), you can consider the Korn shell the same as the Bourne shell. Most versions of the Korn shell also have command editing.

She sells C shells

No, the C shell wasn't written by someone named C. It was written by Bill, the guy we mentioned earlier. (He sells C shells by the C shore? Probably.) We would discuss our opinion of the C shell at length, except that Bill is 6'4", in excellent physical shape, and knows where we live. The C shell's program name is `csh`.

The most notable difference between the C shell and the other leading shell brands is that the C shell has many more magic characters (characters that do something special when you type them). Fortunately, unless you use a number of commands with names like `ed!3x`, these characters aren't a problem.

Many versions of the C shell exist; most of them differ in which bugs are fixed and which are still there. You may run into a program called `tcsh`, a slightly extended C shell with command editing.

Who says the C shell isn't user-friendly?

If you use the C shell, be aware that some punctuation characters do special and fairly useful things.

An exclamation point (!) tells the C shell to do a command again. Two of them (!!) means to repeat the last command you typed. One of them followed by the first few characters of a command means to repeat the last command that started with those characters. For example, to repeat the last `cp` command you gave, type

```
!cp
```

This command is great for lazy typists.

You can also use carets (^) to tell the C shell to repeat a command with some change. If you type this line:

```
^old^new
```

the C shell repeats the last command, substituting "new" for "old" wherever it appears in what you typed. You can use slashes (/) in a similar way, although carets are easier to use. The C shell also uses colons (:) to perform truly confusing editing of previous commands, which we don't get into.

In Chapter 7, the section about history's repeating itself tells you more about reissuing shell commands.

Are Any Good Programs On?

You may be wondering why we refer sometimes to commands and sometimes to programs. What's the difference?

A *command* is something you type that tells UNIX (or actually the shell) what to do. A *program* is a file that contains executable code. The confusion comes because in UNIX, to run a program, you just type its name. (In old-fashioned operating systems, you usually typed something like `RUN BUDGET_ANALYSIS` to run a program called `BUDGET_ANALYSIS`.)

When you type a command, such as `ls` or `cp` or `emacs` (a text editor we talk about in Chapter 10), the shell looks at it carefully. The shell knows how to do a few commands all by itself, including `cd` and `exit`. If the command isn't one that the shell can do by itself, the shell looks around for a program stored in a file by the same name.

DOS users may recognize the way this process works — commands DOS can do itself are called *internal commands,* and commands that require running another program are called *external commands.* Internal commands are also called *built-in commands.*

Finally! You're Ready to Work

We wrap up this chapter with a little advice about hand-to-hand combat with the shell. You can give many commands to your shell. Every shell has about a dozen built-in commands, most of which aren't very useful on a day-to-day basis. All the other commands are the names of other programs. The fact that every UNIX system has hundreds of programs lying around translates into hundreds of possible shell commands.

One nice thing about UNIX shells is that, within a given shell, the way you type commands is completely consistent. If you want to edit a file called `my-calendar`, for example, and use an editor called `e`, you type this line:

```
$ e my-calendar
```

As always, press Enter at the end of the line to tell the shell you have finished. The shell runs the `e` editor, which does whatever it does. When you finish, you return to the shell, where you can issue another command.

Whenever you see a UNIX prompt (either `$` or `%`), a shell is running, waiting to do your bidding. Throughout this book, we usually refer to the entire package — UNIX plus shell — as UNIX. We say, "Use the `ls` command to get UNIX to display a list of files" rather than "Use the `ls` command to get the shell to get UNIX to display a list of files." Okay?

Now you know which kind of UNIX you are using, which shell you are using, and why you care. Let's look at a few UNIX (or shell) commands you can use to begin getting something done.

We could tell you the password, but then we'd have to kill you

When you logged in, you probably hated your password because someone else picked it. Hating your password is a good reason to change it. Another reason you may want to change it is that, to get this far, you enlisted the aid of some sort of expert and had to reveal your password. This section shows how to change your password: Use the `passwd` command.

This stuff is easy. Just type this line:

```
passwd
```

Ending command lines without hard feelings

Remember to end every command line by pressing Enter. UNIX is pretty dumb; in most cases, your pressing Enter is the only way UNIX can tell that you have finished doing something.

With a few programs, notably the text editors `vi`, `pico`, and `emacs`, you don't need to press Enter anywhere; we point out those exceptions. Everywhere else, remember to press the Enter key at the end of every line.

As always, press Enter after typing the command. The `passwd` command asks you to type your current password to make sure that you are really you. (If it didn't check, whenever you wandered off to get some more coffee, someone could sneak over to your desk and change your password. Not good.) Type your current password and press Enter. The password doesn't appear on-screen as you type, in case someone is looking over your shoulder.

Then `passwd` asks for your new password. (Chapter 1 has lots of sage advice about how to choose a password.) You have to type the new password twice so that `passwd` is sure that you typed it correctly. Assuming that you type the new password twice in the same way, `passwd` changes your password. The next time you log in, you are expected to know it.

If you forget your password, you have no way to retrieve it; not even your system administrator can tell you what it is. The administrator can assign you a new one, though, and you can change it again, preferably to something more memorable than the one you forgot.

What's my file?

This section discusses a command you use frequently: the `ls` command, which lists your files. Chapters 5 and 6 talk more about files, directories, and other stuff `ls` helps you with; for now, here's `ls` Lesson 1. Type the following line (we're not telling you to press Enter anymore because we know that you have the hang of it):

```
ls
```

The `ls` command lists the names of the files in the current directory. (Chapter 6 talks about directories.)

Don't turn off the computer if you make a typo!

To repeat something we have hinted at: If you make a mistake and all is not going well, do *not* turn off the computer, unplug it, or otherwise get unnecessarily rough. Although PC users get used to just turning the darned thing off if things aren't going well, UNIX computers don't respond well to this approach.

Instead, suggest politely to UNIX that it stop doing whatever it is you don't like. To stop a command, press Ctrl+C, or, on some systems, the Break key or the Del key.

If the situation is out of control, UNIX is running a program you don't want, and you can't get it to stop, you can use some Advanced and Obscure Techniques to wrestle extremely recalcitrant programs into line. See Chapter 24 if you're desperate.

Oops!

If you are a world-class typist, you can skip this section. If you make thousands of typos a day, as we do, pay close attention. If you type something wrong, you can probably press the Backspace key to back up and retype it. If that doesn't work, though, all is not lost. Try the Delete key, the # key (Shift+3), or Ctrl+H. One of these combinations should work to back you up.

To give up and start the entire line over again (not usually necessary with nice, short commands, such as `ls`), press Ctrl+U. If that doesn't work, press the @ key (Shift+2).

Play it again, Sam

Sometimes, you may want to issue the same command again (because it was so much fun the first time). If you use the C shell, type this line:

```
!!
```

If you use the BASH shell, press the up-arrow key to see the last command you typed and then press Enter.

In the Korn shell, you can type this line to reissue a command:

```
r
```

If you use the Bourne shell, you're out of luck and must type your command again.

The UNIX cast of special characters

One of the more exciting aspects of typing shell commands is that many characters are special. They have special meanings to UNIX; the next few chapters discuss some of them. Special characters include the ones in this list:

```
<   >   '   "   *
{   }   ^   !   \
[   ]   #   |   &
(   )   $   ?   ~
```

Spaces also are considered special because they separate words in a command. If you want to put special characters in a command, you must quote them. You *quote* something by putting quotation marks around it. Suppose that you have a file called `c*` (not a great idea, but sometimes you get these things by mistake). You can edit it by typing

```
e "c*"
```

You can use either single or double quotation marks, as long as you're consistent. You can even quote single quotation marks with double quotation marks and quote double quotation marks with single quotation marks. Is that clear? Never mind.

Everything you wanted to know about typing commands — but were afraid to ask

This list shows a wrap-up of what to do when UNIX displays a prompt (either $ or %) and you want to type a command:

- As you type, the cursor moves along to indicate where you are. The cursor looks like an underline or a box.
- If you make a typing mistake, press Backspace (or try Delete, #, or Ctrl+H).
- To cancel the entire command before you press Enter, press Ctrl+U (or try @).
- When you finish typing a command, press Enter. (If you don't, UNIX — and you — will wait forever.)
- If you issue a command that UNIX (actually, the shell) doesn't know, you see a message like this:

```
blurfle: Command not found.
```

This message means that you typed the command wrong, you typed a command that UNIX doesn't know (maybe a DOS command crept in), or someone hasn't told UNIX the right places to look for programs.

- Don't stick extra spaces in the middle of commands, as in `pass wd`. Type the command exactly as we show it. On the other hand, *do* type a space after the name of the command but before any additional information you have to type on the line (read more about that subject in Chapter 5). Also, do not capitalize except where you know that the command has a capital letter.
- You know that a command resembles a sentence, but you don't end it with a period. UNIX doesn't like the period, and UNIX is extremely unforgiving.

Chapter 3

A Few Lines on Linux

In This Chapter

- ▶ What is Linux?
- ▶ Why should you care?

Linux is the hottest thing to arrive in UNIX-land in years: a wildly popular, completely free version of UNIX. It is (quite deliberately) similar to other versions of UNIX; for the most part, then, everything in this book that applies to other versions of UNIX also applies to Linux.

Out of the Frozen North

In 1992, a guy in Finland named Linus Torvalds took a then-popular, small, educational version of UNIX called Minix, decided it wasn't quite what he wanted, and proceeded to rewrite and extend it so that it was more to his taste. Lots of enthusiastic programmers have started projects like that, but to everyone's astonishment, Linus *actually finished* his. By mid-1993, his system had long since left its Minix roots and was becoming a genuinely usable version of UNIX. Linus's system was picked up with great enthusiasm by programmers, and later by users, all over the Internet. It spread like crazy, to become the fastest-growing part of UNIX-dom.

Linux is popular for three reasons:

- It works well, even on a small, cheap PC. A 386 PC with 4 MB of random-access memory (RAM) and a 40MB hard disk can run Linux — barely. (John bought a computer like that for less than $500, new, from a dealer who had ordered more than he needed.) On a top-of-the-line Pentium PC, its performance approaches that of a full-blown traditional UNIX workstation.
- Lots of enthusiastic people are working on Linux, with wonderful new features and additions available every day. Many of them even work.
- It's free!

The many developers of Linux proudly describe it as a "hacker's system," one written by and for enthusiastic programmers. (This classic meaning of *hacker* should not be confused with the other, media-debased "computer vandal" definition.) These programmers keep up the development of Linux at a brisk pace, and a new "development" version is made available on the Internet every few days. Every once in awhile, the developers decide that they have gotten enough bugs out of their recent developments, and they release a "stable" version, which stays constant for months rather than days. Most normal people use the stable version rather than a development version. Using a development version of Linux is sort of like living in a house inhabited by a large family of carpenters and architects: Every morning when you wake up, the house is a little different. Maybe you have a new turret, or some walls have moved. Or perhaps someone has temporarily removed the floor under your bed. (Oops — sorry about that.)

Linux started life as the operating system of choice for students and other cheapskates, er, users who wanted a UNIX system of their own but couldn't afford a traditional UNIX workstation. As Linux has matured into a stable, reliable UNIX system, this base has expanded to include companies and institutions that *could* afford traditional UNIX workstations, but found that

How free is free?

Linux is *free software.* In the UNIX software biz, "free" has a concrete meaning that is different from public domain and different from shareware.

Linux is made available under the GNU General Public License (GPL), Version 2, the same license the Free Software Foundation uses for most of its programs. The license has seven pages of legalese, much of which is about where copyright notices have to appear and stuff like that, but the basic plan is simple. In short, it says:

- You can copy and distribute Linux and other GPL software, and you can charge for it.
- *But,* anyone to whom you distribute it has the right to give copies away for free.
- *And,* you must include the source code (or make it available for no more than a reproduction fee) in the distribution.

The idea is that people are permitted, even encouraged, to distribute copies of GPL software and to sell maintenance service, as long as the software itself remains freely available.

Don't confuse free software with *shareware,* which is software for which you are supposed to pay the original author if you use it, or with *public domain* software, with which you can do anything you want.

Although the GPL was subject to considerable debate and a fair amount of ridicule when it first came out in about 1990, it has worked pretty much the way its authors intended: GPL software (including Linux) is widely available, and people do indeed constantly work on and improve it.

Linux enabled them to add PC-based workstations at a fraction of the cost. In fact, Linux is now estimated to have more than 6 million users, making it the third most popular operating system in the world (behind Windows and the Macintosh operating system).

What's Old, What's New

The original guts of Linux were written from scratch by Linus Torvalds and have since been greatly changed and extended by other people. He based Linux more or less on System V (on *descriptions* of System V; there's no code from System V). Most programs that people actually use (the shells and other commands) come from the GNU project, which modeled most of them after the Berkeley UNIX versions, so most of the commands are BSD-ish. Because the networking programs are adapted from the Berkeley ones, they also are all BSD-ish.

Technically speaking, Linux refers only to the operating system "kernel." When most people refer to a Linux system, though, they usually mean the whole package: operating system plus the GNU programs that come with it. Like all UNIX systems, Linux systems can run various shells, editors, and other software. Most versions of Linux use BASH as the default shell because it's also new and snazzy.

Keep in mind that because Linux is a moving target, with frequent improvements to the programs, the version of Linux you use is probably not exactly the same as the version described in any book, including this one. At the time we wrote this edition of this book, the latest stable version of Linux was 2.0.34, but even if you have a more recent version, the basic structure is the same.

A look at the various Web sites and Usenet newsgroups dedicated to Linux show a veritable flurry of Linux-related activity. New programs, extensions, and enhancements for Linux appear daily, it seems. Red Hat Linux, for example, now offers a range of snazzy new products, including a secure Web server, a Microsoft Office-like suite of desktop tools called ApplixWare, and a fully graphical integrated desktop (see Chapter 4 for details about UNIX desktops).

If you still have any doubt about whether Linux has arrived, consider this: Red Hat has teamed up with the NASA Goddard Space Flight Center to create something called Extreme Linux, which lets you set up computer clusters — many computers acting like one enormous supercomputer — using parallel processing. You can get the source code, operating system, and management tools for about 30 bucks.

You say to-may-to, I say tomahto

A frequent concern of newcomers to Linux is how to pronounce it correctly, in order not to sound uninformed. It's simple: However you pronounce it is wrong — or right, depending on your audience. Among English speakers in the United States, at least, opinions seem to be divided about evenly between "Line-ucks" and "Linn-ucks."

The name Linux is derived from the first name of its creator, Linus Torvalds. The "Line-ucks" group holds that the pronunciation is based on the usual English pronunciation of Linus. Linus Torvalds himself, though, a Swedish-speaking Finn, has helpfully provided an audio file on the Internet in which he provides the definitive answer in both English and Swedish. (You can find the files at the URL `http://sunsite.unc.edu/LDP/links.html`, way down at the end of the page. See Chapter 18 to find out what a URL is.) In the file, he says, "Hello, this is Lee-noos Torvalds, and I pronounce Lee-nooks as Lee-nooks." It's up to you whether you want to say "Linux" with a Swedish accent, but to our ears his reading sounds much closer to the Anglicized "Linn-ucks," so that's what we use.

In Chapter 14, we talk about the latest releases of the most popular versions of Linux. In Chapter 27, we describe a number of ways you can get additional information about Linux, including reading one of a number of Usenet newsgroups about Linux or subscribing to a Linux magazine.

Where's Linux?

Linux development happens mostly on the Internet, and if you have an Internet connection, you can download the entire system at no charge. You *do* need either a fast connection or great patience because the system takes up about 50 disks full of data. A typical 14.4 Kbps online connection would take about 15 hours to download Linux. Quite a few bulletin-board systems around the world make Linux code available. A more practical approach is to buy or borrow a CD-ROM version of Linux, which you can install in an hour or so.

Sounds great, doesn't it? You can install a version of UNIX on your very own computer! Keep in mind one tiny little snag, however: That makes *you* the system administrator. You have to learn how to create user accounts, deal with disks that fill up, and install and configure software. It's not impossible (far from it — John has done it for years), but you have much to learn.

The details of installing and setting up Linux are way beyond the scope of this book. In Chapter 14, we barely touch on a few basics of administering a Linux system. For more details, take a look at *LINUX For Dummies,* by Craig Witherspoon, Coletta Witherspoon, and Jon Hall; *LINUX Secrets,* 2nd Edition by Naba Barkakati (both published by IDG Books Worldwide, Inc.); and *Running Linux,* by Welsh and Kaufman (O'Reilly & Associates).

Part II

Some Basic Stuff

"WELL THIS HAS SURE TURNED OUT TO BE A MICKEY MOUSE SYSTEM."

In this part . . .

UNIX, like other computer systems, keeps your information in things called *files.* When you work with UNIX, you frequently need to make new files, rename files, make copies of particularly interesting files, get rid of files that have outlived their usefulness, find a file you have temporarily mislaid, or print what's in a file.

This part of the book also talks about *graphical user interfaces* (GUIs), which let you use a mouse to point at things on-screen. Most people find using GUIs a big improvement over typing commands, but you have to know what to point at and click on. You're about to find out!

Chapter 4

Opening Windows on UNIX

In This Chapter

- What's a GUI — and should you care?
- How to tell which type of windows you have
- Window-wrangling skills, Motif and otherwise
- How to get in and out of windows
- How to make UNIX look and act a whole heck of a lot like Those Other Famous Operating Systems

To answer your first question, GUI stands for *graphical user interface* and really *is* pronounced "gooey." We prefer the term WIMP, which stands for *w*indows, *i*cons, and *m*ouse *p*ointing, but for some reason the term never caught on. Fast-track executives would rather be gooey than wimps, we suppose.

A *GUI* is a combination of a graphics screen (one that can show pictures in addition to text), a mouse (or something like it), and a system that divides the screen into several windows that can show different things at the same time. All GUIs work in more or less the same way because they're all based on the same original work done at Xerox about 20 years ago. The details differ enough, though, to make you want to tear your hair out.

UNIX Gets All GUI

The earliest UNIX systems didn't have fancy, screen-oriented windowing systems. They didn't have screens at all, in fact — they used loud, rattling terminals that printed on actual paper. (The historically minded can find these types of terminals in the Computer Museum in Boston and the Smithsonian Institution in Washington, D.C. Yes, really.) As the years went by, UNIX appeared on computers that did have screens (most notably Sun workstations), and various windowing systems appeared.

One thing about the UNIX community you've probably come to appreciate by now is that you can't get everyone to agree on anything, except of course that UNIX is better than every other kind of system and that anyone who thinks otherwise is silly. So, not surprisingly, a variety of incompatible windowing systems arose, each different from the other in various, not particularly interesting, ways. Nearly all the windowing systems were *proprietary* (they belonged to one system vendor or another), and, of course, no vendor would dream of admitting that someone else's window system was better than theirs.

X marks the window

Universities also had a bunch of window system projects. One of the more successful was the X Window project at MIT (alleged to be a successor to the W Window project at Stanford — as far as we know, no one created a V Window project). The X Window system had many virtues, not the least of which were that it worked adequately well and it was available for free to anyone who wanted it. So X became the window system everyone used.

Almost all UNIX systems that have any sort of GUI now use one based on the X Window system (frequently abbreviated to just "X Windows," which has been known to drive UNIX purists crazy because it sounds too much like that *other* famous operating system from Redmond, Washington). Old Sun workstations used systems named SunView or NeWS; NeXT machines use NeXTStep (are tHoSE wOrDS cAPiTaLIzed corREctlY?); other than those exceptions, however, you almost certainly get X Windows.

X (which is an even shorter abbreviation for X Window system) has many advantages as a windowing system:

- It runs on all sorts of computers, not just those that run UNIX.
- It is *policy independent:* A program can make the screen look any way it wants; the screen is not constrained to a single style, as it is on the Macintosh or with Microsoft Windows. (As you may imagine, this capability is not an unmitigated blessing. Read more about this subject in the section "Just my look," later in this chapter.)
- It uses a networked client-server architecture (love those buzzwords). You can run X on one computer, and the programs that display stuff on-screen can be on entirely different computers connected by a network.
- MIT gives it away.

You can imagine which of these important advantages is the one that really made all the computer makers choose X. Even though MIT gives away the base version of X, unless you happen to be using the exact same kind of computer the guys at MIT use (or you feel like compiling and debugging a gazillion lines of C code), you don't get it for free. You must buy a version tailored for the particular kind of screen and adapter on your computer. An exception is XFree86, a free version of X used by PC-based UNIX systems, such as Linux, which is described in Chapter 3.

How your screen looks depends on which GUI you use. The first part of this chapter talks about things that are the same for all GUIs. Later, we talk about how to tell which GUI you are using and how to do things that work differently for each GUI.

"I'm not just a server — I'm also a client!"

X was designed from the beginning to work with computer networks. It makes a clear distinction between the *server* program, which handles the screen, keyboard, and mouse, and the *client* program, which does the actual computing. Although the two programs are running more often than not on the same computer, they don't have to be. (Readers who saw John on *The Internet Show* on public TV a few years ago may recall one demonstration of an online subway map of Paris. That was an X application, with the X server running on a PC in the TV studio in Texas and the client program on a computer in France, connected by way of the Internet.)

The networkability (is that a word?) of X is most useful in two ways. One way is that you can be sitting at an X workstation attached to a local network and have windows attached to client programs running on computers all over the network, often on computers considerably more powerful than yours. The other way is that you can be using an *X terminal,* which is a specialized computer with a screen, a keyboard, a mouse, and network connections that runs only a single program, an X server. The idea of an X terminal is that because it's considerably cheaper than a workstation, you can have a few workstations or larger computers with a flock of inexpensive X terminals attached and get nearly workstation performance for the X terminal users, and at a considerably lower price.

X terminals should be a passing fad because these days a standard PC that runs UNIX, including an X server program, costs about the same as an X terminal and offers more flexibility. (For this same reason, we don't think much of "network computers.") Fortunately, because X terminals and workstations running an X server look and work almost exactly the same, we don't belabor the difference any longer.

Just my look

Most windowing systems on most kinds of computers make programs use a consistent style. All Macintosh programs, for example, look pretty much the same: They all use the same menu, the same little window when you want to select a file, and similar windows to turn options on and off. One Microsoft Windows program looks much like all the others: They all use similar sets of windows.

Do all X Windows programs have a consistent look? Of course not — that would be too easy. This situation is what the X crowd means by *policy independence:* X is utterly agnostic about what windows should look like on-screen, how keystrokes and mouse clicks should be interpreted, and pretty much anything else that affects a user. This lack of policy was part of the original appeal of X because no matter which window system you were used to, you could make X look just like that system. The good news is that X offers great flexibility. The bad news is that the word *inconsistent* barely scratches the surface of what you run into.

Makeup artists for your windows

One of the ways in which X avoids having any policy built in is that it foists much of the general window-management jobs onto a program called a *window manager.* (Catchy name, huh?) The window manager handles jobs such as creating borders around each application's main windows; controlling how you move, resize, switch among, and iconify windows; and most of the other tasks that aren't part of any particular application. It's possible to run X without any window manager, although it's rather unpleasant because, without one, you have no way to do some things, such as move a window.

We've got something in common

A few companies doing UNIX apparently decided that they had gone too far in the customizability department, so they got together with the Open Software Foundation to create something called the Common Open Software Environment, which describes how to build UNIX programs so that they all act and look something like each other (or at least like they come from the same planet). In 1995, this group came out with the Common Desktop Environment, or CDE, which is a UNIX windowing system that bears more than a passing resemblance to the Macintosh and (Microsoft) Windows desktops. Surprisingly, CDE is beginning to catch on, especially among Microsoft Windows and Macintosh users who are new to UNIX or who need to use *both* Windows or Macs alongside their UNIX workstations.

CDE does much more than manage your UNIX windows. We talk about CDE in the section "CDE: A Desktop for All Seasons," later in this chapter.

A field guide to window managers

A bunch of competing window "looks" are on the UNIX market. To tell which one you're stuck with, er, have the pleasure to use, look at the border around the windows on your screen. If they have 3-D-style borders with sharp corners, as shown in Figure 4-1, you're using the Motif Window Manager (MWM); its free lookalike counterpart, FVWM; or DTWM, the Desktop Window Manager that comes with the Common Desktop Environment (CDE). If the borders have rounded corners, as shown in Figure 4-2, you're using OpenLook. If they have a thin border around the sides and bottom and top borders like those shown in Figure 4-3, you're using a program called TWM, which comes with the base version of X and is still sometimes used because it is simple and small.

```
xpcterm
          program, use the commands

              xgrabsc -Z >outfile.pzl
              puzzle -picture outfile.pzl


          To have xgrabsc sleep for three seconds before rubber-
          banding, display processing information, and have the result
          displayed with xwud,

              xgrabsc -Wvs3 | xwud
iecc:ttyp1:johnl>xgrabsc -W > mwmwd
iecc:ttyp1:johnl>xwud mwmwd
usage: /usr/bin/X11/xwud [-in <file>] [-noclick] [-geometry <geom>] [-display <d
isplay>]
        [-new] [-std <maptype>] [-raw] [-vis <vis-type-or-id>]
        [-help] [-rv] [-plane <number>] [-fg <color>] [-bg <color>]
iecc:ttyp1:johnl>xwud -in mwmwd
iecc:ttyp1:johnl>!xgrab
xgrabsc -W > mwmwd
iecc:ttyp1:johnl>!xw
xwud -in mwmwd
iecc:ttyp1:johnl>!xg
xgrabsc -W > mwmwd
```

Figure 4-1: A typical Motif window.

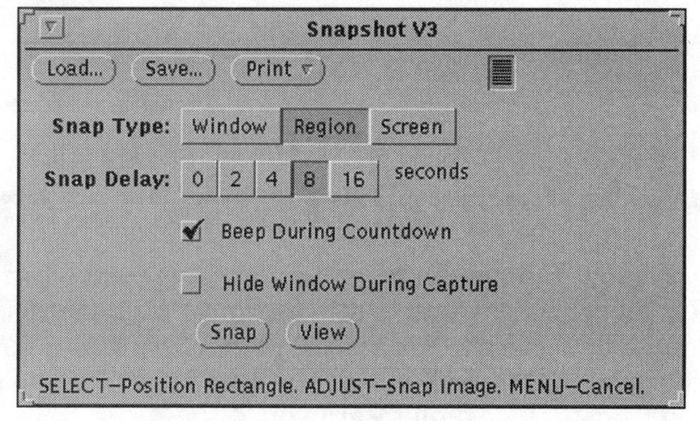

Figure 4-2: A typical OpenLook window.

```
xpcterm
iecc:ttyp1:johnl>who -a
   .          system boot  Dec 12 12:32
   .          run-level 2  Dec 12 12:32     2      0  S
bcheckrc           .       Dec 12 12:33  0:20      5  id=bchk term=0    exit=77
brc                .       Dec 12 12:33  0:20     15  id= brc term=0    exit=0
brc                .       Dec 12 12:33  0:20     19  id=  mt term=0    exit=0
rc2                .       Dec 12 12:49  0:20     23  id=  r2 term=0    exit=0
root          console      Dec 29 20:16  0:01  17956
sleep              .       Dec 12 12:49  0:20    130  id=  wt term=0    exit=0
johnl         vt01         Dec 21 15:19  0:01   5938
LOGIN         vt02         Dec 29 20:16 20:48  17955
LOGIN         ttyd1        Dec 30 16:24  0:52   2827  492-3869
faxserve           .       Dec 26 11:45  0:20  24871  id=  F2
johnl         ttyp2        Dec 30 17:16   .     3053  id=  p2 term=112 exit=2
johnl         ttyp1        Dec 30 16:55   .     3054
johnl         ttyp0        Dec 30 16:55  0:15   3055
johnl         ttyp3        Dec 30 16:56  0:20   3086  id=  p3 term=112 exit=2
johnl         ttyp4        Dec 30 16:12  1:04  19342  id=  p4 term=112 exit=2
johnl         ttyp5        Dec 23 18:41  old   11186  id=  p5 term=112 exit=2
LOGIN              .       Dec 15 15:28  0:20  25517
LOGIN              .       Dec 15 15:30  0:20  25532
LOGIN         ttyd2        Dec 17 18:55  old    5561  id=  02 term=15   exit=0
iecc:ttyp1:john
iecc:ttyp1:johnl>xgrabsc -W > twmwd
```

Figure 4-3: A typical TWM window.

The Open Software Foundation, the same people who provide the OSF/1 version of UNIX, created Motif, based on some work done by their members Hewlett-Packard and Digital Equipment. Motif is much more complete than its competition (it has a provision for handling languages other than English, for example), and because DEC made it cheap for software vendors to use, it has become the primary X Window manager now in use.

People using the Common Desktop Environment (CDE) get the Desktop Window Manager, or DTWM. CDE comes with all kinds of nifty and zoomy programs, although underneath the glitz it's just a version of Motif, so it looks pretty much the same.

Lots of other window managers exist; the ones in this section are the most common ones. After several years of window system warfare, Motif and its clone FVWM have emerged as the clear favorite window systems, so that's what we concentrate on here.

Considerably more than you want to know about window managers, toolkits, and X

If you're dying to know more about how the X Window system works, strap on your safety belts because we get a little technical. If you're dying to know how to *use* your window manager and couldn't care less about how it *works,* skip down to the section "Stupid Window Manager Tricks." If you're sticking with us, just don't say that we didn't warn you.

Déjà vu déjà vu

Readers familiar with Microsoft Windows 95 or Windows NT may find the Motif window manager to be strangely familiar. Its windows don't look all that much like Windows windows, although the mouse and keyboard techniques are extremely similar. That turns out to be no coincidence. Because Hewlett-Packard has a superduper application environment it sells for both Windows and X, it deliberately made its X package (from which much of Motif is derived) as similar to Windows as possible. For users who switch back and forth between Windows and Motif (we authors, for example), this capability is a blessing because the mouse moves and keystrokes our fingers have memorized for one system work by and large in the same way in the other. This practically unprecedented level of compatibility exists between UNIX and something else, so we figure that, deep down, it must have been an oversight.

The X Window system divides the work of controlling what's on-screen among three separate kinds of programs:

- **X server:** Draws pictures on-screen and reads user input from the keyboard and mouse
- **Window manager:** Controls where windows appear on-screen, draws borders around windows, and handles basic window operations, such as moving windows, shrinking windows to an *icon* (a little box representing that window), and expanding icons to windows
- **Clients:** Programs that do some real work

For any particular screen, there's one X server, usually (but not always) one window manager, and a bunch of clients. Every client communicates with the server to tell it what to draw and to find out what you did; the server communicates with the window manager when the user asks for a window-management operation, such as changing the size of a window. Although the server, window manager, and clients usually run on the same computer, X Windows enables them to exist on separate machines connected by a network. It is not unusual to have a setup in which the server runs on an X terminal, the window manager runs on a nearby workstation, and the clients are on various machines scattered around the network.

The window manager is usually (except on a few X terminals) a regular UNIX program. You can stop one window manager and start another if you decide that you don't like the way your windows look. Client programs can ask the X server to ask the window manager to do some specialized operations. A terminal program, for example, can ask the window manager to enable a user to change the size of the window only to a size that is a whole number

FVWM: The chameleon of window managers

Because Motif isn't free, it isn't included with most Linux systems. (Nothing would prevent you from running Motif under Linux, but most people aren't prepared to pay more for a window manager than they paid for the whole operating system and its included software.) Instead, with Linux, you usually find the window manager called FVWM.

The origins of the name FVWM are forever lost in the mists of history. The *VWM* part stands for *v*irtual *w*indow *m*anager. The *F* part is a mystery, though. *Fine* and *feeble* are two frequently offered possibilities.

The "virtual" part of this window manager is one of FVWM's best-loved features. Rather than have just a single desktop, you can have any number of virtual desktops, each with its own independent set of windows open. Because each desktop is the size of the screen, this feature enables you to think of your screen as a porthole looking at part of a much larger screen behind it.

FVWM usually displays a little map of all the virtual desktops at your disposal; Most systems have either four or nine, although theoretically you can have as many or as few as you want. You move around among all your desktops by pressing the Ctrl key and then the arrow key for the direction of the next desktop according to the little map. Is your desktop getting too crowded with windows? No need to close some of them; just pop on over to another desktop. You can have dozens of programs open without getting too crowded; never has slowing your system to a crawl been easier!

FVWM is almost infinitely configurable. You can make it look like practically anything, although its default look is nearly identical to Motif. A version of FVWM known as FVWM95 looks remarkably similar to — you guessed it — Windows 95. (Whether this is A Good Thing is a favorite point of religious arguments among many Linux users.) Not only do its window borders mimic those in Windows 95, but it also even features a Start button with pull-up menus. FVWM95 is found by default on recent releases of Red Hat Linux (discussed in Chapter 14). Another popular mutation of FVWM is called AfterStep, which looks just like the NeXTStep window system.

FVWM has become enormously popular, not only on Linux but also on other free UNIX versions. You can even find it on some large commercial systems.

of lines of text. (This kind of communication starts to resemble that in the ancient Roman Empire, in which proconsuls could officially speak only to procurators, who could speak to senators, and so on. Computers are like that.) If no window manager exists, no window-management operations are available.

Writing an X program is a great deal of work. To make life easier for programmers, a programmer can build on *toolkits* of program code that are already written. MIT sends out X Toolkit (immediately called `Xt` by the usual lazy typists). This toolkit provides a set of basic window functions that most programs use. Starting with `Xt`, different people have produced libraries of *widgets*, or screen elements a program can use. A menu or a file-selection panel is a widget, for example. The Motif widget set is for programs that want to look like Motif. Although the Athena widgets from MIT's Project Athena aren't particularly attractive, many programs use them because (where have we heard this before?) they're available for free. You can also find other toolkits for other, less commonly used window systems.

What all this means is that any particular X client uses one of the widget sets to control what that client's window looks like. A program that uses the Motif toolkit, for example, is a Motif program. Because clients are separate from window managers, however, the Motif window manager (named `mwm` — the lazy typists strike again) can be running and draw a Motif border around the windows of clients using other toolkits.

Because of the constant danger that GUI systems could begin to make sense to users, UNIX people have learned to obfuscate things by using "Motif" to refer to both the Motif window manager and the Motif toolkit, which are, of course, completely separate entities. When people refer to "Motif," therefore, they may be referring to the window manager or maybe to the toolkit. Or both. Often it's difficult to tell. This confusion is all just part of the proud legacy of UNIX evolution.

One school of thought says that we all would be better off if X Windows had picked a window style and stuck with it so that we would have a single window manager and a single set of widgets — as every other window system does — although it's much too late now for that.

Opening a new window

When you run a new X program, generally speaking, it opens a new window. In some cases, you want to tell a program that's already running to open another window (another file for a word processor, for example), although the way you do that is specific to each program. You have to read the manual (gasp!) for the program.

You usually have at least one terminal window running. A *terminal window* isn't as sinister as it sounds: It's a window that acts like a terminal. The usual program is called `xterm`; it acts much like a DEC VT100 terminal. Most systems also have a modified terminal program that acts like the computer maker's favorite terminal. Hewlett-Packard systems have `hpterm`, for example, which acts like an HP terminal, and some PC UNIX systems have `xpcterm`, which acts like a PC console. For most purposes, all these terminal programs act the same. They start up by running a UNIX shell, and you type commands just as we describe in this book.

How do I start Motif, anyway?

You may think that this question would be a simple one to answer, but, because UNIX is involved, it's not. The short answer is "Run mwm" (the Motif Window Manager), although that technique is not useful because you have to run mwm at the right time and place.

If you're lucky, your system manager will have set up everything for you automatically. If you're on an X terminal or a workstation running xdm (the X Display Manager), X is already running when you sit down and waits for you to enter your username and password, and Motif starts as soon as you log in.

The next best thing is that you're at a workstation that has been set up to run X after you log in so that X and Motif start automatically when you log in.

Failing that, you have to start X and Motif yourself after you log in to UNIX. The two most common start-up commands are `startx` and `xinit`. If you're not sure which one to use, try them and see what happens. What should happen is that your screen goes *kerflooie!* for a few seconds when it switches from old, dumb, terminal mode to new, cool, graphical X mode; a few windows appear, running `xterm` (the dumb terminal emulator that runs under X); and Motif starts and draws attractive borders around all the windows.

If none of those things works, we've run out of ideas, and you have to ask your local expert how to start X and Motif on your computer or X terminal.

You can use one of two ways to start a new program that opens a new window: the GUI-oriented, user-friendly way and the easy way.

Follow these steps for the GUI-oriented, user-friendly way:

1. **Move the cursor so that it's not in any of your current windows.**
2. **Click the Menu mouse button.**

   This button is the last one (the rightmost button unless you have a left-handed mouse) in OpenLook and the first button otherwise.
3. **Drag the mouse up and down the menu that pops up until you find the program you want.**
4. **Let go of the button.**

   Sometimes you have nested menus: When you pick an item from the first menu, a second menu pops up, and you must pick an item there too.

The easy way to start a program has only one step:

1. **Go to a terminal window and type the name of the program you want to run.**

About your mouse

Your mouse (or mouse-like thing) has some buttons on it. Take a moment to count the buttons. Finished counting? (How long could it have taken?) We hope that you found three buttons. If you found only two buttons, you have a problem because most X programs were written with three-button mice in mind and don't work well with two-button mice. Some X servers can be configured to enable you to get to all the X features by using only two buttons, although it's much easier to get a three-button mouse. We've found some perfectly usable ones at our local computer store for $10 or less.

This approach is the same one you use to run any other program or to give a command. To display another terminal window, type **xterm** or the name of the terminal program you use.

Then you have the issue of where on-screen the new window appears. Some programs and window managers have strong opinions of their own, and the new window appears wherever the program or window manager thinks that it should. With other, less opinionated programs, you make the call: A ghostly window that appears floats near the middle of the screen. You move the ghost around with the mouse and click when the window is where you want it. At that point, the ghost materializes into the regular window. This latter scheme is usually more convenient because the locations the opinionated programs choose for window placement are rarely where you want them. Beware of one thing, though, while the ghost is on-screen: All other windows are frozen. If you leave the ghost on-screen for a long time (while you're at lunch or overnight), all the others can become rather constipated waiting for the screen to unfreeze so that they can update their windows. If you're using Motif, your local guru can switch your system between opinionated mode and floating-ghost mode.

Some systems have desktop manager programs (unrelated to window manager programs) that attempt to make handling programs and files easier. Desktop managers have sets of icons you click to start common programs. They enable you to click filenames to edit the file, for example — sort of like the Macintosh Desktop. Opinions vary on how useful these desktop managers are. We haven't been crazy about them, although it's worth trying them for a few minutes because some people find them much easier to use than menus and shell commands.

Icon do this with a picture

GUIs are crazy about pictures (they're graphical, after all), especially cute, little ones. The cutest, littlest ones you run into are called icons. An *icon* is a little picture in a little box on-screen that represents a window. When you tell X Windows to "iconify" a window, the window disappears and an icon remains. When you double-click (or single-click if you're not using Motif) the icon, the window comes back just as it was before. Being able to reduce windows to icons enables you to shove programs out of the way and not lose what you were doing — one of the best things about window systems. Figure 4-4 shows a pair of icons, one for an e-mail program and one for a terminal program. If new mail arrives, the little flag on the mail icon flips up, which is almost useful enough to make up for its X-treme cuteness.

Figure 4-4: Icons are windows in a miniature disguise.

Window wrangling à la Motif

Motif (or, more particularly, the Motif window manager) draws a border around every window on your screen, as shown in Figure 4-5. The border gives you considerable control over the window, enabling you to move it, hide it, change its size, and perform other tasks.

The borders of some windows are missing some or all of the buttons we discuss in this section. That's because not all windows allow all functions. If the button's not there, you can't do what it would have done anyway.

You frequently will find that you don't like the way the windows on your screen are arranged. You can do lots of things to alleviate this problem and simultaneously waste lots of time. We have found that, by giving your dedicated attention to window management, you can spend the entire day at the computer apparently working but not accomplishing anything. Because a little rearrangement is inevitable, the following sections are thumbnail sketches of what you can do and how to do it with Motif:

- **Change the layering.** Change which windows are in front of other windows, much like shuffling the papers in the pile on your desk. Unless you're a masochist, you want the active window (the window you're using) to be the one in front.

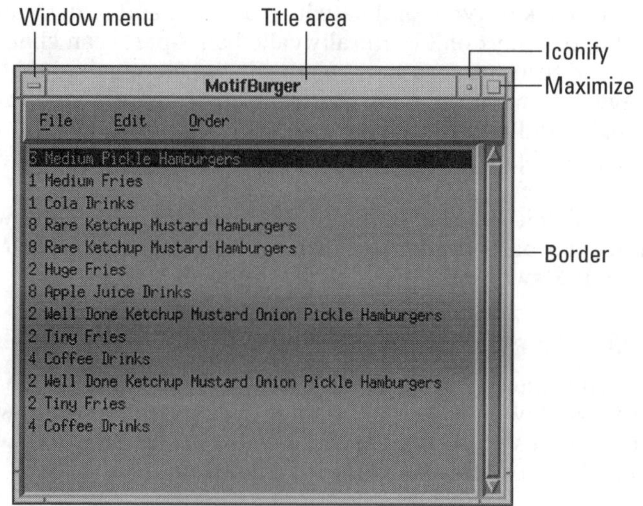

Figure 4-5: A typical Motif window.

- **Move windows around the screen.** This process is even more similar to shuffling the papers on your desk.
- **Turn windows into icons and vice versa.**
- **Change the size of windows.** Create larger areas for long files you're editing, for example.

Switching and layering your windows

Suppose that you have two or three windows on-screen. How do you tell UNIX which window you want to use? The answer is (wait, no — how did you know that this answer was coming?) *it depends.* In line with the standard X rule of never making up its mind about anything, you can switch windows in two different ways:

- **Click-to-type, or explicit focus:** Move the mouse cursor to the window you want to use, and click the mouse in it somewhere. The window moves to the front (any overlapping windows drop behind it so that you can see the entire window).
- **Move-to-type, or pointer focus:** Move the mouse cursor into the window you want to use. Even though the window may be partially obscured by other windows, it becomes active. You can tell when a window is *active* because the border around it changes color. Click the window's title bar if you want to move it to the front. Motif also enables you to move a window up front like this: Move the cursor into the window, hold down the Alt or Meta key, and press F1.

If you have to "click to type" and hate it — or don't and really want to — a guru skilled in the ways of X (naturally called an X-pert) can change some parameters and turn "click to type" on or off. We recommend that you live with whatever you have. So many changeable parameters are available that, after you begin fiddling with them, it can become X-asperating to figure out X-actly how your X-pert left them, and you will utter an X-cess of X-pletives.

You can tell which is the active window because the Motif window manager changes the color of its border to a distinctive darker color. The Motif standard window-switching rule is click-to-type.

"Where, oh, where has my window gone?"

In Motif, you put the cursor on the title bar, press the first mouse button, and drag the window to where you want it (you move the window as you hold down the mouse button). This action also brings the window to the front because you use the same button to do that.

You can move windows so that they are partially off the edge of the screen, sort of like pushing papers to the side of your desk so that they hang over the edge (except that windows are less likely to fall on the floor). This capability is sometimes useful if the interesting stuff in the window is all at the top or all on one side.

Stashing your windows

The title bar of the window has on it little buttons you can click. Near the right of the title bar is a little box that contains a small dot; when you click it, you *iconify* the window; that is, the window turns into an icon.

To get the window back, double-click the icon with the first mouse button.

Icons normally appear in the lower-left corner of the screen, although you can move them around by dragging the icon around with the mouse. After you've moved an icon, if you restore the window and then re-iconify it, the icon reappears where you left it. You can lay out the icons to your taste by iconifying every window on-screen, moving the icons to tasteful positions, and then restoring the ones you want to use.

Curiouser and curiouser: Changing window sizes

The last little bit of window magic involves changing window sizes. Motif has gone to a great deal of trouble to let you change the size of your windows, which tells us that they gave up trying to make them the right size in the first place. Oh, well. Little "grab bars" are in each corner of most windows. (The few windows you can't resize don't have grab bars.) You move the cursor to one of the grab bars, click the first mouse button, drag the corner to where you want it (make the window larger or smaller), and release the button. Then do it again two or three times because you never get it right on the first try. Motif also has grab bars (thin, gray borders) on the top, bottom, and sides of every window, which enable you to change the height of a window without changing the width or vice versa.

Some programs have strong feelings about how big their windows should be. In some cases, they don't let you shrink the window to less than a minimum size. In other cases, you can't change the size. For these programs, attempts to resize just don't work. You can click and drag the borders all you want, but nothing moves.

Motif has a shortcut to enable you to expand a window to fill the entire screen. Click the little box-in-a-box at the right end of the title bar. If you do the same thing again, the window shrinks back to normal size.

In practice, we rarely blow up windows to full-screen size because few UNIX programs take advantage of the entire screen. The full-screen option was much more important when screens were smaller.

Getting rid of windows

Your screen often becomes cluttered with windows you no longer need. You already know how to turn them into icons to get most of the screen space back, but sometimes you just want to make the program go away.

Remember that, if 57 different programs are running, even if most of them are snoozing behind their icons, it can put enough of a load on your computer to slow down the ones you want to use.

Most programs have a natural way to exit. In terminal windows, you log out from the shell by typing **exit** or **logout** in the terminal window. Real windows-oriented programs usually have menus of their own with a Quit or Exit option that cleans up and makes the program stop. Because some programs just won't die, however, you have to take drastic measures.

In Motif, click the little bar in the box at the left end of the title bar; a menu of window operations pops up, as shown in Figure 4-6. The Restore, Move, Size, Minimize, and Maximize choices are equivalent to the border-clicking techniques we just discussed. (Minimize is Motif-ese for "iconify.") The two remaining options can be useful, though. The Lower option pushes the window behind all the rest so that it doesn't obscure any other windows. That option is useful when you want to work on something else for a while. Close closes the window and usually also ends the program that started it. This option can be handy for programs that get stuck or don't have any normal way to exit.

Figure 4-6: The Motif window menu.

Motif offers a set of keyboard equivalents for mouse-haters. To display the window menu, press Shift+Esc or Alt+spacebar. Then either press the cursor keys and Enter to choose one of the entries, or press the underlined letter for the entry you want. For Move and Size, you press the cursor keys to move or resize the window and then press Enter when you're finished.

You can also use the Alt+key equivalents on the menu, such as Alt+F9 for Minimize. If your keyboard has two Alt keys (as most PC keyboards do), you may find that the two Alt keys work differently. Individual programs recognize the left Alt key on our system, and the Motif Window Manager recognizes the right Alt key.

Motif uses confusing and inconsistent names in the window-operations menu. Close destroys the window and the program, and Minimize turns the window into an icon.

Motif widgets on parade

The Motif toolkit is a set of programming tools with prewritten bits of program that programmers can use to build their Motif applications. That information wouldn't be very interesting except that the bits of program it includes are the ones that draw stuff on-screen. These so-called *widgets* include the usual things that windowing programs use, such as menus, pushbuttons, text boxes, and scroll bars. Motif widgets have become a *de facto* standard for X programs and have sprouted up in seemingly every application written for X Windows. Even programs that use something other than Motif widgets often make them look just like Motif programs, with the dull gray menus and buttons UNIX users have gotten used to.

This section quickly describes the most common widgets. Because they're all designed to be easy to use, you can easily — even without reading the instructions — guess how they work.

Menus

Figure 4-7 shows the main window from the MotifBurger sample application that comes with Motif, with one of its pull-down menus selected. You make choices from a Motif menu in an obvious way: Click the place you want on the menu bar at the top of the application's window. If the menu has subentries (as most do), the next-level menu drops down. Click the entry you want.

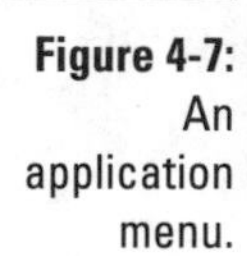
Figure 4-7: An application menu.

You can also drive Motif applications from the keyboard. To choose a menu entry, hold down Alt (the left Alt key if you have two) and press the underlined letter in the menu entry. If submenus are available, press the up- and down-arrow keys to move to the entry you want, and then press Enter to select or Esc to ignore.

Occasionally, you see a couple of other minor variants of menus. *Tear-off* menus are similar to pull-down menus except that they have a dotted line across the top when you pull them down. If you click the dotted line and drag the menu to a convenient place, it stays there indefinitely so that you can use it whenever you want. We don't find this feature useful because it clutters the screen. (The old Motif archrival OpenLook had tear-off-like menus called *pushpins,* and Open Look proponents trumpeted them as a major advantage. Motif probably added them as much to shut up the competition as because anyone really wanted them.) Sometimes, *pop-up* menus also appear when you press the right mouse button, the way the root menu appears when you click outside any window. Pop-up windows work just like pull-down windows after they've popped up.

Radio buttons

Figure 4-8 shows a window from the MotifBurger sample application. This window is somewhat awfully designed because it's full of way too many different kinds of widgets. It was intended as a demonstration of the various kinds of widgets, however, which it does just fine.

Beginning at the left side of the figure, the first type of widget you encounter is the *radio button.* The Hamburgers Rare/Medium/Well Done box is called a radio button box because it sort of resembles the buttons on a car radio. You can click any one of the buttons to select it, and you can select only one radio button in a group.

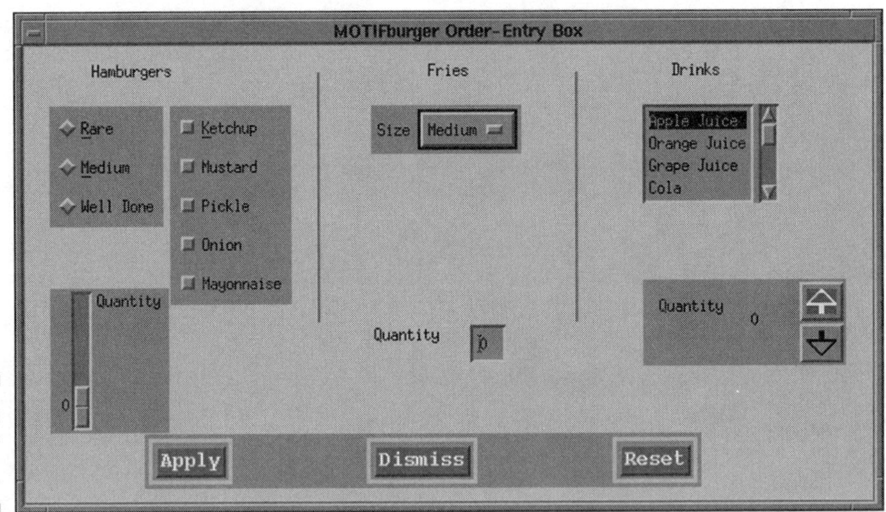

Figure 4-8: A bunch of widgets.

You can recognize radio buttons because they're shaped like little diamonds.

You're supposed to be able to select radio buttons by holding down the Alt key and pressing the underlined letter, although in our experience, that doesn't always work. Use your mouse to be sure.

Toggle buttons

The list of hamburger condiments, from Ketchup to Mayonnaise, shown in Figure 4-8 are *toggle buttons.* When you click one, it turns on if it was off, and it turns off if it was on — sort of like a toggle switch. Unlike radio buttons, any or all of the toggle buttons in a group can be selected at a time.

You can recognize toggle buttons because they're little squares.

Scales or sliders

The hamburger Quantity indicator shown in Figure 4-8 is a *scale.* You can move it up or down with the mouse to control how many hamburgers to order. Although this scale looks silly, in some cases scales are just what you want (the volume control on a sound application, for example).

Scales can be laid out either up and down or left and right. They work the same either way.

Option menus

The fries Size control shown in Figure 4-8 is an *option menu.* When you click it, the complete set of options appears, as shown in Figure 4-9. Move the cursor to the one you want and click. The menu shrinks back down and displays the selected option.

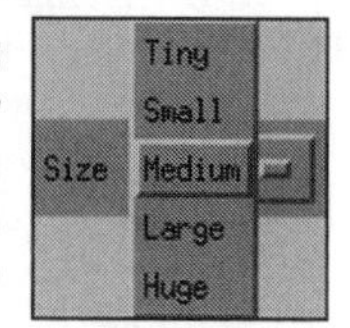

Figure 4-9: How many fries would you like with that?

Text boxes

The little Quantity box shown under Fries in Figure 4-8 is a *text box.* Click the cursor there, and then type the number of orders of fries you want. The usual text-editing characters, such as arrow keys and Backspace, work.

This text box is the smallest one we've ever seen. (Hey, it's just a sample application.) Most text boxes are large enough that the editing keys are useful. Many text windows also have scroll bars, which we discuss in the following section.

Scrollable lists and scroll bars

In Figure 4-8, the list of drinks starting with Apple Juice is a *scrollable list.* You can move the list up and down in its window by clicking the *scroll bar* to the right of the window. The little arrows move the list up and down a small, fixed amount. You can also drag the block between the arrows up and down to move the list directly.

How do I leave Motif, anyway?

This question is only slightly less complicated than the one about starting Motif. As usual, you are the victim of a blizzard of options. Here are some likely possibilities:

- Log out by leaving the Motif Window Manager. In this case, move the mouse cursor outside any windows, click and hold the right mouse button to display the Motif root menu, slide the cursor down to Quit, and release the button. Motif displays an incredulous little box asking whether you really want to leave `mwm`. Click OK.
- Log out by closing the main `xterm` window. The trick is to figure out which window is the main one. If one of them is labeled Login or Console, that's it. Switch to that window by moving the mouse to that window and clicking the left mouse button. Then type `exit` to the shell in that window.

When X and Motif exit, the screen usually *kerflooies!* again when it goes back to dumb terminal mode. (If your system uses the X Display Manager, your system may immediately go back to the login screen, in which case you're finished.) If you end up back at a shell prompt in dumb terminal mode, you then have to exit from that, too, by typing `exit` to that shell.

After you've found the item you want, click it to select and highlight it. (We've selected Apple Juice, although our favorite is Grape Juice because it gives us the classic cool, purple mustache.)

Pushbuttons

The other controls shown in Figure 4-8 are *pushbuttons.* They come in two varieties: buttons with text and buttons with drawings. The two arrows for the drinks quantity are buttons with drawings. The Apply, Dismiss, and Reset buttons at the bottom of the window are buttons with text.

They all work in the same way. To select the button and do whatever the button does, click it.

CDE: A Desktop for All Seasons

If you've ever used a Macintosh or one of those *other* Windows computers, then you know what a *desktop* is. When you start up a computer with the Macintosh or Windows OS installed on it, slick-looking graphics and mouse-clickable icons and menus take over your entire computer screen, giving you a common workspace for all your programs and windows. That's the desktop.

The desktop gives you a slew of ways to keep track of your files and get your work done efficiently and painlessly. You can open multiple windows and switch between them with the click of a mouse button. You can do spiffy stuff such as drag and drop to share files and information among your programs. Graphical tools that come with the desktop give you views into the operating system, your files, and your network (if you're on one). Additional graphical tools let you do neat stuff, such as send and receive mail, manage print jobs, and change the way your desktop looks.

Although window managers (such as Motif) have been around for quite some time, real integrated desktops like the ones built into Windows and the MacOS are just beginning to catch on in the UNIX world. Now you can choose from a whole crop of UNIX desktops. (See the sidebar "A desktop by any other name," later in this chapter, for an overview.) The most widely used UNIX desktops seem to be those based on something called the Common Desktop Environment, or CDE. CDE is the result of an unprecedented outbreak of cooperation among a number of UNIX vendors — including Hewlett-Packard, IBM, Novell, and SunSoft — and the Open Software Foundation (the same people who brought you Motif, remember?).

CDE desktops are not quite as simple, of course, as their Windows and MacOS counterparts. The Mac and Windows desktops are developed and sold only by Apple and Microsoft, respectively. Each company that sells CDE along with UNIX, on the other hand, offers a slightly different version of CDE developed exclusively for its own version of UNIX. Unlike the Mac and Windows desktops, which are built in to the operating system and appear whenever you start up your computer (like it or not), CDE desktops are optional. You don't have to use CDE to use UNIX, and you (or, more likely, your system administrator) can decide whether to have CDE start up when you log in.

A desktop by any other name

Integrated desktops for UNIX are beginning to catch on, in part because they make it fairly easy for Windows and Macintosh users to get their bearings in the sometimes forbidding world of UNIX. UNIX, Windows, and Mac computers often happily coexist on the same network, and it's a big advantage to be able to do things in similar ways no matter which operating system you happen to be using. Another reason for the surge in the purchase of UNIX desktops is the migration of thousands of disgruntled Windows users to Linux, the Young Turk of the UNIX world (it's described in Chapter 3). Integrated desktops ease the shift by letting Windows defectors apply their well-honed techniques and habits to Linux.

CDE desktops come along with the new releases of many of the major versions of UNIX, such as Solaris and HP-UX. Some companies that don't sell their own versions of UNIX have also developed their own versions of CDE. TriTeal sells the TriTeal Enhanced Desktop (affectionately known as TED) for Red Hat Linux 5.1. X Inside sells a version of CDE that works with both Linux and FreeBSD. Hummingbird Software offers a CDE emulator for both Windows 95 and Windows NT named Exceed.

Other, non-CDE desktops for UNIX are out there, too:

- The K Desktop Environment, or KDE, runs on Linux, Solaris, FreeBSD, IRIX, and HP-UX. You can download KDE for free under the terms of the GNU software guidelines, from `ftp://ftp.kde.org`. (The K, by the way, just stands for K.)
- HP-VUE (Visual User Environment) is an alternative to CDE for HP-UX, complete with its own window manager (VUEWM) and distinctive GUI "look." Why does Hewlett-Packard feel the need to offer *both* VUE and CDE desktops with HP-UX? The best answer, as far as we can tell, is "Because it can."
- Red Hat Linux comes with a bunch of desktops, all built on some version of FVWM, for the ultimate in GUI confusion. Depending on which version of Linux you have, you may have a desktop (or desktops) named TheNextLevel, AnotherLevel, Afterstep (for a NextStep look and feel), FVWM 95 (for a Windows 95 look and feel), or Lesstif WM.
- The Caldera Linux distribution includes its own desktop, named the Desktop by some immortal wag in the Caldera marketing department.

Others — many others — are available, you may be sure. Luckily for us mere mortals, all desktops have the same purpose and pretty much the same sets of tools and utilities. Which desktop you end up with is likely determined as much by personal preference as by which flavor of UNIX you happen to be using.

To enhance the confusion to acceptable UNIX-like levels, CDE is infinitely customizable by system administrators and UNIX hackers. You can make far-reaching changes to CDE by switching the CDE default window manager from DTWM to FVWM, for example. You can tell CDE to launch various programs automatically when you log in. You can change the way the keyboard behaves — and so on and so on, ad nauseum.

The good news is that the similarities among versions of CDE far outnumber the differences; after all, it's supposed to be a *common* desktop environment. In practice, and discounting any bizarre modifications an overzealous UNIX system administrator may have made, using one version of CDE is very much like using another.

The following sections give you some idea of how to use the Common Desktop Environment. In the interest of keeping things as simple as possible, we don't worry about which version of CDE you're using, and we figure that you'll make whatever adjustments are necessary to account for the idiosyncrasies of your configuration.

Desktop, here we come!

Bringing up the desktop is much like starting Motif, a subject we cover in the sidebar "How do I start Motif, anyway?" earlier in this chapter. If you're lucky, your system administrator has set up your computer so that the CDE comes up when you turn on your computer or log in. If not, you have to refer to your local UNIX guru or system documentation to find out which command to run in which directory.

No matter what the start-up details are, the desktop heralds its imminent appearance by making your computer screen flicker like Dr. Frankenstein's laboratory on a stormy night and then replacing whatever your screen was displaying with a drab gray background, on top of which appear various tools, toolbars, icons, and programs, depending on how your desktop is configured. You usually see a version of the FrontPanel across the bottom of your computer screen.

Front and center

The FrontPanel is similar to the control center for the desktop. Actually, it's more like the dashboard of a fancy car, which puts all the car's doohickeys and thingums within easy reach of the driver. As with all the elements of the desktop, you can customize the FrontPanel. Figure 4-10 shows a typical set of FrontPanel icons, buttons, and other clickable thingies.

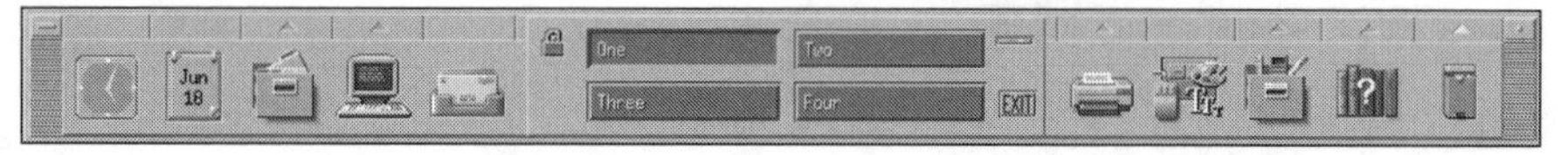

Figure 4-10: The FrontPanel.

At the center of the FrontPanel are four buttons, named One, Two, Three, and Four. These buttons let you manage as many as four *workspaces*. The idea is that the desktop is in reality four times as large as your computer screen; in other words, your computer screen shows only one-quarter of your desktop at a time. Each quarter is a workspace. You can have different icons, program windows, and whatnot set up in each workspace, all of which stay put and reappear just as you left them every time you return to the workspace. For example, you may dedicate one workspace to managing your UNIX environment, one workspace to dealing with all your communications (e-mail, FTP, networking), one workspace to your favorite games, and one workspace to doing work (such as writing the definitive guide to peas and how to eat them). Rename the workspace buttons Looks, Comms, Games, and Peas so that you can remember which workspace is which, and then switch among your workspaces by clicking the buttons. (We recommend switching from Games to Peas whenever your boss comes around the corner.)

Tools you can use

The icons to the left and right of the workspace buttons give you mouse-click access to a typical set of CDE tools. Reading from left to right in Figure 4-10, you see icons for Clock, Group Calendar Manager, File Manager, Terminal Emulator, Mail Tool, Print Manager, Style Manager, Applications Manager, Help Viewer, and Trash.

You can open each tool or tool set by double-clicking its icon in the FrontPanel. If the icon has a little upward-pointing triangle above it, you can click the triangle to pop up a menu of choices (the menu slides out from behind the FrontPanel like a window shade being drawn upward). Drag to the choice you want, and then release the mouse button to select it. You can close a pop-up (or slide-up) menu by clicking the square in the upper-left corner of the menu and choosing Close or by clicking the triangle again (it turned into a downward-pointing triangle while you weren't looking). The menu demurely slides down behind the FrontPanel until it disappears. Figure 4-11 shows the menu that appears when you click the triangle above the Applications Manager icon.

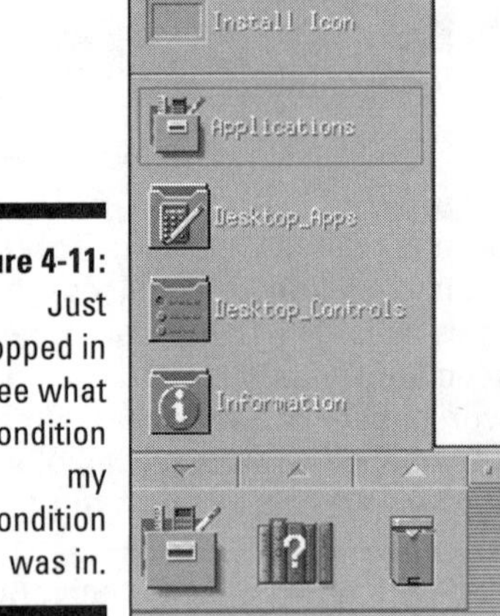

Figure 4-11: Just popped in to see what condition my condition was in.

All the standard UNIX utilities and programs described in Part III of this book (such as `find`, `diff`, `ed`, `vi`, and `emacs`) get zoomy new graphical versions in the CDE, many of which are easier to use than their command-line equivalents (easier, that is, if you're used to using a mouse to do your computing). In fact, CDE desktops come with so many tools and utilities that it would take an entire book just to describe them all.

Filing without tears

The File Manager looks like the window shown in Figure 4-12, which appears when you double-click the File Manager icon on the FrontPanel.

The CDE File Manager is much like the MacOS Finder or Windows Explorer. You can use the CDE File Manager to browse through your files, launch programs, and, as its name implies, manage your files (open, copy, move, or delete them or have them over for dinner). The File Manager shows some kind of icon for each directory and file on your computer. Directory icons look like file folders; file icons look different depending on which type of file it is. Figure 4-12 shows icons for seven text files, which look like pieces of paper with writing on them (clever, no?). The icon with the runner on it launches a program (in this case, a program named Source Safe 5.0).

The "..(go up)" icon lets you travel up the directory tree toward the root directory. The series of folder icons at the top of the window shows your current location (and hence the directory that contains all the stuff you now see in the File Manager) relative to the root directory. You can jump to any directory in the branch of the tree you're on by clicking one of these folders.

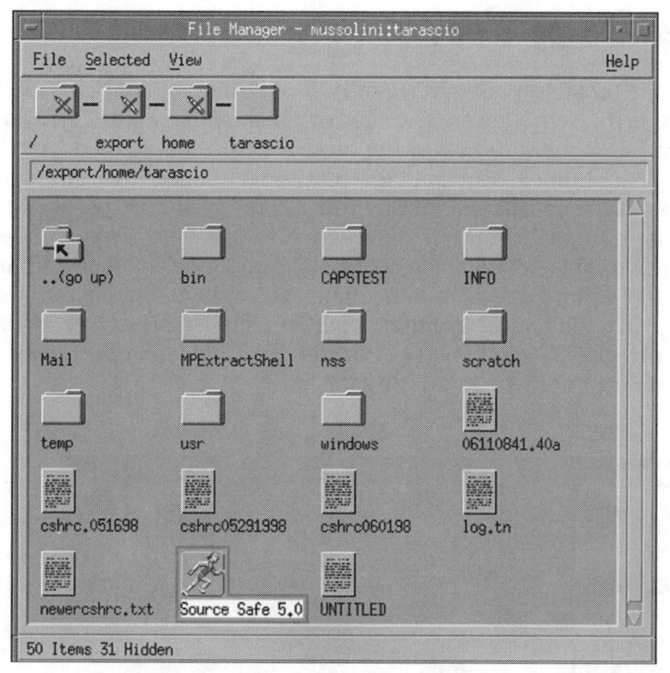

Figure 4-12: Show me some files, man!

Pictograms (little pictures) on the folders tell you something about the directory's permissions; for example, a folder showing a pencil with a line through it means that you don't have write permission in that directory.

You can move files and directories from one location to another by dragging and dropping their icons. Being able to drag and drop in the File Manager means that you can do all kinds of cool and unexpected things. For example, you can drag a text file to the icon for the `emacs` editor to automatically launch `emacs` and open the text file you dragged. You can add icons to the FrontPanel by dragging them from the File Manager and dropping them on the FrontPanel's icon areas.

Not just another pretty face

We don't want to give the impression that the CDE brings only cosmetic enhancements to your UNIX system. The CDE does some heavy lifting, too. Among other features too numerous to mention, the CDE gives you easy and consistent network access, a standard way of printing from any application, session management, advanced collaboration tools such as e-mail clients and group scheduling utilities, GUI toolkits, and all kinds of full-fledged application development tools.

What's up, doc?

One of the most convenient, friendly, and ultimately un-UNIX-like features of the CDE is its Help Viewer. The Viewer, as shown in Figure 4-13, is a graphical help- and documentation-viewing program with full-fledged searching and printing capabilities. You can view all the `man` pages (the online documentation, as described in detail in Chapter 27) for your version of UNIX in a pleasant, readable format (a giant leap for UNIX-kind, as you know if you've ever tried to make extensive use of traditional UNIX `man` pages) and journey hither and yon by means of an expandable and collapsible outline. The Viewer can even handle context-sensitive help (in other words, make a game attempt to guess exactly what information you need at any given moment so that you don't have to go hunting for it).

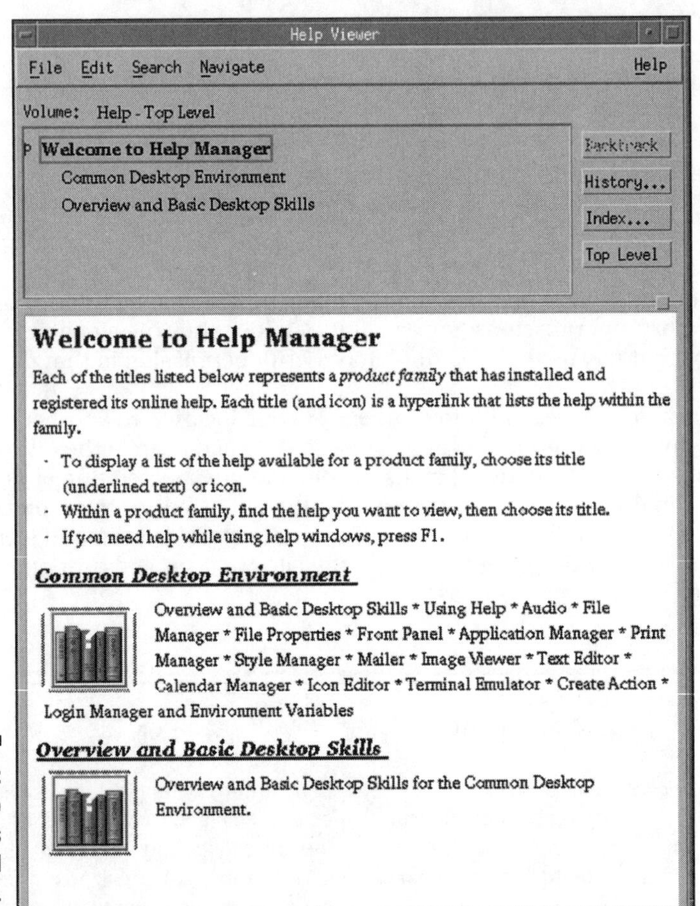

Figure 4-13: The Help Viewer tells you all about itself.

Have it your way

Customize, customize, customize! One of the joys of using the CDE is your ability to change the way your desktop looks and behaves by using the Style Manager (as shown in Figure 4-14). Use up all that pesky extra time by changing the colors of various window elements and text; choosing pretty backdrops to replace your desktop's monotonous gray background; adding pizzazz and generally making your desktop unusable by choosing decorative fonts, reconfiguring your keyboard, changing what the various buttons on your mouse do; and making a thousand other cunning modifications to your computing environment. Go ahead — indulge yourself. You haven't lived until you've spent an entire afternoon designing a desktop scheme that expresses your innermost desires (especially when you should have been doing something else).

Figure 4-14: The Style Manager, for a fashionable desktop.

Talkin' trash

The Trash tool is a great boon to UNIX users susceptible to blowing away important files with unforgiving UNIX commands such as `rm`. When you issue the `rm` command or one of its brethren, the files you deleted are gone, plain and simple. When you're using the File Manager on the desktop, on the other hand, files you delete get put in a virtual trash barrel, where they hang around until you tell UNIX to get rid of them. If you delete a file by mistake, you can bring the file back to life by following these steps:

1. **Double-click the Trash tool icon (the last icon on the right end of the FrontPanel, as shown in Figure 4-10).**
2. **Root around in the trash until you find the file.**
3. **Drag the file from the trash and drop it back into an appropriate location in the File Manager.**

Remember to empty the trash every now and again, or else you eventually run out of disk space.

Desktop, there we go!

The easiest way to get yourself out of the desktop is to click the Exit thingum near the workspace buttons on the FrontPanel, which drops you unceremoniously into good old traditional UNIX character mode.

Terminal Happenings

Even though X Windows enables you to run all the coolest, awesomest, newest, most graphicalest programs, guess which program people use the most? It's called `xterm`, and all it does is act like the kind of VT100 dumb terminal that window systems are supposed to save us from. Such are the ways of progress.

Click, click

One place where `xterm` acts a little better than the dumb terminal it purports to emulate is in mouse handling. You can select text with the mouse and then paste the selected text into either the same or a different `xterm` window.

To select some text, move the mouse to the beginning of the text, press down the first (left) mouse button, and move the mouse to the end of the text. As you move the mouse, the selected text changes color. When you've selected it all, let go of the mouse button. Normally, `xterm` selects text character-by-character; if you double-click rather than just press the mouse button, however, it selects by word, and if you triple-click, it selects by line. Users who don't believe in walking and chewing gum at the same time have an alternative way to select text: Move to the beginning of the selection, click the left button, and then move to the end of the selection and click the right button.

Either way, after you've selected the text, move the mouse to the window where you want to paste it and click the middle button. If, after you've selected the text, a program erases the window, you can't see the selection anymore although it's still there and you can still paste it.

One last stupid xterm trick

If the text in your `xterm` window is insufficiently or excessively legible, you can make the type larger or smaller. Hold down the Ctrl key and press the right mouse button to display the `xterm` VT Fonts menu, from which you can select font sizes ranging from Unreadable to Huge.

Chapter 5
Files for Fun and Profit

In This Chapter

- Listing information about files
- Showing who has permission to use files
- Duplicating a file
- Erasing a file
- Renaming a file
- Looking at what's in a file
- Printing a text file
- Giving a file to someone else

A *file* is a bunch of information stored together, such as a letter to your mom or a database of customer invoices. Every file has a name. You end up with tons of them.

This chapter explains how to work with files, including getting rid of the ones you no longer want.

As a reminder, you must log in (as described in Chapter 1) before you can do any of the nifty things we talk about in this chapter. When you see the UNIX prompt (% or $), you're ready to rock and roll.

What Files Do You Have?

To see a list of your files (actually, a list of the files in the working directory, which Chapter 6 covers), type **ls** and press Enter. (This is positively the last time we nag you to press Enter.)

This command stands for *l*i*s*t, but could the lazy typists who wrote UNIX have used the other two letters? No-o-o-o-o. This command lists all the files in your working directory. (Chapter 6 discusses directories and how to make lots of them.) The `ls` command just shows the names of the files in alphabetical order, like this:

```
bin/    budget-97  budget-98  budget-99  daveg draft
jordan  Mail/      meg        news.junk  zac
```

In some Linux systems, if the directory contains subdirectories, the subdirectory names appear in a different color if your screen handles colors, which is very handy. In BSD UNIX, subdirectory names also have a slash after them. (Chapter 6 talks about subdirectories, if you're wondering what we're talking about.)

Let's see the nitty-gritty details

For more information about your files, use the `-l` option (*long form listing*):

```
ls -l
```

That's a small letter *el,* by the way, not a number *one*. This option tells `ls` to display tons of information about your files. Each line looks like this:

```
-rw-r--r--   1 johnl    users     250 Apr  6 09:57 junk3
```

To switch or not to switch?

Lots of UNIX commands have *options.* (They are also called *switches* because you switch the options on and off by typing or not typing them when you type the command. True geeks call them *flags.*) Options make commands both more versatile and more confusing. Probably the most widely used option is the `-l` option for the `ls` command, which tells `ls` to display lots of information about each file. When you type a command with one or more options, keep this list of rules handy:

- Leave a space after the command name (the command `ls`, for example) and before the option (the `-l` part).
- Type a hyphen as the first character of the option (**-l**, for example).
- Type a space after the option if you want to type more information on the command line after the option.
- If you want to include more than one option, type another space, another hyphen, and the next option. You can usually string multiple options together after one hyphen; for example, `-al` means that you want option `a` and option `l`.

Later in this chapter, in the section "Who can do what?" we explain all the information in this listing. For now, just notice that the right-hand part of the line shows the size of the file (250 characters, in this example), the date and time the file was last modified, and the filename.

Making files come out of hiding

You may have more files in your directory than you think. UNIX enables you to make things called *hidden files,* which are just like regular files except that they don't appear in normal `ls` listings. It's easy to make a hidden file — just start its filename with a period.

You can see your hidden files by typing

```
ls -a
```

To see all the information about your hidden files, type

```
ls -al
```

This command combines the `-a` and `-l` options so that you see the long version of the complete listing of files. You could get the same thing by typing

```
ls -a -l
```

but that would require typing an extra character and an extra space, an anathema to lazy UNIX typists.

Roger, I Copy

You can make an exact duplicate of a file. To do it, you must know the name of the file you want to copy, and you must create a new name to give to the copy. If a file contains your January budget (called `budget.jan`, for example) and you want to make a copy of it to use for the February budget (to be called `budget.feb`, for example), type this line:

```
cp. budget.jan budget.feb
```

The lazy typists strike again. Be sure to leave spaces after the `cp.` command and between the existing and new filenames. This command doesn't change the existing file (`budget.jan`); it just creates a new file with a new name and with the same contents.

A good way to lose some work

What if a file named budget.feb *already* exists? Tough cookies! UNIX blows it away and replaces it with a copy of budget.jan. It truly is an excellent idea to use the ls command first to make sure that you don't already have a file with the new name you have chosen.

In Linux and UNIX System V Release 4, you can use the -i switch to ask cp to inform you whether a file with the new name already exists. If it does, the -i switch asks you whether to proceed. If you have this version of UNIX, type **cp -i** rather than just cp to use this nifty little feature.

If all goes well and cp works correctly, it doesn't show you any message. Blessed silence on the part of UNIX usually means that all is well. You should use the ls command to check that the new file really does exist, just in case.

What's in a name?

When you create a file, you give it a name. UNIX has rules about what makes a good filename:

- Filenames can be pretty long; they're not limited to eight characters and a three-character extension, like some operating systems we could name. In older versions of UNIX, the limit is 14 characters for a filename; newer versions have a huge limit — in the hundreds of characters — so you can call a file Some_notes_I_plan_to_get_around_to_typing_up_eventually_if_I_live_that_long.
- Don't use weird characters that mean something special to UNIX or some shell you may encounter. Stay away from these characters when you name files:

  ```
  < > ' " *
  { } ^ ! \
  [ ] # | &
  ( ) $ ? ~
  ```

  Stick mainly to letters and numbers.
- Don't put spaces in a filename. Although some programs let you put them in, spaces cause nothing but trouble because other programs simply cannot believe that a filename may contain a space. Don't borrow trouble. Most UNIX people use periods to string together words to make filenames, such as budget.jan.98 or pumpkin.soup. Underscores work too.
- UNIX considers uppercase and lowercase letters to be completely different. Budget, budget, BUDGET, and BuDgEt are all different filenames.

Nuking Files Back to the Stone Age

You can also get rid of files by using the command the lazy typists call `rm`. To erase (delete, remove — it's all the same thing) a file, type

```
rm budget.feb
```

If all goes well, UNIX reports nothing and you see another prompt. Use `ls` to see whether the `rm` command worked and the file is gone.

Watch out! Under most circumstances, you have *no way* to get a file back after you delete it.

To be safe, you can use the `-i` option to ask `rm` to ask you to confirm deletion of the file. This is a particularly good idea if you use wildcards to delete a group of files all at one time (see Chapter 7 for more info about wildcards). For example, if you type

```
rm -i last-years-budget
```

UNIX asks:

```
rm: remove 'last-years-budget'
```

Press Y to delete the file or N to leave it alone.

Big, big trouble

If you delete something really, really important and you will be called on to perform ritual seppuku if you can't get it back, don't give up hope. Your local UNIX guru should make things called *backups* on some regular basis. Backups contain copies of some or all of the files on the UNIX system. Your files may be among those on the backup. Go to the guru on bended knee and ask whether the file can be restored. If the file wasn't backed up recently, you may get an older version of it, but hey — it's better than the alternative.

Even before you get yourself into this kind of pickle, you may want to ask your UNIX expert to confirm that regular backups are made. Make sure that your important files are included in the backups. If no one is making regular backups, panic! This is not a safe situation. You had better talk to your system administrator about getting a tape backup system.

Good housekeeping

You should get rid of files you no longer use, for several reasons:

- Having all kinds of files lying around becomes confusing, and it's difficult to remember which ones are important.
- Useless files take up disk space. Whoever is in charge of your UNIX system probably will bother you regularly to "take out the garbage," that is, to get rid of unnecessary files and free up some disk space.

On the other hand, making extra copies of files can be a good idea. If you have been working on a report for three weeks, making an extra copy every day or so isn't a bad idea. That way, if you make some revisions that, in hindsight, were stupid, you can always go back to a previous revision.

What's in a Name (Reprise)

Having given a file a name, you may want to change it later. Maybe you spelled it wrong in the first place. In any case, you can rename a file by using the `mv` (lazy typist-ese for *move*) command.

Suppose that you made a file called `bugdet.march`. Oops — dratted fingers. . . . Type the following line to correct the error in the filename:

```
mv bugdet.march budget.march
```

After `mv`, you type the current name of the file and then the name you want to change it to. Note that it can be harder to retype the same typo than to type the name correctly!

Because you can't have two files with the same name in the same directory, if a file already has the name you want to use, `mv` thoughtfully blows away the existing file (probably not what you want to do). Type carefully. Linux and SVR4 users can use `mv -i` (like `cp -i`) to prevent inadvertent file clobbering.

Want to hide a file so that it doesn't appear in your directory listing? Use a period (`.`) as the first letter of the filename. To see all your files, including hidden files, type

```
ls -al
```

Looking at the Guts of a File

Although you have been slicing and dicing files for a while now, you still haven't seen what's inside one. Two basic types of files exist:

- Files which contain text that UNIX can display nicely on-screen
- Files which contain special codes that look like monkeys have been at the keyboard when you display the files on-screen

The first type of files are called *text files.* The second type is composed of spreadsheet files, database files, program files, and just about everything else. Text editors make text files, as do a few other programs.

To display a text file, type this line:

```
cat eggplant.recipe
```

If you want to see the guts of a file that isn't named *eggplant.recipe*, substitute your file's name. The cat stands for *cat*alog, or maybe *cat*enate — who knows? We're surprised that the lazy typists didn't call it something like q. If you try to use cat with a file that doesn't contain text, your screen looks like a truck ran over it — but you won't hurt anything. Sometimes the garbage in the file can put your terminal in a strange mode in which characters you type don't appear or appear as strange Greek squiggles. See Chapter 22 to learn how to "un-strange" your terminal.

If the file is long, the listing goes whizzing by. (You learn how to look at the file one screen at a time in Chapter 7.) To see just the first few lines of the file, you can type this line:

```
head eggplant.recipe
```

Most versions of the head command display the first ten lines.

You can ask UNIX to guess at what's in a file, by using the file command. If you type

```
file filename
```

(replacing *filename* with the name of the file you're wondering about), UNIX takes a guess at what's in the file, by looking at it. It says something like this:

```
letter.to.jordan:   ascii text
```

or this:

```
unix4d:   directory
```

Is This a Printout I See before Me?

If a file looks okay on-screen when you use the `cat` command, try printing the file. If you use UNIX System V, type this line to print your famous eggplant dish:

```
lp eggplant.recipe
```

If you use BSD UNIX or Linux, type

```
lpr eggplant.recipe
```

Assuming that you have a printer that's hooked up, turned on, and has paper and that your username is set up to use it, the `eggplant.recipe` file prints. If it doesn't, see Chapter 9 to straighten things out.

Who Goes There?

Unlike some operating systems we could name (such as . . . oh, Microsoft Windows, f'rinstance), UNIX was designed from the beginning to be used by more than one person. Like all multiuser systems, UNIX keeps track of who owns what file and who can do what with each file. *Permissions* attached to each file and directory determine who can use them.

Permissions come in three types:

- **Read permission:** Enables you to look at a file or directory. You can use `cat` or a text editor to see what's in a file that has read permission. You also can copy this type of file. Read permission for a directory enables you to list the directory's contents.
- **Write permission:** Enables you to make changes to a file. Even if you can write (change) a file, you can't necessarily delete it or rename it; for those actions, you must be able to write in the directory in which the file resides. If you have write permission in a directory, you can create new files in the directory and delete files from it.
- **Execute permission:** Enables you to run the program contained in the file. The program can be a real program or a shell script. If the file doesn't contain a program, execute permission doesn't do you much good and can provoke the shell to complain bitterly as it tries (from its rather dim point of view) to make sense of your file. For a directory, execute permission enables you to open files in the directory and use `cd` to get to the directory to make it your working directory.

Rock groups, pop groups, and UNIX groups

Every UNIX user is a member of a group. When the system administrator created your username, she assigned you to a group. To see which group you're in, type **id.**

```
id
```

You see something like this:

```
uid=113(margy) gid=102(guest) groups=102(guest),101(book), 103(cheese)
```

Groups usually indicate the kind of work you do. UNIX uses groups to give a bunch of people (the accounting department, for example) the same permissions to use a set of files. All the people who work on a particular project are usually in the same group so that they can look at and perhaps change each other's files.

In Linux and BSD, you can be in several groups at a time, which is handy if you're working on several projects. To find out what groups you're in, type **groups**.

That's mine!

Every file and directory has an owner and a group owner. The *owner* is usually the person who made the file or directory, although the owner can sometimes change the ownership of the file to someone else. The *group owner* is usually the group to which the owner belongs, although the owner can change a file's group owner to another group.

If you use Linux or System V, you can change who owns a file with the `chown` command (described later in this chapter).

Who can do what?

To see who can do what to a file, use the `ls` command with the `-l` option. Type this line:

```
ls -l myfile
```

You see something like this:

```
-rw-r--r--   1 margy   staff    335 Jan 22 13:23 myfile
```

If you don't specify a filename (in this case, `myfile`), UNIX lists all the files in the directory, which is often more useful. For every file, this listing shows all the following information:

- Whether it's a file, symbolic link, or directory. The first character in the line is a hyphen (-) if it's a file, an *l* if it's a symbolic link, and a *d* if it's a directory.
- Whether the owner can read, write, or execute it (as shown by the next three characters, 2 through 4, on the line). The first character is an *r* if the owner has read permission or a hyphen (-) if not. The second character is a *w* if the owner has write permission or a hyphen (-) if not. The third character is an *x* (or sometimes an *s*) if the owner has execute permission or a hyphen (-) if not.
- Whether the members of the group owner can read, write, or execute the file or directory (as indicated by the next three characters, 5 through 7). An *r, w,* or *x* appears if that permission is granted; a hyphen (-) appears if that permission is not granted.
- Whether everyone else can read, write, or execute the file or directory (as indicated by the next three characters, 8 through 10). An *r, w,* or *x* appears if that permission is granted; a hyphen (-) appears if that permission is not granted.
- The link count, that is, how many links (names) this file has. For directories, this number is the number of subdirectories the directory contains plus 2 (don't ask).
- The owner of the file or directory.
- The group to which the file or directory belongs (group owner).
- The size of the file in bytes (characters).
- The date and time the file was last modified.
- The filename — at last!

Permissions by number

It's not too difficult to figure out which permissions a file has by looking at the collection of *r*s, *w*s, and *x*s in the file listing. Sometimes permissions are written another way, however: with numbers. Only UNIX programmers could have thought of this method. (It's an example of lazy typists at their finest.) Numbered permissions are sometimes called *absolute permissions* (perhaps because they are absolutely impossible to remember).

When permissions are expressed as a number, it's a 3-digit number. The first digit is the owner's permissions, the second digit is the group's permissions, and the third digit is everyone else's permissions. Every digit is a number from 0 to 7. Table 5-1 lists what the digits mean.

Table 5-1 Absolute Permissions Decoded

Digit	*Permissions*
0	None
1	Execute only
2	Write only
3	Write and execute
4	Read only
5	Read and execute
6	Read and write
7	Read, write, and execute

If Mom says no, go ask Dad

If you own a file or directory, you can change its permissions. You use the `chmod` (for *ch*ange *mod*e) command to do it. You tell `chmod` the name of the file or directory to change and the new permissions you want the file to have for yourself (the owner), your group, and everyone else. You can either type the numerical absolute permissions (such as **440**) or use letters.

To use letters to type the new permissions, you use a cryptic collection of letters and symbols that consists of the following:

- Whose permissions you are changing: `u` for user (the file's owner), `g` for the group, `o` for other (everyone else), or `a` for all three.
- If the permission should be + (on, yes, okay) or `-` (off, no, don't let them).
- The type of permission you're dealing with: `r` for read, `w` for write, and `x` for execute.

Type the following line, for example, to allow everyone to read a file called `announcements`:

```
chmod a+r announcements
```

This line says that the user or owner, the group, and everyone else can read the file. To not let anyone except the user or owner change the file, type

```
chmod go-w announcements
```

You can also use numeric (absolute) permissions with chmod. To let the user or owner and associated group read or change the file, type

```
chmod 660 announcements
```

This line sets the owner permission to 6 (read and write), the group permission to 6 too, and everyone else's permission to 0 (can't do anything).

You can change the permissions for a directory in exactly the same way you do for a file. Keep in mind that read, write, and execute mean somewhat different things for a directory.

Finding a new owner

When someone gives you a file, he usually copies it to your home directory. As far as UNIX is concerned, the person who copied the file is still the file's owner. In Linux and System V, you can change the ownership of a file you own by using the chown command.

You tell chown the new owner for the file and the filename or filenames whose ownership you are changing, as shown in this example:

```
chown john chapter6
```

This command changes the ownership of the file named chapter6 to john. Keep in mind that only you can give away files you own; if you put a file in someone else's directory, it's polite to chown the file to that user.

Another way to change the owner of a file is to make a copy of the file. Suppose that Fred puts a file in your home directory and he still owns it. You can't use chown to change the ownership because only the owner can do that (you have a chicken-before-the-egg problem here). You *can* get ownership of a file if you copy the file. When you copy a file, you own the new copy. Then delete the original.

File seeks new group; can sing, dance, and do tricks

If you own a file or directory, you can change the group that can access it. The chgrp command enables you to change the name of the group associated with the file, as shown in this example:

```
chgrp acctg billing.list
```

This command changes the group associated with the file billing.list to the group called acctg.

Chapter 6

Directories for Fun and Profit

In This Chapter

- Defining a directory
- Getting to the right directory
- Defining a home directory
- Making a new directory
- Erasing a directory
- Renaming a directory
- Moving a file from one directory to another
- Organizing your files
- A map of UNIX

Files are great — they're where you store all your important information, as well as where UNIX itself and all your programs are stored. UNIX systems have, in fact, tens of thousands of files, even before you create a single one. Imagine typing your `ls` command and getting a list of 10,000 filenames. Not pretty (or fast).

To avoid this situation, UNIX has things called *directories,* which enable you to divide your files into groups. This chapter explains how to organize your UNIX files into directories and how to find things after you have done so.

Good News for Windows and DOS Users

We have good news about UNIX for you experienced Windows and DOS users. It works almost exactly the same as Windows and DOS do when it comes to directories and files. Actually, it's the other way around: A guy named Mark added directories to DOS back in 1982 and ripped off, er, emulated the way UNIX did things — with a few confusing changes, of course.

Briefly, Windows and DOS users should know the following information about UNIX directories:

- All those backslashes (\ ) you learned to type in Windows and DOS turn into regular slashes (/) in UNIX. No one knows why Mark decided that DOS slashes should lean backward. We're sure that he had a very good reason, of course — maybe the / key on his keyboard was broken.
- The UNIX `cd` (*c*hange *d*irectory) command works (more or less) like the DOS CD command; remember not to capitalize it in UNIX.
- The UNIX command for making a directory is `mkdir` rather than the DOS MD command. To remove a directory in UNIX, you use the `rmdir` command rather than the DOS RD command. (Where were the lazy typists when we needed them?) These two commands also work (more or less) like the DOS versions. Don't capitalize these commands, either.
- As always, UNIX believes that uppercase and lowercase letters have nothing to do with each other. Because the two types of letters are completely different, be sure to use the correct capitalization when you type directory names and filenames.
- If you really like DOS commands and want to make UNIX understand them, you can make *shell scripts* (the UNIX equivalent of DOS batch files) that enable you to type DIR or COPY, for example, while you're using UNIX. (Chapter 12 tells you how to make shell scripts.) Or, if you absolutely fall in love with UNIX commands — and who doesn't! — you can make DOS batch files on your PC so that you can type such immortal character combinations as `ls` and `cp` while you're using it.

If you understand directories and paths intuitively from your vast experience with PCs, skip to the sidebar "Getting the big picture," later in this chapter.

What Is a Directory?

A *directory,* for the rest of you people, is a group of files or a work area. (Windows 98, Windows 95, and Macintosh users may recognize it as a *folder.*) You give a directory a name, such as Budget or Letters or Games or Harold. You can put in a directory as many files as you want.

The good thing about directories (also sometimes called *subdirectories,* for no good reason) is that you can use them to keep together groups of related files. If you make a directory for all your budget files, those files are the only ones you see while you're working in that directory. Directories make it easy to concentrate on what you're doing so that you're not distracted by the zillions of other files on the disk.

You can make directories, move files into them, rename directories, and get rid of them. This chapter describes the commands that perform each of these stunts.

Divide and Conquer

Interestingly, a directory can contain other directories. You may have a directory called `Budget`, for example, for your departmental budget. The `Budget` directory may contain several other directories (also called subdirectories) such as `Year1998`, `Year1999`, and `Estimates`. If a directory contains so many files that you can't find things, you should create some subdirectories to divide things up.

Files and directories are stored on disks. Every disk has a main directory that contains everything on the disk. This directory is called the *root directory.* The designers of UNIX were thinking of trees here, not turnips. They imagined an upside-down tree with the root at the top and the branches reaching downward, as shown in Figure 6-1. This arrangement of directories is called a *tree-structured directory.*

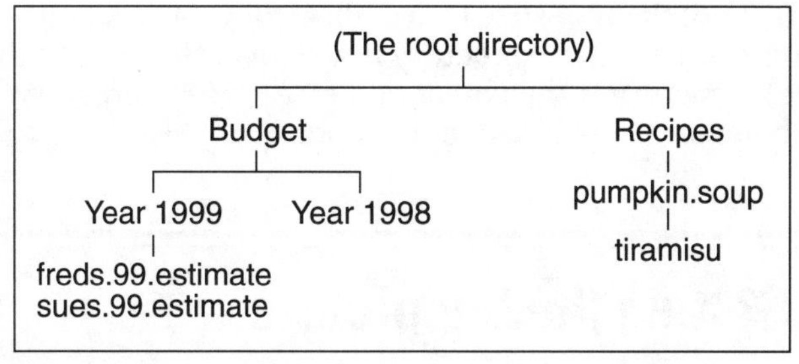

Figure 6-1: A tree-structured directory.

Strangely, you don't type `root` when you're talking about the root directory. Rather, you press /. Just like that: A single slash means "root" in UNIX-ese.

Paths to power

Unfortunately, UNIX never shows you the directory structure as a nice picture, as shown in Figure 6-1. That would be too easy. Rather, to tell UNIX which file you want to use, you type its pathname. The *pathname* is the step-by-step map UNIX follows to get to a file, starting at the root. The pathname for the file named `freds.99.estimate` in Figure 6-1, for example, contains these steps:

`/`	The root, where you start.
`Budget`	The name of the first directory you move to on your way to the file.
`/`	Confusingly, this slash doesn't refer to another root; it's just the character used to separate one name from the next in a pathname.
`Year1999`	The next directory on your way to the file.
`/`	Another separator character.
`freds.99.estimate`	The filename you want.

When you type this pathname, you string it all together, with no spaces:

```
/Budget/Year1999/freds.99.estimate
```

Luckily, you don't often have to type big, long pathnames like this one; it's devilishly hard to get all that right on the first try!

Family matters

You can also think of the tree structure of directories as a family tree. In this way of thinking, the `Year1999` directory is a *child* of the `Budget` directory, and the `Budget` directory is the *parent* of the `Year1999` directory. You see these terms sometimes if you read more about UNIX.

Getting the big picture

If you have a UNIX workstation that's all your own, most or all of the files on its hard disk are yours. If you have a terminal and share a UNIX computer with others, the computer's hard disk has files that belong to all the users. As you can imagine, we are talking about oodles of files. To keep the files — and users! — organized, UNIX has lots of different directories.

UNIX has lots of directories for the UNIX program files themselves, program files for other programs, and other stuff you definitely are not interested in. The files that belong to users (such as yourself) usually are stored in one area. A directory called `/usr` (or sometimes `/home`) contains one subdirectory for every user. If your username is `zacyoung`, for example, the `/usr` directory contains a subdirectory called `zacyoung`, which contains your files.

Names for directories

Choose names for directories in the same way as you choose names for files: Avoid funky characters and spaces, and don't make the name so long that you never type it correctly, for example. Some people capitalize the first letter of directory names so that they can tell what's a directory and what's a file. When you type `ls` to list the contents of a directory, the command lists both filenames and the names of subdirectories. When you use capitalization to distinguish between directory names and filenames, you can quickly tell which are which.

There's No Place Like Home

Every user has a home directory (sweet, isn't it?) in which you store your personal stuff, mail, and so on. When you log in, UNIX starts you working in your home directory, where you work until you move somewhere else. Your home directory is your subdirectory in the `/usr` (or `/home`) directory, so Zac Young's home directory is `/usr/zacyoung`. (Although Zac is only three years old, we're sure that he'll need a home directory shortly.)

Because most UNIX systems involve lots of people sharing disk space and files, UNIX has a security system to prevent people from reading each other's private mail or blowing away each other's work (accidentally, of course). Chapter 5 talks about the security system. In your home directory, you usually have the right to create, edit, and delete all the files and subdirectories. You can't do that in someone else's home directory unless the directory's owner gives you permission.

I've been working in the directory

Whenever you use UNIX, the directory you are working in is the *working* directory. Some people call it the *current* directory, which also makes sense.

When you first log in, your home directory is your working directory. Although you start in your home directory, you can move around. If you move to the `/Budget` directory, for example, the `/Budget` directory becomes the working directory. (Your home directory is still your home directory — it never moves.)

If you forget where you are in the directory structure, you can ask UNIX. Type **pwd** to ask UNIX where you are. That's short for *p*rint *w*orking *d*irectory. UNIX doesn't print the information on paper; it just displays it onscreen. You see something like this:

```
/Budget/Year1999
```

When you use the `ls` command (or most other UNIX commands), UNIX assumes that you want to work with just the files in the working directory. The `ls` command lists just the files in the working directory unless you tell it to look somewhere else.

To move to another directory to do some work (if you're tired of working on the budget and want to get back to that recipe for pumpkin soup, for example), you can change directories. To move from anywhere in the `/Budget` directory to the `/Recipes` directory, type this line:

```
cd /Recipes
```

Remember that `cd` is the *c*hange *d*irectory command. After the `cd` (and a space), you type the directory you want to go to. You can tell UNIX exactly which directory you want in two ways:

- Type a *full pathname,* or *absolute pathname* (the pathname starting at the root, as you did earlier). In the `/Recipes` example, the slash at the beginning of the pathname indicates that the pathname starts at the root.
- Type a *relative pathname* (the pathname starting from where you are now).

This stuff is confusing, we know, but UNIX has to know exactly which directory you want before it makes the move. Because the disk can have more than one directory called `Recipes`, UNIX has to know which one you want. When you type a full pathname starting at the root directory, the pathname starts with a `/`. When you type a relative pathname starting at the working directory, the pathname doesn't start with a `/`. That's how UNIX (and you) can tell which kind of path it is.

If you are in the `/Budget` directory (on the `/Budget` branch of the directory tree) and want to go to the `Year1999` subdirectory (a branchlet off the main `/Budget` branch), for example, just type **cd Year1999**. To go to a different branch or to move upward toward the root, you must type the slashes. To move from the `/Budget/Year1999` branchlet back to the main `/Budget` branch, type **cd /Budget**. For example, to move from the `/Budget` branch to the `/Recipes` branch, type **cd /Recipes**.

If you try to move to a directory that doesn't exist or if you incorrectly type the directory name or pathname, UNIX says:

```
Dudegt: No such file or directory
```

(or whatever directory name you typed).

I want to go home!

If you move to another directory (/Oz, for example) and want to get back to your home directory (/Kansas, that is), you can do so as easily as clicking the heels of your ruby slippers three times. (Or were they glass slippers?) Just type **cd**. When you don't tell UNIX where you want to go, it assumes that you want to go home.

Putting Your Ducks in a Row

As with everything else in life (if we may be so bold as to suggest it), it pays to be organized when you're naming files and putting them in directories. If you don't have at least a little organization, you will never find anything. Think about which types of files you will make and use. (Word-processing files? Spreadsheet files?) Then make a directory for every type of file or for every project you're working on. This section shows you how.

Making directories

Before you create a directory, be sure that you put it in the right place. Remember that you type **pwd** to display your working directory (the current directory).

The most likely place to create a subdirectory is in your home directory. If you're not there already, type **cd** to go back home.

When you create a directory, you give it a name. To create a directory called Temp to hold temporary files, type **mkdir Temp**.

Most people have a directory called Temp to hold files temporarily. These files can be the ones you need to keep just long enough to print, to copy to a floppy disk or tape, or whatever. Anyway, you have one now, too. To confirm that the Temp directory is there, type this line:

```
ls
```

You can even go in there and look around by typing the following (and pressing Enter after typing the first line):

```
cd Temp
ls
```

When you create a directory, it starts out empty (it contains no files).

Most people have directories with names something like these examples:

`Mail`: For electronic mail (see Chapter 17).

`Docs`: For miscellaneous documents, memos, and letters.

`Temp`: For files you don't plan to keep. Use `Temp` to store files you plan to throw away soon. If you put them in some other directory and don't erase them when you finish with them, you may forget what they are and be reluctant to delete them later. Directories commonly fill up with junk in this way. Make it a rule that any files left in the `Temp` directory are considered deletable.

`bin`: For programs that you use but that aren't stored in a central place. Your system administrator may have already made you your own `bin` directory. (See Chapter 12 for information about the `bin` directory and making your own programs.)

You can also make one or more directories to contain actual work.

Dot and dot dot

UNIX has two funny pseudo-directory names you can use — especially with the `cd` and `ls` commands. One is `.` (a single dot), which stands for the current directory. You type the following line, for example, to tell UNIX to list the files in the current directory:

```
ls .
```

This command is pointless, of course, because typing the following line does exactly the same thing:

```
ls
```

Okay, forget about `.` (the single dot). But `..` (the double dot, or dot dot) can be useful. It stands for the parent directory of the working directory. The *parent* directory is the one of which the working directory is a subdirectory. The parent is one level up the tree from where you are now. If you're in the directory `/usr/home/zacyoung/Budget`, for example, the .. (dot dot, or parent) directory is `/usr/home/zacyoung`.

If you type the following line, you see a list of the files in the parent directory of where you are now. This command can save you from some serious typing (and the associated errors):

```
ls ..
```

Performing neat directory operations

After you have some directories, you may want to change their names or get rid of them. You also may want to move a file from one directory to another. This section shows you how to try that first.

Transplanting files

Chapter 5 describes the use of the `mv` command to rename a file. You can use the same command to move files from one directory to another. To get the `mv` command to move files rather than just rename them, you tell it the name of the file you want to move and the name of the path where you want to put the file.

If you want, you can rename the file at the same time you move it, but let's keep things (comparatively) simple. Suppose that you put the file `allens.99.estimates` into the `/Budget/Year1998` directory rather than in `/Budget/Year1999`. The easiest way to move it is to go first to the directory in which it is located. In this example, you type this line:

```
cd /Budget/Year1998
```

Use `ls` to make sure that the file is in the current directory. After you are sure that the file is there, you can move it to the directory you want by typing this line:

```
mv allens.99.estimates /Budget/Year1999
```

Be sure to type one space after `mv` and one space between the name of the file and the place you want to move it to. If you use `ls` again, you discover that the file is no longer in the working directory (`Year1998`). You should change to the directory to which you moved the file and use `ls` to make sure that the file is there. Make one typing mistake in a `mv` command, and you can move a valuable file to some unexpected place.

Amputating unnecessary directories

You can use the `rmdir` command to remove a directory, but what about the files in the directory? Are they left hanging in the air with the ground blown out from under them? Nope; you must either get rid of the files in the directory (delete them) or move them elsewhere before you can hack away at the directory.

To erase a directory, follow these steps:

1. **Use the `rm` command to delete any files you don't want to keep.**

   (See Chapter 5 for the gory details of using this command.)

2. **If you want to keep any of the files, move them to somewhere else by using the `mv` command (as explained in the preceding section).**
3. **Move to some other directory when the directory you want to delete is empty.**

   UNIX doesn't let you delete the working directory. The easiest thing to do is to move to the working directory's parent directory:

   ```
   cd ..
   ```

4. **Remove the directory by typing this line:**

   ```
   rmdir OldStuff
   ```

   Replace `OldStuff` with the name of the directory you want to ax.

5. **Use `ls` to confirm that the directory is gone.**

You can delete a directory and all the files in it or even a directory and all the subdirectories and files in them, but this process is dangerous stuff. You usually are better off sifting through the files and deleting or moving them in smaller groups. If you're interested in a *really* dangerous command, which we shouldn't even be telling you about, you can type `rm -r` to remove a directory and all its files and subdirectories in one fell swoop.

Renaming a directory

If you have used DOS, you will be thrilled to learn that in UNIX you can rename a directory after you create it. (DOS doesn't let you do that, at least not in early versions.) Again, the `mv` command comes to the rescue.

To rename a directory, you tell `mv` the current directory name and the new directory name. Go to the parent directory of the directory you want to rename, and then use the `mv` command. To rename the `/Budget` directory `/Finance`, for example, go to the / directory (type **cd /**) and then type this line:

```
mv Budget Finance
```

Make sure first that a directory with that name isn't already there. If it is, UNIX moves the first-named directory to become a subdirectory of the existing directory. In other words, if a `/Finance` directory is already there, `/Budget` moves to become `/Finance/Budget`. That could be handy, if that's what you have in mind. Then again, it could drive you out of your mind if that's not what you expect.

Chapter 7

The Shell Game

In This Chapter

- Using redirection
- Viewing a file one screen at a time
- Printing the output of any command
- Working with groups of files
- Avoiding retyping commands, especially after typos
- Getting set up each time you log in
- Setting your terminal options

If you've read the preceding chapters in this book, you know how to work with files and how to type some commands to UNIX (you type them to the shell, as you know, but let's not get bogged down in that here). UNIX has a clever way to increase the power of its commands: *redirection.* This chapter shows you how to use redirection and how to use wildcards to work with groups of files.

This Output Is Going to Havana: Redirection

When you use a UNIX command like `ls`, the result (or *output*) of the command is displayed on-screen. The standard place, in fact, for the output of most UNIX commands is the screen. The output even has a name: *standard output.* As you can imagine, you also have *standard input,* usually via the keyboard. You type a command; if it needs more input, you type that, too. The result is output displayed on-screen — all very natural.

You can pervert this natural order by *redirecting* the input or output of a program. A better word is *hijacking.* You say to UNIX, "Don't display this output on-screen — instead, put it somewhere else." Or, "The input for this program is not coming from the keyboard this time — look for it somewhere else."

The "somewhere else" can be any of these sources:

- **A file:** You can store the output of `ls` (your directory listing) in a file, for example.
- **The printer:** It's useful only for output. Getting input from a printer is a losing battle.
- **Another program:** This one gets really interesting, when you take the output from one program and feed it to another program!

Bunches of UNIX programs are designed primarily to use input from a source other than the keyboard and to output stuff to someplace other than the screen. These kinds of programs are called *filters.* Readers old enough to remember what cigarettes are may recall that the advanced ones had a filter between the cigarette and your mouth to make the smoke smoother, mellower, and more sophisticated. UNIX filters work in much the same way, except that they usually aren't made of asbestos.

The only exception to this redirection business is with programs, such as text editors and spreadsheets, that take over the entire screen. Although you can redirect their output to the printer, for example, you won't like the results (nor will your coworkers, as they wait for a pile of your garbage pages to come out of the printer). Full-screen programs write all sorts of special glop (they give instructions) to the screen to control where stuff is displayed and what color to use, for example. These instructions don't work on the printer because printers use their own, different kind of glop. The short form of this tip is that *redirection and editors don't mix.*

Grabbing output

So how do you use this neat redirection stuff, you ask? Naturally, UNIX does it with funny characters. The two characters < and > are used for redirecting input and output to and from files and to the printer. You use another character (|)to redirect the output of one program to the input of another program.

To redirect (or *snag,* in technical parlance) the output of a command, use >. Think of this symbol as a tiny funnel *into which* the output is pouring (hey, we use any gimmick we can to remember which funny character is which). To make a file called `list.of.files` that contains your directory listing, for example, type this line:

```
ls > list.of.files
```

UNIX creates a new file, called `list.of.files` in this case, and puts the output of the `ls` command into it.

If `list.of.files` already exists, UNIX blows away the old version of the file. If you don't want to erase the existing file, you can tell UNIX to add this new information to the end of it (*append* the new information to the existing information). To do it, type this line:

```
ls >> list.of.files
```

The double >> symbol makes the command append the output of `ls` to the `list.of.files` file, if it already exists. If `list.of.files` doesn't exist already, `ls` creates it.

Some (but not all, of course) versions of the C shell check to see whether the file already exists and refuse to let you wreck an existing file with redirection. To overwrite the file if your C shell works this way, use `rm` to get rid of the old version. The command that tells the C shell not to clobber an existing file when you're creating a new file from redirection is `set noclobber`. To turn this protection off, you can use the `unset noclobber` command. We recommend turning on `noclobber` every time you run UNIX (or get a UNIX wizard to help you make this command execute automagically every time UNIX starts up).

Redirecting input

Redirecting input is useful less often than redirecting output, and we can't think of a single, simple example in which you would want to use it. Suffice it to say that you redirect input just like you redirect output except that you use the < character rather than the > character.

Gurgle, Gurgle: Running Data Through Pipes

The process of redirecting the output of one program so that it becomes the input of another program can be quite useful. This process is the electronic equivalent of whisper-down-the-lane, with each program passing information to the next program and doing something to what's being whispered.

To play whisper-down-the-lane with UNIX, you use a *pipe.* The symbol for a pipe is a vertical bar (|). Search your keyboard for this character. It's often on the same key with \ (the backslash). Sometimes the key shows the vertical bar with a gap in the middle, although the gap doesn't matter. If you type two commands separated by a |, you tell UNIX to use the output of the first command as input for the second command.

Gimme just a little at a time

When you have many files in a directory, the output of the `ls` command can go whizzing by too fast to read, which makes it impossible to see the files at the beginning of the list before they disappear off the top of the screen. A UNIX program called `more` solves this problem. The `more` program displays on-screen the input you give it, and it pauses as soon as it fills the screen and waits for you to press a key to continue. To display your list of files one screenful at a time, type this line:

```
ls | more
```

This line tells the `ls` command to send the file listing to the `more` command. The `more` command then displays the listing. You can think of the information from the `ls` command gurgling down through the little pipe to the `more` command (we think of it this way).

The `cat` and the fiddle . . . er, file

As explained in Chapter 5, you can use the `cat` command to display the contents of a text file. If the text file is too long to fit on-screen, however, the beginning of the file disappears too fast to see. You can display a long file on-screen one screenful at a time in these two ways:

- Redirect the output of the `cat` command to `more` by typing this line (assuming, of course, that the file is called `really.long.file`):

```
cat really.long.file | more
```

- Just use the `more` command by typing this line:

```
more really.long.file
```

If you use the `more` command without a pipe (without the `|`), `more` takes the file you suggest and displays it on-screen a page at a time.

Sorting, sort of

A program called `sort` sorts a file line-by-line in alphabetical order. The program alphabetizes all the lines according to the beginning of each line. Each line in the file is unaffected; just the *order* of the lines changes.

Suppose that you have a file called `honors.students`, which looks like this:

```
Meg Young
Shelly Horwitz
Neil Guertin
Stuart Guertin
Sarah Saxon
Zac Young
Gillian Guertin
Tucker Myhre
Andrew Guertin
Megan Riley
Chloe Myhre
```

To sort it line by line into alphabetical order, type this line:

```
sort honors.students
```

The result looks like this:

```
Andrew Guertin
Chloe Myhre
Gillian Guertin
Meg Young
Megan Riley
Neil Guertin
Sarah Saxon
Shelly Horwitz
Stuart Guertin
Tucker Myhre
Zac Young
```

The list appears on-screen, however, and nowhere else. If you want to save the sorted list, type

```
sort honors.students > students.sorted
```

You can also sort the output of a command:

```
ls | sort
```

Because `ls` displays filenames in alphabetical order anyway, of course, this example doesn't do you much good. If you want the filenames in *reverse* alphabetical order, however (we're stretching for an example here), you can use the `-r` option with the `sort` command:

```
ls | sort -r
```

If you're sorting numbers, be sure to tell UNIX. Otherwise, it sorts the numbers alphabetically (the sort of imbecilic and useless trick only a computer would do). To sort numbers, use the `-n` option:

```
sort -n order.numbers
```

Suppose that your file of honors students contains total test scores:

```
10000 Meg Young
8000  Shelly Horwitz
7000  Neil Guertin
5000  Stuart Guertin
9000  Sarah Saxon
5000  Zac Young
8000  Gillian Guertin
7000  Tucker Myhre
11000 Andrew Guertin
6000  Megan Riley
7000  Chloe Myhre
```

When you alphabetize things as letters, not as numbers, a 1 comes before an 8 no matter what, even if it's the first letter of 10. When you alphabetize things as numbers, 10 comes after 8, not before it. If you sort this file as letters, with this command:

```
sort honors.students
```

you get

```
10000 Meg Young
11000 Andrew Guertin
5000  Stuart Guertin
5000  Zac Young
6000  Megan Riley
7000  Chloe Myhre
7000  Neil Guertin
7000  Tucker Myhre
8000  Gillian Guertin
8000  Shelly Horwitz
9000  Sarah Saxon
```

This output does not show the bonus amounts in any useful order. If you sort the file as numbers, with this command:

```
sort -n honors.students
```

you get this more useful listing:

```
5000  Stuart Guertin
5000  Zac Young
6000  Megan Riley
7000  Chloe Myhre
7000  Neil Guertin
7000  Tucker Myhre
8000  Gillian Guertin
8000  Shelly Horwitz
9000  Sarah Saxon
10000 Meg Young
11000 Andrew Guertin
```

If the file contains letters, not numbers, the -n option has no effect.

Can we get that on paper?

Being able to print the output of a command is terrifically useful when you want to send to a printer something that normally appears on-screen. To print a listing of your files, for example, type this line:

```
ls | lp
```

Users of Linux and BSD UNIX use the `lpr` command rather than `lp`. (Chapter 9 explains other stuff about printing.)

You can use more than one pipe if you want to be advanced. To print a listing of your files in reverse order, for example, you can use this convoluted command:

```
ls | sort -r | lp
```

Wild and Crazy Wildcards

When you type a command, you may want to include the names of a bunch of files on the command line. UNIX makes the typing of multiple filenames somewhat easier (as though we should be grateful) by providing wildcards. *Wildcards* are the two special characters (still more of them to remember!) that have a special meaning in filenames:

? Means "any single letter"

* Means "anything at all"

Pick a letter, any letter

You can use one or more ? wildcards in a filename. Each ? stands for exactly one character — no more, no less. To list all your files that have two-letter names, for example, you can type this line:

```
ls ??
```

The command `ls budget??` lists all filenames that start with *budget* and have two — and only two — characters after *budget,* like `budget98` and `budget99`; the combination doesn't match `budget1` or `budget.draft` or `Budget98` (because of the uppercase *B*).

Stars (***) in your eyes

The * wildcard stands for any number of characters. To list all your files that have names starting with a *c*, for example, type

```
ls c*
```

This specification matches files named `customer.letter`, `c3`, and just plain `c`. The specification `budget.*` matches `budget.1999` and `budget.draft`, but not `draft.budget`. The name `*.draft` matches `budget.draft` and `window.draft`, but not `draft.horse` or plain `draft`. By itself, the filename * matches everything (watch out when you let the asterisk go solo!).

Are kings or deuces wild?

Unlike some other kinds of operating systems (we don't name any, although one system's initials are *DOS*), UNIX handles the ? and * wildcards in the same way for every command. You don't have to memorize which commands can handle wildcards and which ones cannot. In UNIX, they all can handle wildcards.

Wildcards commonly are used with the `ls`, `cp`, `rm`, and `mv` commands. For example, to copy all the files from the current directory to the `temp` directory, you can type

```
cp * temp
```

Wildcards for DOS users

Although UNIX wildcards look just like DOS wildcards and they work in almost the same way, they have a few differences:

- Because UNIX filenames don't have the three-letter extensions that DOS filenames use, don't use `*.*` to match all files in a directory. That trick matches only files that have a dot in their names. A simple * does the trick.
- In DOS, you cannot put letters after the * wildcard — DOS ignores the letters following the asterisk. In DOS, *d*mb* is the same as *d**, for example. It's dumb, we know. The good news is that UNIX is not so dumb. In UNIX, *d*mb* works just the way you want it to.

Look before you delete!

The combination of wildcards and the `rm` command is deadly. Use wildcards with care when you delete files. You should look first at the list of files you're deleting to make sure that it's what you had in mind. *Before* you type the following command, for example, to delete a bunch of files:

```
rm *.97
```

type this line and look at the resulting list of files:

```
ls *.97
```

You may see in that list of `.97` files something worth keeping that you forgot about.

The most deadly typo of all is this one ***(do not type this line!)***:

```
rm * .97
```

Notice the space between the `*` wildcard and the `.97`. Although you may have thought that you were deleting all files ending with `.97`, UNIX thinks that you have typed two filenames to delete:

- `*` This "filename" deletes all the files in the directory.
- `.97` This filename deletes a file named `.97` (yes, filenames can start with a period). By the time UNIX tries to delete this (nonexistent) file, it has, of course, already deleted all the files in the directory!

You end up with an empty directory and lots of missing files. Watch out when you use `rm` and `*` together!

History Repeats Itself

We make fun of the C shell often (and rightly so), but when Bill wrote it, he added a lovely feature called `history`. BASH does history too, even more nicely than the C shell. And the Korn shell has a way to do history that is clunky but serviceable.

The `history` command enables you to issue UNIX commands again without having to retype them, a big plus in our book. Bourne shell users may as well skip the rest of this chapter because it will just make you jealous (or it'll make you bite the bullet and switch to the BASH shell, by typing **bash**).

Here's how `history` works. The shell stores in a *history list* a list of the commands you've given. Then you can use the list to repeat commands exactly as you typed them the first time or edit previously used commands so that you can give a similar command.

History in the key of C

In the C shell, you can type **!!** and press Enter to repeat the last command you typed. The shell displays the command and then executes it.

You can also rerun the last command line that begins with a particular bunch of letters. If you type

```
!find
```

the C shell repeats the last command line that began with the text *find*. You don't have to type an entire command. If you type

```
!fi
```

it looks for the last command you typed that started with *fi*, which may be a `find` command or `file` command.

To see the history list, type **history**. You see a list like this:

```
1  20:26   ls
2  20:26   ls -l
3  20:26   ls -al
4  20:26   history
5  20:26   cat junk3
6  20:26   cat .term
7  20:26   history
8  20:27   history
```

This example shows the commands you have just typed, in the order you typed them. Because the list is numbered, you can refer to the commands by number. After the number comes the time you gave the command (if you care), followed by the command you typed.

If you want to repeat a command, you can type **!** followed by the number of the command. For example, if you type

```
!3
```

the C shell repeats command number 3 on the list (in this case, `ls -al`).

You can also repeat a command with a modification. Suppose that you just typed this command:

```
find . -name budget.98 -print
```

Now you want to give the same `find` command, but this time you're looking for a file named `budget.99`. Rather than tediously, arduously retype the line, character by character and keystroke by keystroke, worrying anxiously about a possible typo with every key you press, you can tell the C shell to repeat the last command, substituting *99* for *98*. The command is

```
^98^99
```

You type a caret (^), the old text, another caret, and the text to substitute. Voilà! The C shell displays the new command and then executes it.

BASHing through commands

BASH can do all the cool `history` tricks the C shell can, with some additional acrobatics. When BASH displays your history list, it usually stores the last 500 commands you typed, so the list can be huge. To see it a page at a time, type this command:

```
history | more
```

To see the last nine commands on the history list, type

```
history 9
```

Here comes the neat part — you can press the arrow keys to flip back through your commands. When you press the up-arrow key (or Ctrl+P, for *p*revious), BASH shows you the previous command from the history list. You can press Enter to execute the command. You can keep pressing the up-arrow key (or Ctrl+P) until you get to the command you want. If you go past it, you can move back down your history list by pressing the down-arrow key (or Ctrl+N, for *n*ext).

This feature is downright useful and typo-saving! DOS 6.2 has it too, of course, but who's counting?

After you have displayed on the command line a command from your history list, you can edit the command before you press Enter to execute it. Press the left- and right-arrow keys (or Ctrl+B and Ctrl+F, for *b*ackward and *f*orward) to move the cursor. When you type characters, BASH inserts them on the command line where the cursor is.

The folks at the Free Software Foundation who wrote BASH are big `emacs` fans (as are we) because you can use most `emacs` editing commands to edit the command on the command line. For example, pressing Ctrl+A moves your cursor to the beginning of the line, Ctrl+E moves it to the end of the line, Esc+F moves it forward by a word, and Ctrl+K deletes everything to the right of the cursor. If you, for some reason, prefer `vi` to `emacs`, press Esc+Enter, and BASH changes to a `vi`-like editor, where you search for `history` commands by pressing Ctrl+R and Ctrl+S.

Enough about BASH and `history`. You get the general idea!

A Korn-ucopia of commands

We don't use the Korn shell much because we've become rather fond of BASH, but the Korn shell can do history, too. The `history` command lists your history list, as does the more cryptic `fc -l` command. To repeat the last command, just press **r** and then Enter. That's it — just **r**. To repeat the last `cat` command, type this line:

```
r cat
```

To repeat the last command and replace *98* with *99,* type

```
r 98=99
```

The Korn shell enables you to edit your previous commands in all kinds of fancy ways, although it's confusing to do, so we suggest that you switch to the BASH shell if you long to edit and reissue commands.

Do I Have To Type the Same Things Every Time I Log In?

Most users find that, every time they log in, they type the same commands to set up the computer the way they like it. You may typically change to your favorite directory, for example, and then change the terminal settings (see the following section), check your mail, or do any of a dozen other things.

The Bourne, Korn, and BASH shells look in your home directory for a file called `.profile` when you log in. If the `.profile` file exists, UNIX executes the commands in that file. The C shell has two corresponding files: `.login` (which it runs when you log in) and `.cshrc` (which it runs every time you start a new C shell, either at login time or when you type **csh**).

Your system administrator probably gave you a standard `.profile` or `.login` file when your account first was set up. Messing with stuff that's already there is *definitely* not a good idea. You may end up unable to log in and then have to crawl to your system administrator and beg for help. So don't say that we didn't warn you.

The standard `.profile`, `.login`, and `.cshrc` files vary considerably (why do we even finish this sentence — you know what we're going to say) from one system to another, depending on the tastes of the system administrator. These files usually perform these tasks:

- Sets up the search path the shell uses to look for commands
- Arranges to notify you when you have new mail
- (Sometimes) changes the shell prompt from the usual `$` or `%` to something more informative

If you always type the same commands when you log in, adding new commands at the end of `.profile` or `.login` is fairly safe. If you do most of your work in the directory `bigproject`, for example, you may add the following three lines to the end of the file your shell uses to start up your UNIX session (`.profile` or `.cshrc`):

```
# change to bigproject, added 3/98
cd bigproject
echo Now in directory bigproject.
```

The first line is a comment the computer ignores but is useful for humans trying to figure out who changed what. Any line that starts with a pound sign (#) is a comment. The second line is a regular `cd` command. The third line is an `echo` command that displays a note on-screen to remind you of the directory you're in.

If you use the C shell, a frequently useful command to put in `.login` is this one:

```
set ignoreeof
```

If you press Ctrl+D in the shell, the shell normally assumes that you're finished for the day and logs you out — in keeping with the traditional UNIX "you asked for it, you got it" philosophy. Many people think that you should be more explicit about your intention to log out and use `ignoreeof` to tell the shell to ignore Ctrl+D (the following section tells you what `eof` has to do with Ctrl+D) and log out only when you type **exit** or **logout**.

Terminal Options

About 14 zillion different settings are associated with each terminal or pseudo-terminal attached to a UNIX system, any of which you can change with the `stty` command. More than 13 zillion of the 14 zillion shouldn't be messed with, or else your terminal vanishes in a puff of smoke (as far as UNIX is concerned) and you have to log in all over again or even get your system administrator to undo the damage. You can, however, safely change a few things.

All the special characters that control the terminal, such as Backspace and Ctrl+Z, are changeable. People often find that they prefer characters other than the defaults, for any of several reasons: They became accustomed to something else on another system, the placement of the keys on the keyboard makes some choices more natural than others, or their terminal emulator is dumb about switching Backspace and Delete. The special characters that control the keyboard are described in Table 7-1.

Table 7-1 Terminal-Control Characters

Name	*Typical Character*	*Meaning*
`erase`	Ctrl+H	Erases (backspaces over) the preceding character
`kill`	Ctrl+U	Discards the line typed so far
`eof`	Ctrl+D	Marks the end of input to a program
`swtch`	Ctrl+Z	Pauses the current program (see Chapter 13)
`intr`	Ctrl+C	Interrupts or kills whichever program is running
`quit`	Ctrl+\	Kills the program and writes a `core` file

To tell `stty` to change any of these control characters, you give it the name of the special character to change and the character you want to use. If, as is common, you want to use a control character, you can type a caret (^ — the thing above the 6 on the key in the row of keys across the top of the keyboard) followed by the plain character, both enclosed in quotation marks. As a special case, `^?` represents the Del or Delete key. The Tab key is represented as `^I`. The Backspace key is usually `^H`. To make the Delete key the `erase` character and Ctrl+X the `kill` character, for example, type this line:

```
stty erase '^?' kill '^X'
```

All these `stty` commands usually go in the `.login` or `.profile` file so that the terminal is set up the way you want every time you log in.

Chapter 8

Where's That File?

In This Chapter

- Using the `find` program to find a file when you know the filename
- Telling `find` where to look
- Looking for a file when you know only part of the filename
- Using the `grep` program to find a file when you know what's in it
- Looking for files on other computers on your network
- Looking for a directory
- Knowing what to do with the files you find
- Doing something else while the computer searches for your file
- Sharing files by using the `ln` command so that files appear in more than one directory

Doncha love to set up lots of different directories so that you can organize your files by topic, program, date, or whatever suits you? We do. After you have files in all those directories, however, you can also easily lose them. Is that budget memo in your `Budget` directory, your `Memos` directory, your `ToDo` directory, Fred's `Budget.Stuff` directory, or somewhere else?

Two programs can help you find files: `find` and `grep`. Alternatively, you can use the `ln` command to create links to your files so that a file can appear in several directories at a time and you have that many more opportunities to find it.

The Search Is On

UNIX systems have lots of files. Lots and lots. Tens of thousands, to be more specific. So where's the memo you wrote last week?

Peering into every directory

The first approach to finding a lost file is to use the brute-force method. Starting in your home directory, use `ls` to search through each of your directories. In every directory, type this line:

```
ls important.file
```

Replace *important.file* with the name of the file you're looking for. If the file is in the current directory, `ls` lists it. If the file isn't there, `ls` complains that it can't find the file. This approach can take awhile if you have a large number of directories. An additional drawback is that you won't find the missing file if it has wandered off to someone else's directory.

If you know — or think that you know — that your file is nearby, you can use * (asterisk) wildcards in directory names. (Wildcards are covered in Chapter 7. They enable you to work with lots of files or directories at one time.) To find *important.file* in any of the subdirectories in the working directory, type this line:

```
ls */important.file
```

This technique doesn't work if you have directories within directories: It looks only one level down.

"Hey, I know the filename!"

With luck, you know the name of the file you have lost. If so, you can use the `find` program to find it. When you use `find`, you tell it the name of the file and the place to start looking. The `find` program looks in the directory you indicate and in all that directory's subdirectories.

Links to shadow files

You may run into a situation in which a file seems to be in several directories at one time (*Twilight Zone* music here, please). DOS users know that this situation is patently absurd. Mac users ought to be thinking of *aliases* here; Windows users ought to be thinking of *shortcuts*. UNIX has its own way of letting you keep a file in several places at the same time. To avoid excessive clarity, the file can even have several different names. Seriously, it can be mighty useful for a file to be in, for example, the home directories of several people at one time so that they all can easily share it.

To achieve this magical feat, you use *links*. We discuss links in the section "A File By Any Other Name," later in this chapter. In the meantime, don't panic if you see a file lurking around in one place when you're sure that it belongs somewhere else.

Suppose that you're working in your home directory. You think that a file named `tiramisu` is in there somewhere. Type this line:

```
find . -name tiramisu -print
```

That is, you type these elements:

- **find** (just like you see it here).
- A space.
- The directory in which you want the program to begin looking. If it's the working directory, you can type just a period (which means "right here").
- Another space.
- **-name** (to mean that you will specify a filename).
- Another space.
- The name of the file you want to find (**tiramisu**, in this case).
- Another space.
- **-print** to tell UNIX to print (on-screen) the full name, including the directory name, to let you know where UNIX finds the file. If you omit this step and `find` finds the file, it doesn't tell you. (We know that this situation is stupid, but computers are like that.) If you use UNIX SVR4 or Solaris, you notice that they fixed up the `find` command so that it warns you rather than run the command pointlessly.

The `find` program uses a brute-force approach to locate your file. It checks every file in all your directories. This process can take awhile. After `find` finds the file, it prints the name and keeps going. If the program finds more than one file with that name, `find` finds them and reports them all. After `find` has printed a found file, you usually will want to stop the program (unless you think that it will find more than one match). You stop `find` by pressing Ctrl+C or Delete.

If the `find` command doesn't work and you think that the file may be in some other user's directory, type the same `find` command and replace the . (dot) with a / (slash). This version tells `find` to start looking in the root directory and to search every directory on the disk. As you can imagine, this process can take some time, so try other things first.

"I know where to search (sort of)"

Rather than use a period to tell `find` to begin looking in the working directory, you can use a pathname. You can type this line, for example:

```
find /usr/margy -name tiramisu -print
```

This command searches Margy's home directory and all its subdirectories. (Her home directory name may be something different; see Chapter 6 to find out about home directories.) To search the entire disk, use the slash (/) to represent the root of the directory tree:

```
find / -name tiramisu -print
```

If your disk is large and full of files, a search from the root directory down can take a long time — as long as half an hour on a very large and busy system.

You can even type several directories. To search both Margy's and John's home directories for files named `white.chocolate.mousse`, for example, type this line:

```
find /usr/margy /usr/johnl -name white.chocolate.mousse -print
```

If you use the BASH or C shell, rather than type the home directory name, you can type a tilde (~) and the username; the shell puts in the correct directory name for you:

```
find ~margy ~johnl -name white.chocolate.mousse -print
```

"At least I know part of the filename"

You can use wildcard characters in the filename if you know only part of the filename. (Remember the * and ? characters that act as "jokers" in filenames?) Use ? to stand for any single character; use * to stand for any bunch of characters. There's a trick to this, however: If you use * or ? in the filename, you have to put quotation marks around the filename to keep the shell from thinking that you want it to find matching names in only the current directory.

You can search the entire disk for files that start with `budget`, for example, by typing

```
find / -name "budget*" -print
```

If you leave out the quotation marks, the search may look like it worked, although `find` probably hasn't done the job correctly.

Remote searches

If your system uses NFS (Network File System, as described in Chapter 16), some or all of the directories and files on your machine may really be on other computers. The `find` command doesn't care where files are and

cheerfully searches its way into any directory it can get to. Because getting to files over a network is about half as fast as getting to files stored locally, telling `find` to look through a large number of files stored on a network can take a long time. Consider having a long lunch while `find` does its thing.

Suppose that you're looking for Dave's famous stuffed-squid recipe. The obvious way to look for it is with this line:

```
find ~dave -name stuffed-squid -print
```

If you know that Dave's files are stored on machine `xuxa`, however, this command can be much faster:

```
rsh xuxa "find ~dave -name stuffed-squid -print"
```

See Chapter 16 for details about the `rsh` command.

It's what's inside that counts

"Hmm . . . I don't remember what the file is called, but I'm looking for a letter I wrote to Tonia, so it should contain her mailing address in the heading. That's 1471 Arcadia. How do I find it?"

This situation is made for `grep` — a great program with a terrible name. It stands for, if you can believe it, *g*lobal *r*egular *e*xpression and *p*rint, or some such thing. The `grep` command looks inside files and searches for a series of characters. Every time it finds a line that contains the specified characters, it displays the line on-screen. If it's looking in more than one file, `grep` also tells you the name of the file in which the characters occur. You control which files it looks in and which characters it looks for.

Three `grep` programs exist: `grep`, `egrep`, and `fgrep`. They are similar, so we talk just about `grep`. (`Fgrep` is faster but more limited, and `egrep` is more powerful and more confusing.)

To look in all the files in the working directory (but not in its subdirectories) for the characters `1471 Arcadia`, type this line:

```
grep "1471 Arcadia" *
```

That is, type these elements:

- **grep** (just as you see it here).
- A space.
- The series of characters to look for (also called the *search string*). If the string consists of several words, enclose it in quotation marks so that `grep` doesn't get confused.

- A space.
- The names of the files to look in. If you type * here, grep looks in all the files in the current directory.

The grep program responds with a list of the lines in which it found the search string:

```
ts.doc: 1471 Arcadia Lane
tonia.letter: 1471 Arcadia La.
```

The program lists the name of the file and then the entire line in which it found the search string.

You can do lots of things with grep other than look for files. In fact, we could write entire (small) books about using grep. For our purposes, however, here are some useful options you can use when you use grep to look for files.

If you want to see just the filenames and you don't want grep to show you the lines it found, use the -l (for *l*ist) option. (That's a small letter *l*, not a number 1.) Suppose that you type this line:

```
grep -l "1471 Arcadia" *
```

The grep program responds with just a list of filenames:

```
ts.doc
tonia.letter
```

It may be a good idea to tell grep not to worry about uppercase and lowercase letters. If you use the -i (for *i*gnore case) option, grep doesn't distinguish between uppercase and lowercase letters, as shown in this example:

```
grep -i DOS *
```

With this command, grep, which is extremely literal-minded, finds both references to DOS and some "false hits":

```
fruit.study: salads; in Brazil, avocados are used in desserts.
chapter.26: DOS vs. UNIX
chapter.30: Dos and Don'ts
```

Finally, if you don't know the exact characters that occur in the file, you can use grep's flexible and highly powerful (that is, cryptic and totally confusing) expression-recognition capabilities, known in nerdspeak as *regular expressions.* The grep program has its own set of wildcard characters, sort of but not much like the ones the shell uses to enable you to specify all kinds of amazing search strings. If you're a programmer, this feature can be useful because you frequently need to find occurrences of rather strange-looking stuff.

Directory assistance

You can look for lost directories in addition to lost files. Give the `find` command the option `-type d`:

```
find / -name "Budget*" -type d
   -print
```

This command searches the entire disk for directories that begin with `Budget`.

The reason we mention this subject is that `grep`'s wildcard characters include most punctuation characters — namely:

```
.  * [ ] ^ $
```

If you include any of these characters in a search string, `grep` doesn't do what you expect. To type any of these characters in a search string, precede them with a backslash (\ ). To search for files containing *C.I.A.,* for example, type this line:

```
grep "C\.I\.A\." *
```

The period (.) is `grep`'s wildcard character, like the question mark (?) in the shell. In this example, if you don't precede the periods with backslashes, `grep` would match not only `C.I.A.` but also `CHIFAS` (a Peruvian dialect word meaning "Chinese restaurants," in case you were wondering) and lots of other things. Don't press your luck — use the backslashes with punctuation marks to be safe.

What to Do with Files After You Find Them

After you find the file or files you were looking for, you can do more than just look at their names. If you want, you can tell the `find` command to do something with every file it finds.

Rather than end the `find` command with the `-print` option, you can use the `-exec` option. It tells `find` to execute a UNIX shell command every time it finds a file. The following command, for example, tells the `find` command to look for files with names beginning with `report`:

```
find . -name "report*" -exec lpr {} ";"
```

Every time the command finds that type of file, it runs the lpr program and substitutes the name of the file for the {}. (You type two curly braces, which was some nerd's idea of a convenient placeholder.) The semicolon indicates the end of the UNIX shell command. (You have to put quotation marks around the semicolon, or else the shell hijacks it and thinks that you want to begin a new shell command. If that didn't make sense, take our word for it and remember to put quotation marks around the semicolon when you use find.) Every time find finds a filename beginning with report, this command prints the file it found.

You can use almost any UNIX command with the -exec option, so, after you have found your files, you can print, move, erase, or copy them as a group. A slight variation is to use -ok rather than -exec. The -ok option does the same thing except that, before it executes each command, find prints the command it's about to run, followed by a question mark, and waits for you to agree that that would be a good thing to do. Press Y if you want to do it, and press N if you want it to skip that particular command.

By using find and -exec rm, you can delete many unwanted files in a hurry. If you make the smallest mistake, however, you can delete many important and useful files equally as quickly. We don't recommend that you use find and rm together. If you insist, however, please use -ok to limit the damage.

A File By Any Other Name

Sometimes, it's nice for a file to be in more than one place (that budget file we keep mentioning, for example). If you were working on it with someone else, it would be nice if the file could be in both your home directory and your coworker's home directory so that neither of you would have to use the cd command to get to it.

A nice feature of UNIX (and you thought there weren't any!) is that this situation is possible — even easy to set up. A single file can have more than one name, and the names can be in different directories.

Suppose that two authors are working on a book together (a totally hypothetical example). The chapters of the book are in John's directory: /usr/johnl/book. What about Margy? It's annoying to have to type the following line every time work on the book begins:

```
cd /usr/johnl/book
```

Instead, it would be nice if the files could also be in /usr/margy/book.

How can you be in two places at once when you're not anywhere at all?

You allow a file to be in two places at a time by using the `ln` (for *link*) command. You tell `ln` two things:

- The current name of the file or files you want to create links to
- The new name

Let's start with just one file. Margy wants to make a link to the file named `chapterlog` (it contains the list of chapters). The file is in `/usr/johnl/book`. In her `book` directory, Margy types this line:

```
ln /usr/johnl/book/chapterlog booklog
```

UNIX says absolutely nothing; it just displays another prompt. (No news is good news.) It just created a *link,* or new name, however, to the existing `chapterlog` file. The file now appears also in `/usr/margy/book` as `booklog`. You have only one file (UNIX doesn't make a copy of the file or anything tacky like that) with two names.

How to play the links

After you create a link by using `ln`, the file has two names in two directories. The names are equally valid. It isn't as though the name `/usr/johnl/book/chapterlog` is the "real" name and `/usr/margy/book/booklog` is an alias. UNIX considers both names to be equally important links to the file.

How to delete links

To delete a link, you use the same `rm` command you use to delete a file. In fact, `rm` always just deletes a link. It just so happens that, when no links to a file exist, the file dries up and blows away. When you use `rm` on a file that has just one name (link), the file is deleted. When you use `rm` on a file that has more than one name (link), the command deletes the specified link (name), and the file remains unchanged, along with any other links it may have had.

How to rename a link

You can use the old mv command to rename a link, too. If Margy decides that it would be less confusing for the book-status file to have the same name in both places (as it stands now, it's chapterlog to John and booklog to Margy), she can type this line:

```
mv booklog chapterlog
```

You can even use the mv command to move the file to another directory.

How to link a bunch of files

You can also use ln to link a bunch of files at the same time. In this case, you tell ln two things:

- The bunch of files you want to link, probably using a wildcard character such as chapter*. You also can type a series of filenames or a combination of names and patterns. (UNIX may be obscure, but it's flexible.)
- The name of the directory in which you want to put all the new links.

The ln command uses the same names the files currently have when it makes the new links. It just puts them in a different directory.

The chapterlog business in the preceding example, for example, works so well that Margy decides to link to all the files in /usr/johnl/book. To make links in /usr/margy/book, she types this line:

```
ln /usr/johnl/book/* /usr/margy/book
```

This command tells UNIX to create links for all the files in /usr/johnl/book and to put the new links in /usr/margy/book. Now every file that exists in /usr/johnl/book also exists in /usr/margy/book. Margy uses the ls command to look at a file listing for her new book directory. It contains all the book files. This arrangement makes working on the files much more convenient.

Linking once and linking twice

Here's one caveat. The `ln` command in the example in this section links all the files that exist at the time the command was given. If you add new files to either `/usr/margy/book` or `/usr/johnl/book`, the new files are not automatically linked to the other directory. To fix this situation, you can type the same `ln` command every few days (or whatever frequency makes sense). The command tells you that lots of files are already identical in the two directories and makes links for the new files.

If you have linked to someone else's files, you may have permission to read those files but not to change or write to them. When you ask `ln` to make the new links, if it tries to replace a file you couldn't write to, it says something like this:

```
ln: chapter13: 644 mode?
```

See Chapter 25 for the exact meaning of this uniquely obscure message. Press Y if you want to replace the file, which you probably do in this case. Press N if you don't want to replace the file.

How to link across the great computer divide

All this talk about links assumes that the files you're linking to are on the same file system (that's UNIX-speak for *disk* or *disk partition*). If your computer has several hard disks or if you're on a network and use files on other computers (through NFS or some other system, as explained in Chapter 16), some of the files you work with may be on different file systems.

Here's the bad news: The `ln` command can't create links to files on other file systems. Bummer. We have good news for some readers, however: Linux, BSD, and SVR4 systems (that is, any System V and older AT&T-ish systems) have things called *soft links,* or *symbolic links* (*symlinks,* for short) that are almost as good.

Soft links enable you to use two or more different names for the same file. Unlike regular links (or *hard links*), however, soft links are just imitation links. UNIX doesn't consider them to be the file's real name.

How to make soft links (for users of Linux, UNIX BSD, and SVR4 only)

To make a soft link, add the `-s` option to the `ln` command.

Suppose that you want a link in your home directory to the `recipe.list` file in `/usr/gita`. In your home directory, you type this line:

```
ln /usr/gita/recipe.list gitas.recipes
```

Rather than respond with serene silence, UNIX responds with this line:

```
ln: different file system
```

Drat! Gita's home directory is on a different file system from yours, perhaps even on a different computer. So you make a soft link by sticking an `-s` into the command:

```
ln -s /usr/gita/recipe.list gitas.recipes
```

As usual, no news is good news; `ln` says nothing if it worked. Now a file called `gitas.recipes` seems to be in your home directory — all through the magic of soft links. You still have only file, but there's an extra link to it.

How to use soft links (for users of Linux, UNIX BSD, and SVR4 only)

You can look at, copy, print, and rename a soft-linked file as usual. If you have the proper permissions, you can edit it. If Gita deletes her file, though, the file vanishes. Your soft link now links to an empty hole rather than to a file, and you see an error message if you try to use the file. UNIX knows that the soft link isn't the file's "real" name. When you see a soft link in a long ls listing, UNIX gives the name of the soft link and also the name of the file it refers to.

If you try to use a file and UNIX says that it isn't there, check to see whether it's a dangling soft link (a link to a nonexistent file). Type `ls -l` to see whether the file is a soft link. If it is, use another `ls -l` on the real filename to make sure that the file really exists.

To get rid of a dangling soft link, use the `rm` command to delete it.

Chapter 9

Printing (The Gutenberg Thing)

In This Chapter

- How to send stuff to the printer
- How to find the printer
- Stupid printing tricks

Unless you happen to work in the paperless office of the future (reputed to be down the hall from the paperless bathroom of the future), from time to time you will want to print stuff. The good news is that it's usually easy to do so. The bad news is that nothing is as easy as it should be.

The major extra complication is that the way to print things is different on UNIX BSD and System V systems. (Remember which one you have? Refer to Chapter 2 if you don't. You may have written it on the Cheat Sheet in the front of this book.) We start by explaining how you print something already in a file; then we go on to the fancy stuff.

Printing Stuff: Daemons at Work

From a human being's point of view, printing stuff in UNIX is simplicity itself: You use either the `lp` command or the `lpr` command, depending on your flavor of UNIX.

From your computer's point of view, this arrangement is, of course, way too simple. To make things suitably complex, the print command doesn't print the file. What it does is leave a note for another program buried deep inside UNIX, and this buried program prints your file. This buried program is called a *daemon* (pronounced "demon"). The theory behind this arrangement is that a bunch of people may want to use the printer, and it would be a pain if you had to wait for the printer to be free. The print command puts your file on a list, and the daemon runs down the list and does the printing so that you don't have to wait. The *request ID* is the name the print command gives to the note it leaves for the daemon. You can ignore the request ID unless you change your mind and decide that you don't want to print that file after all.

Printing in System V

If you use UNIX System V, you print stuff with the `lp` command. If you have a file named `myletter`, for example, you print it by typing this line:

```
lp myletter
```

UNIX responds with this important information:

```
request id is dj-2613 (1 file)
```

Usually, that's all you need to do. UNIX responds to your request to print by telling you the request ID of the print job, which you probably don't care about. Sometimes you want to pretty up the way the printout looks by leaving wider margins; we talk about that subject later in this chapter.

Printing in BSD and Linux

If you use Linux or BSD UNIX, printing is just as easy as printing with System V, except that you use the command `lpr` rather than `lp`. If you have a file named `myletter`, for example, you print it by typing

```
lpr myletter
```

Some systems, notably SVR4 and Solaris, have both the `lp` and `lpr` commands. If you have these versions of UNIX, either command should work equally well. Note that the `lpr` command doesn't report a request ID.

Finding Your Printout

As far as UNIX is concerned, its only job is to send your file to the printer. Now the real work begins: *finding* your printout.

If your UNIX system is attached to a network, chances are that your printer is attached to some other computer rather than to yours. You may have to go looking for it to find your printouts.

You may have to ask people in nearby cubicles or stand still in the center of the office and listen for the sound of printing (a gentle whir and click from most laser printers). If all else fails, ask your system administrator. Because your UNIX system may be capable of using more than one printer, your system administrator may be the only person who can tell you which printer your printout is on.

Aha! There's the printer! If you're lucky, no one else has printed anything recently, so the paper on top of the printer is all yours. More likely, lots of people have printed stuff and a pile of paper is on top of the printer — only some of which is yours.

Every printout should have in front of it a sheet that identifies the file that's printed, with the username, time, and other odds and ends that seemed relevant to the person who configured the printer. It's considered tacky to root through the stack, pick out your own pages, and leave the rest in a heap. Instead, separate the printouts and leave them on the table or in printout racks (if available) with the usernames visible. With luck, others will do the same for you. If you can't find your printout on the printer, maybe someone else has already separated and stacked the printouts. Or maybe other users have decided that your printout looked more interesting than theirs and took it off the printer to read it.

Printers, printers, everywhere

A reasonably large installation probably has several printers, either because one printer can't handle all the work or because the installation uses different kinds of printers. When you use the `lp` or `lpr` command, UNIX picks one printer as the default. If you use `lp`, you use the `-d` option (that's a lowercase *d* — remember that UNIX cares about these things) to identify the printer. To print your file on a printer named `draft`, for example, you type

```
lp -ddraft myletter
```

If you use `lpr`, the analogous option is `-P` (that's an uppercase *P*), so the command you type is

```
lpr -Pdraft myletter
```

In either case, don't type a space between the `-d` or `-P` and the printer name.

Calling all printers

The list of available printers depends entirely on the whims of the system administrator. Typically, one day she gets tired of putting up with the slow, illegible, or chronically broken previous printer, storms into the boss's office, gets the necessary signature, and buys the first printer available. Sometimes the old printer is thrown away, sometimes not.

It's generally not too difficult to get a list of printers known to the system. If you use the `lp` command to print, type this line to get a list of available printers:

```
lpstat -a all
```

This line means roughly, "Show me the status of all printers that are active." The `lpstat` program lists the status of all available printers, one per line, like this:

```
dj accepting requests since Thu Apr 25 13:43:50 1991
```

In this case, only one printer, whose name is `dj`, is available. The listing also shows you the vital fact that it was installed on a Thursday afternoon in April 1991. Whoopee.

If you use the `lpr` command to print, try typing this line to get the same information:

```
lpq -a
```

Woodsman, spare that file!

When you tell UNIX to print a file, the file doesn't print immediately. UNIX makes a note to print the file and remembers its filename.

What if you delete the file before UNIX has a chance to print it? If you print with `lp`, you get a nasty message because UNIX can't find the file. If you print with `lpr`, the file is printed normally because UNIX makes a copy of the material to print.

To force `lp` to copy the file, you use the `<` command-line operator. To send a copy of the file `myfile` to the printer, for example, type

```
lp < myfile
```

You can then delete or change `myfile` and not affect the printout.

If you are printing a large file, `lpr` can take a long time to make the copy of the file (which it doesn't really need to do because it's already in a file in the first place, isn't it?). You can use `lpr -s` to tell UNIX to print from the original file to save time and disk space. If you use the `-s` option, be sure not to delete or change the file until it's printed.

You can tell `lpr` to delete the file when it has finished printing it. This capability is sometimes useful when you made the file in the first place only so that you could print it. Use the `-r` option to remove the file after printing:

```
lpr -r myfile
```

For large files, you can use `-r` and `-s` together:

```
lpr -s -r myfile
```

The lpq program responds with a similar list:

```
lp:
      Rank     Owner  Job  Files         Total Size
      1st      johnl  7    longletter   4615 bytes
      ps:
      no entries
```

The lpq command stands for something like *l*ine *p*rinter *q*uery, and -a means *a*ll printers. In this case, two printers are available, named lp and ps, and something is printing on the first one.

Keep in mind that not every printer the lpstat and lpq commands report is usable. System administrators frequently put in the table of printers some test entries that don't really represent printers you can use.

"Help! I've Printed and It Won't Shut Up!"

The first time you print something large, you suddenly will realize that you don't really want to print the file because you have found a horrible mistake on the first page. Fortunately, you can easily tell UNIX that you have changed your mind.

If you tell UNIX to print a file that does not contain text, such as a file that contains a program or a database, in most cases UNIX prints it anyway. In a classic example of Murphy's Law (anything that can go wrong will go wrong), files like that tend to print about 12 random letters on each of 400 pages. Every page has just enough junk on it that you can't use that piece of paper again. As you may expect, people who print a large number of files like that tend to become unpopular, particularly with coworkers whose 2-page memos are in line behind the 400 pages of junk.

Cancel the order, System V

If you used lp to print the file in the first place, you use cancel (we don't know how that name slipped past the lazy typists) to cancel the print job. You have to give the cancel command the request ID that lp assigned to the job. If you're lucky, the lp command is still on-screen and you can see the request ID. If that information has vanished from your screen, remain calm. Remember that the lpstat command lists all the requests waiting for the printer. Type this command:

```
lpstat
```

This command displays a list like the following:

```
dj-2620    johnl   34895      Dec 23 21:12 on dj
```

This list tells you that your request was named `dj-2620`, it was done on behalf of a user named `johnl`, the size of the file to be printed is 34895, and the print command was given on December 23. You can cancel the request with this command:

```
cancel dj-2620
```

UNIX responds with this line:

```
request "dj-2620" cancelled
```

UNIX has a surprisingly convenient (surprising for UNIX, anyway) shortcut you can use. If you give the name of a printer, UNIX cancels whatever is printing on that printer. If you remember that the local printer is named `dj`, you can type the following line to cancel whatever `dj` is printing:

```
cancel dj
```

If you made your printing mistake with the `lpr` command, you use `lpq` to find out the request ID, which — to add confusion — is called a *job number* here. Just type this command:

```
lpq
```

UNIX responds with a list of print jobs:

```
Rank   Owner     Job  Files                     Total Size
1st    johnl     12   blurfle                  34895 bytes
```

You need to note the job number (12, in this case). Use that number with the `lprm` command, which, despite its name, removes the request to print something and not the printer itself:

```
lprm 12
```

The `lprm` command usually reports something about "dequeued" lines; this information is meant to be reassuring, although it's not clear to whom. In response to the `lprm 12` command, for example, UNIX displays this message:

```
dfB012iecc dequeued
cfA012iecc dequeued
```

Some final words about stopping the printer

Most printers have something called an *internal buffer,* which is where data to be printed resides before the printer prints it. An internal buffer is good and bad: It's good because it keeps the printer from stopping and starting if the computer is a little slow in passing your file to it. It's bad because, after data is in the buffer, the computer cannot get it back. So, even after you cancel something you want to print, some of it may still be in the buffer: as much as 2 pages of normal text or about 20 pages of the junk that results from printing a nontext file.

You have no easy way to keep from printing the stuff in the printer buffer. One really bad idea is to turn the printer off in the middle of a page: This method tends to get the paper stuck and, on laser printers, lets loose a bunch of black, smeary stuff that gets all over your hands and on the next 1,000 pages the printer prints. If you insist, press the printer's Stop or Off-line button and wait for the paper to stop moving. Then you can turn the printer off relatively safely.

After your print request is canceled, the printer probably still has half a page of your failed file waiting to print. You can eject that page by pressing a button on the printer labeled something like Form Feed or Print/Check or even Reset.

Prettying Up Your Printouts

If you send a file full of plain text to a printer, the result can look ugly: no margins, titles, or anything else. You can use the `pr` command to make your file look nicer. Use it only with plain text files, however, not with files full of PostScript code, document files from your favorite word processor, or a desktop publishing program.

Titles and page numbers look so official

The simplest thing you can do with the `pr` command is to add titles and page numbers to your printout. By default, the title is the name of the file and the date and time it was last changed. You can use a pipe (defined in Chapter 7 as the vertical bar, `|`) to format with `pr` and print on a single line:

```
pr myfile | lpr
```

(Remember to use the `lp` command rather than `lpr`, if appropriate.) This command tells the `pr` program to pretty up the file and pass the results to the `lpr` program.

You can set your own heading by using the `-h` option with the `pr` command:

```
pr -h "My Deepest Thoughts" myfile | lpr
```

The `pr` command assumes that printer pages are 66 lines long. If that's not true for you, rather than the title's appearing at the top of every page, it sort of oozes down from page to page. You can override the length of the standard page with the `-l` option. Suppose that the page length is 60 lines. You type this line:

```
pr -l 60 myfile | lpr
```

If you want to use `pr` and not have any heading at the top of the page, use the `-t` option:

```
pr -t myfile | lpr
```

(This example doesn't do anything interesting to `myfile`. In the following section, however, you see that it really is useful when you combine it with the margins and stuff.)

Marginally yours

You may frequently put printouts in three-ring binders. Normally, because printing starts very close to the left side of the page, the hole punch may put holes in your text and make the page difficult to read — not to mention make it look stupid. The `-o` option (that's a lowercase letter *o,* not a zero, for *o*ffset) pushes the stuff you print to the right, leaving a left margin. To leave five spaces for a left margin, for example, type this command:

```
pr -o5 myfile | lpr
```

Sometimes it's nice to leave a wider margin at the bottom of the page. You can do that by combining the `-l` option (to set the page length, as described in the preceding section) with the `-f` option that tells `pr` to use a special *form-feed character* to make the printer start a new page *now!* (Normally, the `-l` option uses blank lines to space to the next page, like a typewriter.) Use the following command if you're in this situation:

```
pr -o5 -l 50 -f myfile | lpr
```

This command tells UNIX to print just 50 lines per page, indented five spaces. That amount of space in the margin should be enough for anyone.

Seeing double

The -d option tells pr to double-space the printout. Type this command:

```
pr -d myfile | lpr
```

This command also puts a title on every page. Use -d -t to avoid that:

```
pr -d -t myfile | lpr
```

One column can't contain me

If the lines in your file are short, you can save paper by printing the file in multiple columns. To print your file in two columns, for example, type

```
pr -2 myfile | lpr
```

Astute readers probably can guess what the options -3, -4, and up to -9 do. (If you're not feeling that astute today, these options specify the number of columns you want.) Columns normally run down and then across the page, as they do in newspapers. If your file contains a list of items, one per line, and you want to print them in columns, you may want to change the order in which the lines print. If you want to print items across the page and then move down to the next line, and so on (which is nowhere near as cool), use the -a option in addition to the -2 or -3 option.

Troff, Nroff, Groff!

No, it's not a rabid dog. It's a typesetting program. The troff program is the "*t*ypesetter *runoff*" that has been part of UNIX since the 1970s. The nroff program is "*n*ew *runoff*" (new as of about 1972), which formats documents for simple printers without fancy fonts. The groff program is the GNU (refer to Chapter 2) version of troff, which, like every GNU program, does all the stuff the originals do and about 47 other things, too. Because groff is free, whereas nroff and troff are subject to expensive licenses from whoever owns the original UNIX licensing rights this year, groff is all you see these days.

All the "roff" programs are *batch formatters.* In these programs, you type your document with formatting codes into a text file and then run the text file through groff, which produces a beautifully typeset version of your document, give or take all your typos and coding errors. Then you fix the document, re-groff, and so on. These programs are the antithesis of WYSIWYG (What You See Is What You Get) formatting.

People still use groff, partly because it's free and partly because you can do fancy stuff with highly structured documents that's difficult or impossible with WYSIWYG formatters. We don't expect that you'll write a great many groff documents yourself, but you'll probably run into some on the Internet or in software packages.

Macro mania

Formatting a document by using troff and its cousins requires rather low-level detailed instructions using incomprehensible two-letter codes in the documents — instructions so detailed that even UNIX weenies find them tedious (and that's saying a great deal). To relieve the tedium, most troff documents take advantage of *macro packages* that define higher-level instructions, which people use rather than the low-level stuff. (These macro packages serve roughly the same function as style formats in Microsoft Word.) The troff program has been around for more than 25 years, and many macro packages have come and gone, although a few have stood the test of time. Because all of them have been written by lazy typists, each has a cryptic two-or three-letter name, all starting with -m, the flag code that tells groff to use the macro package. Table 9-1 lists a few popular macro packages.

Table 9-1 Macro Packages

Name	*Description*	*Origin*
-ms	Manuscript macros	Bell Labs
-mm	Different manuscript macros	Another part of Bell Labs
-me	Eric's macros	Somebody's Ph.D. thesis at Berkeley (must have been a good thesis because he's now the head of Novell)
-man	Manual page macros	Same as -ms

To tell groff to format a document with the -ms macros, for example, you type

```
groff -ms filename
```

It's difficult to tell *a priori* what macros were used in what document, unless the author took pity and gave you a clue by naming the file mobydick.ms or the like. Fortunately, the worst that happens if you use the wrong macro package is that the document looks ugly. (It's not totally illegible: The text is still there, but it's formatted incorrectly.) You can try different macro packages and see which one works least badly. As a rule of thumb, documents from academia usually use the -me macro package, whereas those from industry usually use -mm or -ms. Documents about the UNIX system itself usually use -ms because ms was written by some of the same guys who did the original UNIX work and pages from the online manual (what the man command shows you) use -man.

Let's sneak a peek

One of the nicest things about groff is that it's *device independent,* which means that it can reformat your document for any of several output devices. To format your document and display it on a normal, text-only terminal, use the nroff command:

```
nroff -ms filename | more
```

(This command actually calls groff, but tells it to format for plain-text output. Change the -ms to one of the other macro packages if necessary.) The more command displays the result a screen at a time. Press the spacebar to move from screen to screen, or press Q when you've seen enough.

If you're running X Windows, you can tell groff to display a page at a time, beautifully typeset in an X window, by typing this command:

```
groff -TX75 -ms filename
```

In the window that groff creates, press the spacebar to move from screen to screen or press Q when you've seen enough. If the type is too small to read, use -TX100 rather than -TX75 to make the text bigger. (You can't use any other numbers; X comes with one set of fonts for 75 dot-per-inch screens and another for 100 dot-per-inch screens, so that's what groff uses.)

Printing, for the PostScript-Challenged

Earlier in this chapter, we talk about PostScript, the fabulously complicated printer language that enables you to print fabulously complex documents on PostScript printers. But what if you don't have a PostScript printer?

These days, the short answer is "Get one." Although PostScript printers used to cost much more than other kinds of printers, these days you can buy a perfectly decent PostScript laser printer for less than $1,000. Nonetheless, lots of PostScript-free sites are still out there, where Ghostscript comes to the rescue.

Ghostscript is a free, GNU version (see the section that talks about what GNU is in Chapter 2) of PostScript, written by L. Peter Deutsch, a skillful programmer from way back who surely should have been doing something else when he wrote it. When Ghostscript runs, it reads its PostScript input from either a file or the keyboard (not very useful unless you're trying to learn PostScript) and produces its output on one of a zillion possible output devices. If you want to see what the PostScript document looks like, you can tell it to send its output to an X Windows system window. If you want to print the document, you can send its output to your printer.

If you're lucky, your system manager will have installed Ghostscript so that it's semiautomatically called when you print a PostScript file. You typically use the `-v` flag, something like this:

```
lpr -v floogle.ps
```

Failing that, in order to run Ghostscript, you type its name (**gs**) and the name of the PostScript file to display:

```
gs floogle.ps
```

If you just type that line, Ghostscript opens a new X window and displays the first page of `floogle.ps` in that window — probably not what you want. Press Ctrl+C once or twice to stop Ghostscript from displaying the page in a window. To get Ghostscript to do something useful, you have to use switches — lots and lots of switches:

```
gs -sDEVICE=deskjet -dNOPAUSE -sOutputFile=floogle.lj floogle.ps
        quit.ps
```

What's going on here is that we've set the output device (`DEVICE`) to a popular ink-jet printer. We tell it not to pause between pages, we tell it which output file to create and which PostScript file to print, and then we give it another file from the Ghostscript library (`quit.ps`). The `quit.ps` file contains a one-line command which tells Ghostscript that it's finished. You can tailor this command as needed; run `gs -h` to see the available printers.

We expect that you find this subject a wee bit complicated. In practice, unless your system manager has set up Ghostscript to run automatically, your best bet is to find a local expert who can tell you the exact command to use. Lacking an expert, you can still look at PostScript on-screen by using a slick little program named Ghostview.

Part III
Getting Things Done

In this part . . .

In the first two parts of this book, we talk about the computer, files, mice, printers, and the shell — you name it. But what about getting some real work done?

To do useful work, you need software. This part talks about using text editors, word processors, e-mail programs, and other useful programs. We also talk a little about installing software and (for you Linux users) doing a tiny bit of system administration.

Chapter 10

Writing Deathless Prose

In This Chapter

- What is a text editor?
- What is a text formatter?
- What is a word processor?
- What is a desktop publishing program?
- How to use `vi` if you absolutely have to
- How to use `emacs`, which is not that bad, really
- How to use `pico`, which works rather well
- How to use `ed` if you don't have anything better

In the land of UNIX, many programs handle text. Where you come from, you may be accustomed to the idea of using a word processor when you want to type something and print it. Not in UNIX. It has four kinds of programs for this task, just to keep things interesting.

UNIX Has Its Way with Words

The four kinds of UNIX programs that handle text are

- Text editors
- Text formatters
- Word processors
- Desktop publishing programs

Before describing the most commonly used text editors in gory detail, we thought that you would want to know the differences among these four kinds of programs, in case you plan to impersonate a geek at the next meeting of your local UNIX users' group.

Just the text, ma'am

A text editor enables you to

- Create a file full of text
- Edit the text

You can print a file by using the lp or lpr programs, as described in Chapter 9, although text editors can't do boldface, headers or footers, italics, or all that other fancy stuff you need in order to produce modern, overformatted, professional-quality memos.

You may want to use a text editor to write letters and reports. You certainly will use one to send electronic mail, as described in Chapter 17.

The most commonly used text editors in the land of UNIX are ed, vi, emacs, and pico. We have strong opinions about these editors, which becomes abundantly clear in the later sections in this chapter, where we tell you how to use each of them.

Text formatters aren't really editors

Text formatters are programs that read text files and create nice-looking formatted output. You use a text editor to make a text file that contains special little commands only the formatter understands; the .IT command, for example, makes something italic. When you run the text formatter, it reads the text file, reads the special little commands, and creates a formatted file you can then print. You use lp or lpr to print the output of the text formatter.

The most common UNIX text formatter is TeX, pronounced "tecccch" (like yeccccch), an arcane language popular among mathematicians and physicists because of its capability to format large, complex equations, and because it produces more aesthetically pleasing results than any of its competitors. A companion program, LaTeX, is designed to make TeX easier to use (relatively speaking, of course). (See the nearby sidebar, "Howdy, TeX!" for more info about TeX and LaTeX and where to get them.)

Another common text formatter is troff. Some people use nroff (an older version of troff), or groff, a newer GNU version of the program. With luck, you never have to use any of them. If you're luck has run out, you may want to check out the section about troff, nroff, and groff in Chapter 9.

Howdy, TeX!

The popular TeX text formatter was created by one Donald E. Knuth, way back in the late 1970s. According to Knuth himself, TeX is a "typesetting system . . . intended for the creation of beautiful books — and especially for books that contain a lot of mathematics."

Like troff and its cousins nroff and groff, TeX uses *macros* (prewritten bits of formatting code) to shield you (theoretically) from painful, low-level programming chores. In practice, TeX is hard to handle because it can do many, many things in a variety of ways, all proudly anti-intuitive. For people overwhelmed by the sheer complexity of TeX, Knuth created something called plain TeX, which is a slim and trim, stripped-down version of TeX. Because TeX overwhelms almost everyone, almost everyone uses plain TeX rather than TeX itself.

Over the years, various intrepid UNIX hackers have taken it upon themselves to write their own sets of macros that work with TeX. The best known is probably LaTeX (the La part comes from the last name of its creator, Leslie Lamport). To make a long story short, LaTeX simplifies TeX by letting you describe the structure of a document without making you worry about the way the document looks (sort of like using the built-in styles in a word processor, such as Microsoft Word). Other macro packages for TeX include Eplain, Lollipop, pdfTeX (for creating books in Adobe Acrobat), and HyperTeX (for creating hypertext documents, such as Web pages, with TeX).

Like many things UNIX, TeX and the TeX source code and documentation are available for free; you can download them from various FTP and Web sites on the Internet. Also, you can buy one of a number of commercial versions of TeX; you get technical support and, in some cases, additional features in exchange for your money.

The best source of information about TeX, LaTeX, and related subjects is The TeX Users Group home page on the World Wide Web (at http://www.tug.org/) or one of the many TeX Usenet newsgroups, such as comp.text.tex.

Cuisinarts for text: Word processors

Word processors combine the capabilities of text editors and text formatters. Most word processors are (or try to be) WYSIWYG (an acronym for What You See Is What You Get), which enables you to see on-screen how the document (that's what they call their files) will look when you print them.

The most common word processor for UNIX is WordPerfect (available also for PCs and Macintoshes). Most UNIX users think that word processors are for wimps (*w*hat *y*ou *s*ee *i*s *a*ll *y*ou've *g*ot) because they like the unintelligible and unmemorable commands used by text formatters and prefer to imagine what their text will look like when it is printed rather than be able to see it on-screen. Text formatters can do more complex things than word processors can, such as format complicated mathematical expressions, lay out multipage tables, and neatly organize sections and headers of huge, book-length documents. But that's probably not your problem.

Building the perfect word processor

By far the most popular word processing program for UNIX is WordPerfect, from Corel Corporation. The latest version is WordPerfect 7, which costs somewhere in the neighborhood of $500. WordPerfect brings all the features you expect from a graphical word processing package to UNIX computers running X Windows; you can also get a comparable character-based version if your UNIX terminal is graphics-impaired.

WordPerfect runs on just about every version of UNIX available, including versions of Linux later than Version 2.0.25. WordPerfect also has various file-conversion utilities so that you can share your documents with WordPerfect users running DOS and Windows. The marketing buzzword for such ecumenical behavior is *cross-platform capability,* and it's important if you have, for example, UNIX users and Windows users on the same network.

Along with all the usual word processing bells and whistles, WordPerfect 7 comes packaged with Netscape Navigator, a few thousand clip art images and photographs, and more than a hundred fonts. Find out more about WordPerfect on the World Wide Web, at `http://www.wordperfect.com/`, or give Corel a call (in Ottawa), at 613-788-6000.

`vi` *and* `emacs` *and* `pico` *are your friends*

The rest of this chapter explains how to use each of the Big Three text editors (`vi`, `emacs`, and `pico`), along with some words about how to use the prehistoric but not yet extinct `ed` (who, as you will see, is *not* your friend). Even if you use a word processor or desktop publishing program, you may need to use a text editor to do some things, such as these tasks:

- Write electronic mail (see Chapter 16).
- Create or edit text files called *shell scripts,* which enable you to create your own UNIX commands (see Chapter 12).
- Create or edit special text files that control the way your UNIX setup works (see Chapter 7).
- Write C programs (just kidding!).

Shy Vi, the Princess of Text Editors

The `vi` text editor can claim a unique status among UNIX editors: Almost every UNIX system in the universe has `vi`. This fact makes it a good editor to know if you plan to be moving around from system to system, because you can always count on it's being there. Someone may have other reasons for using `vi`, but ease of use is not foremost among them.

To run vi, type **vi**, a space, and the name of the file you want to edit, and then press Enter.

If you get an error message when you try to run vi, talk to your system administrator. If the screen looks weird, your terminal type may not be set right — another reason to talk to your system administrator.

Editor à la mode

The most distinctive feature of vi (and the one that has spawned legions of vi-haters, along with a few devotees) is that it is a *modal* editor. The vi program is always waiting for one of two things: commands or text (also known as input). When vi is waiting for a command, it is in *command mode.* When it is waiting for text, it is in *input mode.* Normally, it is up to you to figure out which mode vi is in at any particular moment — it doesn't give you a clue.

Most vi commands are one letter long. Some are lowercase letters, and others are uppercase letters. When you type vi commands, be sure to use the correct capitalization.

If you're in input mode and want to give a command, press the Esc key.

Whenever we tell you to type a command, it works only if you're in command mode. If you're not sure which mode you're in, press Esc first. If you are already in command mode, pressing Esc just makes vi beep.

To switch from command mode to input mode, you tell vi to add the text after the character the cursor (the point at which you are working) is on (by using the a command) or to insert the text before the current cursor position (by using the i command).

Emergency exit from vi

To escape from vi, follow these steps:

1. **Press Escape at least three times.**

   The computer should beep. Now you are in command mode, for sure.

2. **Type the following line and press Enter:**

   :q!

   This line tells vi to quit and not save any changes.

Help! I need somebody!

The guy who wrote vi (remember Bill, the grouchy guy who's 6'4" and in excellent physical condition? — same guy) didn't believe in help, so there wasn't any.

Fortunately, vi has been used in so many introductory computing courses that Bill eventually relented and added "novice" mode. Rather than type **vi** to run the editor, type **vedit** to get the same editor with some allegedly helpful messages. In particular, whenever you're in input mode rather than command mode, vi displays, at the bottom of your screen, a message such as INPUT MODE, APPEND MODE, CHANGE MODE, or OPEN MODE. All these messages mean the same thing (except to Bill, evidently): Text you type when these messages are visible is added to the file rather than interpreted as commands.

Easy text-entry techniques

Let's make a new file with some more deathless prose so that you can practice entering text in vi. Run vi with a new filename:

```
vi madeline
```

To add text after the current position of the cursor, type the following (you do *not* press Enter after a command):

```
a
```

We tell you in a minute how to move the cursor, when you have some text to move around in. You can press a, for example, to add this text to the newly created xanadu file:

```
In Xanadu did Kubla Khan
        A stately pleasure-dome decree:
        Where Alph, the sacred river, ran
        Through caverns measureless to man
           Down to a sunless sea.
```

To get back to command mode, press Esc. Press Esc whenever you finish typing text so that you are ready to give the next command.

Other commands you can use to enter text include i to insert text *before* the current cursor position, A to add the text at the end of the line the cursor is on, and O to add the text on a new line before the current line.

The vi program shows you a full-screen view of your file. If the file isn't long enough to fill the screen, vi shows tildes (~) on the blank lines beyond the end of the file. Figure 10-1, for example, shows a text file called eating.peas (created in a later discussion about ed) as it would appear in vi.

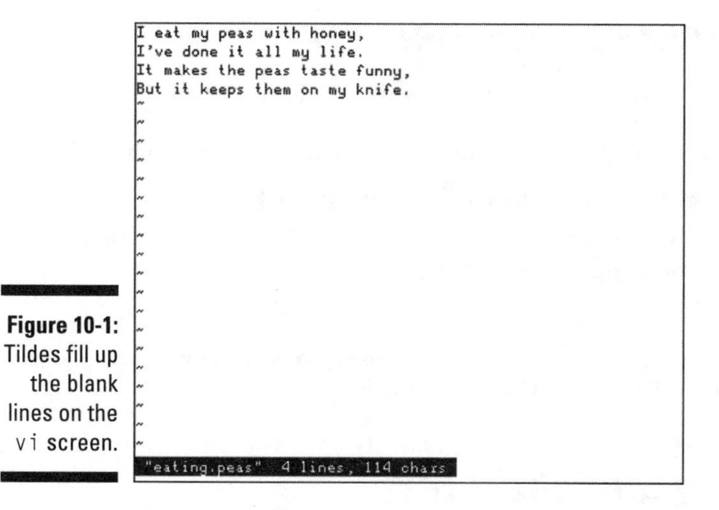

I eat my peas with honey,
I've done it all my life.
It makes the peas taste funny,
But it keeps them on my knife.
"eating.peas" 4 lines, 114 chars

Figure 10-1: Tildes fill up the blank lines on the vi screen.

The cursor appears at the beginning of the first line of the file.

All kinds of ways to move the cursor

You can use dozens of commands to move the cursor around in your file, but you can get to where you want with just a few of them:

- The arrow keys (←, →, ↑, and ↓) usually do what you would expect: They move the cursor in the indicated direction.

  Sadly, on some terminals vi does not understand the arrow keys. If this statement is true for you, press h to move left, j to move down, k to move up, and l to move right. Bill chose these keys on the theory that, because those keys are a touch typist's home position for the fingers on the right hand, you can save valuable milliseconds by not having to move your fingers. Really. In some versions of vi, the arrow keys work only in command mode; in other versions, they also work in input mode.
- Enter or + moves the cursor to the beginning of the next line.
- The hyphen (-) moves the cursor to the beginning of the preceding line.

- G (the uppercase letter) moves the cursor to the end of the file.
- 1G moves the cursor to the beginning of the file. (That's the number 1, not the letter *l*. Why ask why?)

Giving your text a makeover

To modify the text you have typed, follow these steps:

1. **Move the cursor to the beginning of the text you want to change.**
2. **To type over (on top of) the existing text, press R.**
3. **Type the new text. What you type replaces what is already there. Press Esc when you finish replacing text.**
4. **To insert text in front of the current cursor position, press** s**.**
5. **Type the new text. What you type is inserted without replacing any existing text. Press Esc when you finish inserting text.**

Removing unsightly text

To delete text, follow these steps:

1. **Move the cursor to the beginning of the text you want to delete.**
2. **To delete one character, press the letter x. To get rid of five characters, type** xxxxx**. You get the idea.**
3. **To delete text from the current cursor position to the end of the line, press uppercase D.**
4. **To delete the entire line the cursor is on, type dd (the letter *d* twice).**

Nobody undoes it better

Like many text editors, vi has a way to "undo" the most recent change or deletion you made. Type the following to undo the change:

```
u
```

If you type the following line (in uppercase), vi undoes all changes to the current line since you moved the cursor to that line:

```
U
```

Write me or save me — just don't lose me

To save the updated file, type the following (be sure that you have pressed Esc first so that you're in command mode):

```
:w
```

That's a colon and a *w*, and then press Enter. You should give this command every few minutes, in case the confusing nature of `vi` commands makes you delete something important by mistake.

Good-bye, `vi`

To leave `vi`, type

```
ZZ
```

Be sure to press Esc a few times so that you're in command mode before giving this command. To quit and not save the changes you have made, type this line:

```
:q!
```

Then press Enter. This line means, "Leave `vi` and throw away my changes. I know what I'm doing."

Most other letters, numbers, and symbols are also `vi` commands, so watch what you type when you're in command mode. Table 10-1 lists the most common commands you use with `vi`.

Table 10-1 Commands in `vi`

Command	*Description*
Esc	Return to command mode
Enter	Move to beginning of next line
+	Move to beginning of next line
-	Move to beginning of preceding line
a	Add text after cursor
A	Add text at end of current line
dd	Delete entire current line

(continued)

Table 10-1 *(continued)*

Command	*Description*
D	Delete from cursor to end of line
G	Move (go) to end of file
1G	Move to beginning of file
h	Move one space left
i	Add text before cursor
j	Move down one line
k	Move up one line
l	Move right one space
O	Add text on new line before current line
:q! (followed by Enter)	Quit `vi`, even if changes aren't saved
R	Replace text
u	Undo last change
U	Undo changes to current line
x	Delete one character
:w (followed by Enter)	Save (write) file
ZZ	Quit `vi` and save changes

I just love `vi`*!*

If you just love `vi` and want to learn more about it, read Chapter 11 in *MORE UNIX For Dummies,* which we wrote (published by IDG Books Worldwide, Inc.). Or try `emacs` or `pico`, and see whether you still love `vi`.

A Novel Concept in Editing: `emacs` *Makes Sense*

We don't want to get your hopes up, but `emacs` is much easier to use than `vi`. The reason is that it doesn't have the mysterious modes that require you to remember at every moment whether the program is expecting a command or text.

On the other hand, commands in emacs aren't exactly intuitive. Still, we like them better. In case you are wondering, the name *emacs* comes from *e*ditor *mac*ros because the original version of emacs was written as an extension to an early text editor called teco, an editor that makes ed (see the section "Talk to Mr. ed," at the end of this chapter) look like the winner of the Nobel prize for user-friendliness. (Scary thought, isn't it?)

To run emacs, type this line:

```
emacs eating.peas
```

You replace eating.peas with the name of the file you want, of course. If the file you name doesn't exist, emacs creates it. Like vi, emacs displays a full-screen view of your file, as shown in Figure 10-2. On the bottom line of the screen is the *status line,* which tells you the name of the file you are editing and other, less interesting information.

```
I eat my peas with honey,
I've done it all my life.
It makes the peas taste funny,
But it keeps them on the knife.

-- eating.peas [Fundamental] 100% --
```

Figure 10-2: The GNU Emacs display in a text console. emacs displays on the status line (at the bottom) the filename and other mysterious information.

A tale of two emacs

Unlike vi, emacs does not normally come with UNIX. Because most versions of emacs are distributed for free, however, most systems have it or can get it. By far the two most common versions of emacs are GNU Emacs and XEmacs. Despite its name, XEmacs runs under both X Windows and text-based consoles, and so does GNU Emacs. The basic commands are the same for both versions, and the most obvious differences between the two are the button bars and more sophisticated 3-D look to the windows in XEmacs. (Compare the difference in Figures 10-3 and 10-4.) Other than that, it really doesn't matter which you use.

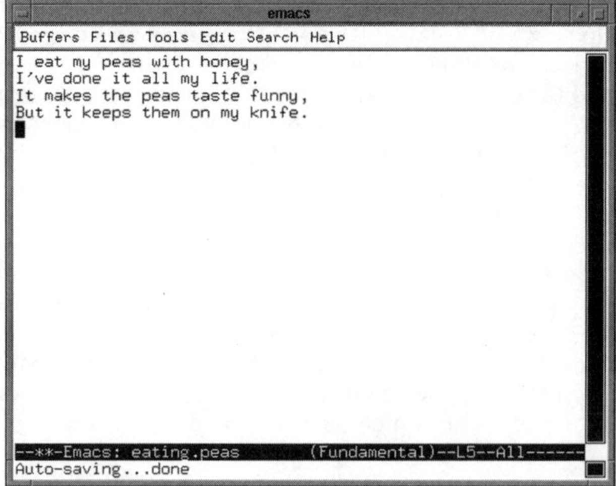

Figure 10-3: The GNU Emacs display in an X window includes pull-down menus for common commands, including save, search, undo, and help.

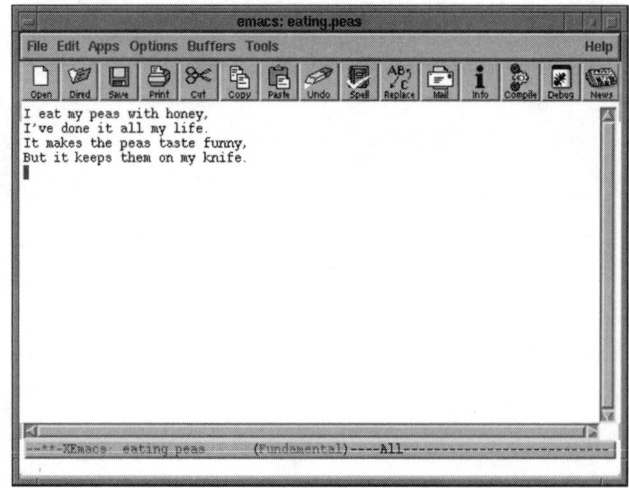

Figure 10-4: The XEmacs display in an X window includes a toolbar in addition to pull-down menus and a 3-D look to the interface.

To run XEmacs on the `eating.peas` file, type the command **xemacs eating.peas**.

- If you get an error message when you try to run `emacs`, ask your system administrator what's up. The `emacs` program may have another name on your system. If your system administrator says that you don't have `emacs`, plead with him or her to get it.
- If `emacs` looks or acts weird (weirder than usual, that is), your terminal type may not be set correctly. Again, ask your system administrator to straighten it out.

More than just a text editor

The emacs program is a cornucopia of bells and whistles, including two different mail packages, a newsreader, a file manager, color text highlighting, and countless other fun and unnecessary features. These features make emacs a much larger package than any other editor (it has been somewhat accurately called an operating system disguised as an editor) and has been known to cause some system administrators to balk at installing it on their UNIX machines. For others, it's almost a way of life, so whether you have access to emacs may depend on how strongly your system administrator feels about those types of things.

Telling emacs *what to do*

Rather than have two modes, as does vi, emacs treats normal letters, numbers, and punctuation as text and sticks them in your file when you type them. (Pretty advanced concept, huh?) Commands are usually given by pressing combinations of the Ctrl (Control) key and a letter. You also give some commands by pressing the Meta key and a letter.

On most computers, the Meta key is the Esc key. If your keyboard has an Alt key, it may be the Meta key. Try Alt to see whether it works. If it doesn't, use Esc. Unlike with Alt, if you use Esc, you must release the Esc key before you type the subsequent letter (Esc, release+letter). In the following section, we tell you to press Esc.

Another novel concept: Type to enter text

To enter text, just start typing! The text is inserted wherever your cursor is.

Getting around in emacs

To move the cursor around in your text, use these keys:

- Arrow keys usually move the cursor up, down, left, and right.

  In a few situations, emacs doesn't understand the arrow keys. If that's true for you, press Ctrl+B to move backward one character, Ctrl+F to move forward one character, Ctrl+P to move to the preceding line, and Ctrl+N to move to the next line. At least they tried to make them mnemonic.

- Ctrl+A moves to the beginning of the line.
- Ctrl+E moves to the end of the line.
- Esc+< (press Esc and then hold down Shift and press the comma key) moves to the beginning of the file.
- Esc+> (press Esc and then hold down Shift and press the period key) moves to the end of the file.

Making changes in emacs

Even though emacs is a better text editor, you still make typos, change your mind, and think of brilliant improvements to your text. To change text, follow these steps:

1. **Move the cursor to the beginning of the text you want to change.**
2. **Type the new text. The text is inserted wherever the cursor is.**
3. **Delete any text you don't want.**

It's that simple. No weird commands required.

Deleting stuff in emacs

emacs has several commands for deleting stuff:

- To delete the character the cursor is on, press Ctrl+D. Or, on many terminals, press the Del key.
- To delete text from the cursor to the end of the word (up to a space or punctuation mark), press Esc and then D.
- To delete from the cursor to the end of the line, press Ctrl+K.

Emergency exit from emacs

To stop using emacs, press Ctrl+X followed by Ctrl+C.

This command doesn't save any changes you made to the file in emacs. It just gets you out. Some versions of emacs may ask whether you want to save the file the editor was looking at or say something like "Buffers not saved. Exit?" (Translation: "Do you really want to quit without saving your changes?") Press Y for yes or N for no, as appropriate. If you just want to get out, press N to the "Do you want to save" question or Y to the "Buffers not saved" question.

Save that file before it's too late!

To save the text in the file, press Ctrl+XS (press and hold down the Ctrl key, press X and S, and then release the Ctrl key). You should save your work every few minutes. Even though `emacs` isn't as frustrating as `vi` (or `ed`, for that matter), lots can still go wrong.

Bidding emacs adieu

When you finish editing and want to leave `emacs`, press Ctrl+XC (press and hold down the Ctrl key, press X and C, and then release the Ctrl key). You leave `emacs` and see the UNIX shell prompt.

If you didn't save your work, `emacs` politely points out that your "buffers" (the stuff you have been working on) aren't saved and asks whether you really want to exit. It suggests N as the safe default in case you want to return to `emacs` to save the file. To leave without saving, press Y and then Enter.

It takes many fewer `emacs` commands to make a file and type some stuff, make a few changes, and then save the file and leave than it does with `ed` or `vi`. The `emacs` program has tons of commands, most of which are utterly useless. Table 10-2 lists the commonly used `emacs` commands.

Table 10-2 Commands in `emacs`

Command	*Description*
Ctrl+A	Move to the beginning of the line
Ctrl+B	Move back one space
Ctrl+D	Delete one character
Ctrl+E	Move to the end of the line
Ctrl+F	Move forward one space
Ctrl+K	Delete to the end of the line
Ctrl+N	Move to the next line
Ctrl+P	Move to the preceding line
Ctrl+XC	Leave `emacs`
Ctrl+XS	Save the file
Esc+<	Move to the beginning of the file
Esc+>	Move to the end of the file
Esc+D	Delete to the end of the word

Moving text in emacs

Although this subject is beyond the scope of this quick introduction to emacs, we tell you how to move text from one place to another in a file. It turns out that when you press Ctrl+K to kill the text from the cursor to the end of the line, the killed information is stored in a temporary place called the *kill buffer.* You can copy the information from the kill buffer back into your file by pressing Ctrl+Y (*y*ank it back into the file). To move some text, kill it with Ctrl+K, move the cursor to the new location, and press Ctrl+Y to insert the text where your cursor is. ("Kill" and "yank" in emacs-ese correspond to "cut" and "paste" in the regular world.)

A Peek at pico

One other editor has become popular: pico. As the Pine mail program has spread like wildfire, the editor that comes with it, pico, has taken off too. pico is the easiest to use, if not the most powerful, of the four text editors we describe in this chapter. It was written by folks at the University of Washington.

To run pico, type this command:

```
pico eating.peas
```

As usual, type the name of the file you want to edit rather than *eating.peas*. If you type a filename that doesn't exist, pico creates a file with that name just for you.

Your system may not have pico — if not, ask your system administrator if she can get it for you. Assure her that if she doesn't, you'll pester her ten times a day for the next year for help with ed or vi.

The pico screen looks like the one shown in Figure 10-5. Amazing — pico shows you at the bottom of the screen a menu of the most commonly used commands! What will they think of next?

You're my type

Typing text into a file by using pico is a breeze. Just type. That's all. No modes, commands, or anything strange.

Figure 10-5: The `pico` editor is easy to use, with a small menu at the bottom of the screen.

You move me

If your cursor keys work in `pico`, great. If not, you can use Ctrl+F to move forward one character, Ctrl+B to move back one character, Ctrl+N to move to the next line, and Ctrl+P to move to the preceding line. The following keys also move you around the screen:

- Ctrl+A moves to the beginning of the line.
- Ctrl+E moves to the end of the line.
- Ctrl+V moves forward one screenful of text (F8 does this too).
- Ctrl+Y moves back one screenful of text (as does F7).

You're a big help

To get help with the `pico` commands, press Ctrl+G. If your keyboard has an F1 key, that should work too. You see pages of helpful information about the program. Press Ctrl+V to see more or Ctrl+X to return to `pico`.

Time for a change

It's also easy to edit your text in pico. Whatever you type is inserted wherever the cursor is. You can use these commands to edit stuff:

- Ctrl+D deletes the character the cursor is on.
- Ctrl+^ (that's Ctrl+Shift+6) marks the beginning of some text you want to work with. You use this command to select a bunch of text to delete or move.
- Ctrl+K (or F9) deletes ("cuts") the text from the mark to the current cursor position. Blammo! — the text is gone and is stored in an invisible holding tank somewhere.
- Ctrl+U (or F10) "uncuts" or "pastes" the last text you cut, making it reappear where the cursor is now.

Thanks for saving my file

To save the text in a file, press Ctrl+O (or press F3). pico asks for the filename to write the text into, suggesting the filename you used when you ran pico in the first place. You can change the name so that the text is written to a new file or leave it as is, to update the existing file. When you press Enter, pico writes the information into the file.

I'm outta here

When you have finished editing and want to leave pico, just press Ctrl+X. If you haven't already saved your file, pico asks whether you really want to leave, because leaving will lose any changes you made to the file since you last saved it. Tell it that you do. Then you're out, and you see the shell prompt.

pico doesn't claim to be an editor with the power of emacs or vi. After all, you can't edit ten files at a time, read your mail, and rename files from pico. Who cares? It's a nice, easy program for editing text. Isn't that what a text editor is supposed to be?

Table 10-3 lists the top pico commands.

Editors galore: NEdit and jed

UNIX being UNIX, you could use many more text editors in addition to the Big Three (and reluctant Fourth) described in this chapter, including such alien-sounding programs as `sed`, `perl`, and `awk`. A few of them, including `NEdit` and `jed`, have graphical user interfaces (GUIs, remember?) that let you use your mouse to get stuff done.

`NEdit` wraps all the fun and frolic of `emacs` and `pico` plain-text editing in a Windows-style GUI. Because `NEdit` is relatively easy to use (you can select and drag-and-drop text with your mouse; imagine that!), it has become one of the most popular editors for UNIX users blessed with some version of X. One of `Nedit`'s coolest features is "unlimited undo," which means that you can undo all your actions right back to the beginning of your `NEdit` session. Programmers like `NEdit` because it's completely customizable and because it has special features that make editing files of various types of computer code easier (features such as syntax highlighting and parenthesis flashing and matching; if you don't know what these are already, you don't care — believe us). `NEdit`, the latest version of which is 5.0.2, is free. You can download versions and source code for just about every flavor of UNIX via FTP from a number of sites, including `ftp://ftp.fnal.gov/pub/nedit`.

`jed` is named after its creator, *J*ohn *E*. *D*avis of MIT (so it's sometimes called `JED`). `jed` is much like `emacs`, but it takes up much less space on your computer. `jed` can do plain-text editing, to be sure; it can also edit binary files just like a decent word processor. In fact, `jed` can do a reasonable imitation (*emulation* is the technical term) of such editors as `emacs`, WordStar, and Brief. Like `NEdit`, `jed` offers a slew of programming modes that help make life a little less trying for programmers trying to edit abstruse computer code in such languages as C, C++, FORTRAN, HTML, and `TeX`. `jed` is free; the latest version number is, curiously, something like 0.98-7. According to Mr. Davis, `jed` isn't up to Release 1.0 "because of lack of adequate documentation," which we're sure doesn't scare you off one bit. You can download `jed` from `ftp://space.mit.edu/pub/davis/jed`, among other FTP sites.

Table 10-3 Commands in `pico`

Command	*Description*
Ctrl+A	Move to the beginning of the line
Ctrl+B	Move back one character
Ctrl+D	Delete one character
Ctrl+E	Move to the end of the line
Ctrl+F	Move forward one character
Ctrl+G (or F1)	Get help (display online help information)

(continued)

Table 10-3 *(continued)*

Command	*Description*
Ctrl+K (or F9)	Kill (delete) selected text (text between the mark and the cursor)
Ctrl+N	Move to the next line
Ctrl+O (or F3)	Output (save) the file
Ctrl+P	Move to the preceding line
Ctrl+U (or F10)	Uncut (paste) the last text that was deleted by using the Ctrl+K command
Ctrl+V (or F8)	Move down one screenful of text
Ctrl+X (or F2)	Exit from pico
Ctrl+Y (or F7)	Move up one screenful of text
Ctrl+^ (Ctrl+Shift+6)	Mark the beginning of selected text

Talk to Mr. ed

The vi editor may seem like a quaint throwback to prehistoric software, but there was a time in the early days of UNIX when even vi didn't exist. In the pre-CRT era of Teletype terminals, *line editors* ruled, and the standard among line editors was (and still is) ed. A *line editor,* such as ed, is one that assigns line numbers to the lines in a file. Every time you do something, you must tell ed which line or lines to do it to. If you have used the EDLIN program in DOS, ed should look familiar. The ed program has been a part of UNIX since the beginning of time. When you use it, you begin to appreciate how far software design has progressed since 1969.

If there is *any way* — repeat — *any way* you can get another text editor to use, do it. If you don't think that ed can really be that bad, just peruse the rest of this section and you will run screaming to your system administrator for vi , pico, or emacs (preferably pico or emacs).

Some systems have a program called ex that is similar to but not quite as horrible as ed. Try typing **ex** to see what happens.

To run ed, type this line:

```
ed important.letter
```

(Type the name of your file rather than *important.letter*.) If no file has the name you specify, ed makes one. UNIX responds to this command with a number, which is the number of characters (letters, numbers, punctuation, and spaces) in the file, just in case you're being paid to write by the letter.

If you receive an error message when you try to run ed, talk to your system administrator. Congratulate her on getting rid of that Neanderthal text editor and find out which text editor you *can* use.

Hey, Wilbur, which command was that?

All ed commands are one-letter long (such as h).

Remember *not* to capitalize ed commands unless we specifically say to. ed commands are almost all lowercase letters.

Relatively recent versions of ed (since, oh, about 1983) have a P command (that's a capital *P*, one of the few uppercase commands) that turns on a prompt. If you type **P** and press Enter, ed prompts you with an asterisk when it's in command mode and waiting for a command. Is that incredibly user-friendly or what? This P command enables you to determine when you're in command mode! Must have snuck that one in when the lazy typists weren't looking.

If you're in input mode and want to give a command, type this character:

```
.
```

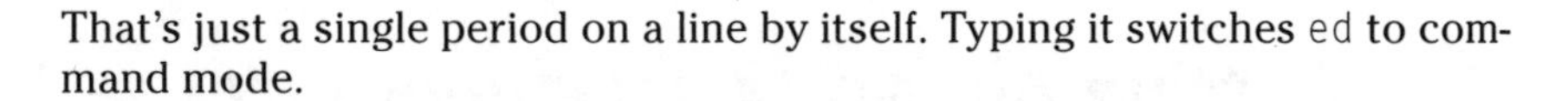

That's just a single period on a line by itself. Typing it switches ed to command mode.

In the remainder of this discussion about using ed, whenever we tell you to type a command, it works only if you're in command mode. If you're not sure, type a period and press Enter first.

If you're in command mode and want to type some text, you switch to text-input mode. First, however, you must decide whether you're going to *append* (by using the a command) after the current line the lines of text you will type or *insert* (by using the i command) before the current line. More about the current line and the a and i commands in a minute.

Feeding text to Mr. ed

Create a file and feed some text to it. Start the process by typing

```
ed eating.peas
```

You can name your file something other than *eating.peas*, if you want. UNIX responds with a question mark, just to keep you on your toes. (This time, the question mark tells you that ed just created a new file for you.)

To add (append) new lines of text to the end of the file — in this case, the end of the file is the same as the beginning because the file is empty — type

```
a
```

UNIX responds by saying nothing, which is your indication that ed is now in input mode and waiting for you to type some text. Type some pearls of wisdom, like this:

```
I eat my peas with honey,
I've done it all my life.
It makes the peas taste funny,
but it keeps them on the knife.
.
```

When you finish typing text, type a period on a line by itself to switch ed from input mode back to command mode. Not that ed gives you a hint that this process is going on, unless you have used the P command to tell it to prompt you.

The lines of text are now in your file. Now would be a good time to save the file, just in case you kick your computer's plug from the wall in your frustration at having to use such a brainless program.

Getting Mr. ed *to save your text*

The following command saves your text in a file with ed. If you're in input mode, remember to type a period on a line by itself to switch to command mode before giving this command:

```
w
```

That's w for *write*. UNIX responds with the number of characters now in the file. Be sure to give this command before leaving ed so that your deathless prose is saved in the file; in this case, eating.peas (or whatever filename you used when you ran ed).

Show me the file, please

Now that you have text in the file, how can you see it or change it? By using the p (print) command. This command doesn't print anything on the printer; it just displays it on-screen — another example of superb software engineering. (Well, it printed on those old Teletypes.) If you type the p command by itself, as follows, ed displays the current line:

```
p
```

In the case of the sample eating.peas file, the current line is the last line in the file. You can also tell ed which lines to display by typing their line numbers. To display lines 1 through 4, for example, type this line:

```
1,4p
```

You can also use the symbol $ to stand for the line number of the last line in the file (in case you don't know how many lines are in the file). The following command always displays the entire file:

```
1,$p
```

A miserable way to edit

You can change the contents of a line of text with ed, although it involves giving commands that look like this:

```
12,13s/wrong/right/
```

This command substitutes right for wrong in lines 12 through 13, inclusive. Totally primitive and painful, isn't it? For the amount of editing you probably do in ed, it's almost easier to delete the line with the typo and insert a new line. We recommend that you immediately ask your system administrator for a better text editor.

Undo your thing, ed!

Wait — ed has one useful, humane command, after all! The u command enables you to "undo" the last (and only the very last) change you made to the file. If you delete a line by mistake with the d command, for example, you can type this line to undo the deletion:

```
u
```

Be sure that you don't make any other changes before using the u command. It undoes only the last thing you did.

Time to ed *out*

When you finish making changes and you want to leave ed (or even if you're not finished making changes and you want to leave ed anyway), type

```
q
```

If you're in input mode, first type a period on a line by itself to get into command mode. Then press q to quit.

If you haven't saved your work by using the w command, ed just doesn't quit. Instead, it displays a question mark to tell you that it was expecting a w command first. To save your changes, type these two commands, pressing Enter after each:

```
w
q
```

If you don't want to save the changes to the file, press q again at the question mark. This time, ed believes that you really want to leave and thus exits. Not a moment too soon!

Chapter 11

Umpteen Useful UNIX Utilities

In This Chapter

- A grab bag of useful programs
- Sorting and comparing files
- Stupid calendar tricks
- Squashing files to make them smaller
- Some other odds and ends

In spite of the fact that we have been making fun of UNIX in this book, we are well aware that UNIX actually has some fairly handy programs lying around. In this chapter, we look briefly at some of them. All these programs have a severe case of what is known as Feature Disease (closely related to the greasy fingerprints mentioned in Chapter 2): They all are bristling with features and options. Most of the features and options aren't worth mentioning, however, so we don't.

Comparing Apples and Oranges

When you have used your UNIX machine for a while, you have piles of files (say that six times quickly) lying around. Often, many of the files are duplicates, or near duplicates, of each other. Two programs can help sort out this mess: `cmp` and `diff`.

The simplest comparison program is `cmp`; it just tells you whether two files are the same or different. To use `cmp` to compare two files, type this line:

```
cmp onefile anotherfile
```

You replace `onefile` and `anotherfile` with the names of the files you want to compare, of course. If the contents of the two files are the same, `cmp` doesn't say anything (in the finest UNIX tradition). If they're different, `cmp` tells how far into the files it got before it found something different. You can compare any two files, regardless of whether they contain text, programs, databases, or whatever, because `cmp` cares only whether they're identical.

A considerably more sophisticated comparison program is `diff`. This program attempts to tell you not only whether two files are different but also how different they are. The files must be plain text, not word processor documents or anything else, or else `diff` becomes horribly confused. Here's an example that uses two versions of a story one of us wrote. We compared files `tse1` and `tse2` by typing this command:

```
diff tse1 tse2
```

Enter the name of the older file first and the name of the new, improved second file. The `diff` program responds:

```
45c45
< steered back around, but the sheep screamed in panic and reared back.
--
> steered back around, but the goats screamed in panic and reared back.
46a47
> handlebars and landed safely in the snow.
```

The changes between `tse1` and `tse2` are that, in line 45, the *sheep* changed to *goats,* and a new Line 47 was added after Line 46.

The `diff` program reports, in its first line of output (`45c45`) that changes (that's what the *c* stands for) have been made in lines 45 through 45 (that is, just line 45). Then it displays the line in the first file, starting with a <, and the line in the second file, starting with a >. We think of this as the `diff` way of saying that you took out the lines starting with < and inserted the lines starting with >. Then `diff` reports that a new line is between lines 46 and 47 in the original file, and it shows the line that was inserted. It's a great way of seeing what changes have been made when you get a new revision of a document you have written.

BSD versions of `diff` (including the version that usually runs under Linux) can compare two directories to tell you which files are present in one and not in the other and to show you the differences between files with corresponding names in the two directories. Run `diff` and give it the names of the two directories.

Assorted Files

Computers are good at putting stuff in order. Indeed, at one time a third of all computer time was spent sorting. UNIX has a quite capable sorting program, cleverly named `sort`, that you may remember meeting briefly in Chapter 7. Here, we talk about some other ways to use the program.

The `sort` command sorts the lines of a file into alphabetical order. From the `sort` point of view, a line is anything that ends with a carriage return (that is, you pressed Enter). If you have a file containing a list, with one item per line, this command alphabetizes the list.

The easiest way to use `sort` is to sort one file into another. In other words, you tell `sort` to place the sorted version of the original file in another file. This way, you don't risk screwing up the original file if the sort runs amok. To sort the original `myfile` into a second file named `sortedfile`, type this command:

```
sort myfile > sortedfile
```

Although you can sort a file back into itself, you can't do it in the obvious way. The following line, for example, doesn't work:

```
sort myfile > myfile
```

The problem with this command is that the UNIX shell clears out *`myfile`* before the sort starts (with the result that, when `sort` tries to sort something, it finds that *`myfile`* is empty). You can use the `-o` (for *o*utput) option to tell `sort` where to put the results, like this:

```
sort myfile -o myfile
```

This command works because `sort` doesn't start to write to the output file until it has read all its input.

Normally, `sort` orders its results based on a strict comparison of the internal ASCII codes the computer uses for storing text. The good news is that this command sorts letters and digits in the correct way, although some peculiarities exist: Normally, uppercase letters are sorted before lowercase letters, so *ZEBRA* precedes *aardvark*. You can use the `-f` (for *f*old cases together) option to sort regardless of uppercase and lowercase letters:

```
sort -f animals -o sortedanimals
```

Although we could have used the > redirection symbol in this example, with `sort`, it's safer to use `-o`. You can use several other options also to tell it to sort:

`-b` Ignore spaces at the beginning of the line.

`-d` Use dictionary order and ignore any punctuation. You usually use this option with `-f`.

`-n` Sort based on the number at the beginning of the line. With this option, 99 precedes 100 rather than follows it, as it does in usual alphabetical order. (Yes, the normal thing the computer does is pretty dumb. Are you surprised?)

`-r` Sort in the reverse order of whatever would have been done otherwise. You can combine this option with any of the others.

We find sorting to be particularly useful in files in which every line starts with a date, as shown in these examples:

```
0505      Tonia's birthday
1204      Meg's birthday
1102      Zac's birthday
0318      Sarah's birthday
```

We could type `sort -n` to sort this file by date. Notice that we wrote May 5 as 0505 (not 55, for example) so that a numeric sort would work.

You can do much more complex sorting and treat every line as a sequence of "fields" that `sort` uses to decide the final sorted order. If you really need to do this, talk to someone who knows something about sorting.

Time Is Money — Steal Some Today!

All UNIX systems have internal clocks. You can ask the system what the date and time are with the `date` command:

```
date
```

UNIX responds with this information:

```
Thu Dec  3 15:43:50 EST 1998
```

Many options enable you to tailor the date format any way you want. Don't waste your time. UNIX has an idea about the time zone too, and it even does daylight savings time automatically.

You can schedule things to be done later by using the `at` command. You say something like this:

```
at 5:15pm Jul 4
sort -r myhugefile -o myhugefile.sort
pr -f -2 myhugefile.sort | lp
```

Then you press Ctrl+D to indicate that you've finished giving commands.

You give the `at` command and specify a time and date. Then you enter the commands you want to run at that date and time. Press Ctrl+D on a separate line to tell UNIX that you're finished listing tasks. In this example, we sort a huge file and then print it in two columns, all on the Fourth of July, when presumably no one is around to complain that it's taking too long. If you omit the date, UNIX assumes that you mean today if the time you give is later than the current time; otherwise, UNIX assumes that you mean tomorrow.

Any output that normally would go to the terminal is sent back to you by electronic mail, so you should at least skim Chapter 17 to find out how to read your mail.

Squashing Your Files

One problem that is common to all UNIX systems — indeed, to nearly all computer systems of any kind — is that you never have enough disk space. UNIX comes with a couple of programs that can alleviate this problem: compress and gzip. They change the data in a file into a more compact form. Although you can't do anything with the file in this compact form except expand it back to its original format, for files you don't need to refer to often, compressing can be a big space saver.

Compress without stress

You use compress and gzip in pretty much the same way. To compress a file named confidential.doc, for example, type this line:

```
compress -v confidential.doc
```

The optional -v (for *v*erbose) option merely tells UNIX to report how much space it saved. If you use it, UNIX responds with this information:

```
confidential.doc: Compression: 49.79% — replaced with confidential.doc.Z
```

The compress program replaces the file with one that has the same name with .Z added to it. The degree of compression depends on what's in the file, although 50 percent compression for text files is typical. For a few files, the compression scheme doesn't save any space, in which case compress is polite enough not to make a .Z file.

To get the compressed file back to its original state, use uncompress:

```
uncompress confidential.doc.Z
```

This command gets rid of the file confidential.doc.Z and gets back confidential.doc. You can also use zcat, a compressed-file version of the cat program, which sends an uncompressed version of a compressed file to the terminal, without storing the uncompressed version in a file. The command is rarely useful by itself but can be quite handy with programs such as more or lp. You use it this way:

```
zcat confidential.doc.Z | more
```

This command enables you to see one page at a time what's in the file. Unlike uncompress, zcat does not get rid of the .Z file.

The GNU crowd weighed in with its own compress-like program named gzip. It works the same way that compress does, but uses a different, slightly better, compression scheme. The gzip program is analogous to compress. gunzip and gzcat uncompress stuff. Use them this way:

```
gzip -v confidential.doc
gunzip confidential.doc.gz
zcat confidential.doc.gz | more
```

Note that the files end with lowercase gz rather than uppercase Z.

Fortunately, gzip knows how to uncompress files produced by compress as well as those produced by several other compression programs, so you can use gunzip as your one-stop uncompression utility.

A similar but older program that uses a different compacting scheme is pack. To use it, type this line:

```
pack confidential.doc
```

UNIX responds with this information:

```
/usr/bin/pack: confidential.doc: 37.1% Compression
```

You get packed files back with unpack. You can look at packed files with pcat. Packed files end in .z (that's a lowercase *z*). Like compress, pack leaves the file untouched if packing doesn't save any space.

Zippedy day-tah

WinZip and PKZIP are widely used compression programs among Windows and DOS users to create *ZIP* files containing one or more files compressed together. You may run into ZIP files if you get information from the Internet or on a disk from a DOS or Windows system. Fortunately, a number of volunteers (led by a perfectly nice guy who goes by the enigmatic handle of Cave Newt) have written free zipping and unzipping programs named zip and unzip. They're both available for free over the Internet.

To unzip a ZIP file, you use unzip:

```
unzip video-list.zip
```

How does file compression work, anyway?

This discussion is pretty technical. Don't say that we didn't warn you.

The issue of *optimal codes* (codes that use the least number of bits for a particular file — or *message* because at that time they were thinking in terms of radioteletypes) was a hot topic in the late 1940s, challenging the deepest thinkers in the field. In 1952, a student named David Huffman published a paper that any high-school student could understand showing how to use simple arithmetic techniques to construct optimal codes. Oops. Ever since then, this kind of code has been known as *Huffman coding.* For many years Huffman coding was the best available, and a UNIX program named `pack` used it.

Normally, every character in a file is stored by using 8 bits (binary digits, 1s and 0s, the smallest unit of data a computer can handle). Suppose that a file contains 800 *A*'s followed by 100 *B*'s and 100 *C*'s. That's 1,000 characters, at 8 bits apiece, or 8,000 bits. For this particular file, a compression program can use much shorter codes. It can use a 1-bit code for *A* and 2-bit codes for *B* and *C*. That makes the total size 800 bits for the *A*'s, and 200 bits apiece for the *B*'s and the *C*'s — a total of 1,200 bits rather than 8,000. The packed file is a little larger than that (1,408 bits) because a table at the front of the packed file indicates which codes correspond to which letters.

The `compress` program uses a dictionary-compression scheme, which is kind of backward from Huffman coding. Rather than try to find the shortest code for every letter, `compress` runs through the file trying to find frequently occurring groups of letters it can encode as a single dictionary entry, or *token.* To compress the same file we packed in the preceding paragraph, `compress` reads letter-by-letter and notes that it has seen *AA* more than once; then it notices that it has seen *AAA* more than once, and so on. It enters longer and longer runs of *A*'s into its dictionary until it has runs of more than 300 *A*'s, each represented by a single dictionary entry and a single token in the compressed file. When `compress` runs into the *B*'s and then the *C*'s, it does the same thing and also enters long runs of *B*'s and *C*'s in the dictionary.

Using a clever technique (at least, it's clever to data-compression wonks), `compress` doesn't have to store the dictionary in the compressed file because `uncompress` can deduce from the sequence of tokens in the compressed file the contents of the dictionary that `compress` was building. As a result, `compress` does a fantastic job on this file and squashes it to a mere 640 bits from the original 8,000.

Compression techniques are still a hot topic in the computer biz, and many techniques have been patented. The particular technique `compress` uses is known as LZW, after Lempel, Ziv, and Welch, the three guys who thought of it. Welch, who works for Unisys and made some improvements to an earlier scheme designed by Lempel and Ziv, has a patent on it. It's such a cool technique, in fact, that two other guys named Miller and Wegman, who work for IBM, invented it at about the same time, and they also have a patent on it. Because the patent office is not supposed to grant two patents on the same invention, some people use this situation to suggest that issuing patents on software isn't a good idea. Fortunately, neither Unisys nor IBM has ever objected to the `compress` program, so you can go ahead and use it. `gzip` and `zip` use a technique that's somewhat similar to LZW but not covered by patents.

The unzip command has a bunch of options, the most useful of which is -l, which tells the program to list the contents of the ZIP file without extracting any of the files. To find out what all the options are, run unzip with no arguments. If you need to create a ZIP file, you can use the equally boringly named zip program:

```
zip video-list *.txt
```

This command says to create a file named video-list.zip (it adds the .zip part if you don't) containing all the files in the current directory whose names end in .txt.

What's in That File?

Sometimes you have a bunch of files and no recollection of what they contain. The file command can give you a hint. It looks at the files you name on the command line and makes its best guess about what's in the files. To have file try to figure out what's in the files in the working directory, type this line:

```
file *
```

UNIX responds with this bunch of seemingly incomprehensible information:

```
sleuthl.doc: data
sleuthl.ms: [nt]roff, tbl, or eqn input text
tsel: ascii text
tse2.Z: compressed file - with 16 bits
```

This mess says that file figured out that the sleuthl.ms file is a text file coded for input to the troff text formatter (those other programs are some of troff's helpers), that tsel contains text, and that tse2.Z is compressed. (The "16 bits" stuff tells basically which version of compress was used; it doesn't really matter because current versions of compress can read any compressed file.) The file program guesses "data" whenever it has no idea what's in a file. Because the first file, sleuthl.doc, was a Microsoft Word document, something file doesn't know about, it guesses that it's data.

Chapter 12

Installing Software Can Be Tricky

In This Chapter

- Where software comes from (the software stork?)
- Where to put software
- How to write shell scripts, or files full of commands
- How to write aliases for your favorite commands
- How to grab software from the Internet
- How to send programs by e-mail
- How to uncompress, uudecode, and otherwise fool with files that contain programs

If you are a Windows or Macintosh user, you probably are thinking: "I can install new programs. What's the big deal? I just stick in a disk or a CD and type INSTALL, right?" No. In UNIX, it's not that simple, of course. You face issues of paths, permissions, and other technical-type stuff we have been protecting you from.

On the other hand, we're not about to train you to be a system programmer. Every user has a few favorite programs, and you wear out your welcome quickly if you go off to your local wizard every time you want to use a new program. Although installing new UNIX programs is much trickier than installing PC or Mac programs, in many cases you *can* do it yourself.

The Software Stork

Interesting software comes from many places:

- Some other user on the same machine already has it for his or her own use and you want to use it too.

- Some other machine on the network has a program you want for yourself. See Chapter 16 for the gory details of copying the program from other machines on the network.

- Someone sends you programs through e-mail. (Yes, it's possible.)
- You create files that contain frequently used commands so that you don't have to type them repeatedly. In UNIX-speak, these files are called *shell scripts.* In essence, you make your own multipurpose UNIX commands.

First, we talk about where you should put your own software. Then we go into more detail about the mechanics of putting it there.

You've `bin` had

Every UNIX user should have a `bin` directory. It's just a directory named `bin` in your home directory. If it's not there, you can make it by going to your home directory and typing this line:

```
mkdir bin
```

The thing that's special about `bin` is that the shell looks for programs there. Most system administrators automatically set up a `bin` directory for users. If not, and you had to create it yourself, you may have to do some fiddling to tell the shell to look for programs there. See the sidebar "Your search path," later in this chapter, for the bad news.

To put programs in your `bin` directory, you just copy them there by using the `cp` command. Alternatively, you can move them there by using the `mv` command, a text editor, or any other way to create or move a file.

Why is it named `bin`?

Early on, `bin` was short for *bin*ary because most programs that people put there were, in fact, compiled binary code. In the late 1970s, a famous professor of cognitive science at the University of California published a paper titled "The Trouble with UNIX," in which he complained bitterly about how difficult it was to use UNIX. One of the items on his list was that `bin` was difficult to remember. One of the UNIX guys at Bell Labs published a witty rebuttal and pointed out that many of the allegedly "more natural" command names the professor suggested were merely the names the computer system at his university used. The UNIX guy reported that many Bell Labs users thought that a bin was the obvious place to stash their programs. So, it's still a bin.

The famous professor, who's now a researcher at Hewlett-Packard, has come around somewhat and is reputed to even use UNIX now and then, although he probably shuts his office door so that no one can see.

You Too Can Be a Script Writer

You can make your own commands (shell scripts) and put them in your `bin` directory. A *shell script* is a text file that contains a list of shell commands — the same commands you type at the shell prompt. You can store a list of commands as a shell script and run the commands any time by typing the name of the shell script. This section tells you how.

How to shell a script

To create a shell script, use any text editor (refer to Chapter 10). Enter the commands one per line, just as you would type them at the shell prompt. Save the file in your `bin` directory.

Here's an example — if you frequently search for files with names that begin with `budget`, you probably are tired of typing this command over and over:

```
find . -name budget* -print
```

(Check out Chapter 8 to see how the `find` command works.) Instead, you can put this command in a shell script and perhaps name the script `findbud`. To do it, create a text file named `findbud` that contains just one line: the command.

First you move to your `bin` directory because that's where your programs live:

```
cd bin
```

Then you use a text editor to create a text file containing the commands you want in your script. In this example, we use `ed`, a creepy editor, but you can use the editor of your choice instead. Type

```
ed findbud
```

UNIX responds with this line:

```
?findbud
```

or maybe

```
findbud: No such file or directory
```

Either way, you are editing the findbud file. Type this command:

```
a
```

This command tells ed to start appending text to the end of the findbud file. (Remember that because you're using ed, you have to type weird commands.)

Then type these two lines:

```
find . -name budget* -print
.
```

The dot on a line by itself tells ed to return to command mode. To save the file, type

```
w
```

UNIX responds with the information that you have saved a file with 29 (or so) characters:

```
29
```

Quit ed by typing this command:

```
q
```

You see the shell prompt again. Great! You've created a shell script!

Getting your script to play

Now you must tell UNIX that the text file you have created is executable — that it's more than a mere text file. Type this line:

```
chmod +x findbud
```

This line marks the findbud file as *executable* (it's a script the shell can run).

Running and rehashing your script

To run the shell script, just type its name:

```
findbud
```

Voilà! You have just created your own UNIX command! UNIX runs the `find` command to look for your budget files.

You're not quite finished, though. Observe what happens when you go to another directory. Type the following two commands to go to your home directory and give the `findbud` command there:

```
cd
findbud
```

UNIX may respond with this message:

```
findbud: Command not found.
```

If so, type this command to get UNIX to do what you want:

```
rehash
```

Now when you type `findbud`, it works.

What's going on? Well, it's Mr. too-smart-for-his-own-good Shell. Because programs don't appear and disappear very often, when the shell starts up, it makes a list of all the commands it can access and where they are. Because five or six command directories frequently exist, this process saves considerable time (the alternative is to check every directory for every command every time you type one). The `rehash` command tells UNIX to rebuild its list (known in geekspeak as a *hash table*) because you have added a new command (the `findbud` file is really a command, remember?). If the command still doesn't work, you have to fiddle with your search path — not a pretty job. See the following sidebar, "Your search path."

Type **rehash** to tell the shell that you have added a new command and that you want it to rebuild its list of available commands to include this one. If you don't give the `rehash` command and you change directories, you can't use the newly created shell script during this login session.

We could write an entire book about shell scripts (others have). In fact, we wrote several chapters about them in *MORE UNIX For Dummies* (published by IDG Books Worldwide, Inc.). The finer points naturally vary depending on which shell you use, although this explanation gives you the general idea. Shell scripts aren't limited to one line: They can be as long as you want, which is handy when you have a long list of commands you want to run regularly.

Your search path

You can ignore this section unless you have put a command in your `bin` directory and the shell can't find it. Still reading? Sorry to hear it. The shell has a list of directories that contain commands; this list is known as the *search path.* On any sensible UNIX system, the `bin` directory is already in your search path. If not, you have to put it there. You do it in two stages: putting it in once and putting it in permanently.

To see what your current search path is, type the following line if you're using the C shell:

```
echo $path
```

If you have BASH or the Bourne or Korn shell, type this line:

```
echo $PATH
```

Yes, one's uppercase and one's lowercase. Arrgh! The C shell responds with something like this:

```
/bin /usr/bin /usr/ucb/
    bin /usr/local/bin
```

BASH or the Bourne or Korn shell shows something like this:

```
/bin:/usr/bin:/usr/ucb/bin:/
    usr/local/bin:.
```

What you have to do is add your bin directory to the path.

If you use the C shell, type this magical incantation:

```
set path=($path ~/bin)
```

That's a tilde (~) in the middle. This line tells the C shell to set the path the same as the current path (`$path`), plus the `bin` subdirectory of your home directory (~).

If you use BASH or the Bourne or Korn shell, type this even more magical incantation:

```
PATH=$PATH:$HOME/
bin export PATH
```

Note that the second time you type `PATH` and `HOME` in the first command, you include a dollar sign ($) in front of them. This line tells the Bourne or Korn shell to set the path the same as the current path ($PATH), plus the bin subdirectory of your home directory ($HOME). Same song, different words.

Now you should be able to run your new script regardless of which directory you're using.

This new, improved path lasts only until you log out. To put your `bin` directory on the path every time you log in, you must add the incantation to the end of the shell script that runs automatically whenever you log in. If you use the C shell, add it to the `.login` file. If you use the Bourne or Korn shell, add it to the `.profile` file.

Yes, these filenames begin with periods. Filenames that start with periods usually don't show up in file listings, which is why you haven't noticed these files in your home directory. Type the following line to list all your files, including these hidden ones:

```
ls -a
```

In principle, you only have to edit the file, go to the end, and add the necessary lines. In practice, it's easy to screw up, so — unless you're feeling particularly brave — you're probably better off asking for expert assistance.

Don't give me any arguments!

Shell scripts can be complete programs. Every shell program has lots of swell programming features you don't want to know about. One is so useful, however, that we're going to tell you anyway: Your shell scripts can use information from the command line. That is, if you type `foogle dog pig`, your script named `foogle` can see that you ran it saying `dog` and `pig`. The things on the line after the name of the command are called *arguments.* The word *dog* is the first argument, and *pig* is the second one. In shell scripts, the first argument is named `$1`; the second, `$2`; and so on. In shorthand, `$*` means "all the arguments."

Suppose that you want to write a script named `2print` that prints files in two-column format. (You do that by using the `pr` command, described in Chapter 9.) Create a file named `2print` that contains this line:

```
pr -f -2 $* | lp
```

Then use the `chmod` and, if necessary, `rehash` commands to make `2print` an executable script. If you want to print several files, one right after the next, in two-column format, you can type this line:

```
2print onefile anotherfile
    yetanotherfile
```

In reality, you are saying

```
pr -f -2 onefile anotherfile
    yetanotherfile | lp
```

This line prints all three files in two-column format. (Note that you may need to use `lpr` rather than `lp` in this shell script. Refer to Chapter 9.)

Borrowing Other People's Programs

Lots of times, someone else has a cool program you want to be able to use. You have two approaches to getting what you want, and both are pretty easy. Suppose that your friend Tracy has a program named `pornotopia` in the `bin` directory. (No, we don't know what it does, either.) How can you run it?

The long way

If you use the C shell, you can run the program from Tracy's directory by typing this line:

```
~tracy/bin/pornotopia
```

If you use BASH or the Bourne or Korn shell, you can type this line:

```
/usr/tracy/bin/pornotopia
```

The easier way

Typing this long string of letters and symbols every time you want to run the program is a pain. A better way is to put in your `bin` directory a *link* to the cool program so that you can run it directly. (Links are described in Chapter 8.) You use the `ln` command to create a link, which makes the file appear to be in your own `bin` directory too.

Try the direct approach. Move to your home directory and create a link:

```
cd
ln ~tracy/bin/pornotopia bin/pornotopia
```

With any luck, this method works, creating a link from Tracy's file to your `bin` directory. Give or take a quick `rehash`, you're all set.

The `ln` command doesn't work, however, if you and Tracy have files on different disks. (All this stuff is explained in Chapters 8 and 16.) In this case, you may get this unhelpful message:

```
ln: different file system
```

If you get this message, it's time for Plan B. Most UNIX systems have *symbolic links* that work across different disks (these links also are explained in Chapter 8). Try this line:

```
ln -s ~tracy/bin/pornotopia bin/pornotopia
```

If it works, it makes a symbolic link to the file you want. You're all set: The link to `pornotopia` refers to Tracy's version. After a `rehash`, you're ready to go.

Using an alias

If you were named pornotopia, you probably would want an alias too. Fortunately, the BASH, Korn, and C shells give you the ability to invent a short name for a long command. (Bourne shell users, you're out of luck. Skip to the next section.)

Time for Plan C. In the BASH and Korn shells, type

```
alias dobudget='/usr/tracy/bin/pornotopia'
```

This line tells the shell that, when you type dobudget, you really want to run Tracy's program. Heh, heh. To avoid inadvertent ease of use, the C shell's alias command works in almost the same way, but it is punctuated slightly differently:

```
alias dobudget '/usr/tracy/bin/pornotopia'
```

(In both cases, the single quotes are optional if the command doesn't contain any spaces or special characters, although it never hurts to use them.)

You can define aliases for any frequently used one-line command. The alias can contain spaces, pipes, and anything else you can type on a command line. In BASH, for example, you can type

```
alias sortnprint='sort -r bigfile | pr -2 | lpr'
```

This line makes the new sortnprint command sort your bigfile in reverse alphabetical order, format it in two columns with pr, and send the result to the printer. Aliases can also be useful if you are subject (as we are) to chronic miswiring of the nerves in your fingers. We always type mroe when we mean more, and the following alias fixes it:

```
alias mroe=more
```

(That's the BASH version; the C shell would have a space rather than an equal sign between mroe and more.)

Aliases you type directly to the shell are lost when you log out. If you want them to be available permanently, you must put the alias commands in your .login or .profile file, in the same way we mentioned earlier in this chapter, in the "Your search path" sidebar.

Using a shell script

If this method doesn't work either, try Plan D to use Tracy's program: a one-line shell script. Although we use the ed program because it's easier to show, you should use a real editor. Start by revving up ed:

```
ed bin/pornotopia
```

You get the following helpful response, or something like it:

```
?bin/pornotopia
```

Now tell ed to add some text to the file, by typing this command:

```
a
```

You are now in append mode. Type the command line you want to include in the shell script, followed by a dot (period) on a line by itself:

```
/usr/tracy/bin/pornotopia
.
```

The dot on a line by itself switches back to ed's command mode. Then type this command:

```
w
```

This command writes the new shell script file and prints the size of the file. Then type the following to quit ed:

```
q
```

Type the next command to make your new shell script runnable:

```
chmod +x pornotopia
```

If necessary, give this command to tell UNIX to redo its hash table:

```
rehash
```

Now your script named pornotopia runs Tracy's original program named pornotopia. At least one of these three plans should work for any program lying around anywhere on your system.

We don't even discuss software copyrights, licenses, and ethics here, but, if you use a copyrighted program, you should pay for it unless you like to think of yourself as a thief.

Stealing Software from the Network

If you are on the Internet, you can get zillions of programs that are free for the taking. You can get copies of programs in the same way you get copies of anything else on the Internet — by either using FTP or downloading files from a Web browser, such as Netscape Communicator. See Chapter 18 for the inside scoop on downloading files from the Internet.

On many UNIX systems, this process is the most common way to get new software. Although most of it is shareware or freeware, even some commercial outfits are now selling their programs to be downloaded from the Internet.

Tar pits

When you download UNIX software from the Internet, nine times out of ten the filename ends in either `.tar`, `.tar.Z`, or `.tar.gz`. (We get to the most common exception in the next section.) Named, oddly enough, *tar files,* they don't have anything to do with black, goopy paving material; *tar* is short for *t*ape *ar*chive. You use this command for backing up (what used to be called "archiving," in the days when people went out of their way to make computers Look Important) UNIX systems to tape. (We discuss this use of `tar` in Chapter 23.)

In this section, though, you're seeing `tar` in its other role, where it moonlights as a software-packaging command. The people who distribute the software use `tar` to glom into one big `tar` file all the files that make up the software package (it can have anywhere from just a few to as many as hundreds of files). This way, you have to download only one big file rather than hundreds of little files. Because `tar` files are generally so big, the software distributors then squish them even more, using either the `compress` command (which results in a file ending in `.tar.Z`) or the `gzip` command (which results in a file ending in `.tar.gz`). Using `compress` used to be the standard, but because `gzip` results in smaller files, it's the compression program most people use these days.

If you're familiar with the Microsoft Windows world, you may have come across *zip files,* which end in `.zip`. These files are the Windows equivalent of `tar` files, except that zip combines the glomming and squishing phases into one command, an example of efficiency that true UNIX die-hards would never stand for.

Suppose that you've found a really cool editor that you've decided you can't live without, and you've download the `tar` file. It probably looks something horrendous, like `really_cool_ed_unix_v.3.4pl6.tar.gz`. To unpack your newly acquired `tar` file, first you have to unsquish it. If the file ends in `.tar.Z`, type this command:

```
uncompress really_cool_ed_unix_v.3.4pl5.tar.Z
```

Otherwise, type this command:

```
gunzip really_cool_ed_unix_v.3.4pl5.tar.gz
```

Either way, you end up with a file named `really_cool_ed_unix_v.3.4pl6.tar`. Notice that the `.Z` or `.gz` is gone? This file is much bigger now that it's unsquished.

Now you have to *untar* the file (that's really the way the UNIX gurus phrase it). This step blows up your tar file into potentially hundreds of little files and puts them into whatever your current directory is. Make sure that your working directory is the directory where you really want all those files to be rather than someplace where you'll have to move them later. (Moving one tar file where you want it is considerably easier than waiting until after you've blown it up into multitudes of files.) Okay, ready? Type this command:

```
tar xvf really_cool_ed_unix_v.3.4pl5.tar
```

The *x* in xvf stands for extract, the *v* means verbose so that you can see all the files being created, and *f* is for file and is followed by the name of the tar file.

Don't get too excited yet, because you still have more to do. Included in the bunch of files you've just created should be a file usually named README or INSTALL. This file has the rest of the installation instructions specific to the package you've just downloaded.

Revving up RPM

For years, the tar file method has been the only game in UNIX-land for distributing software over the Internet. For UNIX administrators who are accustomed to installing software packages, this method has worked just fine. Among everyone else, though, a growing number of disgruntled users have clamored for an easier way to install and maintain software. Their calls were answered by Red Hat Linux, which came up with the Red Hat Package Manager (RPM).

RPM is a software-management system that is a substitute for tar. Rather than download a file ending in .tar.gz, you download one that ends in .rpm. The RPM utility unpacks the file, puts all the resulting little files in their correct places, and updates a database of installed software on the computer. If you later want to install an upgrade, RPM remembers that an older version is already installed and saves any existing configuration files while upgrading the necessary files. This feature is enough to generate grumbling from traditionalists about user-friendliness infiltrating UNIX.

An important caveat about RPM is that you can install software this way only if you are the system administrator, which for most people happens only if they have a PC running Linux, as described in Chapter 14. So far, its use has been limited mainly to systems running Red Hat Linux, although the use of RPM is not necessarily restricted to Linux, and we've heard of people using it on other UNIX systems too.

Sneaking Software through the Mail

You can disguise programs as mail messages so that you can mail them around. This method is often the only way to do *samizdat* (underground, or guerilla) software distribution when networks and system administrators are uncooperative. Two methods are commonly used: shar messages and uuencoded messages. This section gives you the lowdown on both methods.

Sneaky shar

For short programs and shell scripts, the usual way to send stuff is as a *shar message*. A shar message is a shell script that, when you run it, re-creates the files in question. (If you care, shar rhymes with cigar and is lazy-typist-ese for *sh*ell *ar*chive.) Shar files are also a convenient way to mail groups of text files as a unit.

Shar messages usually start with lines like this:

```
#!/bin/sh
# This is a shell archive (produced by shar 3.49)
# To extract the files from this archive, save it to a file, remove
# everything above the "!/bin/sh" line above, and type "sh file_name".
#
# made 01/05/1997 19:41 UTC by johnl@iecc
# Source directory /usr/johnl/bin
```

Recovering the files is a three-step process:

1. **Save the message in a separate file, named something like `incoming-shar`. (See Chapter 17 for instructions.)**
2. **Use any text editor to delete all the lines from the beginning of the file to the first line that starts with a #.**

   If you delete a few of the # lines, don't worry: The shell ignores them anyway.
3. **Feed the edited file to the shell by typing this line:**

   ```
   sh incoming-shar
   ```

This command runs the script in the file and creates the program files or whatever else is in the shar file. (Near the front of most shar messages is a manifest that lists the files contained in the file.) When you see the UNIX prompt, the command is finished. Delete the `incoming-shar` file and move the files it created to the appropriate place, probably to your `bin` directory.

Getting sneaky with uuencode

Shar files don't work well for binary programs, so a widely adopted scheme named `uuencode` disguises them as text. If you receive a file coded in `uuencode`, the message looks something like this:

```
begin 775 pornotopia
M3'$$'!C?&RN:4@"O',"!P"P$+'O"S"P"#'9"#X"O""'$"-"""<
M#4"+G1E>'O"'#O""T"",PL"#O"""""'-I1""'"""("""YD
```

Recovering the binary file from the `uuencode` file is a two-step process:

1. **Save the message in a file with a name along the lines of `uu-incoming`.fs**

   Although UNIX doesn't care what the file is named, choose a name that makes it easy for you to remember that this file is the original uuencoded file.

2. **Feed the file to the `uudecode` program by typing this line:**

   ```
   uudecode uu-incoming
   ```

You don't have to edit the encoded file to delete the first lines in the file because `uudecode` ignores them for you. When you see the UNIX prompt, it is finished. Then get rid of the `uu-incoming` file and move to the appropriate place the binary file that is created.

Making your own sneaky e-mail

What if you want to send a program or other binary file by e-mail? You, too, can create uuencoded files, just like the big guys. Not surprisingly, you use the `uuencode` program. Just follow these steps to create uuencoded files:

1. **Type this command:**

   ```
   uuencode pornotopia strange-program > temp
   ```

   In this command, replace *`pornotopia`* with the file you want to uuencode, *`strange-program`* with the name you want the file to have when it is uudecoded, and *`temp`* with any temporary filename (*`junk`* is another perennial favorite). This command creates a uuencoded file named `temp` that, when it's uudecoded, creates a file named `strange-program` with the same contents as your `pornotopia` file.

2. **Include this uuencoded file at the end of an e-mail message.**

   The text of the message should say that the message contains a uuencoded file and what the file is for. (See Chapter 17 to find out how to send e-mail.)

Chapter 13
Juggling a Bunch of Programs

In This Chapter

- What processes are
- Where processes come from
- What a background program is
- How to shuffle background programs around
- Hints about windows and background programs

If you have a plain old terminal with no windowing system, you may be envious of users with fancy window systems who can pop up a bunch of windows and run umpteen programs at a time.

Don't. Any UNIX system enables you to run as many programs simultaneously as you want. Nearly all the systems let you stop and restart programs and switch around among different programs whenever you want.

If you're used to an old-fashioned, one-program-at-a-time system, such as DOS (without Windows) or the pre-System 7 Mac, you may not see the point of doing several things at a time. Suppose, however, that you're doing something that takes awhile and the computer can manage with little or no supervision from you, such as copying a large file over a network (which can take 10 or 15 minutes). You have no reason to sit and wait for that process to finish — you can do something useful while the copy runs in the background.

Or, suppose that you're in the middle of a program and you want to do something else: You're writing a memo in a text editor and need to check some e-mail you received to make sure that you spelled someone's name right. One way to do that is to save the file, leave the editor, run the mail program, leave the mail program, start the editor again, return to the same place in the file, and pick up where you left off. What a pain. UNIX enables you to stop the editor, run the mail program, and resume the editor exactly where you left it. For that matter, you can run *both* the editor and the mail program and flip between them as necessary.

Lots of X Windows

If you're running Motif or any other X Window graphical user interface (GUI), you've probably already figured out how to run many programs at a time: Open several `xterm` windows and run a program in each one. You create a new window by moving the mouse outside of any window, holding down the left mouse button to get a menu and selecting New Window or something similar. If you're running a version of CDE, running many programs at a time is even easier: Just double-click the icon for each program you want to run. That's it. You don't even have to deal with opening `xterm` windows. Read this chapter anyway, however.

In the interest of fairness, we must point out that *job control,* the feature that enables you to flip back and forth, was written by Bill, the same guy who wrote the C shell, `vi`, and NFS (Network File System, described in Chapter 16). In contrast to our opinion of some of his other efforts, we think that job control is pretty cool.

If you have a process that has run amok, see Chapter 24 to find out how to kill it.

So What Is a Process, Anyway?

All the work UNIX does for you is done by UNIX *processes.* When you log in, the shell is a process. When you run an editor, the editor is a process. Pretty much any command you run is a process.

Processes called *daemons* lurk in the background and wait to do useful things without manual intervention. When you use `lp` or `lpr` to print something, for example, a daemon does the real work of sending the material to the printer.

Normally, all this process stuff happens automatically, and you don't have to pay much attention to it. Sometimes a program gets stuck, however, and you can't make it go away. If you use a personal computer running DOS or a Macintosh, the usual response to a stuck program is to restart the computer. When you run UNIX, resetting the computer is a little extreme for a single stuck program. For one thing, other running programs and other people who are logged in do not appreciate having their computer kicked out from underneath them. Also, UNIX make take awhile to restart from a forced reboot (our system takes about 20 minutes to check all the disks), and you run the risk of losing files that were being updated.

Why processes are not programs and vice versa

Although programs and processes are similar, they're not the same. A *process* is, more or less, a running program. Suppose that you're using X Windows, have two windows onscreen, and are running vi in both of them. Although the same program is running in both windows, they're different processes doing different things (in this case, editing different files).

To add to the confusion, some programs use more than one process apiece. The terminal program cu, for example, uses two processes: one to copy what you type to the remote computer and the other to copy stuff from the remote computer back to your screen. Sometimes, "hidden" processes take place: Many programs have a way you can execute any UNIX command from inside the program. (In vi and ed, for example, you type **!** and the command you want to run.) In addition to the command, a shell process usually interprets the command.

In most cases, it is easy enough to tell in a list of processes which one is which because each one is identified by the command that started it.

Any Processes in the House?

The basic program you use to find out which processes are around is ps (for *p*rocess *s*tatus). Although the details of ps (wait! — how did you know?) vary somewhat from one version of UNIX to another, two main kinds of ps exist: the System V kind and the BSD kind. (SVR4 uses the System V kind of ps, even though SVR4 has a great deal of BSD mixed in. Linux uses a ps that looks more or less like BSD.)

Mind your ps (and qs)

If you run plain ps, no matter which version of UNIX you have, you get a list of the processes running from your terminal (or window, if you're using X Windows). The list looks something like this:

```
PID   TTY     TIME COMMAND
24812 ttyp0   0:01 -csh
25973 ttyp0   0:00 ps
```

The PID column gives the *process identification,* or *process ID.* To help keep processes straight, UNIX assigns every process a unique number as an identifier. The numbers start at 1 and go up. When the PIDs become inconveniently large (about 30,000 or so), UNIX starts over again at 1 and skips numbers that are still in use. To get rid of a stuck process, you have to know its PID to tell the system which process to destroy.

The TTY column lists the terminal from which the process was started. In this case, ttyp0 is the terminal, which happens to be pseudoterminal number 0. (Because UNIX systems were written by and for nerds, they tend to start counting at 0 rather than at 1.) UNIX uses a *pseudoterminal* when you're logged in from a window on your screen or from a remote system through a network rather than through a real, actual, drop-it-on-your-foot-and-it-hurts terminal. For our purposes, all terminals act the same, whether they're real, pseudo, or whatever.

The TIME column is the amount of time the computer has spent running this program. (The time spent waiting for you to type something or waiting for disks and printers and so forth doesn't count.)

The COMMAND column shows, more or less, the name of the command that started the process. If the process is the first one for a particular terminal or pseudoterminal, the command name starts with a hyphen.

The Linux ps

The Linux ps command has one additional column:

```
PID  TTY STAT  TIME COMMAND
1797 pp5 S     0:00 -bash
1855 pp5 R     0:00 ps
```

The STAT column shows the status of the process. According to the man page (online documentation) for the command, *R* means runnable, *S* means sleeping, *D* means uninterruptible sleep, *T* means stopped or traced, and *Z* means a zombie process. Wow! For our purposes, *R* means that it's a command you ran, and other stuff doesn't matter much.

Fancier ps (and qs)

The System V version of ps has lots of options, most of which are useless. One of the more useful is -f, which produces a "full" listing:

```
UID   PID   PPID  C    STIME TTY      TIME COMMAND
johnl 11764  3812  0 14:06:02 ttyp3    0:00 /usr/bin/emacs
johnl 11766 11764  0 14:06:05 ttyp3    0:00 /bin/sh -i
johnl 11769 11766 10 14:06:15 ttyp3    0:00 ps -f
johnl  3812  3804  0  Jan 18  ttyp3    0:04 -sh
```

(We did it from a different window, which you can tell because the PID of the shell is different.)

This listing has a few more columns than does the basic ps listing, and a few columns are different. The UID column is the username — just what it looks like. `PPID` is the *parent PID,* the PID of the process that started this one. We had run `emacs` from the shell and then had told `emacs` to start another shell to run a `ps` command.

The parent PIDs reflect the order in which the processes started each other: The login shell process (number 3812) is the parent of `emacs`, which in turn is the parent of the shell `/bin/sh`, which is the parent of `ps`. (We could explain why the processes aren't listed in order, but — trust us — you don't want to know.) All processes in a UNIX system are arranged in a genealogical hierarchy based on which process started which. The grand ancestor of them all is process number 1, which is named `init`. You can trace the ancestry of any process back to `init`. "Hark! I am yclept Ps, son of Bourne Shell, daughter of Emacs, son of Dash-shell (or is that Dashiell?), great-great-grandson of the ancient and holy Init!"

The C column is a totally technoid number relating to how much the process has been running lately. Ignore it. `STIME` is the *start time,* the time of day the process began. If it began more than 24 hours ago, this column shows the date. `TTY` is the name of the terminal the process is using. If you run a GUI, such as X Windows, and you run the `xterm` program in a window (as we did in this example), the entry for `TTY` doesn't show the terminal you are using. Instead, it lists the "pseudoterminal" assigned to the window (a useless piece of information). Sometimes the TTY column shows a `?`, which means that the process is a daemon that doesn't use a terminal.

The `COMMAND` column shows the full command that began this process, including (in some cases) the full pathname of the program. (Because standard system programs live in the directories `/bin` and `/usr/bin`, you see them frequently in `ps` listings.)

If you're logged in on several terminals or in several windows, you may want to see all your processes, not just the ones for the current terminal. With the System V version of `ps`, you can ask to see all processes for a given user by using this command:

```
ps -u tracy
```

This command lists all processes belonging to user `tracy`. You can ask to see any user's processes, not just your own. You can get a full listing for that user too:

```
ps -fu tracy
```

System V has other, less useful switches for `ps`, notably `-e`, which shows every process in the entire system.

Berkeley ps (and qs)

The basic report from the BSD version of ps looks like this example:

```
  PID TT STAT  TIME COMMAND
 7335 p4 S     0:00  -csh (csh)
 7374 p4 R     0:00 ps
```

The PID, TIME, and COMMAND columns are the same as those you already know about. (In the COMMAND column, the true name of the program is listed in parentheses if a dash or something is in the regular name.) The TT column lists a short form of the terminal name (pseudoterminal 4, in this case). STAT lists the status of the process: R means that the process is running right now; anything else means that it isn't. Usually, you don't care unless you have a stuck process and you wonder whether it's sitting there waiting for you to type something (then its status is I or IW) or running off into the woods (then its status is R).

Adding the -u switch gives a user-oriented report, although perhaps they had a different kind of user than you and we in mind, as you may gather from this example:

```
USER        PID %CPU %MEM   SZ  RSS TT STAT START   TIME COMMAND
johnl      7375 0.0   0.9  196  436 p4 R    14:59  0:00 ps -u
johnl      7335 0.0   0.6  196  316 p4 S    14:56  0:00 -tcsh (tcsh)
```

The %CPU and %MEM columns list the percentage of the available central processor time and system memory the process has taken recently (these numbers are usually close to 0). RSS is Resident Set Size, a measure of how much memory the process is using right now, measured in thousands of bytes (abbreviated as K). The ps command, for example, takes 436K bytes (which is horrifying when you consider that the *entire* UNIX system used to fit into 64K total bytes). The START column lists the time of day the process began.

You can ask for a particular terminal's process list by using the -t option, as shown in this example:

```
ps -tp4
```

With the -t option, you have to use the same two-letter terminal abbreviation ps uses. Have fun guessing it. Try the two-letter abbreviations that appear in the TT column of the ps listing.

The BSD version of ps has lots of other useless options, including -l for a *l*ong technoid listing; -a for *a*ll processes, not just yours; and -x to show processes not using a terminal. You have no way to ask for all processes belonging to a particular user.

To see all the processes you started, type this incantation:

```
ps -aux | grep tracy
```

Replace Tracy's name with your own username. This line redirects the output of the ps command to the grep command (described in Chapter 8), which throws away all the lines except those that contain your username.

Starting Background Processes

Starting a background command is simplicity itself. You can run any program you want in the background: When you type the command, stick a space and an ampersand (&) at the end of the line just before you press Enter.

Suppose that you want to use troff to print a file (even though we warned you not to use it). Because this process is bound to take a long time, for example, typing the ampersand to run it in the background is wise:

```
troff a_really_large_file &
```

The shell starts the command and immediately comes back to ask you for another command. It prints a number, which is the *process ID* (or PID) assigned to the command you just started. (Some shells print a small number, which they call the *job number*, and a larger number, which is the PID.) If you know the PID, you can check up on your background program with the ps command. If you get tired of waiting for the background process, you can get rid of it with the kill command and the PID, as you see in Chapter 24.

You can start as many programs simultaneously as you want in this way. In practice, you rarely want more than three or four. Because only one computer is switching back and forth among the various programs, the more simultaneous things you do, the slower each one runs.

When your background program finishes, the C, Korn, BASH, and SVR4 Bourne shells tell you that it's finished; older versions of the Bourne shell say nothing.

The Magic of Job Control

Quite awhile ago (in about 1979), people (actually, our pal Bill) noticed that, many times, you run a program, realize that it will take longer than you thought, and decide that you want to switch it to a background program. At the time, the only choices you had were to wait or to kill the program and start it over by using an & to run it in the background. Job control enables you to change your mind after you start a program.

The job-control business requires some cooperation from your shell. In SVR4, all three shells handle job control. In some earlier versions of UNIX, only the C shell, or sometimes the C shell and Korn shell, handled job control.

Suppose that you start a big, slow program by typing this line:

```
bigslowprogram somefile anotherfile
```

The program runs in the foreground because you didn't use an ampersand (&). Then you realize that you have better things to do than wait, so you press Ctrl+Z. The shell should respond with the message `Stopped`. (If it doesn't, you don't have a job-control shell. Sorry. Skip the rest of this chapter.) At this point, your program is in limbo. You can do three things to it:

- Continue it in the foreground as though nothing had happened, by typing **fg** (which stands for *f*oreground).
- Stick it in the background by typing **bg** (for *b*ackground), which makes the program act as though you started it with an & in the first place.
- Kill it if you decide that you shouldn't have run it. This method is slightly more complicated. Details follow.

Take this job and . . .

UNIX calls every background program you start a *job*. A job can consist of several processes (which, as you know, are running programs). To print a list of all your files in all your directories with titles, for example, you can type this line:

```
ls -lR | pr -h "My files" | lp &
```

This command lists the files with `ls`, adds titles with `pr`, and sends the mess to the printer with `lp`, all in the background. Although you use three different programs and three separate processes, UNIX considers it one job because each of the three programs needs the other two in order to get work done.

Every regular command (those you issue without an &) is also a job, although, until you use Ctrl+Z to stop it, that's not an interesting piece of information. You can use the `jobs` command to see which jobs are active. Here's a typical response to the `jobs` command:

```
[1]          - Stopped  (signal)   elm
[2]         + Stopped      vi   somefile
```

This listing shows two jobs, both of which have been stopped with Ctrl+Z. One is a copy of `elm`, the mail-reading program; the other job is the `vi` editor. (The difference between `Stopped (signal)` and plain `Stopped` is interesting only to programmers, so we don't discuss it much.) One job is considered the *current job* — the one preceded by a plus sign (+); it's the one most recently started or stopped. All the rest are regular background jobs, and they can be stopped or running.

. . . stick it in the background

You can tell any stopped job to continue in the background by using the `bg` command. A plain `bg` continues the current job (the one marked by a plus sign) in the background. To tell UNIX to continue some other job, you must identify the job. You identify a job by typing a percent sign (%) followed by either the job number reported by `jobs` or enough of the command to uniquely identify it. In this case, the `elm` job can be called `%1`, `%elm`, or `%e` because no other job used a command starting with an *e*. As a special case, `%%` refers to the current job. Although some other `%` combinations are available, no one uses them. Typing **bg %e**, for example, continues the `elm` job in the background.

. . . run it in a window in the foreground

To put a process in the foreground, where it runs normally and can use the terminal, you use the `fg` command. Continuing a job in the foreground is so common that you can use a shortcut: You just type the percent sign and the job identifier. Typing **%1** or **%e**, for example, continues the `elm` job in the foreground. Typing **%v** or **%%**, however, continues the `vi` editor in the foreground.

. . . shove it

To get rid of a stopped or background job, use the `kill` command with the job identifier or (if it's easier, for some reason) the PID. You can get rid of the `vi` editor job by typing this line:

```
kill %v
```

Typically, you start a job, realize that it will take longer than you want to wait, press Ctrl+Z to stop it, and then type **bg** to continue that process in the background.

Alternatively, you interrupt a program by pressing Ctrl+Z, run a second program, and, when the second program is finished, type **fg** or %% to continue the original program.

You don't often bring in the gangster `kill` to turn out the lights on a program, although it's nice to know that you have friends in the underworld who can put a nasty program to sleep for good. Chapter 24 talks more about it.

What happens when two programs try to use the terminal?

Suppose that a program running in the background tries to read some input from your terminal. Severe confusion can result (and did, in pre-job-control versions of UNIX) if both the background program and a foreground program — or even worse, two or three background programs — try to read at the same time. Which one gets the stuff you type? Early versions of UNIX did the worst possible thing: A gremlin inside the computer flipped a coin to decide who got each line of input. That was, to put it mildly, not satisfactory.

With the advent of job control, UNIX enforced a new rule: Background jobs can't read from the terminal. If one tries, it stops, much as though you had pressed Ctrl+Z. Suppose that you try to run the `ed` editor in the background by using this command:

```
ed some.file &
```

UNIX responds:

```
[1]        + Stopped (tty input)   ed
```

As soon as `ed` started and wanted to see whether you were typing anything it should know about, the job stopped. You can continue `ed` as a foreground program by typing **fg** or %% if you want to type something for `ed`. You can kill it (which is all that `ed` deserves) by typing **kill** %%.

Chapter 14
Taming Linux

In This Chapter

- A few basics for the reluctant system administrator
- How a Linux system is structured
- Where to get help

Yeah, we know that it's pronounced "linn-ux" or "leen-ux," not "line-ux," but it still needs taming, and if you look around the office and find nobody other than yourself to fix things, you're the Linux tamer.

Congratulations! You're a System Administrator!

Using Linux is no different from using any other type of UNIX, as long as it's on someone else's computer and they have set you up with an account. When *your* computer is running Linux, however, and *you* are responsible for maintaining it, things become much more complicated. Although we have no way to teach all the complexities of UNIX system administration in a book like this one, we can describe a few key points to get you started.

LINUX For Dummies, 2nd Edition, by Craig Witherspoon, Coletta Witherspoon, and Jon Hall (published by IDG Books Worldwide, Inc.) is a great introduction to Linux and Linux administration. *Running Linux,* by Welsh and Kaufman (published by O'Reilly & Associates), has most of the information you need to *really* administer a Linux system. Also, the World Wide Web is awash in sites devoted to Linux. A good place to start is the Linux home page, at `http://www.linux.org/`. (See Chapter 18 for more information about the World Wide Web if you're uncertain what it means.) Chapter 27 of this book lists a number of other places to go Linux hunting on the World Wide Web.

The root of all UNIX

UNIX is a multiuser world: Lots of people can use the computer at the same time, by connecting from remote locations. The first thing you need to know about administering a Linux system is the difference between the user called *root* and every other user. Root (also grandly called the *superuser*) is the system administrator. This account has all the privileges to change things on the system. If you want to add users, install some software, or even turn off the computer, you must be logged in as `root`. If you're logged in as someone other than `root` and you try to do anything related to system administration, your computer responds with a barrage of "permission denied" messages. It's nothing personal. It's just the computer's way of telling you that in a multiuser environment, it doesn't want just *anyone* messing around with it — only the one person it trusts, which is `root`.

"Fine," you say. "I'll just log in as `root` all the time and not have to worry about running into those pesky permission problems." Bad idea! Using the root account to do non-system-administration tasks is dangerous because sometime — eventually, when you least expect it — you type a command you really didn't want to — oh, say, deleting all the files on the hard disk (it happens more frequently than you may think). If you're logged in as someone other than `root`, the computer replies with a simple "permission denied." If you're `root`, though, the damage is done, and UNIX does not have an "undelete" command! Remember that permissions are your friends!

Adding a user

Assuming that you're convinced about not logging in as `root` unless you really must, you have to add a user account for yourself (or for others) to use for everyday tasks. Suppose that you want to create the username "bobbyjoe" for yourself. To add this user, log in as `root` (because adding users is one of those special, privileged tasks that only `root` can perform) and type the command **adduser bobbyjoe**. The computer creates the new user and then, if you're lucky, reminds you to set the password for the new user. Whether or not the computer reminds you, you have to add the password by typing **passwd bobbyjoe**. Then enter the password when the computer asks for it. It asks you to enter it twice, just to make sure that you typed it correctly.

With some versions of Linux, your computer gives you remedial password advice if it thinks that you need it. If you create a user named `noah` and then try to add the password `ark`, your computer may say `BAD PASSWORD: It's WAY too short`. If you try to fake the computer out by adding the password `arkarkark`, it may say `BAD PASSWORD: it does not contain enough DIFFERENT characters`. If you're not sure what constitutes a good password, go back and read the section in Chapter 1 about password smarts. As a system administrator, you're responsible for the security of the system, so don't say that you haven't been warned.

How do I turn this thing off?

UNIX is very sensitive to impolite treatment on the part of the operator. If you just log out and turn off the machine with the power switch, UNIX reminds you of this rude treatment with a flood of error messages when you next restart the computer. To turn the machine off, you first must execute the `shutdown` command. While logged in as `root`, enter the command **shutdown now** to turn the machine off gracefully. If other users are logged in and you want to give them some warning, you can type the number of minutes until shutdown: `shutdown +10`, for example, waits ten minutes before shutting down and warns any users who are logged in. To reboot the computer, `shutdown -r now` (-r for *r*eboot) shuts down the machine and then restarts it. Some Linux systems also let the "three-finger salute" (Ctrl+Alt+Del, familiar to DOS and Windows users) serve as a shortcut for `shutdown -r now`.

Windows users of the world, unite!

Users who bring experience with other flavors of UNIX to their first encounters with Linux will probably find it relatively easy to get Linux up and running. The large (and growing) community of Windows users who want to add or switch to Linux will likely encounter some fairly rough sledding.

One of the great things about Linux is that it can run on PCs with Intel chips in them. Disgruntled Windows users can therefore switch to Linux without having to buy a new computer. Windows users who are still sufficiently gruntled can check out Linux by installing it, cheek by jowl, on the same computer with Windows (as long as it has enough free disk space, of course).

All well and good, in theory. In practice, however, you can get yourself into trouble with startling efficiency. Even if it's going to coexist on your computer with Windows, Linux needs its own separate file system, which in turn needs its own separate area of your computer's disk. These separate areas are called *partitions,* or *drives,* and you have to have at least two partitions, one for Windows and one for Linux, to get Windows and Linux to live together in peace and harmony.

If you have only one big drive or partition on your computer, you have to create a second partition before you can even begin installing Linux. To do so, you have to run a DOS utility named `fdisk` on your computer. The trouble with `fdisk` is that if you make one false move, everything that's already on your computer gets wiped out, no questions asked. If you already have Windows installed on your computer, do yourself a favor and back up your system before even *thinking* about using `fdisk`. Then carefully follow whatever instructions you have for setting up a computer that can run both Windows and Linux (known as a *dual-boot* system). *LINUX For Dummies,* 2nd Edition (mentioned earlier in this chapter), for example, describes the whole process in gory detail.

A Pride of Linuxes

Complete Linux systems are packaged into "distributions," which describe not how Linux is distributed but rather how the operating system and the GNU programs are bundled. A few distributions are in common use: Slackware, Red Hat, Caldera, and Debian. All are available for free via the Internet or for a small charge on CD-ROM. As a user, it doesn't matter which distribution you use because they all behave in much the same way. As a system administrator, though, you should consider the important differences the distributions have among them.

Slackware, the oldest of the three, has been around since the beginning of Linux. It is the most "traditional" distribution (traditional in the UNIX sense, as in not particularly user-friendly) and has little in the way of utilities to facilitate the management of a Linux system. For this reason, it tends to be favored by those who have been around UNIX systems for a while.

Red Hat Linux is the most popular distribution. It features plenty of tools to make the life of a system administrator easier, most notably the Red Hat Package Manager (RPM), which eases the installation, upgrade, and deletion of software packages, and even the operating system itself. Recently, Red Hat began adding all sorts of extras to its CD distribution. For about $50, you can get the Netscape Communicator Web browser, the latest version of the WordPerfect word processing package, and a whole stack of graphical applications known as ApplixWare.

The *Debian* and *Caldera OpenLinux* distributions, like Red Hat, also provide interfaces that ease the task of a system administrator. Although these distributions are not now as popular as Slackware or Red Hat, their popularity is growing quickly. OpenLinux, probably because of its aggressive marketing campaign, is beginning to give Red Hat a run for its money.

Linux goes commercial

The freely available, "alternative" image of Linux discouraged commercial enterprises from adopting Linux in its early days. Understandably, many companies did not want to deal with an operating system that did not have a corporate entity standing behind it, no matter how reliable or trouble-free the product. To fill this need, a number of companies have stepped in to provide commercial support for Linux. Red Hat Software, Inc., for example, provides a commercial version of its Linux distribution in addition to the free version. Organizations that purchase the commercial Red Hat distribution can therefore turn to Red Hat for support rather than (or in addition to) Usenet. Caldera, Inc., also provides support for commercial users. Purchasers of the Caldera OpenLinux package get user support from Caldera as well as for some additional commercial software packages that Caldera includes.

If you enjoy editing lots of configuration files and moving them around "by hand," the old-fashioned way (believe it or not, some people like to do it that way), you should go with Slackware. Everyone else will find life easier with Red Hat, Debian, or Caldera.

Many other Linux distributions are out there, of course, so you may want to do a little more investigating before deciding on a package:

- **DLX Linux and hal91 Floppy Linux:** For PC users without much free space, these packages offer distributions that fit on a single floppy disk.
- **Linux Pro:** On the other end of the spectrum, it comes complete with seven CDs and a 1,600-page encyclopedia of reference information.
- **LinuxPPC:** It's specifically designed to run on PowerPCs.
- **LinuxWare:** LinuxWare targets the Windows audience by enabling users to start the installation from within Windows 95.
- **S.u.S.E. Linux:** Comes with all kinds of preconfigured software packages, X servers, and graphical utilities for novice users.

"I Need Help!"

What happens when you have a problem with Linux? (It has been known to happen.) If you've shelled out for a commercially distributed CD version, you get possibly a few months of free support if the company has the wherewithal to offer it. Otherwise, no technical-support hotline exists to call when things go wrong.

A huge base of Linux users around the world does exist, though, most of whom have access to the Internet. Usenet is the best place to find help with Linux, as described in Chapter 19. For someone accustomed to calling a commercial entity on the phone for tech support, the idea of posting questions on Usenet may seem foreign, even hopelessly naive. Questions are generally read by so many thousands of people, though, that the odds are overwhelming that someone familiar with your problem will read the question and respond, usually within a day or so. (In fact, many people claim that Usenet-based support is faster and more reliable than some technical-support hotlines!) The Linux community as a group still maintains an attitude of "we're all in this together," and the Usenet support system has mostly worked. The Linux groups, which tend to be some of the most active computer groups on all of Usenet, are listed at the end of Chapter 27.

Part IV
UNIX and the Net

The 5th Wave
By Rich Tennant
©RICHTENNANT
Now take your time and see if you can identify the person who attacked you on e-mail.
8'
7'
6'
5'
4'
2'
1'

In this part . . .

Most computers that run UNIX are connected to other computers. Many are parts of office-wide networks, many have telephone connections to UNIX systems in other places, some are connected to computers running operating systems other than UNIX, and an increasing number are connected to the biggest network of all: the Internet.

This part of the book reveals how to use your UNIX system to send and receive e-mail, browse the World Wide Web, read articles in Usenet newsgroups, transfer files, and log in to other computers over the Internet. We even tell you a few things about how to set up your own Internet site so that you can make files and Web pages on your own computer available to your cohorts in cyberspace.

Chapter 15

Your Computer Is Not Alone

In This Chapter

- Discovering who else is using your computer by using the `finger` command
- Fingering people who use other computers on the Internet
- Communicating with other user computers by using the `write` and talk commands
- Talking to everyone at the same time

From the beginning, UNIX was designed as a multiuser system. In the early years of UNIX computing, it was considered greedy to keep to yourself an entire PDP-11/45 (a 1972 vintage minicomputer about the speed of a PC AT but the size of a trash compactor). It was also kind of expensive. These days, the cost argument is much less compelling — unless your computer is a Cray supercomputer or the like — although UNIX remains multiuser partly because it always was and partly because multiuser systems make it easier to share programs and data.

Even if you have your own workstation but are attached to a network, your machine is potentially multiuser because other people can log in to your machine over the net, as we technoids call a network. (On the other hand, you can log in to their machines too. See Chapter 16 for details.)

Don't confuse *net* — any network of computers — with *the* Net, which is what we technoids call the Internet. In this day and age, all anyone ever talks about is the Internet. If your computer is attached to the Internet, you can talk to literally millions of computers.

In this chapter, you see how you can nose around and find out who's on your system and on other systems to which you're connected. For the most part, we talk about the net — the computer network to which your machine is attached. If we mean *the* Net (also known as the Internet), we say so. After you find out who's out there, you can look into getting in touch with them.

If you are the only person who ever uses your computer and you don't have a network or a phone line (your computer is all alone in the world), skip this chapter — in fact, skip this entire part of the book.

Finding Out Who's on Your Computer

You can use two main commands to find out who's using your machine: `who` and `finger`. The simple way to use either one is just to type **who**.

The typical response is something like this:

```
root       console     Dec 29 20:16
johnl      vt01        Dec 21 15:19
johnl      ttyp2       Jan 6 16:36
johnl      ttyp1       Jan 6 17:20
johnl      ttyp0       Jan 6 16:36
```

You see the user, terminal, and login time. User `johnl` is logged in four times because he has a bunch of X terminal windows, each of which counts as a login session. Although the exact output from `who` varies from one version of UNIX to another, it always contains at least this much. You can also type `who am i`, and UNIX prints just the line for the terminal (or terminal window) in which you typed the command. (A similar UNIX command, `whoami`, prints only the name of the user logged in at the prompt where you typed the command.)

A considerably more informative program is `finger` because it produces a more useful report than `who` does:

```
Login      Name           TTY Idle   When       Office
root     0000-Admin(0000)  co 1:11   Tue 20:16
johnl    John R. Levine    vt 1:11   Mon 15:19 x3712
johnl    John R. Levine    vt 1:35   Tue 16:47 x3712
johnl    John R. Levine    p2 1:11   Wed 16:36 x3712
johnl    John R. Levine    p1        Wed 17:20 x3712
johnl    John R. Levine    p0        Wed 16:36 x3712
```

Although `finger` reports the same stuff as `who` does, it also looks up the user's real name (if it's in the user password file) and tells you how long the terminal has been idle (how long it has been since the user last typed something). If the system administrator has entered the information, `finger` also usually shows an office phone number, room number, or other handy info about where the user works.

You can also use `finger` to ask about a specific user, and UNIX looks up some extra info about that user. In this example, we used it to look up one of the authors of this book:

```
finger johnl
```

UNIX returned this information:

```
Login name: johnl              In real life: John R. Levine
Directory: /usr/johnl          Shell: /bin/sh
On since Dec 21 15:19:45 on vt01 1 hour 27 minutes Idle Time
```

```
Project: Working on "UNIX for Dummies, 4th Ed."
Plan:
Write many books, become famous.
```

The Project and Plan lines are merely the contents of files called `.project` and `.plan` in the login directory. (Yes, the filenames start with periods.) It has become customary to put a clever remark in your `.plan` file, but please don't overdo it. If the user is logged in on more than one terminal or terminal window, `finger` gives a full report for each terminal. The `finger johnl` command we gave reported five times, in fact — one for each login — but we edited it to save paper.

Finding Out Who's on Other Computers

If your machine is on a network, you can use `rwho` and `finger` to find out about other machines. You type the system name you want to check up on after an @ (at sign.) (Chapter 16 has more information about system names.) We can check a nearby system, as shown in this example:

```
finger @gurus.com
```

The `spdcc.com` machine turns out to be not very busy:

```
[gurus.com]
Login    Name           TTY  Idle   When      Office
uucp  Uucp Daemon       02        Wed 20:13
johnl John R. Levine    03        Wed 20:44  Rm 418
dyer  Steve Dyer        p0     1  Wed 08:13
```

You can also ask about an individual by putting that user's name in front of the @:

```
finger johnl@gurus.com
```

This command gives the same sort of report as a local `finger` does:

```
[gurus.com]
Login name: johnl              In real life: John R. Levine
Directory: /var/users/johnl  Shell: /bin/csh
On since Jan 6 9:22:45 on tty02    2 minutes Idle Time
Plan:
no plan
```

If you're on the Internet, you can — in principle — finger any machine on the Internet. Because no rule says that machines must answer when you call, however, in many cases you get a "connection refused" response or even no response.

The UNIX/Windows accords

Sometimes UNIX computers are on networks with computers running other operating systems, such as Windows 98, Windows 95, or Windows NT. So how do you get your UNIX and Windows computers to communicate with each other?

When computers want to speak to one another, they can't just chuck data at one another indiscriminately. They have to use what's known in computerese as protocols. *Protocols* are sets of rules by which computers exchange data and commands. If two computers know the same protocols, they can talk turkey, even if one of those computers is running UNIX and the other is running Windows.

Computers use all kinds of protocols to communicate. On a network, clients connect to servers by using protocols such as TCP/IP (Transmission Control Protocol/Internet Protocol) and IPX (Internetwork Packet eXchange). Computers connected by way of the Internet exchange files by using protocols such as FTP (File Transfer Protocol) and HTTP (HyperText Transfer Protocol).

The particular protocol of interest here is the Server Message Block, or SMB, protocol. SMB has been around in one incarnation or another since 1987, when Microsoft and Intel (the chip maker) first defined it. Because it helped to invent SMB, Microsoft includes an SMB client in all its versions of Windows. Any server that can talk SMB, therefore, can do business with a Windows computer, so the Windows computers can use disks and printers on the server just like on a Windows NT server, for example.

Enter Andrew Tridgell, a UNIX hacker from Canberra, Australia, with a firm grasp of the obvious. He wrote a suite of programs collectively named Samba, which turns almost any version of UNIX you care to mention into an SMB server. Samba lets UNIX and Windows computers do snazzy, friendly stuff, such as access one another's files and share printers. In typical UNIX style, dozens of programmers from around the world have contributed to Samba over the years, and it's distributed for free under the infamous GNU public software guidelines.

SMB is a *request-response* protocol, in which a client makes requests of the server, and the server responds. Because nothing is ever as easy at is seems where computers are concerned, a client has to make several requests of a server before anything useful happens. First, the client has to ask the server which *dialect* of SMB it wants to speak (yup, dialect, just like in real life). Then the client has to get down on bended knee and politely request access to the server by giving the server a username and password. If the server grants the client an audience, the client can start petitioning the server with a series of requests — for example, to locate, open, and print a particular file.

The latest version of Samba is 1.9.1.7 or higher. You can download it from the main Samba site, maintained by the Department of Computer Science at Australian National University, on the Web at `http://samba.anu.edu.au/samba`, or via various FTP sites such as `ftp://ftp.micro.caltech.edu/pub/samba`. (If you don't know what these curious strings of seeming gobbledygook mean, read the "URL!" sidebar in Chapter 18.) Although Samba is free, Andrew Tridgell does appreciate it if you give him pizza. The Samba FAQs (Frequently Asked Questions) at `http://www.samba.bst.tj/samba/docs/faq/sambafaq.html` give you detailed instructions on how to do so even when "the pizza donor is twenty thousand kilometres away." No, we're not making this up.

Some systems, particularly main network machines at universities, have set up `finger` to return user-directory information. Suppose that you ask who's at MIT:

```
finger @mit.edu
```

You get an introduction to the MIT online directory:

```
[mit.edu]
Student data loaded as of Dec 15, Staff data loaded as of Dec 19. Notify the
               Registrar or Personnel as appropriate to change your information.
Our on-line help system describes
How to change data, how the directory works, where to get more info.
For a listing of help topics, enter finger help@mit.edu. Try finger
help_about@mit.edu to read about how the directory works. Please see
             help_url@mit.edu for questions about the new URL field.
```

You can try to finger a particular individual at MIT too:

```
finger chomsky@mit.edu
```

Now you can see the public data about that individual:

```
[mit.edu]
... There was 1 match to your request.  name: Chomsky, Noam A
email: CHOMSKY@MIT.EDU
phone: (617) 555-7819
address: ZZZ-219
department: Linguistics & Philos
title: Linguistics, Institute Professor
alias: N-chomsky
```

You can engage in wholesale nosiness by using `rwho`. This command attempts to compile a list of all the people using all the machines on the local network.

Chatting with Other People on Your Computer

After you have figured out who is on your computer, you may want to send them a message. Message sending has two general schools. The first is the real-time school, in which the message appears on the other user's screen while you wait, presumably because it's an extremely urgent message. The `write` and `talk` commands enable you to do that. Excessive use of real-time messages is a good way to make enemies quickly, however, because you interrupt people's work all over the place. Be sparing in your blather.

The second school is electronic mail, or e-mail, in which you send a message the other user looks at when it's convenient. E-mail is a large topic in its own right, so we save that for Chapter 17.

Real-time terminal communication has been likened to talking to someone on the moon because it's so slow: It's limited by the speed at which people type. Here on Earth, because most of us have telephones, the most sensible thing to do is to send a one-line message asking the other user to call you on the phone.

The simpler real-time communications command is `write`. If someone writes to you, you see something like this on your screen:

```
Message from johnl on iecc (ttyp1) [ Wed Jan 6 20:28:42 ] ...
Time for pizza. Please call me at extension 8649
<EOT>
```

Usually the message appears in the middle of an editor session and scrambles the file on your screen. You will be relieved to know that the scrambling is limited to the screen — the editor has no idea that someone is writing to you. The file is okay.

In either `vi` or `emacs`, you can tell the editor to redraw what's supposed to be on-screen by pressing Ctrl+L (if you're in input mode in `vi`, press Esc first).

To write to a user, use the `write` command and give the name of the user to whom you want to talk:

```
write dguertin
```

After you press Enter, `write` tells you absolutely nothing, which means that it is waiting for your message. Type the message, which can be as many lines long as you want. When you are finished, press Ctrl+D (the general end-of-input character) or the interrupt character, usually Ctrl+C or Delete. Because the `write` command copies every line to the other user's screen as you press Enter, reading a long message sent by way of the `write` command is sort of like reading a poem on old Burma-Shave signs as you drive by each one.

You want to send an important message, for example, to your friend Dave, so you type these lines:

```
write dguertin
Yo, Dave, turn on your radio. WBUR is rebroadcasting
Terry Gross's interview with Nancy Reagan!
```

You press Enter at the end of each line. After the last line, you press Ctrl+D.

I'm talking — where are you?

Sometimes `write` tells you that the user is logged in on several logical terminals:

```
dguertin is logged on more than one place.
You are connected to "vt01".
Other locations are:
ttyp1
ttyp0
ttyp2
```

The `write` command is pretty dumb. If the person you are writing to is logged in on more than one terminal — or, more typically, is using many windows in X — `write` picks one of them at random and writes there. You can be virtually certain that the window or terminal `write` chooses is not the one the user is viewing at the time. To maximize the chances of the user's seeing your message, use the `finger` command to figure out which terminal is most active (the one with the lowest idle time) and write to that window. Remember the results of the `finger` command, for example, from a few pages back:

```
Login       Name           TTY Idle  When  Office
root     0000-Admin(0000)  co  1:11  Tue   20:16
dguertin David S. Guertin  vt  1:11  Mon   15:19
dguertin David S. Guertin  vt  1:35  Tue   16:47
dguertin David S. Guertin  p2  1:11  Wed   16:36
dguertin David S. Guertin  p1        Wed   17:20
dguertin David S. Guertin  p0        Wed   16:36
```

The best candidates to send a message to are `ttyp1` and `ttyp0`. (The `finger` command cuts the `tty` from terminal names.)

To write to a specific terminal, give `write` the terminal name after the username:

```
write dguertin ttyp1
```

If you are writing back to a user who just wrote to you, you should use the terminal name that was sent in his `write` message (in this case, it was also `ttyp1`).

Can we talk?

You can have a somewhat spiffier conversation with the `talk` command, which allows simultaneous two-way typing. You use it the same way you use `write`: by giving a username and, optionally, a terminal name:

```
talk margy
```

The other user sees something like this:

```
Message from Talk_Daemon@iecc at 20:47 ...
talk: connection requested by johnl@IECC
talk: respond with: talk johnl@IECC
```

If someone tries to talk to you and you're interested in responding, type the `talk` command it suggests. If you're in the middle of a text editor or other program, you must exit to the shell first.

Chatting with faraway folks

The `talk` command is designed to "talk" to users on other computers. If the other computer is a long way away, typing rather than talking over the telephone can make sense. As the Internet stretches around the world, you may find yourself exchanging messages with someone for whom English is not a native language. In that case, typing can be faster than trying to understand someone with a strong accent across a noisy phone connection.

Computers have names, too, which are usually called *machine names* (read more about this subject in Chapter 16). To talk to someone on another computer, give `talk` the username and machine name:

```
talk zac@greattapes.com
```

After you're connected, `talk` works just like talking to a local user, except that sometimes it can take several seconds for characters to get from one machine to another on an intercontinental link.

If you want to talk to a number of other people, maybe thousands and thousands of them, you can use a system called Internet Relay Chat (IRC). We don't have room to describe it in this book, but you can read about it at our Web site (if you don't know how to find it, see Chapter 18):

```
http://net.gurus.com/irc
```

Chapter 16

Across a Crowded Network

In This Chapter

- How to log in to other computers
- Computers to check out on the network
- How to tell whether your files are on a different computer

If your computer is on a network, sooner or later you have to use computers other than your own. Although you can do lots and lots of things over a network, the two most widespread activities are remote login and file transfer. If your computer is on a LAN (Local Area Network), you can probably use files directly that are located on other computers.

On a Computer Far, Far Away

Many UNIX systems are attached to the Big Mazooma of networks, the Internet, which hooks together several million computers around the world. Because most of the UNIX network software was originally written at Berkeley specifically for use on the Internet, all the commands discussed in this chapter work just fine on the Internet. The only difference you may notice is that although you can refer to computers on your own network with simple names, such as `pumpkin`, in order to talk to computers on the Internet, you have to give their true names, which can be long and tedious, such as `iecc.cambridge.ma.us` (a name our computer used to have.)

Remote login is no more than logging in to some other computer from your own. While you're logged in to the other computer, whatever you type is passed to the other computer; whatever responses the other computer makes are passed back to you. In the great UNIX tradition of never leaving well enough alone, two slightly different remote-login programs exist: `telnet` and `rlogin`. A variant of `rlogin` called `rsh` enables you to give commands one at a time on other computers.

A *file transfer* copies files from one system to another. You can copy files from other systems to your system and from your system to others. Two different file-transfer programs exist (how did you know that?): `ftp` and `rcp`. We talk about `ftp` in Chapter 18.

Telnet It Like It Is

Telnetting (in English, you can "verb" any word you want) involves no more than typing **telnet** and the name of the computer you want to log in to:

```
telnet pumpkin
```

UNIX tells you that it is making the connection and then gives the usual login prompt:

```
Trying...
Connected to pumpkin.bigcorp.com.
Escape character is '^]'.
 SunOS UNIX (pumpkin.bigcorp.com)
login:
```

At the login prompt, you type your username and then your password. After the other computer connects, you log in exactly as though you were sitting at the other computer. In the following example, we typed **john1** as our username and then gave our secret password:

```
login: johnl
```

```
Password:
Last login: Thu Jan 7 23:03:58 from squash
SunOS Release 4.1.2 (PUMPKIN) #3: Fri Oct 16 00:20:44 EDT
1992 Please confirm (or change) your terminal type.
TERM = (ansi)
```

If the other computer asks you what type of terminal you're using, give the answer appropriate to the terminal you're using. (If you're using an X terminal window, it's `xterm`. Try VT-100, ANSI, or TTY if you're using a dumb terminal or PC.)

The normal way to leave `telnet` is to log out from the other computer:

```
logout
```

What telnet is really useful for

We mostly use telnet to check our mail while we're out of town. If you have access to a computer at a friend's home or office or you wander by a cybercafé, you can telnet back to your home computer to check your mail and otherwise put your digital life in order. It's the next best thing to being there.

UNIX gives you the following message to tell you that the other computer has hung up the phone, so to speak:

```
Bye Bye
Connection closed by foreign host.
```

Sometimes the other computer is recalcitrant and doesn't want to let you go. Remember that you're in control. To force your way out, you first must get the attention of the `telnet` program by pressing Ctrl+] (that's a right square bracket). A few versions of `telnet` use a different escape character to get `telnet`'s attention. (It tells you which character when you first connect to the other system.) After you get `telnet`'s attention, type **quit** to tell `telnet` to wrap things up and return to the shell:

```
Ctrl-]
telnet> quit
```

Terminal type tedium

If you use a full-screen program, such as the UNIX text editors `emacs` and `vi` or the mail programs `elm` and Pine, you have to set your *terminal type.* This problem shouldn't exist in the first place, but it does, so you have to deal with it.

The problem is that about a dozen different conventions exist for screen controls such as *clear screen* and *move to position (x,y).* The program you're using on the remote host has to use the same convention your terminal does (if you're using a terminal) or that your local terminal program does (if you're on a PC or a workstation).

If the conventions are not the same, you get *garbage* (funky-looking characters) on-screen when you try to use a full-screen program. In most cases, the remote system asks you which terminal type to use. The trick is knowing the right answer. Here are a few hints to help you find out:

- If you're using the X Window system, with or without Motif, the answer is more likely to be *VT-100,* a popular terminal from the 1970s that became a de facto standard. You may also try *xterm,* the name of the standard X program that does terminal emulation.
- If you're using a PC and an emulation program, the best answer is usually ANSI because most PC terminal programs use ANSI terminal conventions. (*ANSI* stands for the American National Standards Institute. One of its several thousand standards defines a set of terminal-control conventions that MS-DOS PCs — which otherwise wouldn't know an ANSI standard if they tripped over one — invariably use.)
- In places where a great deal of IBM equipment is used, the terminal type may be *3101,* an early IBM terminal that was also popular.

The ANSI and VT-100 conventions are not much different from each other, so if you use one and your screen is only somewhat screwed up, try the other.

3270: The Attack of the IBM Terminals

All the terminals discussed earlier in this chapter that are handled by `telnet` are basically souped-up Teletypes, with data passed character by character between the terminal and the host. This kind of terminal interaction can be called *Teletype-ish.*

IBM developed an entirely different model for its 3270-series display terminals. The principle is that the computer's in charge. The model works more like filling in paper forms. The computer draws what it wants on-screen, marks which parts of the screen users can type on, and then unlocks the keyboard so that users can fill in whichever blanks they want. Whenever a user presses Enter, the terminal locks the keyboard, transmits the changed parts of the screen to the computer, and awaits additional instructions from headquarters.

To be fair, this method is a perfectly reasonable way to build terminals intended for dedicated data-entry and data-retrieval applications. The terminal on the desks at your bank or the electric company are probably 3270s — or more likely these days, cheap PCs *emulating* 3270s. Because the 3270 terminal protocol squeezes a great deal more on a phone line than Teletype-ish, it's quite common to have all the 3270s in an office sharing the same single phone line, with reasonable performance.

The Internet is a big place, and plenty of IBM mainframes run applications on the Internet. Some of them are quite useful. Most large library catalogs, for example, speak 3270-ish. Usually, if you telnet to a system that wants a 3270, it converts from the Teletype-ish that `telnet` speaks to 3270-ish so that you can use it anyway. Some 3270 systems speak only 3270-ish, however, and if you telnet to them, they connect and disconnect without saying anything in between.

A variant of `telnet` that speaks 3270-ish is called *tn3270.* If a system keeps disconnecting, try typing the command `tn3270` instead. (Large amounts of UPPERCASE LETTERS and references to the IBM operating systems VM or MVS are also tipoffs that you're talking to a 3270.) Even if a 3270 system allows regular `telnet`, you get a snappier response if you use `tn3270` instead.

`rlogin`: The Lazy Man's Remote Login

The `telnet` command is general. You can use it to log in to all sorts of machines — whether or not they're running UNIX. If you want to log in to another UNIX system, the `rlogin` command is usually more convenient because it automates more of the process. You use `rlogin` in much the same way you use `telnet`:

```
rlogin pumpkin
```

UNIX responds:

```
Last login: Fri Jan 8 14:30:28 from squash
SunOS Release 4.1.2 (PUMPKIN) #3: Fri Oct 16 00:20:44 EDT
Please confirm (or change) your terminal type.
TERM = (ansi)
```

Hey! It didn't ask for the username or password. What happened? You frequently have a setup in which a bunch of machines use the same set of usernames. A database called NIS helps keep all the names consistent across all the machines.) In that case, after you log in to one machine, all the others can safely assume that, if you log in to one of them, you will use the same username to log in to others.

The `rlogin` command also passes along the type of terminal you're using so that even if the other system asks you to enter your terminal type, it always guesses correctly if you don't tell it explicitly.

If the remote system doesn't recognize your username, it asks you to type a username and password, just like `telnet` does.

Escaping from `rlogin`

One place where `rlogin` is quite different from `telnet` is in how you escape from a recalcitrant remote system: You type **~.** (a tilde followed by a period) on a line by itself. What you have to press is Enter (or Return), tilde, period, Enter.

Username matching for `rlogin`

This section is pretty nerdy. If you work in an office with a bunch of workstations, you can assume that they all generally share usernames and skip this section.

Two files control `rlogin`'s assumption that you want to use the same username when you're logging in to other machines. The first is called `/etc/hosts.equiv`. On every machine, this file lists all the other machines it can "trust" to have matching usernames. If you look at the file and find lines with + and @ signs, they mean that NIS is providing its own list of trustworthy machines (generally, all the machines in the department or in the entire company).

Individual users may have accounts on machines outside the local group or department. If you are in this situation, you can have your own file called .rhosts, which is sort of a private trusted-machine list. .rhosts has a list of machine names, one per line. If you use rlogin from any of those machines, rlogin forgoes asking for your name and password. If you have different usernames on different machines, edit the file and put the appropriate username after the machine name, as shown in this example:

```
pumpkin
squash
gerbil steph
```

Translation: You have accounts on pumpkin and squash with the same username as on the machine you're using now. You also have an account on gerbil, but your username there is steph.

When you have a different username on the system you're logging in to, you have to use -l to tell rlogin the name to use. Suppose that you want to log in to prune where your login name is sdl:

```
rlogin prune -l sdl
```

Notice that the system name comes first. If you have a .rhosts file on prune that lists both the machine from which you are logging in and your username on that machine, it doesn't ask you for a password.

Dialing out

Another command that acts sort of like telnet is cu (for *c*all *U*NIX). It activates a simple "terminal emulator" program that calls out over the phone. Despite its name, cu can call *any* system that has a modem compatible with the one on your computer. The program is useful for calling online services like MCI Mail and CompuServe.

Your system administrator has to set up the list of system names and phone numbers that cu uses. After they are set up, you call out by simply typing this line:

```
cu systemname
```

You escape from cu and hang up the phone in the same way you escape from rlogin: by typing ~. (a tilde followed by a period on a line by themselves).

rsh: *One Command at a Time*

Sometimes `rlogin` is overkill for what you want to do — you just want to run one command at a time. In this type of situation, the `rsh` command (for *r*emote *sh*ell) does the trick:

```
rsh pumpkin lpq
```

You give `rsh` the name of the system you want to use and the command you want to run on that system. This example runs the command `lpq` on system `pumpkin` (remember that `lpq` asks what's waiting for the printer on `pumpkin`).

The `rsh` command uses the same username strategy `rlogin` does, so if you can use `rlogin` to access a system and not give a username or a password, you can use `rsh` also. Because `rsh` doesn't handle the terminal very cleverly, however, you can't use full-screen commands like `vi` and `emacs`. You can use `ed`, however. Wow.

An old program, also called `rsh`, sometimes conflicts with the `rsh` we talk about here. The old `rsh` is the *r*estricted *sh*ell: a version of the Bourne shell that is of no use to you. If you type `rsh pumpkin` and UNIX responds by displaying `pumpkin: pumpkin: cannot open` or displays a `$` and sits there, you have the old `rsh`. If UNIX displayed the `$`, type **exit** to make it go away. If you have the old `rsh`, what we call `rsh` is probably called `remsh` or `rshell`, so try those names instead.

rcp: *Blatting Files across the Network*

Although `telnet` and `rlogin` may be the next best thing to being there, sometimes there's no place like your home machine. If you want to use files that are on another machine, `rcp` is often the easiest thing to do. (You can also use `ftp` to blat files across the network, but because that's a larger topic, we give it all of Chapter 18.)

The idea behind `rcp` is that it works just like `cp` (the standard copy command) — except that it also works on remote files that you own or that you at least have access to. To refer to a file on another machine, type the machine name and a colon before the filename. To copy a file named `mydata` from the machine named `pumpkin` and call it `pumpkindata`, you type

```
rcp pumpkin:mydata pumpkindata
```

To copy it the other way (from a file called `pumpkindata` on your machine to a file called `mydata` on a machine called `pumpkin`), you type this line:

```
rcp pumpkindata pumpkin:mydata
```

The rcp program uses the same username rules as do rlogin and rsh. If your username on the other system is different from that on your own system, type the username and an @ sign before the machine name:

```
rcp steph@pumpkin:mydata pumpkindata
```

If you want to copy files in another user's directory (tracy, for example) on the other system, place the user's name *after* a ~ (a tilde) *before* the filename. Suppose that you need one of Tracy's files:

```
rcp pumpkin:~tracy/somefile tracyfile
```

To copy an entire directory at a time, you can use the -r (for *r*ecursive) flag to tell rcp to copy the entire contents of a directory:

```
rcp -r pumpkin:projectdir .
```

This command says to copy the directory projectdir on machine pumpkin into the current directory (the period is the nickname for the current directory) on the local machine.

You can combine all this notation in an illegible festival of punctuation:

```
rcp -r steph@pumpkin:~tracy/projectdir tracy-project
```

Translation: "Go to machine pumpkin, where my username is steph, and get from user tracy a directory called projectdir and copy it to a directory on this machine called tracy-project." Whew!

In the finest UNIX tradition, rcp is extremely taciturn: It says nothing unless something goes wrong. If you are copying a large number of files over a network, it can take awhile (a couple of minutes), so you may have to be more patient than usual while waiting for it to do its work. rcp is done when you see the UNIX prompt.

If you copied stuff *to* another machine and want to see whether it worked, use rsh to give an ls command afterward to see which files are on the other machine:

```
rcp -r projectdir pumpkin:squashproject
rsh pumpkin ls -l squashproject
```

Although rcp is reliable (if it didn't complain, the copy almost certainly worked), it never hurts to be sure.

NFS: You'll Never Find Your Stuff

If your computer is on a LAN, the computer is probably set up to share files with other computers. Quite a few different schemes enable computers to use files on other machines. These schemes are named mostly with TLAs (Three Letter Acronyms) such as AFS, RFS, and NFS. This chapter talks mostly about NFS (you'll *n*ever *f*ind your *s*tuff) because that's the most commonly used scheme, even though it works, in many ways, the worst. If you didn't like the C shell or the `vi` editor, you won't like NFS either; it also was written by Bill, the big guy with the strong opinions.

What's NFS?

The NFS (Network File System) program enables you to treat files on another computer in more or less the same way you treat files on your own computer.

You may want to use NFS for several reasons:

- **Often you have a bunch of similar computers scattered around, all running more or less the same programs.** Rather than load every program on every computer, the system administrator loads one copy of everything on one computer (the server) so that all the other computers (the clients) can share the programs.
- **Centralizing the files on a server makes backup and administration easier.** It's much easier to administer one disk of 4,000 megabytes than to administer 10 disks of 400 megabytes apiece. It's also easier to back up everything because everything is all in one place rather than spread around on a dozen machines.
- **Another use of NFS is to make a bunch of workstations function as a shared time-sharing system.** It is reasonably straightforward to set up a bunch of workstations so that you can sit down at any one of them, log in, and use the same set of files regardless of where on the network they physically reside. This capability is a great convenience. Also, by using programs such as `telnet` (discussed earlier in this chapter), you can log in to another machine on the network and work from that machine (which is handy if the other machine is faster than yours or has some special feature you want to use).
- **In heterogeneous networks, NFS is a fancy term for networks with different kinds of computers.** NFS is available for all sorts of computers, from PCs to mainframes. A version of NFS is commonly run on PCs to enable PC users to use files physically located on UNIX or other systems.

Where are those files, anyway?

NFS works by mounting remote directories. *Mounting* means pretending that a directory on another disk or even on another computer is actually part of the directory system on your disk. Files that are stored in lots of different places can then appear to be nicely organized into one tree-structure directory.

Whenever UNIX sees the name of a directory — `/stars/elvis`, for example — it checks to see whether any names in the directory are *mount points,* which are directories in which one disk is logically attached to another.

Your system may have the directory `/stars` mounted from some other machine, for example, and then the directory `elvis` and all the files in it reside on the other machine.

The easiest way to tell which files are where is with the `df` (Disk Free space) command. It prints the amount of free space on every disk and tells you where the disks are. Here's a typical piece of `df` output:

```
Filesystem  kbytes    used   avail capacity Mounted on
/dev/sd0a    30383    6587   20758    24%    /
/dev/sd0g   157658  124254   17639    88%    /usr
/dev/sd0h   364378  261795   66146    80%    /home
/dev/sd3a    15671    1030   13074     7%    /tmp
/dev/sd3g  1175742  758508  299660    72%    /mnt
server-sys:/usr/spool/mail
            300481  190865  79567     71%    /var/spool/mail
server-sys:/usr/lib/news
            300481  190865  79567     71%    /usr/lib/news
server-sys:/usr/spool/news
            298068  243877  24384     91%    /var/spool/news
```

In this example, the directory / resides on a local disk (a disk on your own computer) named `/dev/sd0a`; `/usr` resides on `/dev/sd0g`; `/home` resides on `/dev/sd0h`; and so on. (We don't go into the subject of disk names other than to say that anything in `/dev` is on the local machine.) The directory `/var/spool/mail` is really the directory `/usr/spool/mail` on machine `server-sys`, `/usr/lib/news` is really `/usr/lib/news` on machine `server-sys`, and so on.

Some of the local directory names are the same as the remote machine's directory names — and some aren't. This situation can and often does cause considerable confusion; unfortunately, it's usually unavoidable. A system administrator with any sense at least mounts each directory with a consistent name wherever it's mounted so that `/var/documents/bigproject` is the same no matter which computer you're working on.

Chapter 17

Automating Your Office Gossip

In This Chapter

- What is e-mail?
- What are e-mail addresses?
- Where is your mailbox?
- How to use the Pine program
- How to use the `elm` program
- How to use the `mail` program
- How to use Netscape to read your mail
- How to organize your mail into neat piles

Electronic mail (or *e-mail*) is the high-tech way to automate interoffice chatter, gossip, and innuendo. Using e-mail, you can quickly and efficiently circulate memos and other written information to your coworkers, including directions to the beer bash this Saturday and the latest bad jokes. You can even send and receive e-mail from people outside your organization, if you and they use networked computers.

If your organization uses e-mail, you probably already have some. In fact, vitally important but unread mail may be waiting in your mailbox at this very moment. Probably not, but who knows? You can tell whether unread messages are in your mailbox because UNIX displays this message when you log in:

```
You have mail.
```

What You Need in Order to Use E-Mail

Any UNIX system handles e-mail for users on that system. To exchange e-mail with the outside world, your computer must be on a network — or at least have a phone line and a modem. You definitely don't want to know how to set up a mail network or make connections to other computers — if your computer doesn't already have e-mail on it, it's time to talk to a UNIX wizard.

In the great tradition of UNIX standardization, it has about 14 different mail-sending-and-receiving programs. (Fortunately, they all can exchange mail with each other.) To find out whether your computer can do e-mail, try using the simple `mail` program to see whether you have any mail waiting. Just type this line:

```
mail
```

UNIX says `No mail` if no mail is waiting or blats a copy of the first unread message to your screen. In the latter case, if you don't want to read your mail right now, press x (for e*x*it) and press Enter to get out. We talk more about reading your mail later in this chapter.

To receive mail, you need a mailbox. (Not one of those tasteful roadside mailboxes, in this case. It's an invisible mailbox made up entirely of electronic data.) Your system administrator can make (or already has made) one for you if your organization uses e-mail. The mailbox comes in the form of a file named something like `/var/mail/`*`yourusername`*. It contains your unread mail and any mail you choose to leave lying around. You may also have a directory named `mail` or `Mail` (some systems capitalize it, some don't — sigh) in your home directory that you can use to sort your mail into piles and keep it for historical reference.

To read the mail in your mailbox and send mail, you use a program such as `mail` or `elm` or Pine. If you use Motif or CDE, you can use a fancy X Windows mail program, such as `exmh`.

Addressing the Mail

E-mail, like regular mail (usually referred to by e-mail advocates as *snail mail*) needs an address, usually called a *net address* or *e-mail address*. To send mail to a person, you send it to his or her username (refer to Chapter 1 for information about logging in with a username). If the other user uses a different computer than the one you use, the mail system has to know which computer the other person is on — and the address becomes more complicated.

Sending mail to people on your computer

For people who use the same computer you do (you both use terminals connected to the same computer running UNIX), the mail address is just their username. If you enter `georgew` for your username, that's your mail address too. Make sure that you don't use uppercase letters in the mail address unless the username also does.

Sending mail to people on other computers

You can send mail to people who use other computers if your computer is connected to their computer on a network. For people who use other computers, you send mail by telling the mail system which computer they use.

Computers have names too, you know. They sometimes have boring names that indicate what they are used for, such as `marketing` or `corpacctg`. Sometimes all the computers in an organization are named according to a more interesting scheme, such as naming them all after fish, spices, or cartoon characters. It's traditional in UNIX networks to give the computers tasteful yet memorable names. One company we worked for had computers named `haddock`, `cod`, and `flounder`. Another company used `basil`, `chervil`, `dill`, `fennel`, and `ginger`. At Internet for Dummies Central, they're named `chico`, `astrud`, `xuxa`, `tom`, and `ivan`, after some of our favorite Brazilian singers.

When you're writing to someone on another computer on your network, include the computer name in the mail address by using an at sign (@) to indicate where they are "at." If your friend Nancy, for example, has the username `nancyb` and uses a computer named `ginger`, her mail address is `nancyb@ginger`.

A skillful system administrator can automatically note which computer each user in an organization uses. With luck, you can merely send mail by username, and the system automagically figures out which computer to send it to.

If you have trouble with addresses, the easiest way to send a message to someone is to wait until that someone sends a message to you and then reply to it. All mail programs have a command (usually `r`) that replies to the message you just read. Messages almost always have return addresses, and the `r` command enables you to send a message without typing an address.

Sending mail to people "out there"

If your computer network has phone connections to the outside world, you can probably also send mail to people out in the wide world of The *Internet:* the invisible network of UNIX and other computers that extends worldwide. Check with your system administrator or other e-mail users to find out whether your organization is "on the Net" (connected to the outside world).

To correspond with people on the outside, you need an Internet address for the person you want to send mail to. After you have the address, type it *exactly* the way she wrote it. Internet addresses tend to look like this:

```
ellenz@persimmon.greattapes.com
```

The part in front of the @ is the person's username. The rest of the address is the name of the computer and other information about where the computer is, usually the name of the company. The computer name, company name, and so on are connected by periods. The last three letters frequently tell you what kind of organization it is: com is for companies, for example, and edu is for educational institutions. Sometimes the parts of the address spell out the city, state, and country where the computer is located. It's all very well organized, really.

If your computer is on the Internet, you can also exchange mail with users of commercial services, such as CompuServe and America Online (AOL). For details, see the following sidebar, "Sending mail to people who use online services."

When you're typing Internet addresses, keep these points in mind:

- Be sure that you don't type any spaces in the middle of the address. Don't use spaces in usernames or computer names or on either side of the @ or a period.
- Don't capitalize anything unnecessarily. Check the capitalization of the person's username and computer name. Most addresses are composed entirely of small letters.
- Don't forget the periods that separate the parts of an Internet address.

If your computer is on the Internet and you want to try out network mail, send a message to the authors of this book, at unix4@gurus.com, and tell us what you think of the book. Our computer sends you an automatic reply, and we read your message, too. (If you can get that address right, you're already halfway to being a mail wizard.)

It's dead, Jim

If you get an address wrong, you usually get the message back within a few minutes (for mail on your own computer or your own network) or a few days (for mail that has bounced around the Internet). The dead letter usually has all kinds of cryptic automated error messages in it, but the gist is clear: The message wasn't delivered. Check the address and try again. Generally, the safest way to address a message is to reply to someone else's message.

Sending mail to people who use online services

You can send mail to people who don't use UNIX computers. By using the Internet, you can usually send mail to anyone who uses CompuServe, AOL, and other services.

To send mail to a CompuServe user, do the following:

- Find out his or her CompuServe user ID. It is a nine- or ten-digit number with a comma somewhere in the middle, such as 71234,5678. Most CompuServe user IDs begin with a 7, for reasons we don't claim to understand — probably because of its mystical significance.
- For purposes of sending mail from UNIX, replace the comma in the CompuServe user ID with a period, as in 71234.5678. Because Internet addresses aren't allowed to contain commas, you have to make this change.
- Tack `@compuserve.com` to the end of the number and, voilà! — you have the person's Internet address, as in this example:

```
71234.5678@compuserve.com
```

Some CompuServe users have signed up for usernames so that you can write to them at `JoeBlow@compuserve.com`.

To send mail to an America Online (AOL) user, you do more or less the same thing as for a CompuServe user:

- Find out the AOL screen name, such as Steve Case.
- Take out any spaces and tack `@aol.com` to the end of the number. Voilà! — you have the person's Internet address, as shown here:

```
stevecase@aol.com
```

For users of Prodigy Classic, use the Prodigy username followed by `@prodigy.com`:

```
XYZ666Q@prodigy.com
```

For users of Prodigy Internet, use the Prodigy username followed by `@prodigy.net`:

```
furdle@prodigy.net
```

Sending Stuff Other Than Text

These days, e-mail is getting to be such a widespread practice that you may want to send things other than plain old short text messages. For example, we e-mailed most of the chapters in this book as Microsoft Word documents to our long-suffering editor. Most mail programs now have commands for attaching files to e-mail messages, or at least including text files in messages.

If you want to send a text file by e-mail, just include the text file as part of your message. Note, however, that UNIX e-mail was designed for sending text, not for sending programs, graphics, or formatted word processing files.

Luckily, several ways of cheating have been developed so that the e-mail system doesn't realize that e-mail messages actually contain stuff other than text. The two most widely used methods are

- **Uuencoding:** This method involves using a uuencoding program to convert the file to text and a uudecoding program to convert the text back to the original file. We described uuencoding in Chapter 12, in the section about getting sneaky with uuencode.
- **MIME (Multipurpose Internet Mail Extensions):** This method is much easier to use than uuencoding because many newer mail programs handle it automatically.

When we describe mail programs, we tell you whether they work with MIME. All UNIX mail programs work with uuencoding because *you* have to do the work.

Before sending a file by using a uuencoded or MIME attachment, you may want to send a plain old nonattached e-mail message to the intended recipient, asking whether he can handle uuencoding or MIME.

Exchanging Gossip by Using Pine

Pine was originally a cut-down version of `elm` (which we describe next, for pineless users) intended for novice users, which makes it even easier to use than `elm`. Now it's become much more powerful than `elm` ever was. It has lots of nice menus to remind you of what to do next, and it even uses `pico`, a simple editor, for composing mail.

To run Pine, just type **pine**. You see a display like the one shown in Figure 17-1.

If you're using UNIX by way of a communications program, watch out for which terminal you're emulating. Pine works fine if your program emulates a VT100 terminal, but not so well if it emulates an ANSI terminal. You can usually change which terminal your program emulates.

The figure shows Pine's *main menu,* with a list of its favorite commands. Like `elm`, Pine uses one-letter commands. Note that one of the commands is highlighted — you can also choose commands by pressing the up- and down-arrow keys to move the highlight and then pressing Enter.

```
PINE 3.89   MAIN MENU                              Folder: INBOX  0 Messages

      ?     HELP                  -  Get help using Pine

      C     COMPOSE MESSAGE       -  Compose and send a message

      I     FOLDER INDEX          -  View messages in current folder

      L     FOLDER LIST           -  Select a folder to view

      A     ADDRESS BOOK          -  Update address book

      S     SETUP                 -  Configure or update Pine

      Q     QUIT                  -  Exit the Pine program



  Copyright 1989-1993.  PINE is a trademark of the University of Washington.
                    [Folder "INBOX" opened with 0 messages]
? Help                    P PrevCmd                R RelNotes
O OTHER CMDS L [ListFldrs] N NextCmd                K KBLock
```

Figure 17-1: Pine's menu, listing the most popular commands.

This list shows the commands you're most likely to use:

- Press c to compose (write a new message).
- Press i to see a list of your messages.
- Press q to exit from Pine.
- Press ? for lots of helpful online help.

Into the postbox

To use Pine to send mail, press c. Pine runs `pico`, a nice, simple editor we describe in more detail in Chapter 10. Rather than start with a blank file, you see the headers, ready for you to fill in: `To`, `Cc`, `Attchmnt` (for attaching files to a message — skip that one for now), and `Subject`. Use `pico` to type the header information and the text of your message. Then press Ctrl+X to leave `pico`. Pine sends the message and displays the main menu again.

If you decide not to send the message after all, you can press Ctrl+C to cancel it.

This list shows you some cool things you can do while you're writing your message:

- For lots of helpful information about how to use Pine, you can press Ctrl+G. Pine has complete online help.
- You can even check the spelling of your message — just press Ctrl+T. Pine checks all the words in your message against its dictionary and highlights each word it can't find.

I'm pining for some mail

To read your mail, press i to see the index of messages, as shown in Figure 17-2. The messages are numbered, with codes (N for new messages you haven't read, D for messages you have deleted, and A for messages you have answered) in the left margin. One of the messages is highlighted.

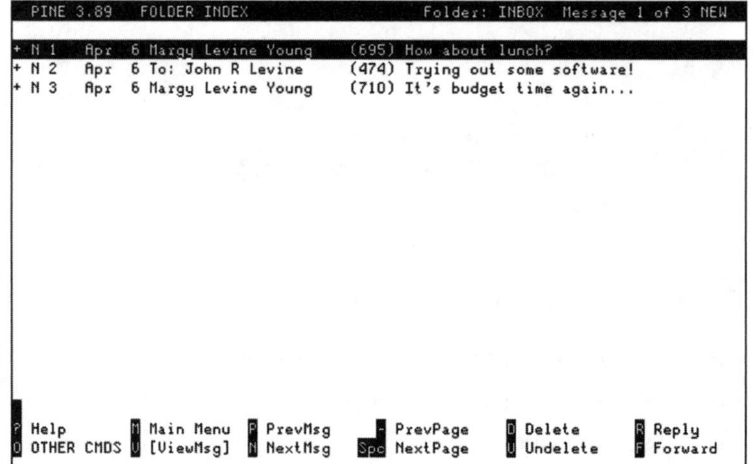

Figure 17-2: A list of your messages, in Pine.

To read a message, move the highlight to it, by pressing the up- and down-arrow keys or by pressing p (for previous) and n (for next). Then press v to view the message.

When you are looking at a message, here are some things you can do:

- Forward the message to someone else, by pressing f. Pine lets you start composing a message, with the text of the original message included in the text of this message.
- Reply to the person who sent the message, by pressing r. Pine automatically addresses the message to the person who sent the original one.
- Delete the message by pressing d. The message doesn't disappear right away, but it is marked with a D on the list of messages. When you exit from Pine, your deleted messages really are deleted. (If you change your mind, you can undelete a message by pressing u.)
- Move on to the next message by pressing n, or move back to the preceding one by pressing p.
- Return to Pine's main menu by pressing m.

Send this file too

Pine can handle MIME attachments with great ease and flair — nothing to it. To attach a file in Pine, move the cursor to the `Attchmnts:` line and press Ctrl+J while you're composing the message. When Pine prompts you for the filename, type it and press Enter. That's all it takes!

Creating your own address book

If you use Pine to send messages to Internet addresses, it can certainly be annoying to type long, complicated Internet addresses. That's a good reason to let Pine do it for you — set up an address book.

When you press a at the Pine menu, you switch to *address book mode.* (It even says `ADDRESS BOOK` at the top of the screen.) If you have already entered some addresses, Pine lists them.

When you finish fooling with your address book, press m to return to Pine's main menu.

To create an entry in your address book when the program is in address book mode, follow these steps:

1. **Press a.**

   Pine asks for the full name of the person.

2. **Type the person's last name, a comma, and then the first name, and then press Enter.**

   Pine asks for a nickname (the name you type when you address mail).

3. **Type the nickname (make it short but easy to remember).**

   Finally, Pine asks for the person's e-mail address.

4. **Enter the e-mail address just as you would when you address a message.**

   Pine stores the entry in your address book and lists it on the address book screen.

If you make a mistake, you can edit an entry later. Just highlight it on the list of addresses, and press e to edit it.

You can also create an address book entry directory from the address of a message. If you're looking at a message from someone whose address you want to save, just press t. Pine prompts you for the person's full name (it may even suggest it, if it's part of the message header), nickname, and e-mail address (Pine suggests the address of the sender of the current message).

Sign here

You can make a *signature file,* a file that contains text for Pine or `elm` to include at the end of every message. The file must be named `.signature` and be in your home directory.

Use your text editor to make a signature file. Keep it short (no more than three lines long), and include your name, your e-mail address, other address information you want everyone to know, and (if you have room) a pithy or philosophical message that characterizes you.

After you've created a signature file, you don't have to type this stuff at the end of every message. To test it, send a message to yourself and see how the signature looks. The signature appears at the bottom of the message when you compose it. To omit the signature information from a message, just delete it.

Saving messages

Pine enables you to create lots of folders in which to put your messages so that you can save them in an organized manner. To save a message in a folder, press s when you're looking at it or when it's highlighted on the list of messages.

If you save a message to a folder that doesn't exist, Pine asks whether you want to create it. Press y to do so. When you move a message to a folder, Pine automatically deletes it from your inbox. Very tidy.

Looking in a folder

After you've put messages in folders, you may want to look at them later. When you see Pine's main menu, you can press l (the lowercase letter *L*) to select which folder to look in. Pine automatically makes several for you, including these:

- **INBOX:** Your incoming messages. Messages remain there until you delete or move them.
- **sent-mail:** Messages you've sent.
- **saved-messages:** A place to save messages before you send them.

Move the highlight to the folder you want, and then press Enter. Pine lists the messages in the folder.

You can make more folders by moving messages into them (as described in the preceding section).

What's all this junk at the beginning of the message?

An e-mail message has a *header* that the mail program (`mail`, `elm`, Pine, or whatever) creates automatically. The header consists of these pieces:

- The `To` address (the person to receive the mail)
- The `From` address (the return address)
- The `Cc` addresses (the addresses to send copies to)
- The `Bcc` address (the addresses to send blind copies to)
- The subject
- Optional information you rarely use, such as expiration date, priority, which mailer mailed the message, and sometimes (for incoming messages) the arcane route the message took to get to you

Don't worry if the header looks like gobbledygook — it is. On incoming mail, the header can have all sorts of extra glop that reports on which systems have passed it along, which program was used to send the mail, and lots of other useless stuff.

You can specify `cc` addresses, the subject, and other information for messages you send.

Exchanging Gossip by Using `elm`

The `elm` mail-reading program is a heck of a lot easier to use than either version of the `mail` program (which we describe later in this chapter, for the desperate), although it's not as nice as Pine. The `elm` program even tells you once in awhile what is going on. Like Pine, it also helps you organize your mail into folders if you plan to save your messages.

To read your mail, send mail, or peruse mail you left lying around the last time, type this line:

```
elm
```

The `elm` program displays a list of your mail messages, as shown in Figure 17-3.

```
Mailbox is '/usr/mail/margy' with 3 messages [ELM 2.3 PL11]Î
   1   Dec 22 John R. Levine     (49)   a few troff hintsÎ
O  2   Dec 23 Jordan M. Young    (12)   Bye, bye, Brazil!Î
N  3   Dec 23 Meg Young          (10)   Hi, cutieÎ
Î
```

Figure 17-3: A list of mail messages in `elm`.

This display is called the *mail index.* The first letter on every line tells you which messages are new (N), old and already read (blank), old and unread (O), and deleted (D). The listing also shows the date the mail was received, who sent it, the number of lines in the message, and the subject. Below the index are instructions, including the one-letter commands you use to read and send mail:

- Use the ↑ and ↓ (or press j and k) to highlight the message you want to read, reply to, delete, or whatever.
- Press Enter to read the highlighted message.
- Press d to delete a message.
- Press u to undelete a message you didn't want to delete.
- Press m to send (mail) a message.
- Press r to reply to a message.
- Press f to forward a message to someone else.
- Press > or press s to save the message in a folder or text file.
- Press p to print the message.
- Press q to quit the `elm` program.
- Press ? for more help.

Compose yourself

To use `elm` to send mail, press m. The program asks you for the address, the subject of the message, and addresses to send copies to. Then it runs a text editor, usually `vi`. (You can arrange for `elm` to run another editor if you loathe `vi` as much as we do — see the tip in the "You send me" section, just a couple of paragraphs from now.) Use the editor to type the text of the message. When you finish, save the message and exit from the editor. (If you're forced to use `vi`, press Esc and type **ZZ** to save the message and exit from `vi`.)

Headers up!

Next, `elm` gives you a chance to edit the message (perhaps to add a P.S.), fool with the header (useful if you decide that your message is so fascinating it should be sent to a wider audience), forget the whole thing, or send the message off.

Press h to edit the header for the message. elm displays all the components of the header, including the addressee and the subject line. You can change most of them or add names of people to receive copies of the message (cc's).

To change each of these things, press the letter shown in front of the parenthesis. To add cc's, for example, press c. elm asks you for the list of addresses to send copies to. Enter the addresses, separated by at least one space, and press Enter. If elm recognizes the address, it displays the person's name in parentheses after the e-mail address. Otherwise, it shows just the address you typed.

When you have finished fooling with the header, press Enter to indicate that you're finished.

You send me

After you're finished fooling with the header, elm asks what to do with the message:

```
And now: s
Choose e)dit message, !)shell, h)eaders, c)opy file, s)end, or f)orget.
```

Press s to send the message. You can also press e to go back and edit some more or h to change the headers (To, Cc, Bcc, and Subject, for example). You don't have to worry about the other, less useful choices.

You can change the editor elm uses for writing and editing mail messages. (Thank goodness, because otherwise you may have to use vi!) When you're using elm and looking at the mail index, follow these steps.

1. **Press o to look at the elm options.**
2. **Press e to change the editor you use.**
3. **Type the name of the editor you usually use to edit text files (we like emacs and pico).**
4. **Press > to save this change.**
5. **Finally, press i to see the mail index again.**

Getting a read on your mail

To read a message, highlight its line in the mail index and press Enter. The `elm` program displays the message — or the first screen of it if it's a long message.

When you finish reading the message, you can do several things with it:

- Delete it (press d).
- Forward it to someone else (press f and tell `elm` the address to forward it to).
- Reply to it (press r).
- Save it. To leave it hanging around in your mailbox, press the spacebar to leave the current message and go to the next message, or press i to leave the current message and return to the mail index. In either case, the message remains unaltered. Alternatively, you can save the message in a folder or text file (see the following sections).

Mail hound

Another UNIX mail program worth mentioning is the humbly named `mutt`. Michael Elkins, a physics undergrad at California's Harvey Mudd College, wrote the original version of `mutt` in 1995 when he finally got fed up with the limitations of `elm`. (`mutt`'s motto for the ages: "All mail clients suck. This one just sucks less.")

Although written from scratch, `mutt` was originally based on `elm`, with various ideas from Pine and other UNIX mail clients thrown in to create a unique hybrid, or mongrel — in short, a `mutt`. (And you thought that `mutt` was an ultranerdy acronym for Mail User Transaction Terminal, didn't you?) Unlike `elm`, which is a basic text-based, one-message-at-a-time affair, `mutt` can handle colors (fancy that!) and message *threads*. Threads group messages based on their subjects so that you can tell which messages are responses to which. Threading is particularly useful if you carry on lengthy e-mail conversations with a number of different correspondents or if you subscribe to especially active mailing lists.

All in all, this `mutt` can hunt. It lets you attach files to e-mail messages by using MIME (`elm` can't, if you recall). It supports PGP (*pretty good privacy*) encoding for keeping your love letters secret. It automatically opens a Web page in your browser when you click a URL in a mail message (if you don't know what that means, try Chapter 18). It has "tons of options." It's small. And in the best UNIX tradition, it's free.

You can download `mutt` from FTP sites all over the Internet, including the FTP archive at the computer science department of Michael Elkins' alma mater. (Check it out at `ftp://ftp.cs.hmc.edu/pub/me`.) It also comes along with various versions of Linux, such as Red Hat Linux and Caldera OpenLinux.

Putting your mail in folders

If you like to save mail messages, you can save them with `elm` in folders, one folder per topic or one folder per sender. You can have lots of folders — each one is just a text file in your `Mail` directory (note the initial uppercase letter).

To save a message to a folder, either highlight the message in the mail index or display the message. Then press > or press s. The `elm` program asks for the name of the folder you want to save the message to. For some reason, folder names begin with = (an equal sign). The `elm` program suggests a folder with the name of the person who sent the message, assuming that you want to save messages organized by sender. You can type any name you want, however (no space and no funny characters other than the = at the beginning).

To see the messages in a folder, return to the mail index and press c to change folders. Type the name of the folder you want to use (or press ? to see a list of your folders). Be sure to type the = at the beginning of the folder name. You see a list of messages just like the mail index of your original mailbox.

All the same commands work in a folder that work in your regular mailbox. After you highlight a message, for example, you can read it by pressing Enter, forward it by pressing f, or delete it by pressing d.

To return to your regular mailbox, press c again and then press ! when `elm` asks for the name of the folder. (Don't ask us why.)

Saving your mail in text files

You can also save a message in a text file so that you can edit it later or include it in a word processing document. Use the `>` or `s` command to move the message, but, rather than type a folder name (which always begins with an =), type a filename (such as **message.text**). The `elm` program creates the file in your home directory and puts the message there. If the file already exists, `elm` adds the message to the end of the existing file so that you can save a series of messages to a single text file.

Printing your mail

To print a message on the printer, highlight the message in the mail index or display the message. Then press p to print it.

Attaching stuff by using elm

Unfortunately, most versions of elm can't attach files to e-mail messages by using the popular MIME system described earlier in this chapter. Bummer, but there it is.

If you want to send a text file, just include it in your e-mail message. The pico command to include another file in a message is Ctrl+R, and the emacs command is Ctrl+XI (that is, press Ctrl+X, release the Ctrl key, and press I).

If you want to send a file that contains something other than text, you can do it with uuencoding. Follow these steps:

1. **Create a uuencoded version of the file you want to send, by typing this command to the shell:**

   ```
   uuencode file-to-send new-name > temp
   ```

   In this command, replace *file-to-send* with the file you want to uuencode, *new-name* with the name you want the file to have when it is uudecoded, and *temp* with any temporary filename (*junk* is another perennial favorite).

2. **Run elm and compose a new message. Address it as usual.**

3. **At the beginning of the message, explain that you are sending a uuencoded message.**

4. **At the end of the message, include the file you created in Step 1 (which is named temp or whatever you typed in place of *temp*).**

   If you use pico as your editor, press Ctrl+R to include the file. If you use emacs as your editor, Press Ctrl+X I to include the file.

5. **Send the message.**

Netiquette

E-mail has been around long enough for an etiquette style to have sprung up around it, just as with real mail. Here are some tips:

Be polite. The written word tends to sound stronger and more dogmatic than speech. Sarcasm and little jokes don't always work.

Don't write anything when you are annoyed. If you get a message that you find totally obnoxious, *don't answer it right away!* You will be sorry if you do, because you will overreact and look just as obnoxious yourself. How do we know this? We used to do it, too. Everyone does at first, until they learn not to take e-mail too seriously. The exchange of needlessly obnoxious messages is so common that it has a name: *flaming.* Don't do it.

Be brief.

Be sure to sign your messages. The header shows where a message comes from, but your recipient may not remember who you are from your cryptic e-mail address.

Use normal punctuation and capitalization. That is, DON'T CAPITALIZE EVERYTHING. It looks as though you are shouting, and that's not polite (see the first tip in this list).

Watch out for acronyms. E-mail is full of them, and you had better know what the common ones mean. A list of acronyms is at the end of this sidebar.

Don't assume that e-mail is private. Any recipient of your mail can easily forward it to other people. Some mail addresses are really mailing lists that redistribute messages to many other people. Also, glitches in the mail system may send your messages to various electronic dead-letter offices. In one famous case, a mistaken mail address sent a message to tens of thousands of readers. It started "Darling, at last we have a way to send messages that is completely private. . . ."

If you need to indicate emotion, most people use *emoticons,* little pictures made up of characters to look like faces. If you see `:-)`, for example, just look at it sideways: You see a little smiley face which usually means that whatever you just read was a joke. (You get a sad face if you use the other parenthesis for the mouth.) Some people — particularly those who use CompuServe — type `<grin>` or `<g>` or `<smile>`. (An opposing viewpoint says that if you need one of those emotion things, it's a better idea to rewrite your message to make it clearer what you mean.)

Here's a list of the most common e-mail acronyms:

BTW	By The Way
IMHO	In My Humble Opinion
IOW	In Other Words
PITA	Pain In The Armpit
PMFJI	Pardon Me For Jumping In
ROFL	Rolling On Floor, Laughing
RSN	Real Soon Now (ha!)
RTFM	Read the Manual (that is, you could have looked it up yourself)
TIA	Thanks In Advance

Dealing with uuencoded stuff

If you receive a message that contains a uuencoded file, here's what to do:

1. **Tell `elm` to run the message through the uudecoder, by typing this command:**

   ```
   |uudecode
   ```

   That's a vertical bar and then the name of the command `uudecode`.

2. **The original file should be reconstituted.**

So what's the new file named? Look on the *begin* line of the uu-incoming file (or the original e-mail message that contained the file) — it shows the length of the file in bytes and the name the uudecoded file will have.

Exchanging Gossip by Using `mail`

The basic `mail` program comes with every brand of UNIX and is an acceptable way to read and send mail. Not great, but acceptable if you have nothing else. It can't deal with MIME attachments, if you're wondering.

Take a letter

Assuming that you want to send mail to your friend Jonathan W., you can send a message with the `mail` program by typing this line:

```
mail jonathanw
```

Some versions of `mail` prompt you to enter a subject line for the message; others respond by doing nothing. You can tell that something is afoot because you don't see a UNIX shell prompt such as `$` or `%` anymore. The `mail` program is waiting for you to type the message. So, type something, as many lines long as you want:

```
Yo. Jonathan! I think I've fiaured out how to use the e-mail on this
          thing!
Send a message back so that I can see if my mailbox works. Thanks.
```

Press Enter when the line reaches the right end of the screen (or window) to make it easier to read. Otherwise, your line wraps around to another line, and UNIX may put the line break in the middle of a word.

When you finish typing the message, type a period on a line by itself to tell the `mail` program that you are finished. The `mail` program confirms that it has sent the message by doing nothing other than displaying a UNIX prompt. (Because some particularly ancient versions of `mail` don't understand the dot, you have to press Ctrl+D to tell it that you're finished.)

Because the `mail` program is so helpful, you may want to consider using a better program, like `elm` or Pine. If you have to use `mail`, send yourself a test message to make sure that it is working. System V computers usually have a really old and awful mail program named `mail` and a somewhat better one named `Mail`. (These guys really had a lot of fun thinking up names for these programs.) If you can use `Mail` rather than `mail`, do so because it's more likely to work the way it's supposed to. (Often, `mail` doesn't even understand Internet mail addresses.)

What's in my mailbox?

To read your mail, reply to letters, and do other mail-related stuff, type this command on a line by itself:

```
mail
```

The `mail` program starts by showing you your unread mail. Some versions print the first unread message or show a list of incoming messages. Then the program displays a prompt:

```
?
```

As you doubtless found intuitively obvious from that prompt, the `mail` program understands many commands and is ready for you to type one.

If `mail` hasn't already showed you a list of messages, press h to tell it to show you a listing of the messages in your mailbox (if there are any).

Figure 17-4 shows what you may see when you start the `mail` program. The little > shows you which message `mail` is working with (the *current message*).

```
3 letters found in /usr/mail/margy, 0 scheduled for deletion, 0 newly arrivedÎ
Î    >Î  3Î    283Î    toniasÎ       Wed Dec 23 11:51:57 1997Î
ÎÎ       2Î    365Î    jordanyÎ      Wed Dec 23 11:51:45 1997Î
ÎÎ       1Î    1738Î   johnlÎ        Tue Dec 22 23:58:50 1997Î
Î    ?Î
Î
```

Figure 17-4: What you may see when you start `mail`.

Ordering `mail` *around*

The `mail` program understands lots of commands, including these:

- Press Enter to see the current message (the one the > points to).
- To move to a different message, type the message number (the first thing on the line in the list of headers).
- Press d to delete the current message (usually after you have read it).
- Press u to undelete a message you didn't want to delete.
- Press m and type ***mailaddress*** to send (mail) a new message. (Use a real username or mail address rather than `mailaddress`.)
- Press r to reply to the current message.
- Press z to see more message headers if you have too many to fit on-screen.
- Press p to print the current message.
- Press q to quit the `mail` program.
- Press ? for more help.

Reading `mail` *messages*

To read a message, type its message number (the number at the beginning of the line). To read the current message (the one with the >), just press Enter. The `mail` program displays the message — or the first screen of it if it's a long message.

When you finish reading the message, you can do several things with it:

- Delete it (press d).
- Reply to it (press r). Then type a message (like the one to Nancy, a few pages ago). End the message by typing **.** (a period) on a line by itself.
- Save it (see the following section).

If you don't make any other arrangements, messages you have read are saved in a file named `mbox`, which can get pretty big if you don't edit it now and then.

Saving your letters for posterity

You can save a message in a text file to edit later or include in a word processing document. To save the current message (the one you are reading or have just finished reading), type this line:

```
s filename
```

Replace *filename* with the name of the text file you want to create. If the text file already exists, `mail` adds the current message to the end of the file; You can save a series of messages to a single text file in this way.

Run that by me again

To print a message (on the screen, not on the printer) press p. You want to do this when you are looking at a list of messages and you want to see the contents of one of them. If you want to see a message other than the current one, put the message number (shown in the list of headers) after the `p`:

```
p 5
```

Bye, `mail`

To quit `mail`, press q. You see the UNIX prompt.

It Slices, It Dices — It's Netscape

Netscape Communicator, the all-singing, all-dancing Web browser, also happens to have a mail program built into it. If you're familiar with Netscape on another kind of computer (Windows or Mac), the UNIX version works almost identically. Because Netscape started distributing Communicator for free, the latest and greatest version (Communicator 4.0) is the most popular. Some excessively loyal (stubborn? lazy?) people still use the older version (Navigator 3.0), but the newer version is so much better and so easy to get that it's hard to feel sorry for them. (If you're still using Navigator, do yourself a favor and download Communicator 4.0 from the Netscape Web site, at `http://www.netscape.com/download`.)

Netscape, as a prime example of the Great Expanding Blob school of software design, can do much more than we have room to describe here. See *The Internet For Dummies,* 5th Edition, and *MORE Internet for Dummies*, 4th Edition (both from IDG Books Worldwide, Inc.), for more details.

Mail bonding with Navigator 3.0

Okay, so you didn't take our advice, and you still insist on using Navigator 3.0. To be fair, perhaps you're in the power of a stubborn system administrator who hasn't got around to making the zoomier Communicator 4.0 available to you, a lowly, disenfranchised X terminal user. In case that's the case, this section's for you.

After you have Netscape running, just choose Window⇨Mail to read or send mail. You see a three-part window, with the names of your mailboxes (Inbox and Trash, unless you've made some new ones) in one part, the titles of the messages in a second part, and the contents of the current message in the third part.

To send a message, click the New Mail Message button on the toolbar. (You can do this in any Netscape window, not just in the mail window.) Netscape opens a new message-composition window. Type the recipient's name in the To field, the message subject in the Subject field, and the body of the message in the large, otherwise empty window. Then click Send to send your message.

To read mail with Netscape, click the Get Mail button on the toolbar to retrieve any waiting mail. Depending on how Netscape is set up, you may have to enter your login password again. It grabs all your mail and puts it into your Inbox and displays the sender and subject of each message.

After the mail is in your Inbox, click on a message to display its contents. After you've displayed a message, you can click the Delete, Reply, Reply All, or Forward buttons. (Reply All composes a reply to the sender and all other recipients of a message.) You can step through the messages in your mailbox by clicking the Next and Previous buttons and print a message with the Print button.

Outlook: Partly cloudy

You may be wondering why we haven't mentioned Outlook Express, the Microsoft answer to Netscape Messenger. Microsoft has pretty much ignored UNIX, except when it has been less than pleasant about UNIX in its Windows NT marketing campaigns. As a result, Microsoft has hardly done any UNIX development of its Internet Explorer Web browser, which contains Outlook Express. So far, Internet Explorer runs only on Solaris 2.5 and up (although a preliminary version is also available for HP-UX). Netscape, in contrast, runs on just about every version of UNIX, including Linux, and many Linux distributions include Netscape Communicator for free. If you don't want the worldwide UNIX community to look down its collective nose at you, use Netscape. (In case you're wondering, the Solaris version of Outlook Express works exactly the same as the Windows version, except that the Solaris version is buggier.)

Mail bonding with Communicator 4.0

After people had figured out how Netscape 3.0 worked, the Netscape developers addressed that deplorable situation by inventing the new, incompatible Netscape Communicator. Fortunately, although the screens have all changed, the functions are pretty much the same.

To start Messenger, the mail part of Communicator, choose Communicator⇨Messenger Mailbox. This action opens the Inbox, which you can see in Figure 17-5. The layout of the window has changed somewhat, so now the top half lists the messages in the current mailbox, and the bottom shows the current message.

To send a message, click the New Msg (New Message) button on the toolbar. The window that opens is chock-full of incomprehensible icons, although you can ignore most of them. First, you have to enter the name of your recipient. At the top of the window are a couple of lines that look sort of like lined notebook paper. Near the left end of the line may be an entry that says To or Cc or Bcc. If it says anything other than To, click the little arrow to the left of the Cc or Bcc and switch it to To. Having done that, type your recipient's address on the right half of your freshly updated To: line. If you have other recipients, you can enter them on the next lines, one per line.

Having done that, you can move on to the subject. This process is easier — type the subject in the Subject box. Now you can enter your message into the rest of the window.

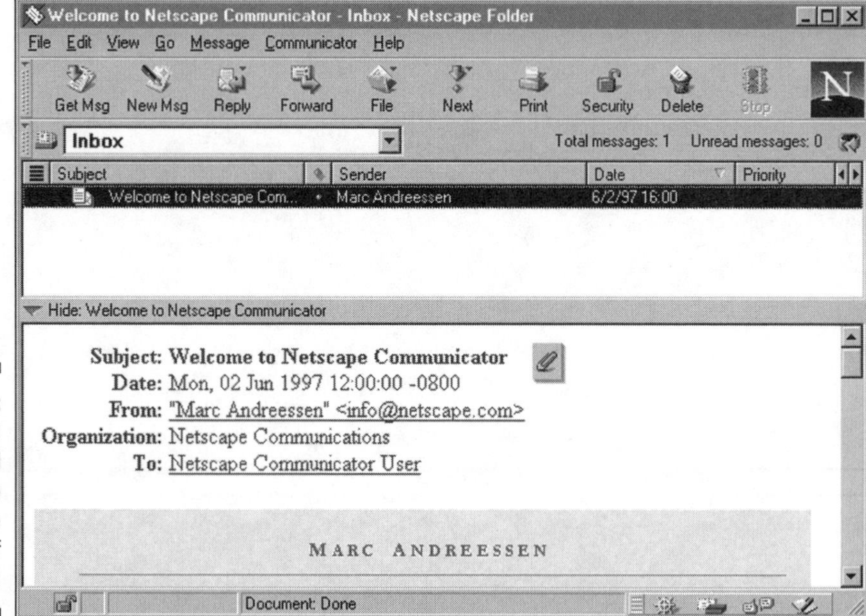

Figure 17-5: Hey, look! A personal message from the CEO of Netscape!

Messenger offers a fantasia of fantastic formatting features. *Don't use any of them unless you are 110 percent sure that your recipient uses Netscape 4.0.* Anyone else sees illegible pseudo-Web-page glop and will likely throw your message away.

After you have created your message, click the Send button. If you've used any of the formatting features, or even if you haven't, Netscape pops up a window warning you that your recipient may not be able to handle the beautiful formatting and gives you some options. Pick the middle option, Send in Plain Text Only, and click Send. Whew!

To see your new mail, click the Get Msg button on the toolbar. (You may be prompted for your login password, depending on your mail setup.) After you have mail in your mailbox, double-click on a message in the message listing to see that message in a new window. Again, the Reply, Forward, Next, and Previous buttons do what they look like they should.

Chapter 18

Web Surfing for UNIX Users

In This Chapter

- What is the Web?
- Using Lynx
- Using Netscape Navigator
- Finding great Web pages

The World Wide Web (WWW, or just the Web) is the zoomiest, coolest Internet facility around. It contains lots of information, including pictures and other non-text stuff, in the form of *hypertext.* As you read through the information, therefore, you can click (or otherwise select) words, pictures, or buttons to zoom right to related information. These clickable words, pictures, and buttons are called *links.*

The amazing thing about all these linked pages is that a page may be stored on any Internet host computer in the world. If you're looking at a page stored on a computer in Brookline, Massachusetts, a link on that page may jump you to a page stored in Basel, Switzerland. You never even notice, unless you look carefully at the names of the Web pages.

What's a Browser?

You read the World Wide Web by using a *browser.* If you're stuck with a plain old text-based terminal (for example, if you have connected to a remote UNIX host with `telnet`), you can use a text-only browser named Lynx. "Text-only" means that you don't get to see any of the cool pictures, animations, and sounds that have made the Web the phenomenally popular success that it is. If you use X Windows, you can use a graphical browser such as Netscape, currently the most popular browser for UNIX. With a graphical browser, you get to see all the cool stuff as well as the text. (Does this type of browser make the browsing experience any more educational or enriching? In some cases, maybe, but mostly it just makes it more fun.) This chapter describes both Netscape and Lynx.

URL!

The World Wide Web brought us the extremely useful concept of Uniform Resource Locators, or URLs. The point of a URL is to have a simple and consistent way to name Internet resources that tells you both the type of the resource and where to find it. A URL consists of a resource type, a colon, and a location. URLs look horrendous. In most cases, the location is two slashes, the hostname where the resource can be found, a slash, and a filename on that host.

Commonly used resource types are shown in this list:

http: A HyperText Transfer Protocol document; that is, something in native Web format

ftp: A directory or file on an FTP server

news: A Usenet news item (unsupported by many Web browsers)

gopher: A gopher menu (an early Internet-based information system that is dwindling as quickly as the Web is expanding)

Here's a typical URL:

```
http://net.gurus.com/
    toc-u4d4.html
```

The reason that most URLs look more like run-on typos than actual locations is that they were originally designed to be read by computers rather than actual human beings. Still, their structure has an underlying order, and understanding that order helps to demystify them (a little). The sample URL is a Web document. Reading backward, the part after the last slash is the filename: `toc-u4d4.html`. The part following the two slashes is the hostname of the computer: `net.gurus.com`. Finally, back at the beginning, you see `http:`, which just tells the browser to use the `http` resource type (the Web) to view this file.

Although URLs were originally intended as a way for computers to pass around resource names, they've also become widely used as a way to tell people about Internet resources, and that's how we use them in this section of the book. It's unfortunate that they're so difficult to type!

When you start Netscape or Lynx, you can begin with the Web page it suggests and find your way to the information you want by following the hypertext links. (Don't worry — we tell you how.) Alternatively, you can jump directly to a Web page if you know its name. These names are called *URLs* (for Uniform Resource Locators) — see the preceding sidebar, "URL!" to read about them.

A Day on the Lynx

Lynx is a boring-looking, character-based, graphics-impaired Web browser, but by gosh, it works. For most UNIX users (except those with GUI interfaces), Lynx is the only browser they can use. It was created at the University of Kansas. This chapter describes Version 2.8.

There's no place like home

You hear a great deal these days about home pages. Everyone who is anyone has a home page. So what are they?

A *home page* is a page on the World Wide Web that serves as a starting point for information about something. If, for example, you want information about our *...For Dummies* books, you may want to start at the Internet Gurus Central home page, which is at `http://net.gurus.com`.

Home pages generally contain introductory information about the entity whose home page it is, along with lots of links to other pages. Many home pages for organizations have URLs such as `http://www.`*`something`*, where *`something`* is the Internet domain name for the organization. Guess whose home page is `http://www.microsoft.com`?

If your UNIX system doesn't have Lynx, you (or your system administrator) can get it for free by anonymous FTP from `ftp2.cc.ukans.edu` in the `pub/lynx` directory. For up-to-date information about Lynx, you can subscribe to the Lynx mailing list by sending the message `subscribe lynx-dev` *`your-name`* to `listserv@ukanaix.cc.ukans.edu` (be sure to replace *your-name* with your actual name).

Coming and going

To run Lynx, just type **lynx**. You see a Web page (for example, the page shown in Figure 18-1). This particular page is the home page of The World, a Boston-based Internet provider.

When you're in Lynx, you can exit at any time by pressing q. Lynx asks whether you really want to leave — press y.

If you don't want Lynx to ask you whether you really, really, truly want to leave, press Q (capitalized) or press Ctrl+D to quit.

Anatomy of a page

Lynx tells you the name of the Web page (in words, not the URL) in the upper-right corner of the screen. The bottom two lines of the screen comprise a cryptic little menu that reminds you about which keys do what. The third line from the bottom displays various helpful messages. In Figure 18-1, it tells you that this Web page is too long to fit on-screen and how to see the rest of it. The rest of the screen is the Web page itself.

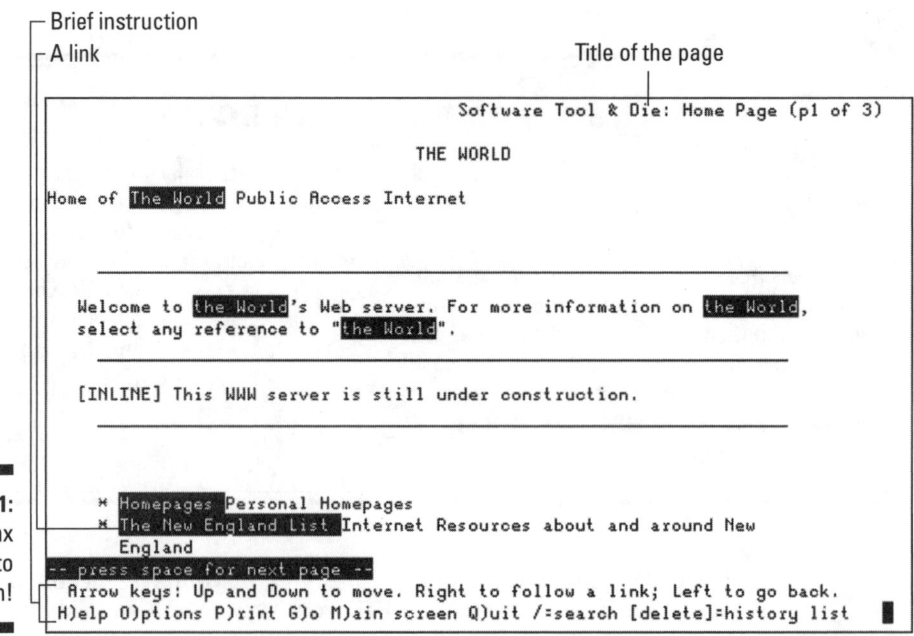
Brief instruction
A link
Title of the page
Software Tool & Die: Home Page (p1 of 3)
THE WORLD
Home of The World Public Access Internet
Welcome to the World's Web server. For more information on the World,
select any reference to "the World".
[INLINE] This WWW server is still under construction.
* Homepages Personal Homepages
* The New England List Internet Resources about and around New
England
-- press space for next page --
Arrow keys: Up and Down to move. Right to follow a link; Left to go back.
H)elp O)ptions P)rint G)o M)ain screen Q)uit /=search [delete]=history list

Figure 18-1: Lynx springs into action!

A Web page can contain text, links, pictures, sounds, and movies. Unfortunately, Lynx can deal with only text and links. Text looks (not surprisingly) like text. Hypertext links (things you can click to view a related Web page) are displayed in reverse video. Graphics, sound, and movies aren't displayed. Instead, Lynx shows you something such as `[INLINE]` or `[IMAGE]`. This technique is Lynx's way of saying, "Nyaah, nyaah, nyaah! I see a picture here, but I'm not going to show it to you!"

Skating the Web

Each link (highlighted word or phrase) on the Web page connects to another page on a related topic. The links that say `The World`, for example, connect to a page that describes Software Tool & Die's World Internet service. The `Homepages` link connects to a list of home pages about individual people.

One of the links appears in a different color on-screen. (This color difference doesn't show up worth a darn on paper, so in Figure 18-1 you can't tell that the first link is displayed in white letters on black and that the others are in yellow on black. Your colors may differ.) This link is the selected link. To select a link, follow these steps:

1. **Press the arrow keys so that the link you want is selected.**
2. **Press the right-arrow key or Enter to jump to the linked page.**

The linked page appears (sometimes after a short delay while Lynx retrieves the page over the Internet).

So that's it! To "surf the Web," you just move from page to page until you find something interesting. Here are some surfing pointers:

- The links you see may be numbered — if they are, you can choose a link by typing its number and pressing Enter.
- To return to the page you were looking at previously, press the left-arrow key.
- To return to the first screen you saw when you started Lynx, you can press m at any time. Lynx calls this first screen your *main screen.*
- To display a good starting point for surfing, press i for index. The Web page that Lynx displays depends on the one your system administrator chose. One popular index page is the `Welcome to the World-Wide Web` page at CERN, the laboratory near Geneva, Switzerland, where the Web was invented (see Figure 18-2).
- Sometimes a link doesn't take you to a different Web page. Sometimes it takes you to another part of the same page. It is common (and convenient) for long Web pages to contain a table of contents at the top of the page, with links to the major headings.

```
                                   Welcome to the World-Wide Web (p1 of 2)
                             THE WORLD-WIDE WEB

  This is just one of many access points to the web, the universe of
  information available over networks. To follow references, just type
  the number then hit the return (enter) key.

  The features you have by connecting to this telnet server are very
  primitive compared to the features you have when you run a W3 "client"
  program on your own computer. If you possibly can, please pick up a
  client for your platform to reduce the load on this service and
  experience the web in its full splendor.

  For more information, select by number:
     * A list of available W3 client programs
     * Everything about the W3 project
     * Places to start exploring

  Have fun!

-- press space for next page --
 Arrow keys: Up and Down to move. Right to follow a link; Left to go back.
H)elp O)ptions P)rint G)o M)ain screen Q)uit /=search [delete]=history list
```

Figure 18-2: One of the World Wide Web's own home pages.

Where do all these pages come from?

Web pages don't all come from any one source. Lots of universities and companies have Web pages — right now it's the in thing for anyone and everyone to have a Web page about themselves (so much for humility). Most Internet providers run *Web servers,* or programs that store Web pages and make them available to any Web browser that wants to display them. If you get the urge to have your own Web page, read Chapter 21 for encouragement (or discouragement, as the case may be).

Web pages are usually stored as ASCII text files. In addition to the text the Web browser displays, special instructions are written in a language called HTML (Hypertext Markup Language), which is discussed in the sidebar "Here's HTML in your eye!" later in this chapter. These instructions include marking headings and lists, links to other pages, and information about nontextual stuff, such as pictures and sounds. Several books are available that tell you how to write Web pages in HTML, including our *MORE Internet For Dummies,* 4th Edition (IDG Books Worldwide, Inc.).

Before you rush to create your own Web page, however, with a picture of your dog and a list of your kids' latest cute utterances, consider this question: How will people find your page? Sure, your friends will see your page after they type the URL you proudly give them. But will anyone else ever see it? Remember that the way most people display most pages is by selecting a link to the page. Will any other pages contain links to your page? Probably not.

Handling long pages

Some Web pages just fit on the screen, and others are miles long (or they seem like it). You can press the PgUp and PgDn keys to move around the page one screenful at a time. Pressing the Home and End keys (if your keyboard has them) moves you to the very top and the very bottom of the page (we let you guess which does which).

If you're looking for something in particular on a very long page, you may want to try the Lynx search commands. The page shown in Figure 18-2, for example, is 14 screens long and can be tedious to look through for a specific topic.

Instead, press the slash key (/) to begin a search. Lynx says `Enter a search string`. Type a word or phrase and press Enter. Lynx skips to the part of the page that includes the word or phrase, if it occurs on the page.

Getting help

If you want help, you can see hypertext help pages by pressing H (be sure to capitalize it). You see a page like the one shown in Figure 18-3.

```
                                  Help! - Press the Left arrow key to exit help

                                LYNX HELP FILES

Choose a subject

     * Key-stroke commands
     * About Lynx
     * Lynx users guide version 2.3.7
     * New, improved Key-stroke commands for version 2.3.7
     * Lynx users guide version 2.3
     * Help on version 2.3
     * Help on HTML
     * HTML Quick Reference Guide
     * Help on URL's

Commands: Use arrow keys to move, '?' for help, 'q' to quit, '<-' to go back
  Arrow keys: Up and Down to move. Right to follow a link; Left to go back.
 H)elp O)ptions P)rint G)o M)ain screen Q)uit /=search [delete]=history list
```

Figure 18-3: Help! I'm being attacked by a lynx!

The help pages are themselves Web pages, so move around them as you would any Web page. If you need help navigating the Web, of course, this process may not be so easy!

Where have I been?

Lynx keeps a list of the pages you have seen, in order. It needs this list to make the left-arrow key back you up through the pages. You can also see the list of pages by pressing the Del key (if it doesn't work, try the Backspace key). You see the Lynx History Page, as shown in Figure 18-4.

The pages you've seen are listed, and you can jump to any of them by choosing the link and pressing the right-arrow key. (If the links are numbered, you can also type the number and press Enter.)

```
                                                     Lynx History Page
                      YOU HAVE REACHED THE HISTORY PAGE

5.  -- You selected:  The World-Wide Web Virtual Library: Beer & Brewing

4.  -- You selected:  The World-Wide Web Virtual Library: Subject Catalogue

3.  -- You selected:  Data sources classified by access protocol

2.  -- You selected:  Overview of the Web

1.  -- You selected:  Welcome to the World-Wide Web

0.  -- You selected:  Software Tool & Die: Home Page

Commands: Use arrow keys to move, '?' for help, 'q' to quit, '<-' to go back
  Arrow keys: Up and Down to move. Right to follow a link; Left to go back.
 H)elp O)ptions P)rint G)o M)ain screen Q)uit /=search [delete]=history list
```

Figure 18-4: The history of Lynx.

Here's HTML in your eye!

As you may know, Web pages are written in a language called *HTML,* which includes instructions to tell the browser about text, headings, links, graphics, and anything else a Web page may contain. Each browser reads the HTML information about a page, formats it tastefully, and displays it. Different browsers use different formatting.

If you want to see the actual HTML version of a page in Lynx, just press the backslash (\ ) key. You see something like this:

```
<HTML>
<HEAD>
<TITLE>Great Tapes for Kids!
www.greattapes.com </TITLE>
<!— Changed by: Margy Levine
Young, 11-Nov-1998 —>
</HEAD>

<BODY BGCOLOR="#FFFFFF"
BACKGROUND="back.gif">
<CENTER><IMG SRC="title.gif"
HEIGHT=30 WIDTH=500></CENTER>

<H1>Great Tapes for Kids: A
Catalog of the Best Children's
Video
    and Audio Tapes</H1>

Have you ever seen a terrific,
    educational tape at a
    friend's house, a tape that
    your kids loved, and then
    never been able to find the
    tape for sale? Many of the
    best kids' video- and
    audiotapes aren't in your
    local video store, but you
    can order them here!
```

All those brackets surround HTML markings, which tell Lynx (and other Web browsers) about how to format the text and where to put pictures and links. If you want more information about HTML, the Lynx help system includes an introduction to HTML. The CERN home page also has links to HTML introductory documents.

Going right to a URL

If you know the URL of the Web page you want to see, and if you have the stomach to attempt to type it, press g (for goto). Type the URL, and be careful about both the punctuation and the capitalization (yes, capitalization counts). Then press Enter. Lynx gets the page you want.

Printing or saving good stuff

What if you want to print what's on a Web page? If you press p, you see the Lynx Printing Options page, which looks something like the one shown in Figure 18-5. The exact options on this page depend on your Lynx installation.

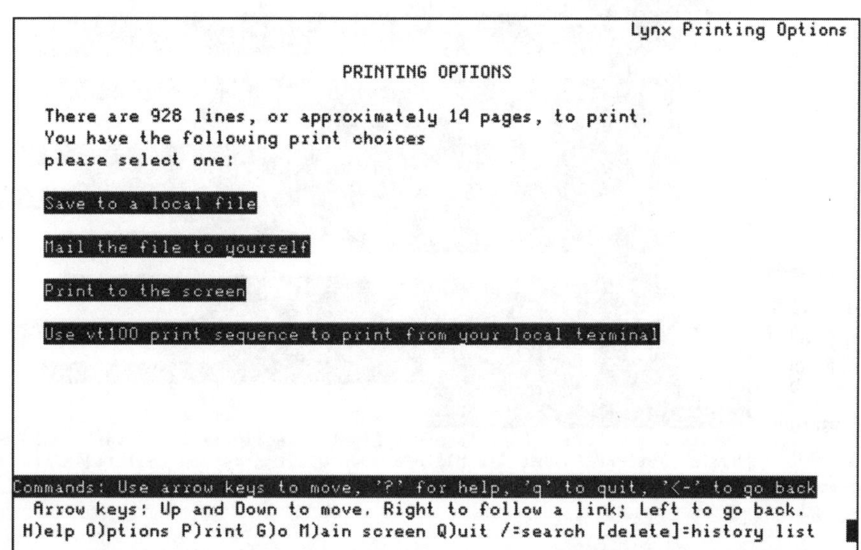

Lynx Printing Options
PRINTING OPTIONS
There are 928 lines, or approximately 14 pages, to print.
You have the following print choices
please select one:
Save to a local file
Mail the file to yourself
Print to the screen
Use vt100 print sequence to print from your local terminal
Commands: Use arrow keys to move, '?' for help, 'q' to quit, '<-' to go back
Arrow keys: Up and Down to move. Right to follow a link; Left to go back.
H)elp O)ptions P)rint G)o M)ain screen Q)uit /=search [delete]=history list

Figure 18-5: How do you want to save this page?

Some of the options on this page enable you to save the text of the page in a file rather than print it.

Fake Web pages

As you wander around the Web, you may stumble across a Usenet newsgroup, telnet session, or list of files on an FTP server. How did that stuff sneak onto the Web, you may ask. Lynx, like most Web browsers, can display not only Web pages but also information from other Internet services. Lynx makes the information look like a Web page, but it's not.

Using "fake" Web pages in this way is a wonderfully clever way to make lots of information about a topic accessible by way of a single program (your browser). Lynx can display Usenet newsgroups, FTP sites, Gopher menus, and telnet sessions for you. How convenient!

News of the weird

Figure 18-6 shows you how a Usenet newsgroup looks in Lynx. It lists the latest 30 or so articles, with a link at the top of the page to display earlier articles. (See Chapter 19 for background information about Usenet.)

```
                          Newsgroup misc.rural,  Articles 16918-16947 (p1 of 2)

  (Earlier articles...) Articles in misc.rural
     * "Re: How can I make pressure treated wood?" - Geoffrey Leach
     * "Well, I have a nice friend looking for a rural mate." - Dean
       Hughson
     * "Re: How can I make pressure treated wood?" - Tropical Steve
     * "Re: Septic Problem?" - an48068@anon.penet.fi
     * "Re: Septic Helpers" - Joshua_Putnam
     * "Re: Propose new group: alt.living.tightwad" - Neil McLaughlin
     * "Re: Propose new group: alt.living.tightwad" - Cara Vandy
     * "Re: How can I make pressure treated wood?" - Denison Rich, 3-5105
     * "Re: Squirrels in garden" - Denison Rich, 3-5105
     * "Re: Propose new group: alt.living.tightwad" - Walter Vose
       Jeffries
     * "Re: Propose new group: alt.living.tightwad" - B.M. Paquet
     * "Re: moving to the country" - John A. Stanley
     * "Re: Propose new group: alt.living.tightwad" - Richard & Marsha
     * "please snail me yer rosehips" - FLORIBUNDA
     * "Re: Propose new group: alt.living.tightwad" - Paul J. Lucas
     * "Re: STUMPS!!" - Jon Fox
-- press space for next page --
  Arrow keys: Up and Down to move. Right to follow a link; Left to go back.
 H)elp O)ptions P)rint G)o M)ain screen Q)uit /=search [delete]=history list
```

Figure 18-6: Here's a list of articles in the newsgroup `misc.rural`.

To read an article, just select its link, and you see something like Figure 18-7. Lynx shows you all the newsgroups to which the article was posted and enables you to jump to them.

The first link, `Reply to:` *author*, enables you to send e-mail to the person who wrote the article. If you choose this link, Lynx asks for your name, e-mail address, and the subject of the e-mail, and then it runs an editor so that you can type your post. (See the section "Controlling your Lynx," later in this chapter, to learn how to tell Lynx which editor to run.) If you specified an editor, Lynx runs the editor and enables you to type the message. Save and exit as you usually do, using that editor. If you didn't specify an editor, Lynx enables you to type the lines one line at a time and lets you type a period on a line by itself to signal that you are finished. After you type the message, Lynx asks you whether you really want to mail it. If it's angry, petty, or not funny, think again.

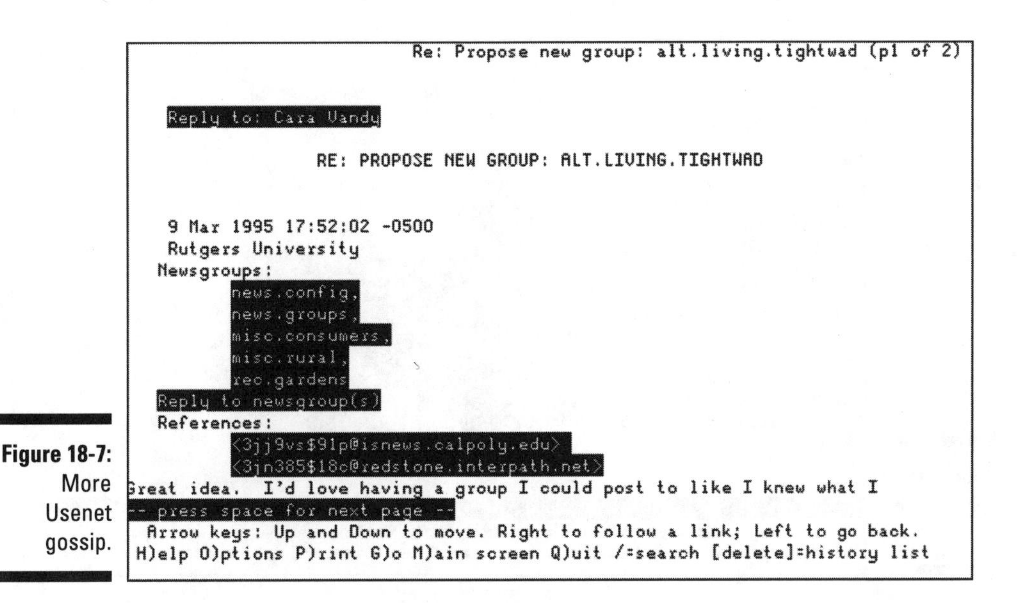

Re: Propose new group: alt.living.tightwad (p1 of 2)
Reply to: Cara Vandy
RE: PROPOSE NEW GROUP: ALT.LIVING.TIGHTWAD
9 Mar 1995 17:52:02 -0500
Rutgers University
Newsgroups:
news.config,
news.groups,
misc.consumers,
misc.rural,
rec.gardens
Reply to newsgroup(s)
References:
<3jj9vs$91p@isnews.calpoly.edu>
<3jn385$18c@redstone.interpath.net>
Great idea. I'd love having a group I could post to like I knew what I
-- press space for next page --
Arrow keys: Up and Down to move. Right to follow a link; Left to go back.
H)elp O)ptions P)rint G)o M)ain screen Q)uit /=search [delete]=history list

Figure 18-7: More Usenet gossip.

Another link, `Reply to newsgroup(s)`, posts a follow-up article. If you choose this link, Lynx asks for your e-mail address, the subject of the post, and whether you want to include the original message, and then it runs an editor to enable you to type your post. After you type the message, Lynx asks whether you really want to post it. Think twice — will it really be of interest to lots of people in the newsgroup, not just to you and the person who wrote the post to which you are replying?

Although Lynx is a pretty good Web browser, it's a lousy news program. If you spend much time reading news, switch to a real news program, such as `trn`, `nn`, or `tin`. See Chapter 19 for details.

Downloading files via Lynx

With Lynx, you don't need a separate FTP program for downloading files. If a Web page contains a link to an FTP server and you choose that link, you see the message `Retrieving FTP directory`, and Lynx displays the files on the FTP server as a Web page, similar to the one shown in Figure 18-8.

You see one directory on the FTP server. For each item in the directory, Lynx displays its date and time, which type of thing it is (directory or file), its name, and its size. For files, it guesses which type of file it is. Follow these steps:

```
                                                          Welcome  directory

                                   WELCOME

Apr 14  1993  text/plain        [1].notar
Apr 10  1994  Directory         [2]bin
Apr 14  1993  Directory         [3]dev
Aug 18  1994  Directory         [4]etc
Apr 14  1993  Symbolic Link     [5]ftp
Mar 20 07:57  text/plain        [6]Index-byname  1847Kb
Mar 20 07:57  GNU Compressed    [7]Index-byname.gz  273Kb
Mar 20 07:58  text/plain        [8]Index-bytime  1847Kb
Mar 20 07:58  GNU Compressed    [9]Index-bytime.gz  165Kb
Nov 10  1993  text/plain        [10]Index.README  249 bytes
Mar  7 17:16  Directory         [11]installkits
Mar 20 08:12  UNIX Compressed   [12]ls-lR.Z  529Kb
Feb 25 21:55  Directory         [13]pub

Commands: Use arrow keys to move, '?' for help, 'q' to quit, '<-' to go back
  Arrow keys: Up and Down to move. Right to follow a link; Left to go back.
 H)elp O)ptions P)rint G)o M)ain screen Q)uit /=search [delete]=history list
```

Figure 18-8: Files on the Web.

1. **Move to the directory that contains the file you want.**

   If you select a directory, you see the contents of the directory. All directories except the root (/) have a link that enables you move up to the directory's parent directory.

2. **When you see the file you want, select it.**

   If the file is a text file or contains a Web page, Lynx displays it. You are finished.

   If the file is anything else (not text), Lynx says that this file can't be displayed on this terminal. True enough. You don't want to display it — you want to store it in a file on your system. Lynx asks what you what to do with it — download it to a file or cancel.

3. **Press d to download the file.**

   Lynx displays the menu shown in Figure 18-9.

4. **Choose one of the options for downloading a binary file.**

   (We recommend the last option on the menu, downloading by using ZMODEM to download a binary file, because it's the fastest.)

   Lynx asks for the name to give the file on your system. It suggests the same name the file now has, but you can change it.

5. **Type the filename and press Enter when you are finished.**

   The download begins! That is, Lynx and FTP begin transferring the file to your disk. You see various messages, depending on which type of transfer you chose in Step 4.

```
                                                    Lynx Download Options

                          DOWNLOAD OPTIONS

  You have the following download choices
  please select one:

  [1]Save to disk

  [2]Use Kermit to download a file

  [3]Use Xmodem to download a text file

  [4]Use Xmodem to download a binary file

  [5]Use Ymodem to download a text file

  [6]Use Ymodem to download a binary file

  [7]Use Zmodem to download a text file

-- press space for next page --
  Arrow keys: Up and Down to move. Right to follow a link; Left to go back.
H)elp O)ptions P)rint G)o M)ain screen Q)uit /=search [delete]=history list
```

Figure 18-9: How do you want to download this file?

Here are a few tips for downloading files with Lynx:

- It may take some time to connect to the FTP server. Many FTP servers are overburdened and overbooked — you may not be able to connect in some cases.
- If you start at the root directory of the FTP server, you may have to press PgDn once or twice before you get to the directories you are looking for. (Many FTP servers store their publicly accessible files in a directory named `/pub`.)
- If you want to use Lynx to access an FTP site, just press g and then type **ftp://*ftpsite*/**, replacing *`ftpsite`* with the name of the site. To look at the files at `gatekeeper.dec.com`, for example, you type `ftp://gatekeeper.dec.com/`.
- If the file transfer doesn't seem to work, try another type of transfer, as described in Step 4. You may have to exit from Lynx and use the `ls` command to see whether the file has in fact arrived. If the transfer still doesn't work, it's time to make a note of the FTP server name and the file you want and then fire up the regular FTP program.

Lynx can act like telnet too

Chapter 16 explains how you can log in to other computers to get information. Some of the computers are mentioned on Web pages, and amazingly enough, you can use Lynx to telnet to them.

When you click a telnet link, Lynx automatically connects by way of telnet. You have to log in and so on, just as you would if you were using the telnet program. When you're finished, be sure to log out — you can press q to tell Lynx to log you out. When you see the `Connection closed by foreign host` message, you are logged out.

Remembering the good parts

The World Wide Web has tens of millions of pages on it, and thousands are added every day (well, almost). When you find one that looks interesting and useful (or fun), it would be nice to be able to return to it easily. Otherwise, finding it again may be impossible!

You can return to it! You can create a *bookmark* for the page — that is, add its address (its URL) to a list of your favorite Web pages.

Before you can begin making your own bookmarks, you have to tell Lynx where to store them. Press O (the letter) to see the Options menu, which is described in more detail in the following section. The third option is the name of the file in which bookmarks are stored. If you see a filename for this option, fine — just leave it alone. It may already be set to something such as `lynx_bookmarks.html`. If no filename appears, press B, type a filename, and then press Enter. To leave the Options menu, press > (Shift+.) to save your changes and then press r to return to the normal Lynx screen.

Now you have a file just waiting to contain some bookmarks. To add a page to your bookmark file, press a. Lynx asks whether you want to make a bookmark for that page you are viewing (if so, press d) or to the page you would see if you chose the selected link (if so, press l — the letter). All that seems to happen is that Lynx displays the friendly, upbeat message `Done!`

Behind the scenes, however, Lynx has added the URL of the current page or link to your bookmark file. To see your list of bookmarks, press v. You see a page like the one shown in Figure 18-10. To go to a Web page on your list of bookmarks, just select its link. It's like having your own Web page full of your favorite links!

Controlling your Lynx

Lynx has some options you can set to control some things about how it works. When you press o, you see the Lynx Options menu.

```
                                                          Bookmark file

  You can delete links using the new remove bookmark command. it is
  usually the 'R' key but may have been remapped by you or your system
  administrator.
  This file may also be edited with a standard text editor. Outdated or
  invalid links may be removed by simply deleting the line the link
  appears on in this file. Please refer to the Lynx documentation or
  help files for the HTML link syntax.
    1. [1]Virtual Library by Subject
    2. [2]subject
    3. [3]Lynx Users Guide v2.3.7B
    4. [4]Data sources classified by access protocol









Commands: Use arrow keys to move, '?' for help, 'q' to quit, '<-' to go back
  Arrow keys: Up and Down to move. Right to follow a link; Left to go back.
 H)elp O)ptions P)rint G)o M)ain screen Q)uit /=search [delete]=history list
```

Figure 18-10: Some of our favorite places.

To change an option, type the capitalized letter in the option name. For some options, you then type the setting you want (such as the name of your favorite editor for the Editor option). For other options, only a few possibilities exist, and you can press any key (except Enter) to flip among them. Then press Enter when you see the one you want.

When you finish setting your options, press > to save them. Then press **r** to return to what you were doing in Lynx.

Here are some options you may want to fool with:

- **Editor:** This option controls which editor Lynx runs when you use it for sending mail. We recommend `emacs` because it's our favorite, although you may prefer `pico` or `vi`. Type the full pathname of your editor. You can send e-mail to the owners of most Web pages by using the Lynx **c** command.
- **Personal mail address:** Set this option to your own, complete e-mail address. Lynx uses it when you mail Web pages to yourself or as your return address when you mail things to others.
- **Keypad as arrows or numbered links:** If you set this option to numbered links, each link in a page is numbered, and you can choose a link by typing its number.

After you change this option, exit from Lynx and start it up again.

- **User mode:** This option is usually set to Novice, so that Lynx displays two lines of helpful menu items at the bottom of the screen. If you already know all the Lynx commands you need and would rather see two more lines of Web page, set this option to Intermediate. If you want to see the URL of each Web page, set it to Advanced.

Problems

The third line from the bottom of the screen displays various messages to tell you what to do or to let you know what's going on. Here are a few messages you may see:

- `Making HTTP connection to kufacts.cc.ukans.edu`. This message means that Lynx is asking `kufacts.cc.ukans.edu`, or whatever host computer it mentions, for the Web page you want.
- `http request sent: waiting for response`. If the Internet is very busy, a message like this one tells you that you're experiencing a brief delay. Lynx has spoken (metaphorically) to the host on which the Web page lives and is waiting to get the actual page.
- `Alert! Unable to connect to remote host` or `Alert! Unable to access document`. If you see this message, the host on which the information is stored is so busy that it doesn't have time for you. Or maybe it's down for repairs. Either way, try again later.

Browsing with Pictures: Netscape

Other browsers are available for UNIX, although Netscape currently wins the prize for most ubiquitous Web browser for UNIX computers. Versions of Netscape exist for UNIX, Windows, and the Macintosh. They all work in more or less the same way.

The Netscape Corporation calls its browser Netscape "Navigator" to distinguish it from Netscape Messenger (the Netscape e-mail program; see Chapter 17) and Netscape Collabra (the Netscape Usenet newsreader, which we cover in Chapter 19), but everyone else just calls the browser "Netscape."

Netscape has dubbed the 4.0 version of its browser software "Netscape Communicator." This package bundles the Navigator browser with a bunch of other software that you may or may not find useful. Aside from having a completely new interface (did we say confusing?), other programs in addition to the Navigator browser, and an appetite for lots more disk space and memory, Version 4.0 does much the same stuff as Version 3.0. The commands we mention in this section are for Version 4.0.

Hey! What about Internet Explorer??!?

At the time we wrote this edition of the book, Microsoft Internet Explorer, Netscape's chief rival in PC Land, has a shaky toehold in the UNIX world. Why? Partly because it's available for only one version of UNIX (Solaris 2.5 or higher), partly because of Microsoft's thinly veiled fear of and contempt for all things UNIX, partly because Internet Explorer for UNIX is full of bugs, and partly because Netscape gets distributed for free with various versions of UNIX and Linux. Apparently, a version of Internet Explorer for HP-UX is in the works, but Microsoft has yet to make a serious commitment to supporting the UNIX community.

(Don't bother) configuring Netscape

Because Netscape is an X and Motif application, it uses dozens and dozens of X resources you can customize. Here's our advice: Forget it. The standard configuration works fine, and our sad experience is that most changes you can make only make it worse.

Starting it up

You start Netscape by typing **netscape** in your shell. (Or, with luck, maybe you have a Netscape entry on your Motif or CDE menu.)

Netscape automatically loads the Netscape home page from its headquarters. You see a window like the one shown in Figure 18-11.

If you have a slow Internet connection, it may take quite awhile to load the attractive nautical graphic at the top of the window. If you get impatient, choose Edit⇨Preferences, choose Advanced, and uncheck Automatically Load Images to tell it not to bother loading the images in pages you retrieve. In that case, it replaces the images with little graphic icons. Netscape is relatively smart about remembering which images it already has, so if a page uses an image it already has, it automatically displays the image.

Leaving

When you finish using Netscape, choose File⇨Exit from the menu. (You can also use the keyboard shortcut Alt+Q.)

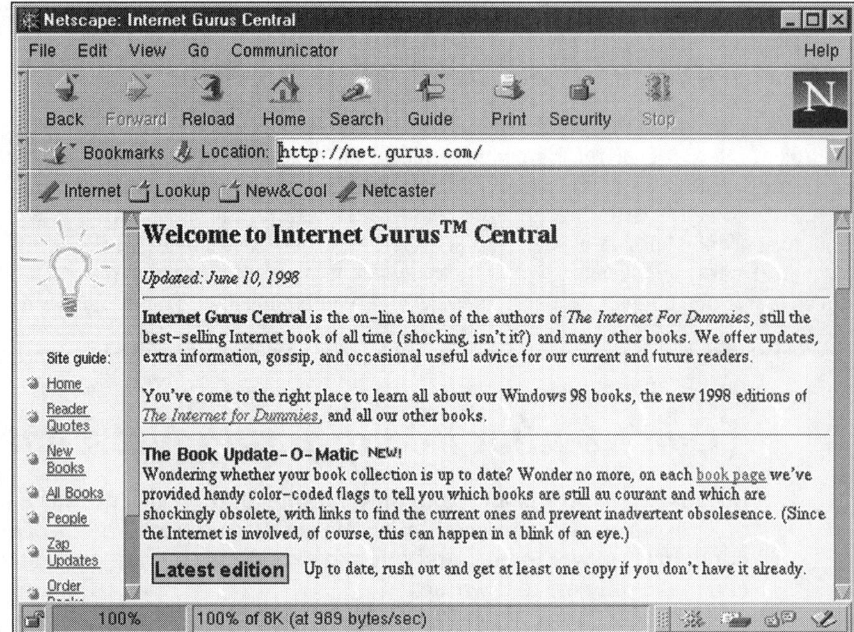

Figure 18-11: Netscape Mission Control.

Jumping around the Web

When you're looking at a Web page, some words and phrases are underlined and displayed in a different color (usually, but not always, blue). These things, called *links,* refer to another, related Web page about that topic. For example, if you see *Netscape* underlined and in blue, it's a link to a Web page about (not surprisingly) Netscape.

A link may not necessarily lead to another Web page — instead, it may connect to a Gopher menu, a Usenet newsgroup, or an FTP site. In any case, the information is related to the topic you click, and Netscape can display it just fine.

When you point to a link on a Netscape page, the URL of the link appears on the status line at the bottom of the Netscape window.

You may occasionally get an error message when you try to retrieve a page. If it happens, try it again because it frequently works on the second or third try.

You can also use buttons on the navigation toolbar at the top of the screen to move around:

- **Back:** Takes you to the preceding page you retrieved. If the button is gray, you have no page to back up to.
- **Forward:** After you have backed up by using the Back button, Netscape displays the next page you retrieved. If the button is gray, no next page exists yet.
- **Reload:** Reloads the current Web page. Click it if Netscape can't load a page correctly or if you think that the page may have changed since the last time Netscape loaded it and you want to try again.
- **Home:** Returns you to your home page, which is usually a page about Netscape, unless your system manager has made it something else.
- **Search:** Search the World Wide Web for a topic. This button takes you to a page where you can select from among several different search engines.
- **Guide:** Enables you to go to various places on the Internet that Netscape has deemed interesting.
- **Print:** Prints the current page.
- **Security:** Options for the paranoid: This button enables you to change security settings, such as encryption of Web pages and e-mail. Unless you're really into network security issues, it's probably best to leave these unchanged.
- **Stop button:** If Netscape takes forever to retrieve something, click this to tell it to forget it.

Finding other Web pages

If you know the URL (the official technical name) of a Web page you want to see, you can tell Netscape to go directly to it:

1. **Choose File⇨Open Page from the menu (or press Alt+O).**

   Netscape asks for the URL name, using the dialog box shown in Figure 18-12.

2. **In the URL box, type the URL.**

   With luck, you have the URL in a file on your computer somewhere so that you can copy it by using copy-and-paste with the mouse.

3. **Click Open In Navigator.**

   Netscape retrieves the URL you requested.

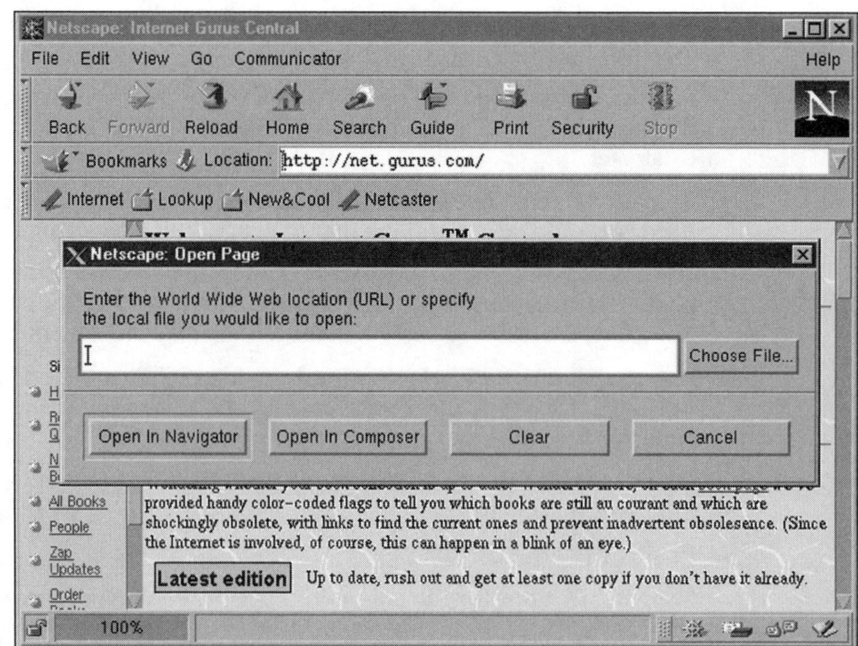

Figure 18-12: Where to now?

The URL of the page you're looking at is displayed in the Location box at the top of the Netscape window. To go to a new URL, you can just type it in this box rather than use the File➪Open Page menu item.

Often you get e-mail or read a Usenet item that contains a URL. Rather than retype the URL, highlight the URL in the mail or news window, and then switch to Netscape, click Open, click Clear (if some text is already in the text window), and then click the *middle* mouse button in the text window to paste in the URL you selected.

If you want to go to a URL that has the form `http://www.something.com`, Netscape offers a shortcut: You can simply type the `something` part of the URL in the Location box, and Netscape fills in the rest automatically.

Clicking the shooting-star N logo in the upper-right corner takes you to the Netscape home page. It's where you check for new releases and developments in Netscape.

Printing, saving, or copying good stuff

To print the displayed page, choose File➪Print from the menu. It suggests a print command, which you generally should leave alone, and asks whether you want to print to the printer or to a file. If you select file, a box enables you to set the filename. Then click the Print button in that window to send the page to the printer.

Remembering good places

When you find a particularly interesting page, you can add it to your list of Bookmarks of favorite Web pages. Choose Bookmarks➪Add Bookmark from the Location toolbar (or Communicator➪Bookmarks➪Add Bookmark from the main menu, or press Alt+D) to remember the current page.

To go to a page on your Bookmark list, follow these steps:

1. **Choose Bookmarks from the Location toolbar.**

   It's next to Location and below all the other buttons at the top of the window.

2. **Scroll down to the entry you want on the bookmark list.**
3. **Release the mouse button.**

To delete a bookmark or change its name, choose Bookmarks➪Edit Bookmarks (or Alt+B), as shown in Figure 18-13.

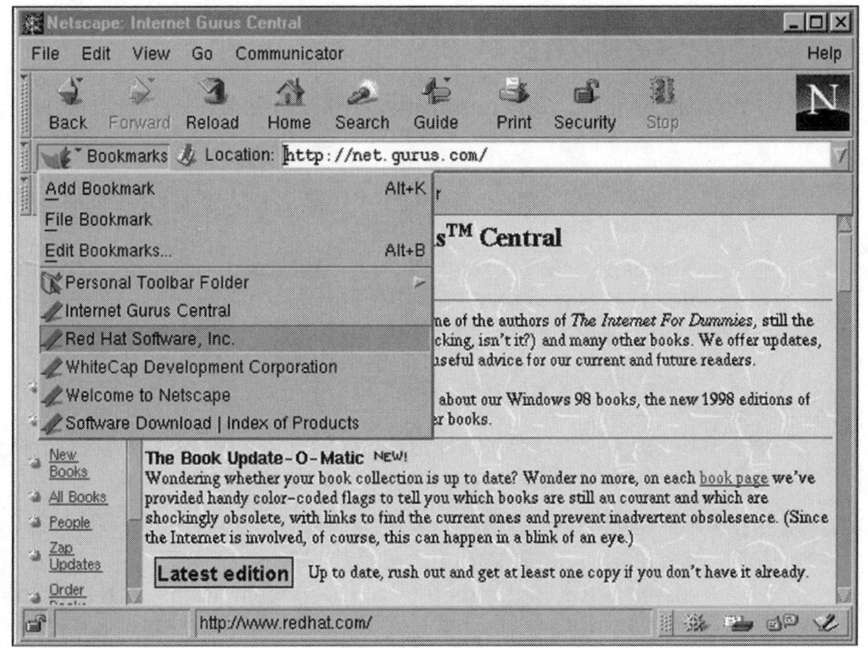

Figure 18-13: Select and edit Netscape bookmarks.

Highlight the bookmark you want to edit, and select Edit⇨Bookmark Properties to change it or Edit⇨Delete to delete it.

Searching for info

Of all the Web directories (or *search engines,* as they're known), the best is AltaVista, at `http://altavista.digital.com/`. Enter keywords you want to search for, and Alta Vista begins searching through millions of Web pages around the world.

Another good bet is Yahoo, at `http://www.yahoo.com/`. The Yahoo home page has links to categories and subcategories and, a couple of levels down, to interesting pages all over the Internet.

Several search engines are available to you by clicking the Search button on the toolbar.

For a list of the search pages we find useful, check out `http://net.gurus.com/favorite.phtml` — you see a list of some of our favorite Web sites too.

If you think that you'll use AltaVista or Yahoo a great deal, add them to your bookmarks by choosing Bookmarks⇨Add Bookmark from the menu.

Files on the Web

You can use Netscape to download files from FTP servers. Follow these steps:

1. **Choose File⇨Open Page (or press Alt+O or click the Location box near the top of the window).**

   Netscape asks for the URL of the information you want, using the dialog box that was shown in Figure 18-12.

2. **In the URL box, enter a URL like this:**

   ```
   ftp://hostmachine/
   ```

   In place of *`hostmachine`*, type the name of the FTP server. Don't forget the two slashes before it and one slash after it.

3. **Click OK.**

   Netscape connects to the FTP server, logs in as `anonymous`, and displays the root directory of the system. Items with a little folder icon are directories, and clicking them moves to that directory. Items with little paper icons are text files. Items with a little block of ones and zeroes are binary information.

4. **Move to the directory that contains the file you want.**
5. **Click the file with the right mouse button to download it.**

   Using the right button pops up a menu instead of displaying the link. From the menu, choose Save Link As. Netscape asks where to put the file and then retrieves the file and stores it on your disk.

Telnetting with Netscape

If you see a URL that begins with `telnet`, you can use Netscape to run a telnet program for you and look at particular information on other systems:

1. **Choose File⇨Open Page (or press Ctrl+O).**
2. **In the URL box, enter the URL that begins with `telnet`.**

   Netscape starts an `xterm` window running telnet, which connects to the Internet host computer, asks you for the username and password to use, and displays whatever the information that the URL describes.

This telnet program is the same one you can run directly. See Chapter 16 for details.

Chapter 19
Turbocharge Your Newsreading

In This Chapter

- What is Usenet?
- What's a newsreader?
- Running `trn`
- Selecting newsgroups
- Selecting threads
- Reading articles
- Responding to articles
- Killing the boring stuff
- Understanding how `tin` works
- Understanding how Netscape Collabra works

Not long after e-mail was invented, some people in North Carolina thought that having a distributed bulletin-board system would be neat. People could send messages from their local machine, the messages would be distributed to a couple of other machines, and users on all the machines could see all the messages. These folks figured that this system would be popular and could handle dozens of messages per day.

They were right: It's popular. Most of the machines are now connected via the Internet, although plenty of dial-up links still exist, and more than 100,000 machines are now hooked up, with sites on every continent. (We hear that a machine is even on the Internet at one of the research stations in Antarctica.) The system handles about 100,000 messages totaling more than a gigabyte (that's a billion keystrokes) of text every day. This monster is known as *Usenet,* or sometimes *net news.*

How to Read So Much Electronic Gossip That You Have No Time Left to Work

Usenet messages are filed in topic categories called *newsgroups,* of which more than 20,000 exist. Newsgroup topics range from technical discussions of computer architecture to gossip about old trains, nudism, and interminable political arguments. Reading all this stuff could take a large chunk of your workday (about 24 hours daily, or perhaps slightly more). Fortunately, the standard newsreading programs enable you to specify which groups you want to see and which ones you don't. You can identify, within groups, the topics and authors in which you are or are not interested.

Because many of the computers that run Usenet are UNIX systems, many newsgroups discuss UNIX topics. Usenet can be a good way to find other people with questions and comments about UNIX. In Chapter 27, we list some UNIX-related newsgroups.

If you get Usenet, you can probably send out your own Usenet messages. Please resist the urge to do so until you have been reading news for a few weeks, so that you have an idea of what's appropriate to send and what isn't. Also read the newsgroup called `news.announce.newusers`; it contains helpful advice for new Usenet users.

The most amazing thing about Usenet is who's in charge of it: no one. It's just a big, informal, cooperative setup. The programs most commonly used to file and transfer news were written by a guy in Cambridge, Massachusetts, who probably should have been working on his regular job instead. The various newsreading programs come from educational and commercial sites all over the world. The money to pay for the network time is, by and large, hidden in corporate telephone budgets. It's the definitive example of pioneer networking.

For general information about Usenet newsgroups, see Chapter 13 in *MORE Internet For Dummies,* 4th Edition, which we wrote (IDG Books Worldwide, Inc.).

To use Usenet, you have to learn these three Important News Skills:

- How to read the news that interests you
- How not to read the news that doesn't interest you, because much more news is sent every day than any single human could ever read
- How to post articles of your own (definitely optional)

Not every UNIX system gets Usenet newsgroups. Some employers have the benighted idea that spending hours every day reading `alt.fan.power.rangers` and `rec.sports.baseball.ny-mets` may not be the absolute best use of your time. If none of the newsreaders in this chapter works on your system, come up with some plausible reason to read newsgroups and talk to your system administrator or Internet provider. ("Gee, I really need up-to-date information about widgets, so I have to be able to read the `comp.gizmos.widgets` newsgroup every day.")

How Do I Read It?

Most UNIX systems have at least one program for reading Usenet newsgroups — these programs are called *newsreaders*. The most basic is `rn`; more powerful versions are called things such as `trn` and `nn` and `tin`. This chapter describes `trn` in detail because it's our favorite and describes `tin` a little, too. Many systems provide at least one of these programs for reading Usenet newsgroups. At the end of this chapter, we nod in the direction of graphical newsreaders, such as Netscape Collabra, for you X Windows users.

Note: UNIX newsreading programs tend to be really, really picky about the capitalization of the commands you type. For example, pressing the lowercase letter r may do one thing, and pressing an uppercase R may do another. In this chapter, we tell you for each and every command whether to type a lowercase or uppercase letter. When in doubt, type just what you see in this book.

Running `trn`

The `trn` program is a major improvement over `rn`, on which it is based, because it is *threaded* (in fact, its name stands for *t*hreaded *r*ead*n*ews). In newsgroup lingo, a *thread* is an article along with all its follow-up articles, including follow-ups to follow-ups, and so on. The program can organize all the articles in a newsgroup into threads, list them, and enable you to choose the topics that look interesting. This capability makes it easy to find the wheat from among the chaff (the articles of interest amid all the surrounding dreck).

Editor swamp alert

If you decide to respond to articles, either by e-mail or by posting a follow-up article, your newsreader runs a text-editing program. We can't predict which one it is because it depends on the way the system is set up. It's probably either `vi` or `emacs`. Neither is particularly easy to use (refer to Chapter 10).

To run `trn`, just type **trn** — simple enough. If your system doesn't have it, tough luck. Skip ahead for information about `nn` or `tin`. This section describes `trn` Version 3.6, by the way.

If you find that `trn` can't perform all the commands we tell you about in this chapter, you may have to tell it specifically that you plan to use all of its features. To do so, type **trn -x -X** to run it.

Remember your first time?

The first time you run `trn`, it checks in your home directory to see whether you have a file named `.newsrc`. (Yes, the filename begins with a period.) You may not have noticed the file because the period at the beginning of the filename makes it hidden in normal file listings. The `.newsrc` file stores information about which newsgroups you subscribe to and which messages you've already read in each one. (For the gory details about `.newsrc`, see the section "Remembering where you've been and what you've done," later in this chapter.)

If you've ever run any newsreader, it created this file. If not, `trn` just makes you a brand-new one, in your home directory. It also figures that you must be a newbie, so it displays some (allegedly) helpful messages. Press the spacebar to make them go away.

This new `.newsrc` file is a list of every blessed newsgroup your system carries, and the list can be long. This first time you run `trn`, you have to go through them and unsubscribe to the groups you don't plan to read. Don't worry — you can change your mind later and subscribe again. For each newsgroup in the list, it asks whether you want to read it, to which you reply y or n. If you get tired of answering questions, press Shift+N to tell it not to subscribe to any more groups. (You can go back later and pick up ones you may have missed.)

After the first time

After you've run `trn` once, it remembers which newsgroups you are interested in and asks you about only those you subscribe to.

When new newsgroups are created, which happens every day now that Usenet is getting to be so popular, you have to decide whether to add them to your `.newsrc` file. You see a message similar to the following one, depending on the name of the new newsgroup:

```
Newsgroup alt.binaries.sounds.utilities not in .newsrc -- subscribe? [ynYN]
```

To subscribe to the newsgroup and begin reading it now, press y (that's a lowercase *y*). To skip it forever, press n (again, a lowercase one). To add all the new newsgroups, press Shift+Y. To tell `trn` not to ask you about any of the new groups, press Shift+N.

If you choose to subscribe to a newsgroup, you see this message:

```
Put newsgroup where? [$^.Lq]
```

The various potions in the square brackets control exactly where in your `.newsrc` file you want to put this newsgroup. To put it at the end, just press the spacebar.

The `trn` program thoughtfully lets you know whether you have e-mail waiting. If so, it says `(Mail)` at the beginning of some prompts.

Choosing Newsgroups to Read

For each newsgroup in your `.newsrc` list, `trn` suggests that you read its articles. If this is your first time, the newsgroup is probably `news.announce.newusers`, the newsgroup for folks who are new to newsgroups. It's not a bad idea to peruse these articles, but we get to that topic later. The way `trn` suggests a newsgroup is with this message:

```
67 unread articles in news.announce.newusers -- read now? [+ynq]
```

(The number of messages varies.) The `[+ynq]` tells you possible responses:

- Press + (the plus sign, which is usually Shift+=) to see the list of threads for this newsgroup so that you can select which threads to read. (If you choose this option, skip down to the section "Picking Up the Threads," later in this chapter.)
- Press y (lowercase) to go ahead and look at the newsgroup article by article. (If you choose this one, skip down to the section "Reading the News," later in this chapter.)
- Press n (lowercase) to not read this newsgroup, at least not now. You see the next newsgroup on its list.
- Press q (lowercase) to quit `trn` altogether.

You can also press u (lowercase) to unsubscribe from the newsgroup so that you're never bothered by it again.

If you always like to look at the thread selector for a newsgroup, you can make pressing + (go to the thread selector first) the default for the newsgroup rather than y (go directly to reading articles). When `trn` asks whether you want to read the newsgroup, press t (lowercase). This choice turns thread selection on for this newsgroup, assuming that it was off. (If it was already on, this choice turns it off.) For each newsgroup, `trn` remembers whether you like to select threads first and presents the appropriate default so that if you press the spacebar, you get what you want. We invariably prefer to see the thread selector unless the group has so few messages that it's easier to look at all of them.

Commanding `trn`

When `trn` gives you a list of possible commands in square brackets (such as `[+ynq]`), you generally can press any of the options that are listed. Don't press Enter — `trn` moves along right away as soon as you press a key. Also, you can press the spacebar to choose the first option in the square brackets (this one is the default option).

Occasionally, commands are more than one letter long, usually because they enable you to specify extra information, such as a filename in which to save a message. Commands that are longer than one letter must be followed by pressing Enter so that `trn` knows when you're finished typing.

While you're reading the news, `trn` always does one of four things:

- Offers a newsgroup to read
- Displays a list of threads to choose among
- Offers an article to display
- Pauses while it displays an article that is too long to fit on-screen

Confusingly, different commands work in these four situations. Luckily, you don't have to use many commands very often, and `trn` suggests the most likely options.

You can press h (lowercase) at any time to see `trn`'s online help. It's rather concise but can certainly be helpful, especially as a reminder.

Picking Up the Threads

It's about time to read some news! When `trn` asks whether you want to read a newsgroup and offers the options `[+ynq]`, press + (the plus sign) to see the list of threads for the newsgroup. You see a list of threads (topics) like the one shown in Figure 19-1.

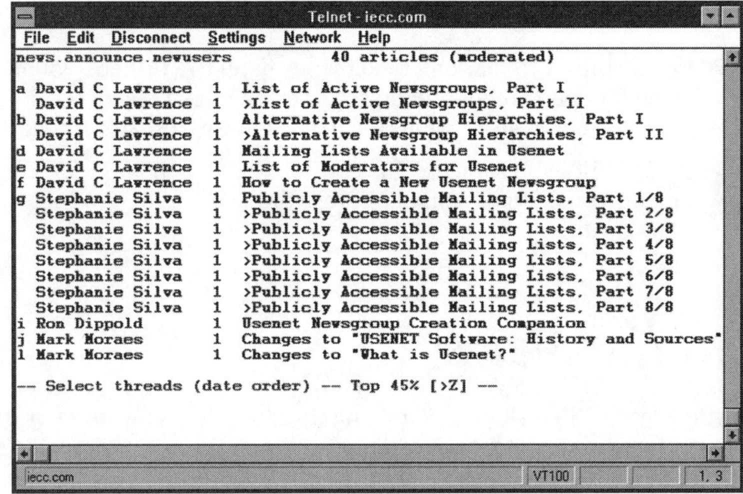

Figure 19-1: What topics are we talking about?

The top line of the screen shows the name of the newsgroup (in this example, it's `news.announce.newusers`), along with the number of articles waiting to be read and whether it is moderated. (*Moderated* newsgroups have editors who control which messages get posted.)

Underneath that is a list of articles, organized into threads. Each thread is assigned a letter, down the left edge of the screen. (The list skips some letters, which are used for commands.) For each article, you see the author and the subject line.

The bottom line of the display tells you to choose some threads and tells you whether there are more articles than will fit on the screen (there usually are). For example, Figure 19-1 contains the top 45 percent of the articles in the newsgroup.

If you want to read the articles in a thread, press the letter assigned to the thread. A plus sign appears next to the thread letter, showing that this thread has been chosen. (If you change your mind, press the thread's letter again to deselect it.)

To see more threads, press > (which is usually Shift+. [period]). You can tell when you get to the end of the list of threads when you see `Bot` on the bottom line of text.

To back up and see previous pages of threads, press < (which is usually Shift+, [comma]). To begin at the beginning again, press ^ (Shift+6), or to go to the end, press $ (Shift+4).

When you've chosen the threads you want, use one of these commands:

- Press Shift+X to mark all the articles in all the threads you *didn't* choose as having been read already so that trn doesn't ask you about them again. Then begin reading the articles in the threads you *did* pick.
- Press Shift+N to forget all about this newsgroup and look at the next one on your .newsrc list. Or press Shift+P to move to the preceding newsgroup.

Reading the News

If you pressed Shift+X after choosing the threads you wanted or if you pressed y when trn first asked about the newsgroup, trn begins showing you the articles one at a time. First, it shows you the article's headers, as shown in Figure 19-2.

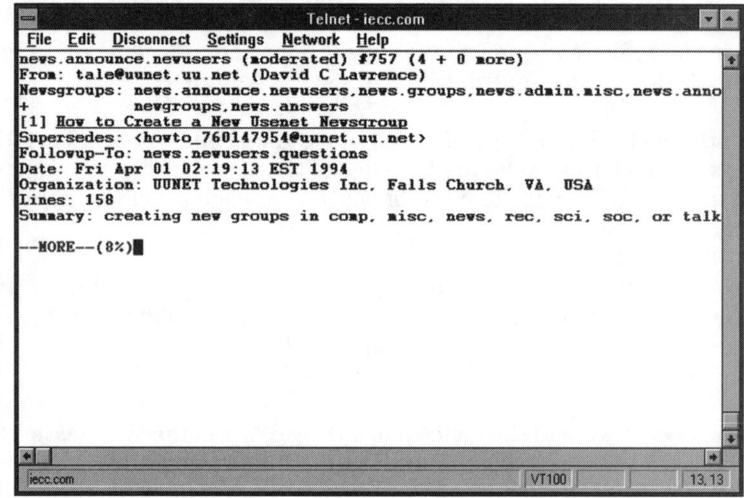

Figure 19-2: Cryptic headers at the beginning of an article.

You have several options:

- To see the rest of the article (or at least the next screenful), press the spacebar. You see the next page of text. If the article is several pages long, you see a MORE prompt at the end of each page, until you get to the end of the article.

You can get a sense of how long the article is by looking at how much you've read. The MORE prompt tells you what percentage of the article you've seen so that you can tell how far you have to go.

- If the article doesn't interest you, press j (a lowercase *j*) to "junk" the article. This choice marks the article as read (so that it doesn't offer it to you again later) and goes to the end of the article.
- If the entire topic is boring and you don't want to see any more articles that have the same subject line, press k (a lowercase *k*) to kill the topic. You skip any articles in this thread (or any other thread) that have the same text in the subject line.
- To quit looking at this newsgroup (for now, anyway), press q. The program asks you about the next newsgroup in your list.

At the end of the article, `trn` asks:

```
End of article 757 (of 818) -- what next? [npq]
```

Again, you have lots of options:

- To see the next article you haven't read yet, press n (lowercase) or press the spacebar.
- To see the preceding unread article, press p (lowercase). (If you've already read all the previous articles, nothing happens.)
- To see the same article again, press Ctrl+R.
- To move the first article in the next selected thread, press > (Shift+. [period]).
- To quit reading this newsgroup, press q (lowercase). The program asks whether you want to read the next newsgroup in your list.
- To kill (mark as read) all articles that have this subject line, press k (lowercase *k*).
- To kill the entire thread, including articles with a different subject line, press Shift+J.

Rot what?

Usenet has a system for protecting you from gross, disgusting, obscene, or otherwise offensive articles. Offensive articles can be posted by using a simple code called *Rot 13*. If you try to read an article and it appears as gibberish, you can press Ctrl+X to start the article over and decode it as it goes. But don't complain to us (or anyone else) if it offends you! Incidentally, if you press Ctrl+X by mistake and want to read the article *au naturel*, press Ctrl+R to redraw it normally.

Searching for something

You can use trn's search command to find articles that contain a particular word or set of characters in the subject line, anywhere in the header, or anywhere in the article. To search for articles that contain *text* in the subject line, type this command:

```
/text
```

If you want to look for articles that contain *text* anywhere in the header, type this command:

```
/text/h
```

For articles that contain *text* anywhere in the text of the articles themselves, as well as in the headers, type this command:

```
/text/a
```

To search backward through previous articles, press ? rather than / in any of these commands.

- If you are way behind on reading this newsgroup and you want to give up the idea of ever catching up, press c (that's a lowercase *c*). The program marks all the unread articles in the newsgroup as read. The next time you read this group, you see only the new articles.
- If you have lost interest in this newsgroup, press u (lowercase *u*) to unsubscribe from it.

File It, Please

You can save the text of an article in a file if you want to transfer it to another machine, include it in a word-processing document, or just plain keep it. Follow these steps:

1. **When you are at the end of an article you want to save, type this command:**

```
s filename
```

Press lowercase s, and replace *filename* with the name you want to give to the file that contains the article.

If the file already exists, trn sticks the article at the end of it. (This feature works well when you want to save an entire series of articles in a file: As you save each article, trn adds it to the end of the file.)

If the file doesn't exist, trn asks which kind of file to make:

```
  File /usr/margy/News/save.it doesn't exist--
use mailbox format? [ynq]
```

2. **To save the article in a regular text file, press** n **(lowercase). To save it in the kind of file in which mail programs store e-mail messages, press y (lowercase).**

If you don't tell `trn` otherwise, it saves files in a directory named `News` in your home directory. You can enter a pathname if you want to put the file elsewhere. Use a tilde (~) to tell `trn` to put a file in your home directory:

```
s ~/article.about.chickens
```

We find that saving messages in mailbox format is most convenient because then we can use a mail program such as Pine or `elm` to handle files of saved articles. (The only difference between a mailbox file and a non-mailbox file is that a mailbox has a separator line before each message.)

When Is an Article Not Really an Article?

Sometimes a news article contains not plain text, but rather a coded version of a binary file or group of files. You can sneak files into articles in two common ways: *uuencoding* and using *shar* files.

We introduce uuencoding and shar files in Chapter 12, where we explain how to attach files to e-mail messages; in case you skipped that chapter, however, we describe them again here. In a *uuencoded* message, a single binary file is turned into a bunch of ugly-looking text:

```
begin 644 sample
M5V]W(2!)9B!Y;W4@86-T=6%L;'D@='EP960@:6X@=&AI<R!W:&]L92!F:6QE
M(&%N9"!U=61E8V]D960@:70@<W5C8V5S<V9U;&QY+'T*>6]U)W)E(&$@<F5A
M;&QY(&1E9&EC871E9"!R96%D97(N("!$<F]P('5S(&$@;F]T92!A=”!M;W)E
M=6YI>$!I96-C+F-O;2!A;FO-"FUE;G1I;VX@<V5C<F5T(&-09&4@6#$S+@T*
"#0H*
'
end
```

Usually, uuencoded files are much longer than this one, although they're all equally ugly. Really long ones are often split across several news messages to keep each individual article to a reasonable size. Uuencoded files are most often found in groups such as `comp.binaries.ms-windows`, in which case they're runnable programs, or in groups such as `alt.binaries.pictures.erotica`, in which case they're digitized pictures of, er, various stuff.

A *shar file* (short for *sh*ell *ar*chive) contains a group of files. Although the files most often contain program source code, they can contain any text files. Here's a short example:

```
#!/bin/sh
# This is a shell archive (produced by shar 3.49)
# To extract the files from this archive, save it to a file, remove
# everything above the "!/bin/sh" line above, and type "sh
             file_name".
#
# made 05/25/1997 01:43 UTC by johnl@iecc
# Source directory /usr/johnl
#
# existing files will NOT be overwritten unless -c is specified
#
# This shar contains:
# length  mode       name
# ------ ---------- ------------------------------------------
#    112 -rw-rw-r-- poem
#
# ============= poem ==============
if test -f 'poem' -a X"$1" != X"-c"; then
             echo 'x - skipping poem (File already exists)'
else
echo 'x - extracting poem (Text)'
sed 's/^X//' << 'SHAR_EOF' > 'poem' &&
I eat my peas with honey
I've done it all my life
It makes them taste real funny
But it keeps them on my knife.
SHAR_EOF
chmod 0664 poem ||
echo 'restore of poem failed'
Wc_c="`wc -c < 'poem'`"
test 112 -eq "$Wc_c" ||
             echo 'poem: original size 112, current size' "$Wc_c"
fi
exit 0
```

The `trn` program makes it easy to extract the useful bits from uuencoded or shar files. When you see this type of message, you can extract its contents by pressing e (lowercase) followed by the name of the directory in which to extract it. (If you just press e and then press Enter, `trn` uses your `News` directory.) Multipart uuencoded files are also handled more or less automatically. After you extract the contents of the first part of a uuencoded message, `trn` says `(continued)`, and it's up to you to find the next part and press e again. After the last part, it says `Done`. Shar files are extracted in the same way as uuencoded files, except that there's no such thing as a multipart shar file. (Large programs may be multipart messages, but each one is a separate shar file.)

Shar and uuencode files present some enormous potential security holes. Shar files are really no more than lists of commands for the UNIX shell that create the files to be extracted. Although this setup offers considerable flexibility, it also means that a prankster can stick in some commands you would just as soon not execute, such as ones that delete all your files. Shar files from *moderated* groups (groups in which all the messages are examined and approved by a third party before being sent out) are generally okay, but the files in other groups are only as reliable as the people sending them. Shar scanning programs are available that scan shar files for untoward commands. Check with your system manager to see whether any of these programs is available on your system.

Uuencoded files of pictures are unlikely to cause any trouble, other than the hair on your palms you may get from looking at some of them. Uuencoded binary programs should be treated with the same skepticism as any other binary programs. Again, the ones that come from moderated groups are pretty safe; others are less so. A scan with a virus checker is always appropriate.

Dealing with Articles That Demand a Response

If you read an article that demands a response, you have two options: Respond privately by sending e-mail to the person who wrote it, or post a follow-up article to the newsgroup. This list shows you how to decide which way to go:

- If your response will be of interest to only the person who wrote the article, send e-mail.
- If you are really mad, take a walk before doing anything. If you're still mad and you just *have* to reply, send e-mail.
- If the original article contains errors that everyone reading it should know about, post a follow-up article, but only after checking that 12 other people haven't already done the same thing.
- If you have additional information about the subject that will be of universal interest to those reading the original article, post a follow-up article.

Responding privately by e-mail

When you are at the end of an article to which you want to respond privately, these steps show you what to do:

1. **Decide whether you want to quote parts of the article in your e-mail.**

   If you do, press Shift+R. Otherwise, press r (lowercase).

   You see a bunch of confusing messages, followed by a question about including a prepared file.

2. **Assuming that you have not prepared a text file in advance that you now want to include in your e-mail, press Enter to tell `trn` not to include any file.**

   The program now asks which editor you want to use.

3. **If you don't like the editor it suggests, type the command you use to start your editor. Otherwise, just press Enter.**

   The `trn` program runs the editor. If you chose to include the text of the original article, it is already sitting on-screen, indented to show that you are quoting it. The headers for the e-mail are at the top of the screen too.

4. **Delete unnecessary text.**

   Be sure to delete the boring header lines from the original article (not the ones that address your e-mail message, at the top of the screen — the ones that are quoted from the original article). Also delete parts of the article that you don't plan to discuss in your e-mail message. Pare the quoted text to the minimum, just enough to remind the person what article it is you just read and are responding to.

5. **Type your reply. Be clear, polite, and reasonable.**

6. **Save your message and exit from the editor, using whatever commands work in your editor.**

   The program asks:

   ```
   Check spelling, Send, Abort, Edit, or List?
   ```

7. **To run a spelling checker, press c (lowercase). To forget all about sending this e-mail, press a (lowercase). To return to the editor to make one more little change, press e (lowercase). To send the message, press s (lowercase). Then press Enter.**

   The program asks whether you want it to stick your signature file at the end of the message. (A signature file is a file called `.signature` in your home directory, and it contains your name, return address, and other info.)

8. **Press y or n (both lowercase) and press Enter.**

   You return to you where you left off — right at the end of the article you just responded to.

You can press r (lowercase) to send an e-mail message to anyone, not just to the person who wrote the article you just read. If you suddenly get the urge to write a note to your mom, press r and follow the steps to enter the editor. After you are editing your response, you can change the `To` line to any address you want, rather than to the article's author, and the `Subject` line to any subject.

Possibly making a fool of yourself

Okay, you've decided to take the plunge. You have something so interesting to say that you want to post it publicly, where it can be read, appreciated, savored, misconstrued, or laughed at. Here's how to do it:

1. **Press Shift+F to tell `trn` that you want to post a follow-up article, and include some or all of the original article.**

   The program gives you a sage warning:

   ```
   This program posts news to thousands of machines throughout the entire
             civilized world. Your message will cost the net hundreds if not
             thousands of dollars to send everywhere. Please be sure you know
             what you are doing.
   Are you absolutely sure that you want to do this? [ny]
   ```

2. **If you have thought better of it, pres `n` and press Enter. You can always send an e-mail message to the article's author and then decide to go public later. If you still want to post an article, press y. Then press Enter.**

   The program asks whether you want to include a *prepared file* (a text file you've already written).

3. **Assuming that you have not prepared in advance a text file you now want to include in your article, press Enter to tell `trn` not to include any file.**

   The program may ask which editor you want to use. Or it may just dump you into an editor, probably `vi`.

4. **If you don't like the editor it suggests, type the command you use to start your editor. Otherwise, just press Enter.**

   The `trn` program runs the editor. If you chose to include the text of the original article, it is already sitting on-screen, indented to show that you are quoting it. The headers for your follow-up article are at the top of the screen, too.

Look at the `Newsgroups:` line at the top of the message. It lists the newsgroups to which this article will be posted.

5. **Delete any newsgroups that wouldn't be interested in your article.**
6. **Move down to the beginning of the text of the article you are replying to, and delete unnecessary text.**

   Be sure to delete the boring header lines along with any parts of the article you don't plan to refer to. Pare the quoted text to the minimum, just enough to remind newsgroup readers what exactly you are responding to.
7. **Type your reply. Be clear, polite, and reasonable.**
8. **Save your message and exit from the editor, using whatever commands work in your editor.**

   Lines in Usenet articles are usually limited to 70 characters. If any of the lines in your article is longer than that, `trn` warns you about it so that you can go back and fix it. Then `trn` gives you this choice:

   ```
   Check spelling, Send, Abort, Edit, or List?
   ```
9. **To run a spelling checker, press c. To forget all about posting this article, press a. To return to the editor to make one more little change, press e. To send the message, press s. Then press Enter.**

   Your article wings out across the universe, and `trn` displays a message confirming it. Then you are back at the end of the article you responded to.

When you post an article to an unmoderated newsgroup, the article is distributed directly all over the Internet. When you post to a moderated newsgroup, the article is e-mailed to the person (or group) who moderates the newsgroup. The moderator decides whether the article is appropriate to post. You generally get an automated response from the moderator's computer and sometimes follow-up mail from the moderator.

Before sending a real posting to a real newsgroup, experiment in the `misc.test` newsgroup, which exists exactly for this purpose. You won't annoy anyone by posting to `misc.test` — no one reads the message there anyway.

Being Original

You can post an article that isn't a follow-up to any other message. That is, you can launch a brand-new thread on a brand-new topic, if you want.

To do so, press f when you are reading the newsgroup to which you want to post the article. The program asks whether you want to respond to the article you just read or start a new topic. Press **y** to start a new topic, and type the subject of the article when trn asks.

Fiddling with Your Newsgroups

When trn offers a newsgroup for you to read, you can give dozens of commands. In addition to the four commands listed earlier in the chapter (+, y, n, and q), you can use this command to add or delete newsgroups from your list:

- To delete a newsgroup from your list (that is, to unsubscribe to it), press u (that's a lowercase *U*).
- To add a newsgroup that's not on your .newsrc list, type this command:

  ```
  g newsgroupname
  ```

  Replace newsgroupname with the exact name of the newsgroup. For example, if you are interested in naturist activities, type this command:

  ```
  g rec.nude
  ```

- If you are not sure of the exact name of the newsgroup you are looking for, type

  ```
  a text
  ```

  Replace text with a word or part of a word. For example, if you are interested in gardening, type

  ```
  a garden
  ```

  If trn finds any newsgroups with names that contain those characters, it asks whether you want to subscribe to each one. Press y or n to subscribe or not. When trn asks where to put the newsgroup, just press the spacebar.

Remembering where you've been and what you've done

All newsreading programs store information about your particular preferences and situation, including which newsgroups you subscribe to and which messages you've already read. (Because messages in each newsgroup are numbered, the newsreader can just remember the range of message

numbers you've seen.) The information is stored in a file named `.newsrc`. Whether you use `rn`, `trn`, or `nn` to read the news, they all share the information in the `.newsrc` file. This file is the way most newsreading programs don't forget all about what you've subscribed to and what you've already read.

To look at your `.newsrc` file, when `trn` asks whether you want to look at a newsgroup, press Shift+L. You see a listing like this:

```
#  Status   Newsgroup
  0  (READ)  local.risks! 1-5548,5551-5556
  1 (UNSUB)  local.pcdigest! 1-7197
  2 (UNSUB)  comp.binaries.ibm.pc.d! 1-17823
  3 (UNSUB)  comp.sys.ibm.pc.digest! 1-580
  4 (UNSUB)  comp.text.desktop! 1-2558
  5 (UNSUB)  rec.food.veg! 1-36863,37791,37958
  6      37  rec.humor.funny! 1-3424
  7 (UNSUB)  rec.humor! 1-105750,106727,107119
  8     152  rec.arts.startrek.info! 1-1942
  9 (UNSUB)  news.lists.ps-maps! 1-1111
 10 (UNSUB)  comp.sys.ibm.pc.programmer! 1-5748
 11 (UNSUB)  comp.specification! 1-1337
 12 (UNSUB)  comp.text.tex! 1-35685
```

The first column of the listing just numbers the groups for your reference. The second column specifies

- A number: You subscribe to the group, and that's how many unread articles are waiting for you.
- `READ`: You subscribe to the group and have read all its articles.
- `UNSUB`: You once subscribed to it but unsubscribed in disgust.
- `BOGUS`: It's not in the official list of real newsgroups.
- `JUNK`: Means nothing (`trn` ignores lines that say *JUNK* here).

A colon after a newsgroup name means that you're subscribed to the group, and an exclamation point means that you're not. The number ranges are the article numbers of the articles marked as having been read.

Reading the best ones first

The `trn` program goes down the list of newsgroups in your `.newsrc` file, asking you about each one in order. If your `.newsrc` file has many newsgroups in it, it's a good idea to put first the ones you read most often. Putting your most interesting newsgroups first on the list avoids having to skip over the less interesting ones each time.

When trn asks whether you want to read a newsgroup and you want to move this newsgroup to a different location in your list of newsgroups, press m and then Enter. Then press one of these options:

- Press ^ to put it first.
- Press $ to put it last.
- Press a number to tell trn what line number to put it on in your .newsrc file.
- Press + and the name of another newsgroup to put it after that newsgroup.
- Press q (lowercase) to forget the whole thing.

Killing Articles That Displease You

We abhor violence as much as you do, but sometimes you gotta do what you gotta do. An ugly fact of Usenet life is that a great deal of garbage appears in newsgroups, mixed in with the good stuff. One powerful method of avoiding the garbage is to use trn's thread selector, described earlier in this chapter, in the section "Choosing Newsgroups to Read." A more permanent method is the *kill file*.

What's a kill file?

The trn program has two kinds of kill files: your global kill file, which applies to all your newsgroups, and kill files for each newsgroup. Both types of kill files contain information about which types of Usenet messages you never, never want to see. Because trn simply skips over messages described in your kill files, they never bother you.

For example, what if some idiot decides that it is very funny to send gross and useless messages to a newsgroup you like to read. You can skip over them, true, but wouldn't it be nice to just tell trn, "Look, if you get any message from that idiot, ignore them! I don't want to see them!" With kill files, you can.

Alternatively, if you are interested in only a small subset of the articles in a newsgroup, you can tell trn, "In this newsgroup, I want to see only articles that contain thus-and-such in the subject." Rather than kill a group of articles, you can kill all except a group of articles. You can use kill files to select articles, too.

The global kill file contains a list of commands that trn executes every time you begin reading a newsgroup. Newsgroup kill files contain the commands that trn executes when you enter that particular newsgroup. The commands usually tell trn which articles to kill (that is, ignore and never show you) or select (that is, ignore all the *other* articles). Your global kill file is stored in your News directory and is named KILL.

The kill files for each newsgroup are stored in subdirectories of your News directory. For example, your kill file for the rec.humor.funny newsgroup is stored in News/rec/humor/funny/KILL.

Using newsgroup kill files is usually better than using the global kill files because the types of articles you want to kill or to select tend to differ widely from newsgroup to newsgroup. If trn has to execute a bunch of unnecessary commands at the beginning of each newsgroup, it can slow down your newsreading. On the other hand, an unfortunate spate of advertisements has been posted to every newsgroup in the known universe (a practice known as *spamming,* which is an insult to the Spam brand meat-type product) for which a global kill file is the best response.

Killing newsgroup articles has nothing to do with killing UNIX processes with the kill command, as described in Chapter 24. Just thought you may be wondering.

License to kill

You can add commands to your newsgroup kill file when you are choosing the threads to read, but the best time is when you are reading articles. When you are looking at a particularly obnoxious article, here's how to draw some blood:

1. **Press Shift+A.**

   This step adds a command to the newsgroup kill file, telling trn what to do with all articles that have the same subject as this article, both now and in the future, forever.

   The program then asks [+j . ,] (surely one of the most inspired prompts of all time) — this is its way of asking what exactly you want to do with these articles.

2. **To kill (skip) all the articles, press j (lowercase). To kill all the articles as well as any replies to them, press , (a comma).**

A faster way of killing articles on the same subject as the current article is by pressing Shift+K. This method is the same as typing **Aj**.

Narrowing your view

Alternatively, you may want to tell `trn` that you are interested *only* in articles about a certain subject, now and forever. When you are looking at an article on that subject, press Shift+A (uppercase). Then press + to look at only articles about that subject. Or press **.** (period) to look at only those articles and replies to them.

Editing the kill file

You can use a text editor to look at what's in your kill file and make some changes. To edit your global kill file, wait until `trn` is asking whether you want to read a newsgroup. Rather than answer, press Ctrl+K. To edit a newsgroup kill file, when you are reading that newsgroup, press Ctrl+K. Either way, `trn` runs a text editor and loads up the appropriate kill file.

Each line in a kill file contains one command, telling `trn` to either skip all articles that fit a certain description or to look only at articles that fit a description. The first line in a kill file tells `trn` the message number of the latest message that `trn` has looked at, as in this example:

```
THRU 13567
```

Commands look like this:

```
/Buzz off, buddy!/:j
```

The text between the slashes tells `trn` what text to look for in the subjects of articles. The character after the colon (a *j*, in this example) tells `trn` what do with the articles: *j* to junk them, a comma to junk them and their replies, a + to select only them, and a period to select only them and their replies. Not exactly easy to remember!

Here's another example: Suppose that you read the newsgroup `news.groups`, which is where discussions about new newsgroups take place. However, it can have several hundred messages a day. You are interested only in articles that have anything to do with cats. To see only those articles, you can add the following line to the kill file for the `news.groups` kill file:

```
/cat/:+
```

This command selects all articles with a subject line that contains the word *cat*.

New hope for the dead

If you add a command to a kill file and then change your mind, the only way to get rid of it is to edit the kill file. When you are in the newsgroups, press Ctrl+K to edit the file. Look for the command (if it's the last one you created, it's at the end of the file). Using your editor's commands, delete the whole line or modify it until it does what you want.

Using `tin`

Another newsreader worth looking at is `tin`, written by Iain Lea, at Siemens in Germany. Because this program makes superior use of a terminal screen, many users prefer it over the other leading brands.

Start `tin` by typing **tin** (tricky, eh?). You see a screen like the one shown in Figure 19-3.

File Edit Disconnect Settings Script Network Help

```
                              Group Selection (125)                  Type 'h' for help

->     21  news.groups                                  13
       22  news.groups.reviews                          1
       23  news.lists
       24  news.lists.ps-maps
       25  comp.arch
       26  comp.archives                                148
       27  comp.compilers
       28  comp.compression
       29  comp.compression.research
       30  comp.dcom.lans.ethernet
       31  comp.dcom.telecom                            19
       32  comp.dcom.telecom.tech                       2
       33  local.telecom
       34  alt.dcom.telecom                             1
       35  alt.snail-mail
       36  local.teletech                               2
       37  comp.society.privacy                         1
       38  comp.doc
       39  comp.doc.techreports
       40  comp.internet.library
```

Ready | VT100 | 24, 1

Figure 19-3: `tin` shows you some newsgroups.

Choosing newsgroups

Your subscribed groups are listed with a line number on the left and the number of unread articles on the right. You can move up and down by pressing the cursor keys and PgUp and PgDn or by typing the line number. To look at the articles in a group, move the cursor to that group's line and press Enter.

The `tin` program updates the index files it keeps for the group (which can take awhile for a busy group) and then displays a list of articles.

Choosing and reading articles

For each topic, you see a line number, a plus sign if unread articles are under that topic, the number of follow-ups to the article, the title, and the author.

To read a particular article, move to the article by pressing the cursor keys or typing the line number, and then press Enter. Pressing Tab to go to the next unread article is usually more convenient.

In an article, you can use these keys:

- Pressing Tab displays the next page of the article or, on the last page, the next unread article. On the last page of the last unread article, pressing Tab displays the next group with unread news. (Perhaps we should offer a "`tin` convenience keyboard" that has only a giant Tab key.)
- If you want to skip to the next article without reading the rest of the current one, press n to move to the next article or press Shift+N to move to the next unread article.
- Press i to go back to the article index (the list of article names) and press i again to return to the index of newsgroups.
- Most other commands are similar to `trn` and `nn`: For example, you press r or Shift+R to reply to the author of an article, f or Shift+F to post a follow-up, and c to catch up a group (pretend that you've read it all).
- Press h at any point for a surprisingly readable help screen.

Getting uuencoded and shar files out of articles

One thing `tin` does quite differently is extract uuencoded and shar files. It's not hard, but it's not obvious. Follow these steps:

1. **Display the article index for the group with the articles you want to extract.**
2. **Move to each article to be extracted (just one for a shar file or one or more for a multipart uuencoded file) and tag each one by pressing Shift+T.**

   The program displays sequential numbers for each article tagged.
3. **Tell `tin` to save the tagged articles in a temporary file by pressing s.**
4. **When tin asks for a filename, give it one.**

   A traditional temporary file name is `foo`.

   After `tin` saves the articles, it asks what to do with them.
5. **Press s to extract a shar file or u to extract a uuencoded file.**

   The program thoughtfully deletes the temporary file if the extract worked.
6. **Press Shift+U to untag the articles you just saved and extracted.**

Leaving `tin`

Press q for *q*uit. (You probably guessed that.) The program asks whether it should catch up all the groups you looked at (that is, mark all unread articles as read). Press n, and you're finished.

Using Graphical Newsreaders

Several graphical newsreaders are available for UNIX. They don't necessarily do the job of reading newsgroups any better than their text-based counterparts, but they're certainly prettier and arguably easier to learn. If you prefer clicking buttons with the mouse to typing obscure commands, see whether any of these is available on your system. The most commonly encountered graphical newsreaders that run under X Windows are `knews`, `nn-tk` (which, as its name suggests, is based on `nn`), and Qnews.

Newsreading with Collabra

The Netscape Collabra newsreader comes bundled with the Netscape Communicator package. Although it's not a great newsreader, it's free, it requires no extra setup, and it's conveniently located on your browser's main menu.

After you have Netscape running, you can open the Netscape Message Center by choosing Communicator⇨Message Center or Communicator⇨Collabra Discussion Groups. In a stroke of design genius, both commands do exactly the same thing: They open the Netscape Message Center (as shown in Figure 19-4), a sort of centralized launching pad from which you can open any of your Messenger mailboxes or newsgroups to which you may have already subscribed.

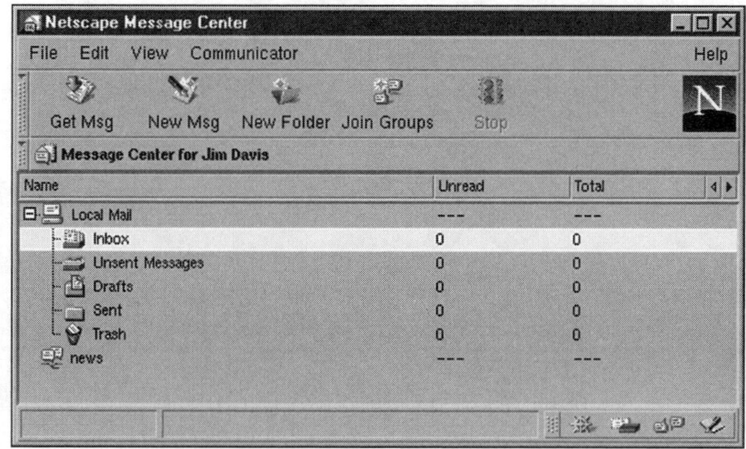

Figure 19-4: The Netscape Message Center: Where the news is.

To see any newsgroups to which you're subscribed, click the plus sign to the left of the news entry in the Message Center.

If Netscape doesn't show you any newsgroups, you may not be connected to a news server. To make the connection, choose Edit⇨Preferences from the menu, expand Mail & Groups (by clicking the plus sign), click Groups Server, and fill in the name of your Internet provider's news (NNTP) server.

To browse through a list of available newsgroups, click the Subscribe button. You see a window, like the one shown in Figure 19-5, that lists all the groups available on your news server.

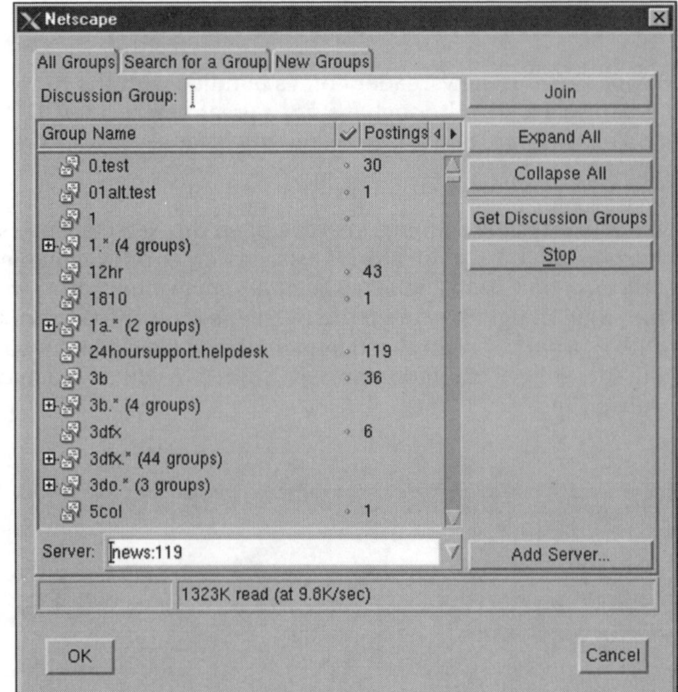

Figure 19-5: All the news that's fit to subscribe to.

Deja Deja News News

If you have a Web browser but no news server, you can read Usenet via the Web. The Deja News Web site, at `http://www.dejanews.com`, lets you sift through both new news messages and a Usenet archive going back several years. You too can post messages, after you go through a simple registration process.

If you're a serious Usenet reader, you'll want to use a program like `trn` or `tin` that you can customize to show just what you want; to get a flavor of Usenet or to look for specific messages that may have been posted a long time ago, however, Deja News is the way to go.

Chapter 20

Grabbing Files from the Net

In This Chapter

- Getting files from all over the Internet
- Stashing files all over the Internet
- Lotsa swell stuff for FTP
- Navigating in anonymous land
- Finding files by name

In Chapter 18, we explain how to use your Web browser to grab files stored on the Internet. Web browsers are definitely the easiest way to download files to your computer; just find a Web page with a link to the file and click the link.

If you want to copy to or from a non-UNIX machine, however, or if you want to retrieve files from a public file archive on a machine on which you don't have a personal account, you need an industrial-strength file-copying program. Your Web browser just can't cut the mustard (whatever that means). Instead, you can use the File Transfer Protocol (FTP) system, which is widely used on computers all over the Internet.

You can use FTP to transfer files to or from computers on which you have accounts. You can also use FTP to *download* (transfer to your computer) files from any of a bunch of publicly available FTP servers out there on the Internet. Thousands of public FTP servers are on the Internet, each with hundreds of files that may be of use, including text, pictures, and programs. It's just a matter of locating them and downloading them!

After we tell you about how to use FTP, we list some of the big FTP servers you may want to use.

You're a Copying Machine

It's simple to copy a file from one place to another (but don't forget — computers are involved). Here's how it works: Log in to the other computer for FTP, and tell it what you want to copy and where you want it copied.

Getting connected

To run the ftp program, you type **ftp** and the name of the host computer where the FTP server you want is:

```
ftp ftp.iecc.com
```

(That's John's computer. It has files, but perhaps not all that many in which you're interested, unless you care deeply about techniques for translating one programming language to another.) Substitute the FTP server's name for ftp.iecc.com.

Assuming that the FTP server is not too busy to let you connect, it greets you with a message like this:

```
Connected to ftp.iecc.com.
220 iecc FTP server (Version 4.1 8/1/91) ready.
```

The computer asks for your username and password on the host computer. If you don't have an account on the computer, don't panic. See the section "No Names, Please," later in this chapter. (On this particular computer, unless you happen to be one of the authors of this book, it's extremely unlikely that you have an account. We're using it as an example.)

If the FTP server likes you, it says something like this:

```
230 User johnl logged in.
ftp>
```

The ftp> is the FTP prompt, telling you that it's ready for you to type a command.

Getting your file

To copy a file from the FTP server (the host computer) to your own computer, use the get command:

```
get README
```

Substitute the name of the file in place of README in this command. FTP says something like this:

```
150 Opening ASCII mode data connection for README (12686 bytes).
226 Transfer complete.
local: README remote: README
12979 bytes received in 28 seconds (0.44 Kbytes/s)
```

FTP always tells you much more than you want to know about the transfer. When it says that the transfer is complete, you have the file.

You have to type the filename by using the syntax the server uses. In particular, if the server is a UNIX system (as most are), upper- and lowercase are different, so README, Readme, and readme are different filenames.

Getting out

When you finish transferring files, type the command **quit**. FTP responds with this heartfelt message:

```
221 Goodbye.
```

Files with Finesse

That's basically how FTP works, although you need to know, of course, about 400 other odds and ends to use FTP effectively.

When is a file not a file?

When it's a text file. The FTP definition specifies six different kinds of files, of which only two types are useful: ASCII and binary. An *ASCII file* is a text file. A *binary file* is anything else. FTP has two modes, ASCII and binary (also called *image* mode), to transfer the two kinds of files. When you transfer an ASCII file between different kinds of computers that store files differently, ASCII mode automatically adjusts the file during the transfer so that the file is a valid text file when it's stored on the receiving end. A binary file is left alone and transferred verbatim.

You tell FTP which mode to use with the binary and ascii commands (user input is shown in bold):

```
ftp> binary
200 Type set to I.
ftp> ascii
200 Type set to A.
```

In the preceding example, the *I* is for binary or image mode (after 25 years, the Internet protocol czars still can't make up their minds what to call it), and the *A* is for ASCII mode. Like most FTP commands, `binary` and `ascii` can be abbreviated by lazy typists to the first three letters — so `bin` and `asc` suffice.

How to foul up your files in FTP

The most common FTP error that inexperienced Internet users (and experienced users, for that matter) make is transferring a file in the wrong mode. If you transfer a text file in binary mode from a UNIX system to a DOS, Windows, or Macintosh system, the file looks something like this (on a DOS or Windows machine):

```
This file
          should have been
                           copied in
                                      ASCII mode.
```

On a Mac, the entire file looks like it's on one line. When you look at the file with a text editor on a UNIX system, you see strange `^M` symbols at the end of each line. You don't necessarily have to retransfer the file. Many networking packages come with programs that do ex post facto conversion from one format to the other.

If, on the other hand, you copy something that isn't a text file in ASCII mode, it gets scrambled. Compressed files don't decompress; executable files don't execute (or they crash or hang the machine); images look unimaginably bad. When a file is corrupted, the first thing you should suspect is the wrong mode in FTP.

If you are FTP-ing (Is that a verb? It is now) files between two computers of the same type, such as from one UNIX system to another, you can and should do all your transfers in binary mode. Whether you're transferring a text file or a nontext file, it doesn't require any conversion, so binary mode does the right thing.

Patience is a virtue

The Internet is pretty fast, but not infinitely so. When you're copying stuff between two computers on the same local network, information can move at about 200,000 characters per second. When the two machines are separated by a great deal of intervening Internet, the speed drops — often to 1,000 characters per second or fewer. If you're copying a file that's 500,000 characters long, it takes only a few seconds over a local network, but it can take several minutes over a long-haul connection.

It's often comforting to get a directory listing before issuing a `get` or `put` command, so that you can have an idea of how long the copy will take.

The directory thicket

Every machine you can contact for FTP stores its files in many different directories, which means that to find what you want, you have to learn the rudiments of directory navigation. Fortunately, you wander around directories in FTP in pretty much the same way as you do on your own system. The command you use to list the files in the current directory is `dir`, and to change to another directory you use the command `cd`, as in this example:

```
ftp> dir
200 PORT command successful.
150 Opening ASCII mode data connection for /bin/ls.
total 23
drwxrwxr-x  19 root    archive     512 Jun 24 12:09 doc
drwxrwxr-x   5 root    archive     512 May 18 08:14 edu
drwxr-xr-x  31 root    wheel       512 Jul 12 10:37 systems
drwxr-xr-x   3 root    archive     512 Jun 25 1992 vendorware
... lots of other stuff ...
226 Transfer complete.
1341 bytes received in 0.77 seconds (1.7 Kbytes/s)
ftp> cd edu
250 CWD command successful.
ftp> dir
200 PORT command successful.
150 Opening ASCII mode data connection for /bin/ls.
total 3
 -rw-rw-r--   1 root    archive  87019 Dec 13 1996 R
 -rw-rw-r--   1 root    archive  41062 Dec 13 1996 RS
 -rw-rw-r--   1 root    archive 554833 Dec 13 1996 Rings
drwxr-xr-x   2 root    archive    512 May 18 09:31 administrative
drwxr-xr-x   3 root    archive    512 May 11 06:44 ee
drwxrwxr-x   8 root    234        512 Jun 28 06:00 math
226 Transfer complete.
200 bytes received in 63 seconds (0.0031 Kbytes/s)
ftp> quit
221 Goodbye.
```

In a standard UNIX directory listing, the first letter on the line tells you whether something is a file or a directory. `d` means that it's a directory — anything else is a file. In the directory `edu` in the preceding example, the first three entries are files, and the last three are other directories. Generally, you FTP to a host, get a directory listing, change to another directory, get a listing there, and so on until you find the files you want. Then you use the `get` command to retrieve them.

You often find that the directory on your machine in which you start the FTP program is not the one in which you want to store the files you retrieve. In that case, use the lcd command to change the directory on the local machine.

To review: cd changes directories on the other host; lcd changes directories on your own machine. (You may expect cd to change directories correspondingly on both machines, but it doesn't.)

What's that name again?

Sometimes on your machine, you have to give a file a name that's different from the name it has on a remote machine. (This statement is particularly true on DOS machines, on which many UNIX names are just plain illegal, as well as when you're retrieving Macintosh, Windows 95, or Windows NT files, which can contain spaces and special characters.) Also, if you need to get a bunch of files, it can be tedious to type all the get commands. Fortunately, FTP has work-arounds for both those problems. Suppose that you've found a file named rose and you want to download it as rose.gif because it contains a GIF-format image. First, make sure that you're in binary mode, and then retrieve the file with the get command. This time, however, you give two names to get — the name of the file on the remote host and the local name — so that it renames the file as the file arrives. You do this as shown in this interaction:

```
ftp> bin
200 Type set to I.
ftp> get rose2 rose2.gif
200 PORT command successful.
150 Opening BINARY mode data connection for rose2 (47935 bytes).
226 Transfer complete.
local: rose2.gif remote: rose2
47935 bytes received in 39 seconds (1.2 Kbytes/s)
```

Next, suppose that you want to get a bunch of the files that begin with ru. In that case, you use the mget (which stands for *m*ultiple *GET*) command to retrieve them. The names you type after mget can be either plain filenames or wildcard patterns that match a bunch of filenames. For each matching name, FTP asks whether you want to retrieve that file:

```
ftp> mget ru*
mget ruby? n
mget ruby2? n
mget ruger_pistol? n
mget rugfur01? n
mget rush? y
```

```
200 PORT command successful.
150 Opening BINARY mode data connection for rush (18257 bytes).
226 Transfer complete.
local: rush remote: rush
18257 bytes received in 16 seconds (1.1 Kbytes/s)
mget rush01? y
200 PORT command successful.
150 Opening BINARY mode data connection for rush01 (205738 bytes).
local: rush01 remote: rush01
205738 bytes received in 200.7 seconds (1.2 Kbytes/s)
mget rush02?
```

If you find that `mget` matches more files than you expected, you can stop it with the usual interrupt character for your system — typically Ctrl+C or Del:

```
^C
Continue with mget? n
ftp> quit
221 Goodbye.
```

You can even interrupt in the middle of a transfer if a file takes longer to transfer than you want to wait.

You also can do an *express* `mget`, which doesn't ask any questions and enables you to find exactly the files you want. To tell FTP not to ask you about each file, use the `prompt` command before you give the `mget` command, as this example shows:

```
ftp> prompt
Interactive mode off.
ftp> mget 92-1*
200 PORT command successful.
150 Opening BINARY mode data connection for 92-10.gz (123728 bytes).
226 Transfer complete.
local: 92-10.gz remote: 92-10.gz 123728 bytes received in 2.8 seconds
           (43 Kbytes/s)
200 PORT command successful.
150 Opening BINARY mode data connection for 92-11.gz (113523 bytes).
226 Transfer complete.
local: 92-11.gz remote: 92-11.gz 113523 bytes received in 3.3 seconds
           (34 Kbytes/s)
200 PORT command successful.
150 Opening BINARY mode data connection for 92-12.gz (106290 bytes).
226 Transfer complete.
local: 92-12.gz remote: 92-12.gz 106290 bytes received in 2.2 seconds
          (47 Kbytes/s)
```

Here's a file in your eye

Okay, now you know how to retrieve files from other computers. How about copying the other way? It's just about the same procedure, except that you use put rather than get. The following example shows how to copy a local file called rnr to a remote file called rnr.new:

```
ftp> put rnr rnr.new
200 PORT command successful.
150 Opening ASCII mode data connection for rnr.new.
226 Transfer complete.
local: rnr remote: rnr.new
168 bytes sent in 0.014 seconds (12 Kbytes/s)
```

(As with get, if you want to use the same name when you make the copy, leave out the second name.)

The mput command works just like the mget command does, only in the other direction. If you have a bunch of files whose names begin with uu and you want to copy most of them, issue the mput command, as shown in this example:

```
ftp> mput uu*
mput uupick? y
200 PORT command successful.
150 Opening ASCII mode data connection for uupick.
226 Transfer complete.
local: uupick remote: uupick
156 bytes sent in 0.023 seconds (6.6 Kbytes/s)
mput uupoll? y
200 PORT command successful.
150 Opening ASCII mode data connection for uupoll.
226 Transfer complete.
local: uupoll remote: uupoll
200 bytes sent in 0.013 seconds (15 Kbytes/s)
mput uurn? n
```

(As with mget, you can use the prompt command to tell it to go ahead and not to ask any questions.)

Most systems have protections on their files and directories that limit where you can copy files. Generally, you can use FTP only to put a file anywhere that you could create a file if you were logged in directly. If you're using anonymous FTP (see the section "No Names, Please," later in this chapter), you usually can't put any files to the other host.

A bunch of other file-manipulation commands are sometimes useful, as in this example of the `delete` command:

```
delete somefile
```

(Replace *somefile* with the name of the file you want to delete.) This command deletes the file on the remote computer, assuming that the file permissions enable you to do so. The `mdelete` command deletes multiple files and works like `mget` and `mput` do. The `mkdir` command makes a new directory on the remote system (again assuming that you have permissions to do so):

```
mkdir newdir
```

(Replace *newdir* with the name of the directory you want to make.) After you create a directory, you still have to use `cd` to change to that directory before you use `put` or `mput` to store files in it.

If you plan to do much file deleting, directory creation, and the like, it's usually much quicker to log in to the other system by using `telnet` (discussed in gory detail in Chapter 16) to do your work and using the usual local commands.

No Names, Please

The first part of this chapter shows you how to FTP to systems where you already have an account. What about the other 99.9 percent of the hosts on the Internet, where no one has ever heard of you?

You're in luck. On thousands of systems, you can log in with the username `anonymous`. For the password, enter your e-mail address. (This arrangement is strictly on the honor system — if you lie, they still let you log in.) When you log in for *anonymous FTP,* most hosts restrict your access to only certain directories that are allowed to anonymous users. You can hardly complain, though, because anonymous FTP is provided free, out of sheer generosity.

Hello, anonymous!

When you log in, you frequently get a friendly message, like this one:

```
230-  If your FTP client crashes or hangs shortly after login please try
230-  using a dash (-) as the first character of your password.  This will
230-  turn off the informational messages that may be confusing your FTP
```

(continued)

(continued)

```
230-  client.
230-
230-  This system may be used 24 hours a day, 7 days a week.  The local
230-  time is Wed Aug 12 12:15:10 1998.
230-
230-  You are user number 204 out of a possible total of 250.
230-
230-  All transfers to and from wuarchive are logged.  If you don't like
230-  this then disconnect now!
230-
230-  Wuarchive is currently a DEC Alpha AXP 3000, Model 400.  Thanks to
230-  Digital Equipment Corporation for their generous support of wuarchive.
230-
230-Please read the file README
230-  it was last modified on Sat May 17 15:02:13 1997 - 452 days ago
230 Guest login ok, access restrictions apply.
```

When you're logged in, you use the same commands to move around and retrieve files as you always do.

An FTP cheat sheet

Command	***Description***
`get` *old new*	Copies remote file *old* to local file *new;* can omit *new* if same name as *old*
`put` *old new*	Copies local file *old* to remote file *new;* can omit *new* if same name as *old*
`del` *xxx*	Deletes file *xxx* on remote system
`cd` *newdir*	Changes to directory *newdir* on the remote machine
`cdup`	Changes to next higher directory
`lcd` *newdir*	Changes to directory *newdir* on the local machine
`asc`	Transfers files in ASCII mode (use for text files)
`bin`	Transfers files in binary or image mode (all other files)
`quit`	Leaves FTP
`dir` *pat*	Lists files whose names match pattern *pat;* if no *pat,* lists all files
`mget` *pat*	Gets files whose names match pattern *pat*
`mput` *pat*	Puts files whose names match pattern *pat*
`mdel` *pat*	Deletes remote files whose names match pattern *pat*
`prompt`	Turn name prompting on or off in `mget` and `mput`

URLs for FTPing

URLs? Yikes! It's that three-letter acronym from Chapter 18. More than just a way to denote hypertext Web pages, URLs are ways of naming general Internet resources, including FTP sites. Here's the way you describe a file you can get over the Internet by using the `ftp` program:

```
ftp://hostname/pathname
```

Suppose that you see this URL:

```
ftp://rtfm.mit.edu/pub/net/
    internet.txt
```

That means to FTP to `rtfm.mit.edu`, move to the `/pub/net` directory, and get the `internet.txt` file.

Great Stuff on FTP

Hundreds of gigabytes of stuff are available for FTP, if you know where to find them. Before you start cruising FTP sites, however, here are a few words about strategy.

A word from those etiquette ladies again

Please recall that all *anonymous FTP* servers (hosts that enable you to log in for FTP without requiring that you have an account there) exist purely because someone feels generous. Any or all can go away if the provider feels taken advantage of, so remember these rules:

- Pay attention to restrictions on access times noted in the welcome message. Remember that servers are in time zones all over the world. If the server says to use it only between 6 p.m. and 8 a.m., but it's in Germany and you're in Seattle, you can use it between 9 a.m. and 11 p.m. your time.
- Do not upload material unless you're invited to. (And don't upload material inappropriate to a particular archive — we hope that this advice would be obvious, but experience suggests otherwise.)

A few words about navigation

All the FTP servers discussed in this chapter require you to log in using the username anonymous. For the password, use your e-mail address.

Many servers have a small file called readme that you should retrieve the first time you use the server. This file usually contains a description of the material that's available and the rules for using the server.

If you log in to an FTP server and don't see any interesting files, look for a directory called pub (for public). For reasons lost in the mists of history, UNIX systems by tradition put all the good stuff there.

The FTP Hit Parade

This section lists some available FTP systems, including the name and location of the system, particular rules for its use, and what's there.

UUNET

ftp.uu.net
UUNET Communications, Virginia
Accepts FTP only from hosts with registered names

UUNET is probably the largest archive available on the Internet. It has masses of software (mostly for UNIX in source form), archives of material posted on Usenet, files and documents from many publishers and vendors, and mirrors of many other archives around the Internet.

SIMTEL

Mirrored at wuarchive.wustl.edu, oak.oakland.edu, ftp.uu.net, nic.funet.fi, src.doc.ic.ac.uk, archie.au, and nic.switch.ch

SIMTEL, the premier archive for MS-DOS material, also has a great deal of stuff for Macs, CP/M (remember that?), and UNIX. SIMTEL itself was an ancient DEC-20 computer at an Army base in New Mexico. Although it has long since shut down, mirror systems are still available, and someone is still updating and maintaining the archive.

WUARCHIVE

wuarchive.wustl.edu
Washington University, Missouri

This large program and file archive includes mirrors of many other programming archives, with megabytes of stuff for DOS, Windows, Macintosh, and other popular computer systems. WUARCHIVE also contains the largest collection of GIF and JPEG pictures (all suitable for family viewing, by the way) on the Internet.

RTFM

rtfm.mit.edu
Massachusetts Institute of Technology, Massachusetts

RTFM is the definitive archive of all the *FAQ* (Frequently Asked Questions) messages on Usenet. Hence, RTFM is a treasure trove of information for everything from the state-of-the-art in data compression to how to apply for a mortgage to sources of patterns for Civil War uniforms. Look in the directories `pub/usenet-by-group` and `pub/usenet-by-hierarchy`.

RTFM also has an experimental Usenet address database, containing the e-mail address of every person who has posted a message to Usenet in the past several years. That database is in `pub/usenet-addresses`.

Because RTFM is an extremely popular site and limits itself to 50 simultaneous non-MIT connections, it can be extremely difficult to get into. Sometimes it has taken us several days.

INTERNIC

ftp.internic.net
Internet Network Information Center, Virginia

This central repository for information about the Internet includes copies of all the standards and RFC documents that define the network. Also, INTERNIC has information about many other FTP archives available on the Internet.

NSFNET

nic.nsf.net
National Science Foundation c/o MERIT, Michigan

The NSFNET is (or at least used to be) the largest backbone network on the Internet. It has a great deal of boring administrative stuff and some interesting statistics about how big the Internet is and how fast it's growing. Look in `statistics/nsfnet`.

NSF publications not related to the NSFNET can be found at `stis.nsf.gov`, or the mail server `stisserv@nsf.gov`.

The list of lists

sri.com
SRI International, California

Look in the directory `netinfo` for the file `interest-groups`. It's one of the largest available lists of public mailing lists on various topics. The contents of this list are published in book form and sold for about $25, but you can get it via FTP or e-mail for free!

Chapter 21

Now Serving the Internet

In This Chapter

- Getting yourself an Internet presence
- What domains are
- How to choose Web server software
- What you need to serve e-mail, FTP, and other cool Internet resources
- A few words about Webmastering

In the preceding few chapters, we tell you everything you ever wanted to know (more, probably) about how to use your UNIX computer to take advantage of popular Internet resources such as telnet, e-mail, newsgroups, FTP, and the World Wide Web. Well, you have something to offer the world yourself, dadgum it! You're wondering how all those *other* people got their stuff on the Internet, and whether you can do it, too.

Of *course* you can do it, too. With UNIX, in fact, you have ways to get yourself on the Internet rather inexpensively, assuming that your ambitions are modest. No matter what approach you end up taking, getting on the Internet is a matter of setting up, or at least getting access to, some kind of Internet *server*. To be more specific, you have to set up (or get someone else to set up for you) server programs for each kind of Internet resource you want to provide. If you want to serve your own e-mail, you need POP (Post Office Protocol) and SMTP (Simple Mail Transfer Protocol) servers. If you want your computer to act as a telnet site, you need a telnet server. If you want to make interesting files available for people to download to their own computers, you need an FTP server. If you want people to read your exquisite, erudite, and potentially moneymaking Web pages, you need a Web server.

In this chapter, we talk mostly about Web servers, not because we think that e-mail, telnet, FTP, and other non-Web resources are unimportant, but because full-featured Web servers like the ones we tell you about in this chapter usually come with all the software you need in order to set up those other Internet resources.

The Internet, at Your Service

What you do on the Internet is a function of who you are and what you want to accomplish. An Internet presence can be as simple as a set of Web pages that trumpet to the world your personal tastes in music and literature. It can be as complex as a full-fledged online catalog sales company, replete with shopping carts, virtual cashiers, automatic e-mail notification, password-protected customer accounts, and encryption capabilities to ensure secure transactions.

If you're interested in doing something as foolhardy, er, complex as setting up your own online catalog sales company, you need much more information than we have space to provide in this book about UNIX. Allow us to suggest *Selling Online For Dummies,* by Leslie Heeter Lundquist, as a good place to start. (It's from IDG Books Worldwide, so it *has* to be good.)

To make things as simple as possible, you have only two realistic approaches to getting yourself an Internet presence. The approach that's right for you depends on what you want to do, how much time and money you're willing to spend, and the height of your technical pain threshold:

- **Host your own site:** To host your own site, you need at least one dedicated computer, permanently connected to the Internet and running some brand of Web server software. Hosting your own site requires you to act as your own system administrator and Webmaster (the author and manager of your Web site). Although administering and maintaining your own Web site is not for the technically faint of heart, it's well within the powers of a mere mortal such as yourself. In exchange for the money you spend to buy the stuff you need and the time you spend to set everything up and keep it running, you get complete freedom and total control over whatever it is you want to do on the Internet. Because the permanent Net connection costs at least several hundred dollars per month, you probably don't want to choose this approach until you're sure that you're serious about your Web site.
- **Get someone to host your site for you.** In practice, that "someone" usually turns out to be an Internet service provider, or ISP. *ISPs* are the people who sell you basic Internet services, such as e-mail and Web access. Many ISPs also offer Web-hosting services: For a monthly fee, they do all the technical heavy lifting for you. If you don't need your own dedicated server, you can usually buy a few megabytes of space on one of your ISP's servers for about $20 a month (less, in some cases) and upload your Web pages via FTP.

A complete discussion of setting up your own Web site is well beyond the scope of this book. It's a book in it's own right, in fact. Nonetheless, in the following sections, we try to give you some pointers to get you started on the right foot.

Domainia

If your Web site supports a business or other official organization, you may want to consider applying and paying for your own domain name. *A domain name* is a unique name that identifies a computer or group of computers on the Internet. For example, we registered the domain name `gurus.com`, so our Web site is named `www.gurus.com` and our FTP site is named `ftp.gurus.com`. Registering a domain name costs $35 per year, and on top of that you need at least two separate servers — a main server and a backup server — with permanent Internet connections to qualify for a domain name. Your server has to have DNS (domain name system) software running on it so that it can respond to requests for a name in your domain. If you don't want to deal with the gory technical details, you can pay an Internet service provider to act as your domain server. (Most ISPs are only too happy to find a reason to take your money, and in this case it's probably money well spent.)

The part of a domain name to the right of the last dot is called the *zone*. A number of so-called generic domains also exist: `com` for profit-taking enterprises, `org` for nonprofit outfits, `gov` for the U.S. government, `edu` for educational institutions, are some examples. Two-letter country domains also exist — `fr` for France, `mx` for Mexico, and `us` for United States, for example.

The organization that handles generic domain name registrations is InterNIC. If you plan to register your own generic domain name, you send a form to InterNIC via e-mail. Complete instructions and registration forms are available from the InterNIC Web site, at `http://www.internic.net/`.

For a discussion of Webmastering that doesn't shy away from the gory details, see *Setting Up an Internet Site For Dummies*, 3rd Edition, by Jason Coombs, Ted Coombs, David Crowder, and Rhonda Crowder (IDG Books Worldwide, Inc.).

Serving Yourself

If you're hosting your own Web site, you have to have a computer with a permanent, dedicated connection to the Internet. The speed, or *bandwidth,* of your connection depends on such factors as how much traffic you expect your Web site to get and how much money you have to spend. For example, a full-time dial-up connection offering standard speeds of 28.8 to 56 kilobytes per second (a kilobyte is a thousand bytes) costs somewhere in the neighborhood of $100 a month. A T1 line, at 1.5 megabytes per second, is more than 25 times as fast as the fastest dial-up connection. As you may expect, a T1 line costs more than 25 times as much as dial-up connection. If you're serving a modest little Web site, a dial-up connection works just fine, thank you. If you're running your business online, you have to bite the bullet and get a T1 if you expect more than a few customers at any one time. (A T3 line gives you a speed of 45 megabits per second. These babies cost at least $10,000 a month, so we figure that you're not planning to run one to your home computer any time soon.)

After you have your connection squared away, you have to install the software that turns your computer into a Web server. A *Web server* is simply a computer that hosts Web pages. The Web server computer runs a program that fulfills requests from other computers for Web pages stored on the Web server's disks. A UNIX machine makes a great Web server because the Web was designed using UNIX programs.

For example, John has computer named `net.gurus.com` on the Internet. It runs Apache (an excellent choice on John's part because Apache is fast, reliable, and — most important — free). When you view the author team's Web site, at `http://net.gurus.com`, your computer sends a request for a Web page to the Apache program on `net.gurus.com`, and Apache sends the page back to your computer so that you can see it on your screen. Other popular Web servers include Netscape's and the NCSA server (Apache's grandfather). We talk more about UNIX Web servers later in this chapter.

After you've installed a Web server on your UNIX system, you tell the Web server the directory where the Web pages will be stored (the Web directory). You can store Web pages in that directory and its subdirectories. To make a Web page accessible to the world, you create the page with a Web-authoring program (or with any text editor), test it on your own system to avoid embarrassing typos, and move or copy the page to your Web directory. After the page is in the Web directory, anyone can see the page if they know its URL (Web address).

If you're learning about UNIX to be a Webmaster, you need to know how to

- Install, configure, and maintain your Web server program
- Create and modify Web pages

Getting Served

Suppose that you've decided to forego the expense and hassle of hosting your own site. You've opted to pay your Internet service provider a reasonable monthly fee (probably around $20) to give you some space on one of its Web servers. On your own computer, you create and store the Web pages you want to put out, or *post,* on the Internet. You can see them by using your own Web browser, although no one else can see them until you upload them to your ISP's server.

Usually, you upload your Web pages to a Web server by using FTP (see Chapter 20 to find out how to transfer files). Ask your Internet service provider (or whoever runs the Web server you are using) where to put your Web page files. Also ask whether you need to give any special commands to tell the Web server about your files.

Here are some tips for uploading Web pages:

- Because Web pages are text, you upload your Web pages as ASCII (not binary) files. Graphics files are not text, so upload them as binary files.
- UNIX cares about capitalization in filenames. If you create Web pages on a PC or Mac and upload them to a UNIX-based Web server, check the capitalization of your filenames.
- Name your main Web page with the name `index.html`, which is the default Web page name. If you omit the filename from a URL when you're retrieving a Web page, your Web browser usually gets the page `index.html`. For example, if someone types the URL `http://www.greattapes.com/`, the Web browser displays the `index.html` file on that computer.

Web Servers Galore

If you're hosting your own Web site, you have to get a Web server, install it, configure it, and keep it running. Choosing the UNIX Web server package that's best for you is a question of finding the right set of features at the right price. (In the case of Apache, the right price happens to be free.)

Some of the more comprehensive Linux distributions include, for free, a Web server along with server software for other Internet resources such as e-mail, news, and FTP. For example, Red Hat Linux 5.1 includes the Apache Web server, an e-mail server, a domain name server (for translating domain names into the IP addresses that network software needs), a news server, and an FTP server. Caldera's OpenLinux 2.1 includes the Netscape FastTrack Web server.

Apache is king

The Apache Web server is free and fast and popular. It runs on every UNIX you can think of, including Linux. (Versions for Windows 95 and Windows NT are also in the works.) In fact, it's the most popular Web server of any kind in use today. If you're on the Web, surf to the home page of the Apache HTTP Server Project, at `http://www.apache.org`, for all information and downloads. You can also check out *Apache Server For Dummies,* by Ken A.L. Coar (IDG Books Worldwide, Inc.).

Netscape is a many-splendored thing

Netscape, the maker of the popular Communicator and Navigator Web browsers, offers various Web servers that run on UNIX (see `http://home.netscape.com/servers/index.html` on the Web). Its flagship server, Enterprise Server, runs on Digital UNIX, HP-UX, AIX, IRIX, and Solaris (as well as Windows NT). Netscape Enterprise Server sets you back from $1,300 to $2,000, depending on the options you choose. If you want to serve e-mail and news along with the Web, you have to consider shelling out $4,100 for Netscape's SuiteSpot Standard edition. If you don't have that kind of money, the Netscape FastTrack server dispenses with all the bells and whistles (as well as with the Netscape FTP server) for only $300 — or for nothing, if you buy Caldera's OpenLinux. (Such a deal!)

A Web site named "hoohoo"

The National Center for Supercomputing Applications at the University of Illinois offers, for free, the famous NCSA HTTPd server (the most recent version of which is 1.5.2a). You can read about it and download it from the NCSA Web site, at `http://hoohoo.ncsa.uiuc.edu`. Although the HTTPd server is still popular, it's unsupported — in other words, you have no one to guarantee that it works or to bail you out if run into problems. It's also somewhat outdated because it sort of morphed into Apache after its creator left the University of Illinois.

A cup of Java

As you may expect, Sun Microsystems (the maker of the Solaris OS) has its own UNIX Web server, the Java Web Server, which runs on UNIX, Linux, Windows NT, and OS/2. You can check it out on the Web at `http://jserv.java.sun.com/products/webserver/index.html`.

Daemons Run Amok

Providing most Internet services is a matter of installing, configuring, and running daemons. A *daemon* is simply a program you configure, start up, and then forget about. It runs in the background, where you can't see it. The only time you have to deal with it is when something goes wrong with it (a mercifully rare occurrence) or when you want to change the way it behaves. We introduce daemons in Chapter 9, where we talk about the daemon that handles UNIX print jobs.

Some Internet resource servers, such as telnet and FTP, are standard parts of all UNIX distributions. Some UNIX (and Linux) distributions also include Internet servers for other resources, such as e-mail and news. In some cases, these servers are included with your Web server. If neither your UNIX nor Web server package includes the servers you need, you have to find or purchase them separately. Fortunately, free versions abound on Web sites and FTP sites on the Internet.

Here are a few tips about what you may need to help get you started:

- **E-mail:** If you want to serve your own e-mail, you need an SMTP server and a POP or IMAP server. *SMTP (Simple Mail Transfer Protocol)* defines the way computers pass a mail message to each other until it gets delivered to a user's mailbox. *POP (Post Office Protocol)* and *IMAP (Internet Mail Access Protocol)* define how the user who got the message retrieves it from the mailbox. Some mail clients require POP; others, such as Pine, require IMAP instead. The most popular, although not the best, SMTP server is called sendmail, and large books are devoted to its care and feeding.
- **Telnet and FTP:** Use the telnet and FTP daemons included in your UNIX or Linux distribution. Because security issues are always a major concern when you give unknown computers access to your computer, be vigilant about potential security breaches.
- **News:** Providing news requires that you set up an NNTP (Network News Transfer Protocol) server and news database. News servers are less frequently included with OS and Web server distributions. Fortunately, a number of free news servers are available for downloading, such as INN (Internet News Software Consortium, which is responsible for INN development, recently released as Version 2.0). Be forewarned: Hosting Usenet news requires a serious amount of disk space (3 gigabytes per week is in the ballpark) and enough bandwidth to handle the traffic (56K is the minimum).

Other resources you may consider providing are the highly addictive Internet Relay Chat, equally addictive games such as MUDs (Multi-User Dungeons) and MUSHes (Multi-User Shared Hallucinations), Gopher, and streaming video and audio. As with the basic services, you have to determine whether your OS or Web server package includes the server software you need.

A Few Tips for Webmasters

Now you've done it: You've gone ahead and decided to host your own Web site. You've registered a domain name, shelled out big bucks for computers and Internet connections, installed and configured server software, and even posted your first home page on the World Wide Web. Your job here is finished, right?

Not on your life. Your job is just beginning. For Web surfers, the beauty of the Internet is that it's available 24 hours a day, seven days a week. For Webmasters, the round-the-clock nature of the Internet can become a maintenance nightmare. If your site is down for a few hours or longer or if it goes down for short periods on a regular basis, you quickly lose your audience. If you're trying to run a business online, these types of outages can be disastrous.

Both the Apache and NCSA HTTPd servers are extremely reliable, which, along with being free, are good reasons to use them. Problems do occur, however, and you have to know how to recover from them quickly. Make sure that your backup server is an accurate copy, or *mirror,* of your main server so that you can cut over to it in case your main server fails. You should also make sure that you can log on to your computer from a remote location so that you can do server administration (troubleshooting, shutdowns, restarts) without having to be in the same room with your computer. Your vacation in Fiji will be ruined if the server running your catalog sales company quits working and you have to fly home to deal with it.

Often, problems with a Web site occur because of gremlins running around in your Web pages. *HTML,* the language you use to define your Web pages, is extremely literal and unforgiving. Make sure that you have a good HTML reference and a way to test your pages before casting them on the waters of the Web. The Netscape Communicator package has a graphical Web page program called Composer, which has an HTML editor that novice Web page designers may find easy to use. We recommend that you use a text editor with at least syntax highlighting to make your coding job easier (see Chapter 10 for some suggestions).

Our last tip is perhaps our most important: Whatever you do, keep it simple. Updating and maintaining your site's content is a big job. If you're going it alone, you have to become a graphics designer, writer, software developer, and system administrator all rolled into one — not an easy task for anyone. If you run into trouble, ask for help. Many people in situations similar to yours are only too happy to share with you their horror stories and hard-earned wisdom. A good place to look for help is Usenet, where you can find and communicate with UNIX Webmasters in newsgroups such as `comp.infosystems.www.servers.unix`. (See Chapter 19 for more information about Usenet, and Chapter 27 for a listing of UNIX-related newsgroups.)

Part V
Help!

The 5th Wave **By Rich Tennant**

©RICHTENNANT
THAT'S RIGHT, THE UPPER CASE BUTTON WORKS ON-SCREEN, BUT THEY'RE NOT COMING OUT ON THE DANG PRINTER! HOLD? SURE, I'LL HOLD.

Poet e.e. cummings makes his last service call.

In this part . . .

The point of this book is to help you when things go wrong. That's what makes it different from "good news" books that talk only about how everything *should* work in a perfect world. If you've read the first four parts of this book, you know that "good news" and "UNIX" rarely appear in the same sentence. This part of the book lists things that go wrong, error messages you may see, and what you can do about them.

Chapter 22
Disaster Relief

In This Chapter

- "My computer won't turn on"
- "My mouse is acting glitchy"
- "The network is gone"
- "These aren't my files!"
- "It's not listening!"
- Wrecked X
- "I give up"

The tiny, infinitesimal chance that you may run into some kind of problem with your computer always exists. The problem can be something major (such as losing the funniest interoffice memo you have seen in years) or minor (perhaps accidentally deleting the analysis you have spent two months creating). Some computer problems you can fix — some you can't. The situation is similar to cars: You can pump gas yourself and maybe change the oil, but when it's time to rebuild the engine, call for help. (We do, anyway.)

"My Computer Won't Turn On"

You come in to the office one morning, flip the switch on your computer, and nothing happens. Uh-oh. Lots of things could have happened:

- **Is your computer plugged in?** It sounds stupid, but we have had computer problems when the people who clean the office bumped their vacuum cleaners into the outlet all our equipment was plugged in to. If you're using a terminal or X terminal, this check applies to both the terminal and the computer.
- **Check the power-strip switch.** If the computer is plugged in to a power strip that has its own on-off switch, check that switch's position. People have been known to turn off the switch inadvertently with their toes.

- **Is the computer still attached?** Are the cables that connect the computer, keyboard, screen, and whatever else still connected? If your terminal is connected to a network, is the network cable firmly attached to the computer? Try wiggling it a little, even if it looks okay.
- **Does the rest of the office have power?** Plug a lamp into the same outlet as the computer and make sure that the lamp turns on. (True story: "Hello, help desk? My computer won't turn on." "Is it plugged in correctly?" "I can't tell. The power failed, and none of the lights work.")
- **Is the picture on the screen turned off?** The computer can be turned on, and the screen can even be on, but the picture on the screen can be dimmed. Fool with the brightness knob (remember where the knob was positioned when you started fiddling with it).
- **Does your computer have a screen-blanker program?** Press a key to make sure that a screen-blanker program hasn't blacked out your screen as a favor to you. (We like to press the Shift key because it has no other effect on the computer.) Moving the mouse a little also unblanks the screen.

If the problem isn't the power, it's probably not something you can fix yourself. Call your system administrator for help. Some component may have burned out. Stay calm — it does *not* mean that the files stored on your disk are gone. They are probably fine: Disks remember data perfectly well with the power off.

"My Mouse Is Acting Glitchy"

If you have a computer with a male mouse (a mouse with a ball underneath), dust or crumbs inside it can prevent the ball from rolling smoothly. Most mice with balls have a way to remove the ball for cleaning, usually by turning a plastic ring that surrounds the opening for the ball or by sliding the ring to the front or side. (We don't begin to suggest appropriate names for that ring.) Turn the mouse over so that the ball falls into your hand and not on the floor, gently wipe off the grit, and snap it all back together. Female mice (optical mice, with no balls) appreciate it if you occasionally wipe off the mouse pad with a tissue. Also, look at the bottom of your female mouse: If it's turned on and working, you should be able to see a little, red lamp through one of the openings.

"The Network Is Gone"

Trying to solve most network problems is not for the faint of heart. One thing you can try is to check the cables in the back of your computer. Is the network cable firmly attached to the computer? Try wiggling it a little, even if it looks okay. Otherwise, it's time to call in the experts.

"These Aren't My Files!"

Normally, when you log in, you start working in your home directory. If you type **cd**, you return to the home directory from whichever directory you may have roamed to.

If `cd` doesn't get you back home, you may not be who you think you are. Try typing **whoami** or **who am i**. If someone else's username appears, your computer thinks that that's who you are! A coworker may have logged in to your computer to do some work for a moment. Here are your options:

- Send some malicious e-mail, which will arrive looking as though your coworker sent it. Delete all her files that look important, and then log out and pretend that nothing happened.
- Log out without fouling anything up, and then log in as yourself. Type **logout.**

  Maybe you have to type **exit** or just press Ctrl+D. At any rate, when you see the login screen, log in as yourself.

Most courses in business ethics tell you that the second option is preferred by all except the slimiest of bottom-feeding MBAs, but the urge to send goofy e-mail is sometimes irresistible. ***Remember:*** You may be caught.

Wrecked X

If you use Motif or another X Window variant, now and then you may find your screen in a most peculiar state, one in which you can move the mouse pointer around, but none of the windows changes and you can't type anything in any windows. Often you can fix this problem by restarting the window manager, which is the program that controls which window gets what. Move the mouse pointer outside any window and click and hold the left or right mouse button (which one depends on which window manager you're using) to display the window manager menu. That menu should have an item such as "Restart mwm" or "Restart fvwm". Choose that option. With luck, everything will be fixed.

"It's Not Listening!"

The computer is on, you're working away, and suddenly it doesn't respond to anything you type. It's the Abominable Frozen Computer.

The computer is probably fine — it's a program that has frozen up. Try these things to try to get the program's attention:

- Press Esc a bunch of times.
- Press Ctrl+C a bunch of times.
- Press Ctrl+D a bunch of times.
- Press Ctrl+S and then Ctrl+Q a bunch of times. (You never know what will work.)
- If you are running Motif, CDE, or another X Windows-based system, see whether you can use the mouse to select another window or whether you can type a command or two in a shell window. If you can, you can probably arrange to murder the frozen program and start it up again (see the following section).
- If your window system is completely stuck, you can usually murder the window system and start it over again without having to restart your computer.

If your computer is on a network or has more than one terminal, you can ask a computer guru to kill the program. If you're feeling brave, you can kill the program yourself. When you kill a program, you lose any work you were doing in that program since the last time you saved data to the disk.

"I Give Up"

Sometimes discretion is the better part of valor (whatever that means). If you need to call for help, be sure to do the following:

- **Don't turn off the computer**. Unless flames are coming from the screen and threatening to engulf your entire office, this option is not a good idea.
- **Know the symptoms.** Be ready to tell someone what happened and which actions you took to fix the problem.
- **Know what has changed recently.** Did you install new software? Did you run something you have not run before? New things are always suspicious.
- If you call for help by phone, *call from within reach of your computer.* Your savior may want you to try a few maneuvers at the keyboard.

Chapter 23

The Case of the Missing Files

In This Chapter

- Four easy ways to lose files
- Some ways to get files back
- Three almost-as-easy ways not to lose files

Sooner or later, you will delete a file by mistake. Scratch that "later": Sooner than you think, you will delete a file by mistake. In far too many cases, you are out of luck, although you can do a few things to avoid disaster.

How You Clobber Files

Contrary to the usual image of UNIX users being radically technical and without a creative bone in their bodies, we submit that typical UNIX users are immensely creative: They can come up with a zillion inventive ways to avoid the computer altogether and, when they are forced to sit down to stare the computer in the face, they can come up with a dozen more inventive reasons for why things went wrong. UNIX programmers have written thousands of useful freeware and shareware programs, when they should have been getting some work done. You can make files disappear in lots of ways (either intentionally or accidentally). This section lists the four main ways you can trash files — although you can probably come up with a dozen new and creative ways to do the vanishing act with your files.

Clobbering files with `rm`

Because disks are not infinitely large, sooner or later you have to get rid of some files. (Some wag once commented that the only thing that's standard among UNIX systems is the message-of-the-day reminding users to delete unneeded files.)

The normal way to get rid of files is the rm (for *r*emove) command. Until (notice that we didn't say *unless*) you screw up, rm removes only what you want it to. Recall that you tell rm the names of the files you want to remove:

```
rm thisfile thatfile somedir/anotherfile
```

You can remove more than one file at a time, and you can specify files in other directories (rm removes just the file and not the directory).

This method is usually pretty safe. The tricky part comes when you use wildcards. If you use a word processor that leaves backup files with names ending in .bak, for example, you can get rid of all of them with this command:

```
rm *.bak
```

That's no problem — unless you put in an extra space *(Do not type this line!)*:

```
rm * .bak
```

Note the little, tiny space between the asterisk and the dot. In response to this command, UNIX says

```
rm: .bak non-existent
```

Uh-oh. UNIX decided that you wanted to delete two things: * and .bak. Because the asterisk wildcard matches every single filename in the working directory, every single filename in the working directory is deleted. Then UNIX tries to delete a file named .bak, which isn't there. Bad move.

At this point, we recommend that you panic, gnash your teeth, and throw Nerf balls at the computer. After you calm down a little, read the rest of this chapter for some possible ways to get your files back.

You can also make slightly less destructive but still aggravating mistakes when you forget just which files you have. Suppose that you have files named section01, section02, and so on, up to section19. You want to get rid of all of them, so you type this line:

```
rm sec*
```

Now suppose that you forgot that you have a file named second.version, which you want to keep. Oops. Bye-bye, second.version.

The obvious solution is to delete things one at a time. Unless you're an extremely fast and steady typist, however, that's not practical. In the following sections, we make some suggestions about that, too.

Clobbering files with `cp`*,* `mv`*, and* `ln`

Are you feeling paranoid yet, as though every time you press the R and M keys you're going to blow away a year's worth of work? Wait — it gets worse.

The `cp`, `mv`, and `ln` commands can also clobber files by mistake: If you use one of these programs to copy, rename, or link a file (respectively) and a file already has the new name, the existing file gets clobbered. Suppose that you type this command:

```
mv elbow armpit
```

If you already had a file named `armpit` — *blam!* It's gone! The same thing happens if you copy or link. Copying is a *little* different: Here's an example of the most annoying case of blasting away good files with trash when you use the copy command:

```
cp important.file.save important.file
```

As a responsible and paranoid computer user, you want to save a copy of an important file before you make some changes. But your fingers work a little faster than your brain and you get the two names switched (left-handed users are particularly prone to getting names sdrawkcab) — and *blam!* (again) you've just copied an obsolete saved version over the current version. Fortunately, you can arrange your file-saving habits to make this kind of mistake harmless, or at least mostly harmless.

Creaming files by using redirection

A third popular way to blow away valuable files is by using redirection. If you *redirect* the output of a command to a file that already exists, whammo! UNIX blows away the existing file and replaces it with your redirected output.

For example, if you type this command:

```
ls -al > dirlist
```

and you already have a file named `dirlist`, it's gone now, replaced by the new listing.

If you use the BASH shell, you can give this command:

```
noclobber=1
```

If you use the C shell, you can give this incantation:

```
set noclobber
```

Better yet, get a UNIX wizard to help you include this command in your `.cshrc` or `.profile` file so that the command is given automatically every time you start the shell. This command tells the shell to *ask* you before using redirection to clobber files.

When you redirect output to a file, you can tell UNIX to add the output to the end of an existing file. Rather than type one >, you type two:

```
ls -al >> dirlist
```

You have little reason not to use >> every time you think of using >.

Wrecking files with text editors

The fourth way you're likely to smash files is in a botched editor session. The problem usually comes up after you have been editing a file for a while and realize that you have screwed up: The changes you have made are not what you want, so you decide to leave the editor. On the way out, however, you write the botched changes to the disk and wreck the original file. A similar problem occurs when you use an editor to look at a file: Although you may not intend to change anything, you may make some inadvertent changes anyway. (This can easily happen in `emacs`, where pretty much anything you type goes straight into the file.) If you're not careful, you can write the changes to the disk by mistake.

If you use `vi`, you can avoid the accidental-clobber problem by typing **view** rather than **vi**. The `view` editor is the same as the `vi` editor (`vi` and `view` are links to the same program). The `view` editor works the same as `vi` except that it doesn't let you write changes to the file. Keep it in mind.

Although some versions of `emacs` can mark files as read-only so that you can't make changes to the files, the methods of doing so aren't entirely standardized. In GNU Emacs, you press Ctrl+X, Ctrl+R in a file window, and Emacs puts an inscrutable `%%` on the status line at the bottom of the screen. To be even more careful, you can press Ctrl+X and then Ctrl+R to open a file as read-only in the first place.

Ways to Try to Get Files Back

Now you've done it: You've clobbered something important, and you really, *really* want it back. Let's see what you can do.

If you're used to other systems, such as Windows 95, in which you can magically get deleted stuff back from the Recycle Bin, we're sorry to tell you that UNIX doesn't let you do that (unless you're lucky enough to be using a UNIX desktop with a Trash tool; see the sidebar in Chapter 4 about talkin' trash). If it's gone, it's gone. (A version of the Norton Utilities that includes an unerase command is available for some versions of UNIX, although it isn't widely used.)

Copies, copies, everywhere

Maybe you have stashed away in a different directory other copies of the file you deleted. For our important files, we stick copies in a directory named `save` (or something similar). Also, sometimes you can reconstruct the information from a different form. If you clobber a word processor file, for example, you may have a backup version (the `.bak` files mentioned earlier in this chapter) that's close to the current version. You may have printed the deleted file to a file (rather than directly to the printer) and can edit the print file back into document form.

If you share your computer with other people or use a network, see whether someone else has a copy. It's a rare file that exists in only one place.

Call in the backup squad

It's really gone, huh? Now it's time for the final line of defense: backups. You *do* have backups, don't you?

We interrupt this chapter for a stern lecture: *Always make backups.* If your system administrator is on the ball, tape backups are made automatically every night. All you have to do is go to the administrator, with chocolate-chip cookies in hand, and ask politely for some help in getting your valuable file back from the previous night's backups. If no backups exist, it's fair to jump up and down and scream that someone had better get on the ball.

Seriously, backups are a standard part of any administrator's job, by either making the backups personally or overseeing operators who do the backing up. (After the procedures are set up, making backup tapes is so simple that you can practically train your dog to do it. One reason that it sometimes doesn't get done is that backing up is boring.)

Why you need backups

Making backups is a pain. The question isn't *whether* you will lose data — it's *when.* Here are some events that have sent us heading for the backup tapes:

- The obvious one: We deleted a file by mistake.
- Just as we were saving a file, the power failed and scrambled both the old and new versions of the file. Yikes!
- One day, while working on the insides of the computer (one of us is a closet nerd), we accidentally dropped a screwdriver on the disk controller. Exciting sparks came out and fried the controller card that attaches the disk to the rest of the computer. We got a new controller card and found that, although the disk was physically fine, the new controller wasn't quite compatible with the old one, and we had to reformat the disk and restore everything from tape.
- We remembered hearing that we should absolutely, positively run a "disk-head parking" program before moving our hard disk, so we ran one. Unfortunately, it was a version that was incompatible with the hard disk, so it parked the disk head right off the edge of the disk, way out past what you may call the Long-Term Parking Area. We could hear the disk head banging on the side of the hard disk as it tried to get back on. Rats!
- Back in the good old days, computers weighed about 15,000 pounds and you needed a forklift to move one. Now they weigh about 25 pounds, which means that if the cleaning people bump into one with a vacuum cleaner, they can knock it over with a clunk that can put an unreadable ding into the disk. Oops — sorry, lady.

Although you probably have horror stories of your own, they all have the same moral: Make those backups.

If your system administrator doesn't make backups, you had better learn how to do it yourself. If you have a tape unit on your machine, the procedure is usually as follows:

1. **Put a tape in the tape unit and flip the latch to seat the tape firmly.**
2. **Give a command to copy files to the tape, usually the `tar` (*t*ape *ar*chive) or `pax` (*p*ortable *a*rchive e*x*change) program.**

   On Sun workstations, the program is `bar` (*b*ackup *ar*chive). The exact things you have to say to the `tar` program vary from one system to another, mostly because of the peculiarities of different kinds of tape units. You can't use the regular `cp` command because tapes aren't logically organized the same way disks are. This process can take awhile — maybe an hour for a largish disk.
3. **Take the tape out of the tape unit.**

4. **Write the current date on the label so that you know that it's a current backup.**

   (The sensibly paranoid alternate several tapes, in case one of them goes bad. We describe this subject in more detail in the "Backup strategies" sidebar, later in this chapter.)

5. **Put the tape back in its box, and put the box back on the shelf.**
6. **Once a week (or some other frequency), take the backup tape and store it off-site, such as in another office or at someone's house or, if you're really serious, in your safe-deposit box. (We do that.)**

The usual way to back up stuff on Linux is to use `tar`. To back up to tape, type this fabulously memorable command:

```
tar cvf /dev/rft0 *
```

The `cvf` means Create, Verbose Report, to File, and `/dev/rft0` is the name of the tape unit. The * means to back up all the files in your directory; if you have a large number of them, you can list specific files and directories instead.

Some systems don't have tapes; they have disks. Disks are a major pain for backup use for two reasons: You need a stack of them, and you must format them first.

Before you can use a disk, you must format it, which means that the computer writes some bookkeeping junk on it to mark where to put the data and in the process checks to be sure that no bad spots are on the disk. Fortunately, you have to do this only one time per disk. Formatting disks is easy but tedious and (sing along with us as we say this) varies, of course, from one system to another. You stick the blank disk in the computer and type the formatting command, and UNIX formats it. If you're stuck with disk backups, ask your administrator for help in setting up the procedure, and while you're feeding all the disks into the drive, consider getting a tape drive.

If you back up to disks, type this line in Linux:

```
tar cvMf /dev/fd0 *
```

The `M` means *m*ultiple disks because you can't put much stuff on one disk. Linux tells you when to swap disks. Be sure to write the backup date and the disk number on each disk so that they don't get out of order.

If you have a large number of files, copying everything to tape can take awhile (perhaps an hour or so). You may want to do the backup over lunch. Or do what we do, and have your administrator arrange to run the `tar` program automatically every morning at about 3 a.m. We leave a tape in the tape unit every night. When we come back the next morning, the backup has been done, and we take the tape out and put it away. The tar command creates a report that is e-mailed to us so that we can check to see whether the tape was written correctly.

Thank goodness it's backed up!

Getting stuff back from a tape also involves the use of tar but is somewhat trickier because you want to restore just the files you clobbered. Ask for help — at least the first time. Generally speaking, you put the tape in the drive in the same way you did to make the backup, and then you type a tar or pax command similar to one of these:

```
tar xvf /dev/tape somedir/clobberedfile
pax -rv -f /dev/tape somedir/clobberedfile
```

In the tar command, xvf stands for e*x*tract *v*erbosely *f*rom. In the pax command, -rv -f similarly means *r*ead *v*erbosely *f*rom. Either way, the command is followed by the name of your tape drive (it's often /dev/tape, except on Linux, where it's usually /dev/rft0) and the name of the file to look for. The tape spins as tar or pax runs down the tape looking for the file you want. When it finds the file, it reads the file to the disk, reports that it did so, and stops. If you clobbered a bunch of files, you can use wildcards:

```
tar xvf /dev/tape "somedir/*"
pax -rv -f /dev/tape "somedir/*"
```

You have to use quotation marks around the wildcards because the files to match are on the tape, where tar or pax can find them, not on the disk where the shell (which normally handles wildcards) can find them.

To restore files on Linux from a tape, type

```
tar xvf /dev/rft0 "somedir/*"
```

To restore from disks, type

```
tar xvMf /dev/fd0 "somedir/*"
```

If you want to see which files are on the tape and not restore any of them just now, use one of these commands:

```
tar tvf /dev/tape
pax -v -f /dev/tape
```

You should try to run the restore command from the same directory where the program that made the backup tape ran. If it's a system backup, that's probably the root directory (/).

Backup strategies

The obvious way to do tape backups is to copy the entire contents of the disk to a tape every night. Here are a couple reasons, however, that it may not be the best approach:

- The disk may contain too much stuff to fit on a tape. Tape and disk manufacturers continually battle to see which one can outstrip the other. The battle is evenly matched — as we write, they're both in the 4 gigabyte (4,000 megabyte) range, although many people are still using 150MB tapes, which are smaller than most disks on UNIX systems.
- Because you may not notice for a day or two that you clobbered something important, a scheme that gives you a few days' grace to get your data back would be nice.
- Murphy's Law says that the system will fail as it's writing a backup tape, so you had better not depend on one tape.

The best scheme is a combination of rotating and incremental backups. With *rotating backups,* a set of tapes is used in rotation; five tapes, for example, one written every Monday, one every Tuesday, and so on. Because each tape is written only once a week, if you delete a file by mistake on Tuesday, for example, the file is still on the Monday tape until the following Monday. You then have nearly a week to realize that it's gone and get it back. The number of tapes you use depends on your budget and your paranoia. Some people use as few as two, some as many as seven. (We use four because we bought a four-pack of tapes.)

With *incremental backups,* you back up only what has changed. Generally, you do a full backup of everything on the disk at infrequent intervals — once a month, for example. This process may take five or six tapes, but because you do it only once a month, it's not that bad of a job. For the daily incremental backup, you back up only what has changed since the last full backup (it should fit on a single tape). Any given file is then either on the full backup (if it hasn't changed in a long time) or on the current backup, so you have only two places to look.

If you have a large tape budget, you may want to have two sets of tapes you use alternately for full backups, in case your system fails while it is writing the full backups. Sometimes full backups are stored off-site in a bank vault or other safe place, but a trade-off exists: the security of the vault versus the inconvenience of going to the bank when you need to recover a file. If you're paranoid, you can have two full backups: one off-site and one on-site.

Your system administrator should handle all this, of course. It's useful to understand at least the rudiments of backup theory, however, so that when the administrator hands you several different tapes that may contain your file, you understand why.

Three Ways Not to Lose Files

Now you're probably quaking in your boots (or sandals, depending on where you live). You figure that, if you so much as touch the keyboard, you will do horrible, irreparable damage and spend the next week spinning tapes. It's not that bad. This section tells you some tricks to avoid deleting files by mistake in the first place.

Are you sure you wanna clobber this one?

When you delete files with `rm`, use the `-i` (for *i*nteractive) switch:

```
rm -i s*
```

This line tells `rm` to ask you before it deletes each file, prompting you with the filename and a question mark. You answer y if you want to delete it, and anything else to tell UNIX not to delete. (Remember that the question UNIX asks is, "Should I delete this?" and not "Do you want to keep this?")

The main problem with `-i` is that it can become tedious when you want to delete a large number of files. When you do that, you probably use wildcards. To be safe, check that the wildcards refer to the files you think they do. To make that check, use the `ls` command with the same wildcard. If you want to delete all the files that start with *section,* for example, and you think that you can get away with typing only *sec* and an asterisk, you had better check what *sec** refers to. First give this command:

```
ls sec*
```

UNIX responds with an appropriate list:

```
second.version  section04  section08  section12  section16
section01       section05  section09  section13  section17
section02       section06  section10  section14  section18
section03       section07  section11  section15  section19
```

Hey, look! There's that file `second.version`. You don't want to delete it, so it looks like you have to type **section*** to get the correct files in this case.

Idiotproofing save files

The best way to make temporary backup copies of files is to make a directory named `save` and put all saved copies of files there, as shown in this example:

```
mkdir save
cp important.file save
```

These commands tell UNIX to make a directory named `save` and then to make a copy of `important.file` to `save/important.file`. If you reverse the order of the names, nothing happens. Suppose that you type this line instead:

```
cp save important.file
```

UNIX makes this observation:

```
cp : <save> directory
```

UNIX is saying that you can copy a file to a directory but that you can't copy a directory to a file. As a result, UNIX doesn't copy anything. To copy a file back from the `save` directory, you have to use its full name: `save/important.file`.

A variation of this process is a two-step delete. Suppose that you have a bunch of files you want to get rid of but some good files are mixed in the same directory. Make a directory named `trash`, and then use `mv` to move to the trash directory the files you plan to delete:

```
mkdir trash
mv thisfile thatfile these* trash
mv otherfile somefile trash
```

Then use the `ls` command to check the contents of `trash`. If something you want is in that directory, move it back to the current directory by using this command:

```
mv trash/these.are.still.good .
```

(The dot at the end means to put the file back in the current directory.) After you're sure that nothing other than trash is in `trash`, you can use `rm` with the `-r` option:

```
rm -r trash
```

This line tells `rm` to get rid of `trash` and everything in it.

Don't write on that!

Another thing you can do to avoid damage to important files is to make them read-only. When you make files read-only, you prevent `cp` and text editors from changing them. You can still delete them, although `rm`, `mv`, and `ln` ask you before doing so. The `chmod` command changes the "mode" of a file (as explained in the section "If Mom Says No, Go Ask Dad" in Chapter 5). Here's how to use `chmod` to make a file read-only:

```
chmod -w crucial-file
```

The `-w` means *not writable.* To make changes to the file later, do another `chmod` but use `+w` instead. (This stuff doesn't involve inspired command syntax, but the old syntax was even worse and used octal digits.) After a file is made not writable, editors can't change it. The `vi` program and some versions of emacs even display a note on-screen that the file is read-only. If you try to delete it, rm, mv, or ln asks you in a uniquely user-hostile way whether that's really what you had in mind. Suppose that you type the following line and crucial-file is a read-only file:

```
rm crucial-file
```

UNIX responds with this line:

```
crucial-file: 444 mode ?
```

The number may not be 444: It may be 440 or 400 (depending on whether your system administrator has set things up so that people can normally see the contents of other people's files). As with rm -i, you type **y** if you want to delete the file, or anything else to say that you don't want to delete this valuable data.

Chapter 24

Some Programs Just Won't Die

In This Chapter

- Killing a process with a keystroke or two
- Killing a process by using the `ps` command
- Bringing dead terminals to life

You can almost always get rid of recalcitrant programs without rebooting. In this chapter, we talk about how to figure out which processes you have and how to make unwanted ones go away. Before reading this chapter, be sure that you've read Chapter 13, where we talk about how you can juggle processes and do neat tricks, such as stop one program, run another one, go back to the first one, and pick up exactly where you left off.

Why Killing Is Sometimes Justified

Why kill a process? Don't even the smallest processes deserve to live?

In a word, no. Sometimes a program hangs, and your computer just sits there, inert. Or sometimes a program get stuck in some kind of loop and never ends. Or sometimes you give the wrong command and realize that you don't want to run that program after all. To stop the process in which the program is running, you kill the process.

Suppose that you're running along, minding your own business, and you find that you have a program that just won't stop. Vell, ve haff vays to make eet stop. First, we discuss the normal ways to kill a process, and then we get into some serious artillery.

What Process? (Reprise)

In Chapter 13, in the section about whether any processes are in the house, we tell you how to use the `ps` command to see which processes you have running. In case you're too weak from struggling with UNIX to turn back to Chapter 13, just type the **ps** command to see a list of your processes. Note the PID (*p*rocess *ID*) of the process you want to kill. You can identify which process is the one that needs to be offed, because `ps` shows you the command line that started each process.

Fifty Ways to Kill Your Process

The usual way to get rid of a process is to press the *interrupt character,* which is usually Ctrl+C, although sometimes it's Delete. In most cases, the rogue program gives up peaceably and you end up back in the shell. Sometimes, though, the program arranges to handle Ctrl+C itself. If you use the `ed` editor (if you're a masochist) and you press Ctrl+C, for example, `ed` returns to command mode rather than give up and throw away any work you have done. To exit `ed`, you have to use the `q` command.

If the interrupt character doesn't work, you can up the ante and use the *quit character,* generally Ctrl+ \ (a reverse slash or backslash — not the regular forward slash). The quit character not only kills the program but also saves the dead body of the process (this description is awfully morbid, but we didn't invent these terms) in a file named, for arcane historical reasons, `core` (or maybe *programname*`.core`). The shell then gives this requiem:

```
Quit (core dumped)
```

This message tells you that the process is dead and that its body has been put on ice with the filename `core`.

Most programs that catch Ctrl+C give up under the greater onslaught of Ctrl+ \. If the program you were running is one written locally, your system administrator may appreciate your saving the `core` file, because it includes clues about what was going wrong when you killed the program. Otherwise, delete any `core` files with `rm` because they're a waste of space.

Because a program can immunize itself to Ctrl+ \ (`ed`, for example, just ignores it), the next possibility is the *stop character* (always Ctrl+Z). The stop character doesn't kill the program, it just puts it to sleep and returns you to the shell. (See Chapter 13 for more information about what Ctrl+Z really does and how it can be useful even with programs you like.) After you're back in the shell, you can apply the stronger medicine described in the following section.

For Ctrl+Z to work, your shell must do some of the work. Many versions of the Bourne shell aren't up to it and ignore Ctrl+Z. The C, BASH, and Korn shells are Ctrl+Z-aware.

Dirty Deeds, Done Dirt Cheap

No more Mister Nice Guy: It's time for merciless slaughter. If you were successful in the preceding section at putting the process to sleep with Ctrl+Z, go ahead and kill it with the procedure in this section.

All the following techniques require that you have a terminal or window in which you can type some commands to do the dirty deeds. If Ctrl+Z didn't work to put the process to sleep, you may not have a shell prompt at which to type the requisite commands. Here are other places you can type the commands to kill the process:

- If you're running X Windows, any window other than the one with the stuck program will do.
- Otherwise, you may have to find another terminal attached to your computer or go to another computer on the network and use telnet or `rlogin` to get into your computer.
- If no other terminal or window is available and you have no other way into the machine, you're out of luck and probably have to reboot. Before you reboot, check with your system administrator, who may know some other tricks.

This simple two-step procedure murders a rogue process:

1. **Find out the rogue process's true name.**
2. **Utter the true name in an appropriate spell to murder it.**

The true name of a process is its PID, one of the things `ps` reports. First do a `ps` command to find out the PID of your victim. To find out the PID, follow these steps:

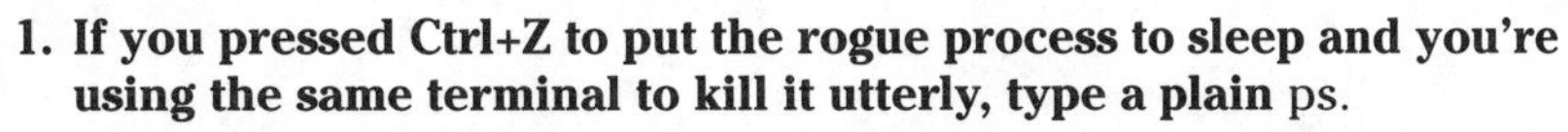

1. **If you pressed Ctrl+Z to put the rogue process to sleep and you're using the same terminal to kill it utterly, type a plain** ps.

   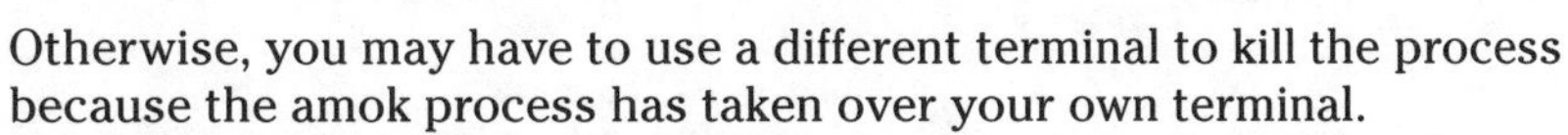

   Otherwise, you may have to use a different terminal to kill the process because the amok process has taken over your own terminal.

2. **In this case, you have to tell** `ps` **which user's processes you want to see. If you use Linux, type this command:**

   ```
   ps -u username
   ```

Replace *username* with your own login name so that you see the processes you're running.

If you use System V, type this command:

```
ps -fu username
```

If you use BSD, type

```
ps -a
```

Suppose that you see the following listing after typing `ps -fu johnl`, which lists all the processes for user `johnl` (the listing is shortened to save space):

```
UID    PID   PPID  C  STIME   TTY   TIME COMMAND
johnl  24806 24799 0  Jan 18  ?     0:39 xclock
```

The PID of the process you want to kill is 24806. You kill it by typing the `kill` command:

```
kill 24806
```

The normal type of kill sends a request to a process: "Please, nice Mr. Process, would you be so kind as to croak?" Although this method usually works, occasionally a program doesn't take the hint. Another kind of kill, the ominously named Number-Nine kill, offers the victim no choice. Type this command:

```
kill -9 24806
```

If you stop a particularly uncooperative program with Ctrl+Z, a regular `kill` may provoke it to retaliate by trying to take over your terminal (something the shell, fortunately, prevents). The following example shows a true-life transcript of our attempts to murder our old text editor pal, `ed`. First, we pressed Ctrl+Z, which put it to sleep. Then we tried a regular `kill`. When `ed` tried to strike back, we did a Number Nine. Sayonara, Bud.

```
% ed badfile
?badfile
Ctrl-Z
Stopped
% ps
   PID TTY      TIME COMMAND
 12746 ttyp1    0:00 ed
 12747 ttyp1    0:00 ps
 11643 ttyp1    0:02 -csh
% kill 12746
?
[1]  + Stopped (tty input)    ed badfile
% kill -9 12746
[1]    Killed                 ed badfile
```

Resuscitating a terminal

If you blow away a program that reads a character at a time from your terminal, such as vi or emacs, the dead process leaves your terminal in a rather peculiar state that makes it hard to get any work done. The following three-step method usually brings the terminal back:

1. **Press Ctrl+J.**

   The shell may complain about strangely named nonexistent commands. Ignore its whining.

2. **Type stty, a space, and sane (as opposed to the insane state your terminal is in). Press Enter.**

   You may not see anything on-screen. Remain calm.

3. **Press Ctrl+J again.**

   This step should put your terminal back into a usable state.

When X Goes Bad

If you're using X Windows in any of its multiple guises (particularly Motif) on a workstation or PC running UNIX and are especially unlucky, X itself may freeze the entire screen. If you can get into your computer through another terminal or a network, you can get rid of X Windows. Doing so makes all the programs using X go away so that you have to log in all over again. The trick is to figure out which program is X Windows. Here's an edited ps report from a System V system:

```
UID    PID   PPID  C  STIME  TTY   TIME  COMMAND
johnl 24788 19593  0  Jan 18  vt01  0:00  /usr/bin/X11/xinit
johnl 24789 24788  5  Jan 18  ptmx  38:10 Xgp :0
```

In this case, X is called Xgp because the particular computer happened to have a graphics processor running the screen.

Here's the equivalent from a Sun workstation:

```
PID TT STAT TIME   COMMAND
224 co IW   0:00   /bin/sh /usr/openwin/bin/openwin
228 co IW   0:00   /usr/openwin/bin/xinit -- /usr/openwin/bin/xnews :0
229 co S  149:23   /usr/openwin/bin/xnews :0 -auth /usr/johnl/.xnews
```

You can find out which process is X in two easy ways:

- The command line has the strange code `:0`, which turns out to be X-ese for "the screen right there on the computer."
- The amount of computer time used (in the `STAT` column) is large because X is, computationally speaking, a pig.

After you figure out which process is X, you can give it the old Number-Nine kill and probably be able to log back in.

If you're using an X terminal, the Number-Nine kill doesn't apply because X itself runs in the terminal and not in the main computer. In this case, you kill X by restarting the X terminal. In the worst case, you turn the terminal off and back on, although your system administrator can probably tell you an easier way.

Chapter 25

"My Computer Hates Me"

In This Chapter

- Lots of error messages
- What they mean
- What to do about them

Question: You type a command. UNIX says something incomprehensible. What does it mean? What should you do?

Answer: Look in this chapter for the error message. We tell you what the message means and what you can do to fix the problem.

Most error messages start with the name of the command you tried to use. If you want to use the cp command to copy a file, for example, but you spell the name of the file incorrectly, cp can't find a file with the name you typed, so it says something like this:

```
cp: No such file or directory
```

At the beginning of the line is the name of the command that failed to work. After the colon comes the UNIX error message — UNIX's attempt to explain the problem.

This chapter contains the most common error messages, in alphabetical order. In some of our explanations, we refer to things called *arguments,* not because we are feeling argumentative but because that's the technical name for the information you type on the command line after the command. Suppose that you type this line:

```
cp proof.that.elvis.lives save
```

cp is the command, proof.that.elvis.lives is the first argument, and save is the second argument. You can have lots of arguments on the line: The number you need depends on the command you use (cp requires two). Type a space between arguments.

UNIX also has things called *options,* which tell the command how you want it to work. Options always start with a hyphen (-). Suppose that you type this line:

```
ls -l
```

The `-l` tells the `ls` command how you want it to display the files. Options don't count as arguments. If you type this line:

```
ls -l *
```

the `-l` is an option, and `*` is the first (not the second) argument.

This stuff is nitpicky, but, if UNIX complains about a particular argument or option, knowing exactly which item it doesn't like comes in handy.

And now (drum roll, please), the error messages!

Arg list too long

Meaning: The list of *arguments* (stuff on the command line after the name of the command) is too long.

Probable cause: When you type a wildcard character as part of a filename or pathname, UNIX replaces it with the list of filenames and then calls the command. If you go wild with the asterisks, the result is a very long list. The list can be more than 5,000 characters long, so it's unlikely that you typed too long a list of filenames, unless you're an unusually fast typist.

Example: You are in the root directory (/) and type this line:

```
ls */*
```

If a large number of files is in the root directory and its subdirectories, `*/*` turns into a really long list.

Solution: Check the wildcards you used in the command, and use fewer of them.

Newer versions of UNIX allow much longer argument lists than older ones did. If you're using a modern system, such as Linux or BSD/OS, and get this message, something strange is probably going on.

Broken pipe

Meaning: You are running two programs connected by a pipe, and the program at the receiving end of the pipe exited before it received all its data (refer to Chapter 7).

Probable cause: You get this error occasionally when you use a pipe (|) to redirect the output of a program into the `more` program and then press q to cancel the `more` program before you see all the output. The program has no place to put its output because you canceled the `more` program, so you get this error. In this case, it's harmless.

Example: You type this line:

```
man furgle | more
```

The `man` program (which displays frequently incomprehensible UNIX manual pages) shows you screen after screen of boring information. You press q to cancel the `more` program, but the `man` program gives you the error message.

Solution: Nothing to do — it's not really an error!

Cannot access

See the section "No such file or directory," later in this chapter.

Cross-device link

See the section "Different file system," later in this chapter.

Device or resource busy

Meaning: A device, such as a terminal or printer, is in use by another program.

Probable cause: Sometimes you see this message when you try to use `cu` or `tip` to access a terminal that's already in use by another program or user.

Example: You type this line:

```
cu somesystem
```

Solution: Wait until the other user finishes.

Different file system

Meaning: You're using the `ln` command to create a link to a file in a different file system (a different disk or a disk on a different computer).

Probable cause: If your system can't do soft links (see Chapter 7), you can't create a link from one file system to another. The file you want to link to is probably in a different file system from the directory in which you want to make the link (usually the working directory).

Solution: Use the `df` command to find out which disks your computer has and which directories are on which disk.

If your version of UNIX can't do soft links, you're out of luck. The only solution may be to make a copy of the file rather than create a link to it.

File exists

Meaning: A file by that name already exists.

Probable cause: When UNIX expected the name of the file you want to create, you typed the name of a file that already exists.

Solution: You rarely see this message, because most UNIX commands blow away an existing file when they want to create a new one by the same name (which is not always what you want).

File table overflow

Meaning: The system is way too busy and can't juggle as many files simultaneously as all the users have asked it to.

Probable cause: The system isn't configured correctly, or someone is doing way too much work.

Solution: Complain to the system administrator.

File too large

Meaning: You are trying to make a file that is too big.

Probable cause: The maximum file size is set by your system administrator. A maximum file size prevents a messed-up program from making a file that uses up the entire disk by mistake. You're not likely to really want to make a file this big. It usually happens when you use >> to add a copy of a file to itself, so you end up copying the file over and over until it passes the preset size limit.

Example: You type the line shown here:

```
pr myfile >> myfile
```

Solution: Check the command and make sure that you're saying what you mean. If you're sure that you want to make a really big file, talk your system administrator into upping your file-size limit.

Illegal option

Meaning: You typed an option that doesn't work with this command. (*Options* tell the command how you want it to work. They begin with a hyphen.)

Probable cause: You typed a hyphen in front of a filename, or you typed the wrong option.

Example: You type this line:

```
ls -j
```

Because the `ls` command has no `-j` option, you get an error message. Frequently, after the `illegal option` message, UNIX also prints a line about `usage`, which is its cryptic way of reminding you about which options *do* work with the command. (See the "Usage" section, later in this chapter.)

Solution: Check your typing. Look up the command in this book to make sure that you know which option you want. Alternatively, use the `man` command to display an exhaustive and exhausting list of every option the command may possibly understand.

Insufficient arguments

Meaning: You left out some information.

Probable cause: The command you are using needs more arguments than the ones you typed. UNIX may also print a `usage` message in its attempt to tell you which arguments you should have typed. (See the "Usage" section, later in this chapter.)

Example: The `cp` command needs two arguments: The first one tells it what to copy from, and the second one tells it what to copy to. You can't leave out either one.

Solution: Check your typing. If the command is one you don't use often, check to make sure that you've used the correct arguments and options.

I/O error

Meaning: *I/O* is computerese for *i*nput and *o*utput. Some physical problem has occurred during the reading or writing of information on a disk, tape, screen, or wherever your information lives.

Probable cause: Broken disk drive.

Solution: Tell your system administrator. You may have big trouble ahead.

Is a directory

Meaning: You typed the name of a directory when UNIX wanted a filename.

Probable cause: The command you typed is trying to do something to a directory rather than to a file. You can look at a directory by using a text editor, but it looks like binary junk with filenames mixed in. You can't change a directory by editing it.

Note that `emacs` has a special mode (called `dired` mode) for "editing" directories. But `emacs` has its own special way to create, rename, and delete files, too.

Solution: Make sure that you type a filename, not the name of a directory.

Login incorrect

Meaning: You are trying to log in and didn't enter a correct username or corresponding password.

Probable cause: Two possibilities exist: One is that you typed your password incorrectly, and the other is that you typed your username incorrectly.

Solution: Type slowly and deliberately, especially when you type your password and can't see what you are doing. If you have trouble remembering your password, use the `passwd` command to change it to something more memorable, as described in Chapter 2.

No more processes

Meaning: Your system can't create any more new processes.

Probable cause: This message appears when you tell UNIX to create a new process, and UNIX can't do it. Refer to Chapter 24 for information about processes.

Possible reasons for this message are that the system doesn't have any more space for this kind of thing. Occasionally you get this message on very busy systems when you try to run something or if you start dozens of background processes (refer to Chapter 13).

Solution: Wait a minute and try the command again. If you have lots of background processes, get rid of some of them. If you see this message often, complain to your system administrator.

No process can be found

See the section "No such process," later in this chapter.

No space left on device

Meaning: The disk is full.

Probable cause: Either your files take up too much space or someone else's do.

Solution: Delete something to make space. If you don't think that you can or you don't have any large files, talk to your system administrator. She has probably already gotten the same message and is checking to see who is taking up all the space.

No such file or directory

Meaning: UNIX can't find a file or directory with the name you typed.

Probable cause: You spelled a filename or pathname wrong. This problem happens to most of us ten times a day. If you typed a pathname, you may have misspelled any of the directory names it contains. You may also have capitalized something incorrectly.

Example: You type this line:

```
cp june.bugdet save
```

The file isn't named `june.bugdet`, however — it's `june.budget`.

Solution: Check your spelling and capitalization. Use the `ls` command to see how the file and directory names are spelled and whether they have any uppercase letters. For the pathname, check to see whether it should begin with a slash (which means that it is an absolute pathname that describes the path from the root directory) or not (which means that it is a relative pathname that describes the path from the working directory). See Chapter 6 for more information about pathnames.

No such process

Meaning: UNIX can't find the process you are referring to.

Probable cause: You have given a command that talks about processes, probably a `kill` command to stop a runaway process. (Chapter 24 describes what a process is and why you may want to kill the poor thing.)

Solution: The process may already have gone away, in which case no problem exists. You may have mistyped the PID that specifies which process to do in. Check your typing and use the `ps` command to check the PID.

Not a directory

Meaning: UNIX needed the name of a directory, but you typed a filename or the name of something else.

Probable cause: Either you spelled a directory name incorrectly or you forgot to create a new directory.

Example: You type this line:

```
cd /gillian
```

but no directory is named `/gillian`.

Solution: If you are referring to a new directory you planned to create, make it first by using the `mkdir` command. If you are referring to an existing directory, get the spelling right. Use the `ls` command to see how it's spelled.

Permission denied

Meaning: You don't have permission to do whatever the last command you issued tried to do.

Probable cause: You are trying to change, move, or delete a file you don't own.

Example: You type this line:

```
rm /usr/bill/resignation.letter
```

But you are not Bill. Because you don't have permission to delete this file, UNIX doesn't let you.

Solution: Use the `ls -l` command to find out who owns the file and what its permissions are (refer to Chapter 5 for information about permissions). If you think that you ought to be able to mess with the file, make your own copy of it or talk to the owner of the file or your system administrator.

RE error

Meaning: You are using the grep program and it doesn't understand what you're searching for. (RE stands for *r*egular *e*xpression.)

Probable cause: You probably have to use backslashes in front of a character that is a wildcard in grep.

Example: You type this line:

```
grep '[x' myfile
```

Solution: Put a backslash in front of any character that has a special wildcard meaning in grep (grep wildcards include periods, asterisks, square brackets, dollar signs, and carets). If you are searching for text that contains special characters, put single quotation marks around the text to match.

Read-only file system

Meaning: You are trying to change a file that UNIX is not allowed to change.

Probable cause: Some disks, particularly NFS remote disks, are marked read-only so that you can't create, delete, or change files on them. It doesn't matter what the permissions are for the individual files: The entire file system can't be changed.

Solution: Talk to your system administrator. Alternatively, make a copy of the file you want to change and change the copy.

Too many links

Meaning: You are trying to make so many links to a file that you have exceeded the maximum number of links to a file.

Probable cause: The maximum number of links to a file is 1,000. You must be a heck of a typist to get this message, or more likely you were running a script that linked a little more enthusiastically than you had intended. Because the parent directory is linked to each of its subdirectories, you also get this message if you try to make more than 1,000 subdirectories in one directory.

Solution: Stop making links.

Usage

Meaning: UNIX doesn't like the number or types of arguments you typed after the command. It is telling you (in its own cryptic way) the correct way to use the command.

Probable cause: UNIX usually displays this message with another, more specific message. Check out the other message to see what the real problem was. The `usage` message is the UNIX reminder about how to use the command. After `usage`, you see the command, followed by the options and arguments you can use with the command. Unfortunately, you get no clue about what the options do.

Example: You type this line:

```
kill abc
```

UNIX responds with this message:

```
usage: kill [signo ] pid
```

This line means that the correct way to use the `kill` command is to type **kill**, a space, (optionally) the type of signal you want to send to the process, another space, and then the process ID. Don't type the [ ] — we stuck them in to let you know which part of the command is optional — not that it's entirely clear from the message!

Solution: Check your typing, as always. Make sure that spaces are between things on the line (between filenames or between a filename and an option, for example). If you don't use this command often, check to make sure that you have the correct arguments (filenames and so on) and options (things that begin with a dash, such as the *-l* in `ls -l`). Look up the command in this book or consult the UNIX manual page about it (see Chapter 27 for instructions on how to display manual pages).

444 mode? (or some other three-digit number)

Meaning: You don't have permission to change this file, but you have told UNIX to delete it.

Probable cause: You are using `rm`, `mv`, or `ln` to remove or replace a read-only protected file or a file that belongs to someone else. (Refer to Chapter 5 for information about permissions.) Rather than refuse outright to do what you asked, UNIX asks whether you really want to do it.

Example: You used the `chmod` command to make an important file read-only. Then you decide to delete it by typing this line:

```
rm important.file
```

UNIX asks whether you really want to delete it, even though the file is read-only.

Solution: The question mark at the end of this message indicates that UNIX is asking you a question. By divine intuition, you are supposed to guess that UNIX is asking whether you want to complete the command anyway. Press y if you want to go ahead and do the command. Press anything else if you want to cancel it (for this file, anyway).

If you own the file, you can change its permissions by typing this line:

```
chmod 644 filename
```

Rather than type `filename`, type the real filename. This command has the result of allowing anyone to read or write to the file.

Part VI
The Part of Tens

The 5th Wave
By Rich Tennant
©RICHTENNANT
SURE, HE'S A LITTLE DIFFERENT, BUT HE WORKS HARD AND KEEPS THE SYSTEM FREE OF BUGS.

In this part . . .

UNIX uses many commands, programs, options, and other stuff — much more than we can pack into this book. The real, official manuals for a UNIX system take up about three feet of shelf space. (For cost savings, all the pages of these manuals are blank because no one ever reads them, but if you don't tell, neither will we.)

In this part of the book, we organize facts into neat lists of ten (actually, two lists) so that they're easier to remember. Astute readers may claim that neither of these lists contains exactly ten items. Well, we were using mixed radix arithmetic (survivors of new math in school may remember some of this subject from fourth grade), so a chapter with eight items has ten items counting in base 12, and a chapter — what? You say that we can't bamboozle you with such nonsense? Truth is, we can't count.

Read on — good stuff is in this part, regardless of the numbers.

Chapter 26

Ten Common Mistakes

In This Chapter

- Mistyping commands
- Believing that it will be easy
- Pressing Enter or not pressing Enter
- Working in the wrong directory
- Not keeping backup copies
- Not keeping files organized
- Turning off your computer
- Writing your password on a note next to your computer
- Sending angry electronic mail (flaming)

Here are ten (or so) of the most common user mistakes we have run into. Although you will probably invent some new ones yourself, at least avoid the ones on this list.

Believing That It Will Be Easy

UNIX was designed a long, long time ago in computer time (computer years are similar to dog years, except that 50 computer years equal a human year). Software design has made a great deal of progress since 1972, and UNIX has not. If you are used to a Macintosh or a PC with Windows, or even a PC with DOS, UNIX isn't easy to use.

On the other hand, UNIX has a certain cachet and glamour; it takes a macho person (of either gender) to face it. You should give yourself major kudos, and maybe even one or two of those cookies you made to bribe your UNIX wizard, every time you get UNIX to do something useful.

Mistyping Commands

If you type a command the UNIX shell doesn't understand, it says that it can't find the command. The reason is that it looks high and low for a file with the name you just typed, hoping to find the program you want to run. And then it says

```
eatmylunch: Command not found.
```

Or perhaps it says

```
eatmylunch: not found
```

The exact wording varies from shell to shell (we would bet that you already guessed that). To make sure that you type a command properly:

- **Check your spelling (as always).** You may have typed a correctly spelled English word rather than the garbled set of letters that comprise the name of the program.
- **Check your capitalization.** Capital and small letters count as completely different things in filenames and, therefore, in commands. Nearly every command uses only small letters.
- **Change directories (maybe).** You may have given the right command, but UNIX may not know where to look for the file containing the program. If you know where the program file is, move to that directory and give the command again. If you don't know where the file is, either look for it (as described in Chapter 23) or give up and ask your system administrator or local wizard.

To Press Enter, or Not to Press Enter

Depending on which program you are using, sometimes you must press Enter (or Return) after a command, and sometimes you don't. In the UNIX shell, you *always* have to press Enter or Return before UNIX performs the command. If you don't, UNIX waits forever for you to do so.

In other programs, particularly in text editors like `emacs` and `vi`, as soon as you press the command (Ctrl+K to delete a line in `emacs`, for example), the program does it right away. If you press Enter or Return after the command, `emacs` sticks a new line in your file, and `vi` moves down to the next line.

When you use a program you're not familiar with, hesitate a moment before pressing Enter or Return to see whether the computer may already be performing the command. If nothing is happening, press Enter or Return.

Working in the Wrong Directory

If you use separate directories to organize your files, make sure that you are in the proper directory when you begin working. Otherwise, UNIX won't find the files you want to work on.

To find out which directory you're in, type **pwd**. Remember that this command stands for *p*rint *w*orking *d*irectory.

If you're really lost, you can type **whoami**. This command tells you your username.

To move back to your home directory, type **cd**.

Not Keeping Backup Copies

Sooner or later, it happens. You give an `rm` command to delete a file, and UNIX deletes the wrong file or deletes everything in the directory. Chances are that you typed an extra space or spelled a filename wrong, but the point is — what now?

See Chapter 23 to find out how to proceed if you delete something important. The best approach is to keep extra copies of important files: in another directory, on a floppy disk, or on a backup tape that either you or your system administrator makes. If you haven't talked to your system administrator about backups, now is a good time to find out whether your files are backed up automatically; you can also tell him which of your directories contain files you want to have backed up.

Not Keeping Files Organized

Unless you do all your work on one or two files, you will run into trouble if you don't do the following:

- **Make directories for the groups of files you use.** (Refer to Chapter 6 to find out how.) Directories help you separate your files into groups of files you use together.
- **Use filenames that mean something.** UNIX lets you name your files with nice long names, so take advantage of it (up to a point, anyway). Filenames should tell you what's inside the file rather than make you guess.

Turning Off Your Computer

Leaving your computer on all the time is better than turning it off at the wrong time. Chapter 1 talks about this subject in detail. UNIX can get messed up if you turn off your computer (if you kick the plug out by mistake, for example) without warning it that you are going to do so.

If you use UNIX from a terminal rather than directly with a workstation, it may make sense to turn off the terminal (not the computer) at night. Check with your system administrator.

Writing Your Password on a Sticky Note

Okay, maybe this one doesn't apply if you work at home, live alone, and don't have any friends, cleaning people, or burglars. Otherwise, you should keep your password to yourself. Not that anyone has malicious intent — let's not get paranoid — but people can get curious around computers. And you never know when an inquisitive 14-year-old who knows more about UNIX than you do will appear on the scene. If you can't remember your password, choose a new one that is more memorable. (Refer to Chapter 1 for hints.)

Sending Angry Electronic Mail (Flaming)

Electronic mail can bring out your insidious side. There you are, sitting alone in your cubicle with your computer, and you get ticked off at something, usually some stupid message sent by a coworker. Before you know it, you have composed and sent a tactless, not to say downright rude, response.

It's easy to say things in e-mail that you would never say in person or even write in a memo. But e-mail has an off-the-cuff, spontaneous style in most organizations, and it can get you into trouble.

Sarcasm seldom works in e-mail — instead, you just sound mean. Gentle suggestions can turn into strident demands just because they appear in ugly computer type on a computer screen. Rude mouthing off via e-mail even has a special name: *flaming.* A message full of tactless, pointless complaints is referred to as a *flame*. A series of flames between two or more people is called a *flame war*. You get the idea.

Recipients of your mail can easily forward copies of it to anyone else, so imagine that everyone in the office may read your missives. Think twice before sending e-mail containing negative remarks! Then don't send it. Remember that the best way to end an unpleasant exchange is to let the other person have the last word.

Chapter 27

Ten Times More Information than You Want about UNIX

In This Chapter

- How to use the `man` command for online help
- What's on a manual page
- Other books about UNIX
- UNIX information on the Internet

We wish that this book contained every single thing you may ever want to know about UNIX. We considered writing the book that way, but our publisher frowned on printing a book with 25,000 pages. (Books like that are hard to bind, not to mention hard to pick up off the floor.) So, we tried to include just the information that new UNIX users really need to know. If you read this entire book, however, you'll be well on your way to becoming a seasoned UNIX veteran. For additional seasoning, this chapter points you in the direction of more advanced facts about UNIX.

Let's Hear It from the `man`

You thought that UNIX was completely unhelpful. For the most part, you're absolutely right. A standard UNIX command called `man` (for *man*ual), however, can give you online help.

Sound good? Well, yes and no. The information is there, all right, but it's written in a rather nerdy style and can be difficult to decipher. Each part of the online manual is written, of course, on the assumption that you have read all the other parts and know what all the commands are called. The `man` command is definitely worth knowing about, though, when you just can't remember the options for a command or what to type where on the command line after the command name.

The man's online manual contains *manual pages* for every UNIX command, and other pages about internal functions that programmers use, formats for various system file types, descriptions of some of the hardware that can be attached to your UNIX system, and other odds and ends. When you type the man command, you indicate which page or pages you want.

All manual pages have a standard format. Figure 27-1 shows part of the manual page for dcheck, a program a system administrator may use to deal with people whose files take up too much space on the disk.

```
DCHECK()                  Diskhog                    DCHECK(1)
NAME
   dcheck - send mail to potential disk hogs
SYNOPSIS
   dcheck
DESCRIPTION
   dcheck is normally run from the crons procedure to check
   if users are taking up too much space. It creates a tag
   file for such users, will send them warning mail, and
   also sends mail to the system administrator about what
   it's done.
SEE ALSO
   diskhog(1).
FILES
   $DQUOTAS/hogs/$LOGNAME  -   tag file indicating that
                               diskhog should be run
WARNINGS
   Should know about multiple file systems.
BUGS
   None.
```

Figure 27-1: Part of the man page for dcheck, a truly arcane command.

The parts of the manual page include

- **The title (the first line):** It includes the name and page number of the manual page on the left and right ends of the line. Centered on the line may be the name of the system the command is a part of. In Figure 27-1, the dcheck command is part of the diskhog system.
- **NAME:** The one-line name of the manual page. The name is usually the command or commands the page talks about, as well as a brief description.
- **SYNOPSIS:** What you type when you give the command, with a terse and cryptic example of every option available. This part often makes no sense until you read the description that follows. Sometimes it still makes no sense.

- DESCRIPTION: A few paragraphs about the command. For commands with a large number of options, the description can run for a few pages. A list of options usually is included, with an explanation of every one. Sometimes you see examples, although not often enough.
- SEE ALSO: Lists names of related manual pages, if any.
- WARNINGS **and** BUGS: May list a command's known bugs or common problems. Then again, it may not.
- FILES: A list of the files this command uses. The elm and mail commands, for example, use your Mail directory, the central list of mailboxes, and other files. (Your system administrator usually sets up these files — they're rarely something you want to fool with yourself.) The manual pages for elm and mail mention these files.

Reading manual pages

To see a manual page, type this line:

```
man unixcommand
```

Except, of course, you substitute for unixcommand the name of the UNIX command you're interested in. Some versions of man present the manual page a screen at a time. Other versions just whip the page by at maximum speed, assuming that you can read 150,000 words per minute. If that happens (and you can't read that fast), you can use the usual more command to display the manual page a screen at a time by typing this command:

```
man unixcommand | more
```

On the other hand, if you're on a system that normally presents manual pages a screen at a time and you want it to whip by at full speed because you just finished a speed-reading course — so you *can* read 150,000 words per minute (or, more likely, because your terminal is a PC and you're capturing the terminal output to a file) — type the following line (the dash tells UNIX that you're a fast reader):

```
man - unixcommand
```

Printing manual pages

You can also print the manual pages for later perusal. To print the manual pages, type this line:

```
man unixcommand | lpr
```

Remember to use `lp`, if that is the command you use to print. A better technique may be to put the manual pages in a file first, remove the information you don't want, and print the result. You could type the following line, for example (remember to substitute for `filename` the name of the file you want the information in):

```
man unixcommand > filename
```

Then edit the file with a text editor (refer to Chapter 10) and print it (refer to Chapter 9). Before you print the file, however, keep in mind that the online manual pages are generally identical to the printed manual pages in the dusty UNIX manuals on the shelf, except that the printed manual pages are typeset so that they're easier to read. Rather than print the online page, it's often better to look it up in the paper manual. (Bet you didn't think we would *ever* tell you to do that!)

If you have a laser printer, you can often print the manual pages with nice fonts and italics and such rather than the typewriter-like version you see on-screen. Ask your local guru for advice. Usually, you use `troff` or `groff` typesetting programs.

Finding the manual page you want

If you use the `man` command, you have no good way to find out which manual pages are available. Sometimes, it can be difficult to find the one you want. Suppose that you type this line:

```
man ln | more
```

UNIX shows you this message:

```
man: ln not found
```

The `ln` command has no separate manual page. Instead, it shares a set of pages with `cp` and `mv`. You get information about `ln` by typing this line:

```
man cp | more
```

(Typical UNIX ease of use!) If `man` doesn't display anything about the command you want, try some similar commands. BSD UNIX systems have an `apropos` command that suggests manual pages relevant to a particular topic, so you can type **apropos ln** to see what it has to say.

In addition to manual pages about commands, you can find lots of pages about other topics. You can type this line, for example:

```
man ascii
```

If necessary, you can type this line:

```
man ascii | more
```

This command shows you a table of the ASCII-character codes for all the characters text files can contain. Although you probably aren't interested in them, it does look impressively technoid.

It's a bird, it's a plane, it's `xman`!

If you use X Windows or Motif, you can use the `xman` command to look at manual pages. The nice thing about `xman` is that it displays a list of the available manual pages. When you run `xman`, it pops up a little box with three buttons, one of which is labeled Manual Page. If you click that button, a larger window then displays a manual page describing `xman`. Choose Display Directory from the Options menu on that page, or press Ctrl+D as a shortcut, to see a screen of all the manual pages it has — probably more than 100 of them. Click the one you want to see, and `xman` switches to that page. Press Ctrl+D again to return to the directory of manual pages. Read the initial description of `xman` for other tricks you can get `xman` to do, such as show you two or three different pages at a time or search for keywords in manual-page titles.

Scanning the Networks

If your system is connected to the Internet or if you have dial-up access to an Internet provider, you can connect to *Usenet,* a gigantic, distributed online bulletin-board system described in Chapter 19. Because most systems on Usenet are running on UNIX systems, Usenet has a great deal of discussion of UNIX issues and questions.

Your basic UNIX news

Usenet discussions are loosely organized into about 10,000 topic areas, or *newsgroups.* Table 27-1 lists some newsgroups that discuss UNIX topics.

Table 27-1 UNIX-Related Newsgroups

Group	*Description*
comp.unix.admin	UNIX system administration.
comp.unix.advocacy	Arguments about how wonderful UNIX is.
comp.unix.aix	AIX, the IBM version of UNIX.
comp.unix.amiga	UNIX on the Commodore Amiga.
comp.unix.aux	The Apple AUX for the Macintosh.
comp.unix.bsd.386bsd.announce	Announcements about the 386BSD version of UNIX.
comp.unix.bsd.386bsd.misc	Discussions about the 386BSD operating system.
comp.unix.bsd.bsdi.announce	Announcements about BSD/OS.
comp.unix.bsd.bsdi.misc	Discussions of BSD/OS.
comp.unix.bsd.freebsd.announce	Announcements about the FreeBSD version of UNIX.
comp.unix.bsd.freebsd.misc	Discussions of FreeBSD.
comp.unix.bsd.misc	Various BSD versions of UNIX.
comp.unix.bsd.netbsd.announce	Announcements about the NetBSD version of UNIX.
comp.unix.bsd.netbsd.misc	Discussions of NetBSD.
comp.unix.bsd.openbsd.announce	Announcements about the OpenBSD version of UNIX.
comp.unix.bsd.openbsd.misc	Discussions of OpenBSD.
comp.unix.cde	Discussions of the Common Desktop Environment.
comp.unix.cray	UNIX on Cray supercomputers.
comp.unix.dos-under-unix	Running MS-DOS programs under UNIX.
comp.unix.internals	The technical internals of UNIX.
comp.unix.large	UNIX on large systems.
comp.unix.misc	Random UNIX discussions.
comp.unix.osf.misc	Discussions of the OSF/1 version of UNIX.
comp.unix.osf.osf1	OSF/1 version of UNIX.

Group	Description
comp.unix.pc-clone.16bit	UNIX on 16-bit IBM PC compatibles.
comp.unix.pc-clone.32bit	UNIX on 32-bit IBM PC compatibles.
comp.unix.programmer	Programming on UNIX.
comp.unix.questions	Questions about UNIX. The best place to ask questions. Look at articles first to see whether someone has just asked the same question.
comp.unix.shell	UNIX shells.
comp.unix.solaris	The Sun Solaris version of UNIX.
comp.unix.sys5.r3	SVR3 version of UNIX.
comp.unix.sys5.r4	SVR4 version of UNIX.
comp.unix.ultrix	The Digital Ultrix version of UNIX.
comp.unix.unixware.announce	Announcements about Novell UnixWare.
comp.unix.unixware.misc	Discussions about Novell UnixWare.
comp.unix.wizards	Technical discussions among UNIX wizards.
comp.unix.xenix.sco	SCO Xenix, an old, popular version of UNIX for IBM PC clones.
comp.security.unix	UNIX security issues.

Just for Linux

Because Linux is so popular, Table 27-2 lists a bunch of discussion groups of its own.

Table 27-2 Linux-Related Newsgroups

Group	Description
alt.os.linux.caldera	All about Caldera OpenLinux
alt.os.linux.slackware	All about Slackware Linux
comp.os.linux.admin	Linux system administration
comp.os.linux.advocacy	Discussions of how great Linux is
comp.os.linux.announce	Announcements of new versions of Linux

(continued)

Table 27-2 *(continued)*

Group	*Description*
comp.os.linux.answers	Answers to Frequently Asked Questions; a good place to look
comp.os.linux.development.apps	Development of application programs
comp.os.linux.development.system	Development of the underlying Linux system
comp.os.linux.hardware	Making Linux work with various kinds of hardware
comp.os.linux.help	More answers to Frequently Asked Questions
comp.os.linux.misc	Linux discussions that don't fit anywhere else
comp.os.linux.networking	Networking issues
comp.os.linux.help	Even more answers to Frequently Asked Questions
comp.os.linux.setup	Setting up Linux
comp.os.linux.x	X Windows on Linux
linux.redhat.install	Help with (or at least a great deal of complaining about) installing Red Hat Linux

On the Web

Sites with information about UNIX and Linux have been proliferating on the World Wide Web at an astonishing rate. Point your Web browser at any of the useful, colorful, frequently updated sites in this section.

UNIX OS

- **Berkeley Software Design, Inc.:** The maker of BSD/OS, the commercially supported version of BSD, has a Web site at `http://www.bsdi.com/`.
- **BSDNet:** Maintained by a nonprofit group of BSD enthusiasts, BSDNet has tons of information about all flavors of BSD (at `http://www.bsdnet.org/`).
- **Sun Microsystems:** The maker of Solaris, it has a Web site at the bizarrely named `http://wwwwswest2.sun.com/`.
- **Hewlett Packard:** This site tells you all about HP-UX, at `http://www.hp.com/esy/`. Click UNIX News and then Software & Applications and then HP-UX.

Linux

- **Linux Online!:** This site, at http://www.linux.org/, is *the* source for Linux information on the Web, maintained by a nonprofit organization of Linux users.
- **The Linux Resource Kit:** At http://www.secretagent.com/, this site has very good installation, networking, administration, and programming how-to's for Linux and Apache. It has links to major sources of Linux distributions, downloads, and news and is a well-designed site.
- **The Linux Documentation Project:** The project (at http://sunsite.unc.edu/mdw/) has tons of Linux documentation, news, links, and downloads.
- **Red Hat:** Red Hat maintains a site (at http://www.redhat.com/) that serves as a clearinghouse for all kinds of information about Linux.
- **The Debian GNU/Linux site:** This site (at http://www.debian.org/) is also worth checking out.
- **LinuxMall.com:** "Get it all at the Linux Mall!" The Linux Superstore is at http://www.linuxmall.com/.

X Windows and such

- **The Open Group:** Formerly the Open Software Foundation, or OSF (based in Cambridge, Massachusetts), this nonprofit organization helps develop standards for such UNIX-related technologies as Motif, X Windows, and the Common Desktop Environment. Its desktop home page, at http://www.camb.opengroup.org/tech/desktop/, has all kinds of introductory and technical information about graphical UNIX systems.
- **The Motif Zone:** The Motif Zone has everything you ever wanted to know about Motif (at http://www.motifzone.com/).
- **The XFree86 Project:** Its home is at http://www.xfree86.org/.

Web browsers

- **The Lynx Users' Guide:** Maintained by the Academic Computing Services group at the University of Kansas, the guide is yours for the viewing, at http://www.cc.ukans.edu/lynx_help/Lynx_users_guide.html.
- **Netscape:** Netscape maintains information and downloads for its Communicator browser for UNIX at http://home.netscape.com/eng/mozilla/4.0/relnotes/unix-4.0.html.
- **Microsoft Internet Explorer:** Although we don't recommend it, Internet Explorer is indeed available for Solaris 2.5 and later. You can read about it for yourself and download it from http://www.microsoft.com/ie/unix/.

Other stuff

- **The Apache Project:** It's the official Web site (`http://www.apache.org/`) of the most popular Web server in the world. Get documentation, FAQs, the latest news, and free downloads.
- **Apache RTFM:** This site has a great set of reference pages on how to use the Apache server and is especially useful for beginners (`http://www.jlk.net/apache/`).
- **Samba:** Check out the worldwide home of *the* package that lets your UNIX system provide networked logical disks to Windows PCs (at `http://www.samba.bst.tj/samba/samba.html`), with documentation, FAQs, how-to's, news, and downloads. Includes pizza supply details for paying Samba's creator in the only kind of currency he seems to recognize.

Other Sources of Information

Your system administrator or nearby UNIX users probably have copies of UNIX manuals lying around. The pages of some of these manuals usually look much like the manual pages you get with `man`.

The advantage of the printed manual is that an index is in the front (or the back). It is usually a permuted or KWIC index (an overly clever abbreviation for *k*ey *w*ord *i*n *c*ontext), which means that you can find an entry by looking under any of the words in the title except for boring ones, such as *the*. To find the page for the `cp` command (the title of the manual page is *cp, ln, mv* — *c*o*p*y, *l*i*n*k, or *m*o*v*e files), for example, you can look in the permuted index under *cp, ln, mv, copy, link, move,* or *files.*

Then again, it's not a bad idea to try typing **help**, just to see what happens. Someone may have installed some kind of help system — you never know.

UNIX is used widely enough that a growing industry of UNIX books, magazines, user groups, and conferences has sprung up. Any of them can provide additional help and information.

Read a magazine

Several weekly or monthly magazines cover UNIX. Most of them include in their titles either the name UNIX or the code phrase Open Systems (for systems that act like UNIX but haven't licensed the UNIX trademark).

Because you probably have already thrown away mail inviting you to subscribe to most of them, we don't belabor the point. The major brands of workstations (Sun, Hewlett-Packard, and IBM) also have magazines that specifically cover those product lines. Although some of these magazines tend to be awfully technical, they can be interesting for product reviews and announcements about new UNIX hardware and software packages.

If you use Linux, take a look at the *Linux Journal,* the magazine for and about Linux. (Its address is P.O. Box 55549, Seattle, WA 98155-0549 USA; phone 206-782-7733; e-mail, `linux@ssc.com`.) The technical level varies from totally introductory to fairly technical.

Read a book

Yeah, we know: You may have (or not) just read this book. We mean read *another* book. Here are a few you may like:

- Levine and Young, *More UNIX For Dummies;* IDG Books Worldwide, Inc. (Big surprise, huh?) Get more info about UNIX shells, script-writing languages, and the use of the Internet from UNIX.
- Levine and Young, *UNIX For Dummies Quick Reference,* 3rd Edition; IDG Books Worldwide. (Equally big surprise.) The Quick Reference has essential information from the book you're reading and a detailed command reference, squashed down into a smaller, less expensive, pocket-size form.
- Daniel Gilly, *UNIX in a Nutshell;* O'Reilly. A complete UNIX reference, the one we turn to when memory fails. It comes in various editions for different versions of UNIX and is intended for more advanced users than our *UNIX For Dummies Quick Reference.*

- Witherspoon, Witherspoon, and Hall, *LINUX For Dummies,* 2nd Edition; IDG Books Worldwide. This one tells how to survive installing, using, administering, and networking Linux, for beginners with some technical tolerance.
- Welsh and Kaufman, *Running LINUX;* O'Reilly. All about installing and using Linux, it's medium technical but quite informative.
- Naba Barkakati, *LINUX Secrets,* 2nd Edition; IDG Books Worldwide. This one covers a wide range of topics, from hardware debugging to using Linux in your business.
- *The Linux Bible,* Yggdrasil Computing. The online Linux documents are neatly printed and bound — all 1,200 pages of them.

Join a user group

Two major UNIX user groups exist. The older one, called *Usenix,* dates back to about 1976; it is traditionally for technical users. The other is *Uniforum,* formerly `/usr/group`, which is more for business users. Each one sponsors annual conferences and publishes a newsletter. You can also find local and regional UNIX user groups; you tend to find out about these groups from notes posted on physical or electronic bulletin boards. User groups can be great sources of help because chances are good that someone out there has already run into many of the same problems you have and has some ideas that may help.

Index

• Numbers and Symbols •

• A •

• B •

(continued)

• G •

• H •

• I •

• J •

• K •

• L •

• M •

(continued)

• N •

(continued)

• Q •

• R •

• S •

• U •

• V •

• W •

IDG BOOKS WORLDWIDE BOOK REGISTRATION

We want to hear from you!

Visit **http://my2cents.dummies.com** to register this book and tell us how you liked it!

- Get entered in our monthly prize giveaway.
- Give us feedback about this book — tell us what you like best, what you like least, or maybe what you'd like to ask the author and us to change!
- Let us know any other *...For Dummies®* topics that interest you.

Your feedback helps us determine what books to publish, tells us what coverage to add as we revise our books, and lets us know whether we're meeting your needs as a *...For Dummies* reader. You're our most valuable resource, and what you have to say is important to us!

Not on the Web yet? It's easy to get started with *Dummies 101®: The Internet For Windows® 98* or *The Internet For Dummies®*, 5th Edition, at local retailers everywhere.

Or let us know what you think by sending us a letter at the following address:

...For Dummies Book Registration
Dummies Press
7260 Shadeland Station, Suite 100
Indianapolis, IN 46256-3945
Fax 317-596-5498